Oh My Goddess!

ああっ女神さまっ MYSTERY CHILD

Oh My Goddess!

ああっ女神さま

MYSTERY CHILD

v.16

STORY AND ART BY

Kosuke Fujishima

TRANSLATION BY

Dana Lewis & Toren Smith

LETTERING AND TOUCH-UP BY

Susie Lee with Betty Dong & Tom2K

DARK HORSE COMICS®

PUBLISHER
Mike Richardson

SERIES EDITOR
Tim Ervin-Gore

COLLECTION EDITOR
Chris Warner

COLLECTION DESIGNER
Amy Arendts

ART DIRECTOR
Mark Cox

English-language version produced by Studio Proteus
for Dark Horse Comics, Inc.

OH MY GODDESS Vol. XVI: Mystery Child

This volume collects issues three through ten of the Dark Horse comic book series *Oh My
Goddess! Part XI.*

Published by
Dark Horse Comics, Inc.
10956 SE Main Street
Milwaukie, OR 97222

www.darkhorse.com

To find a comics shop in your area, call the Comic Shop
Locator Service toll-free at 1-888-266-4226

First edition: May 2003
ISBN: 1-56971-950-0

1 3 5 7 9 10 8 6 4 2
Printed in Canada

THE BOY WHO COULD SEE GODDESSES

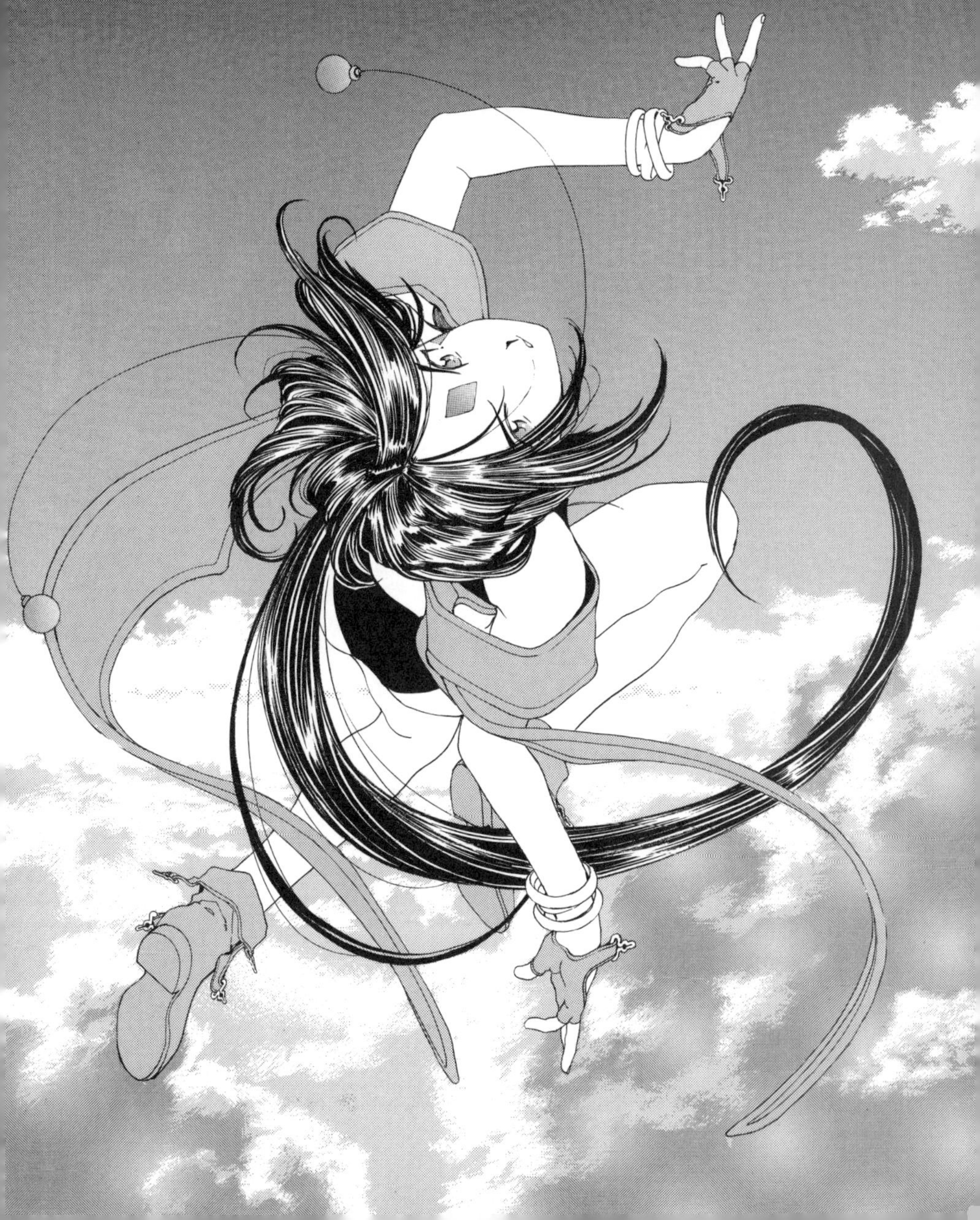

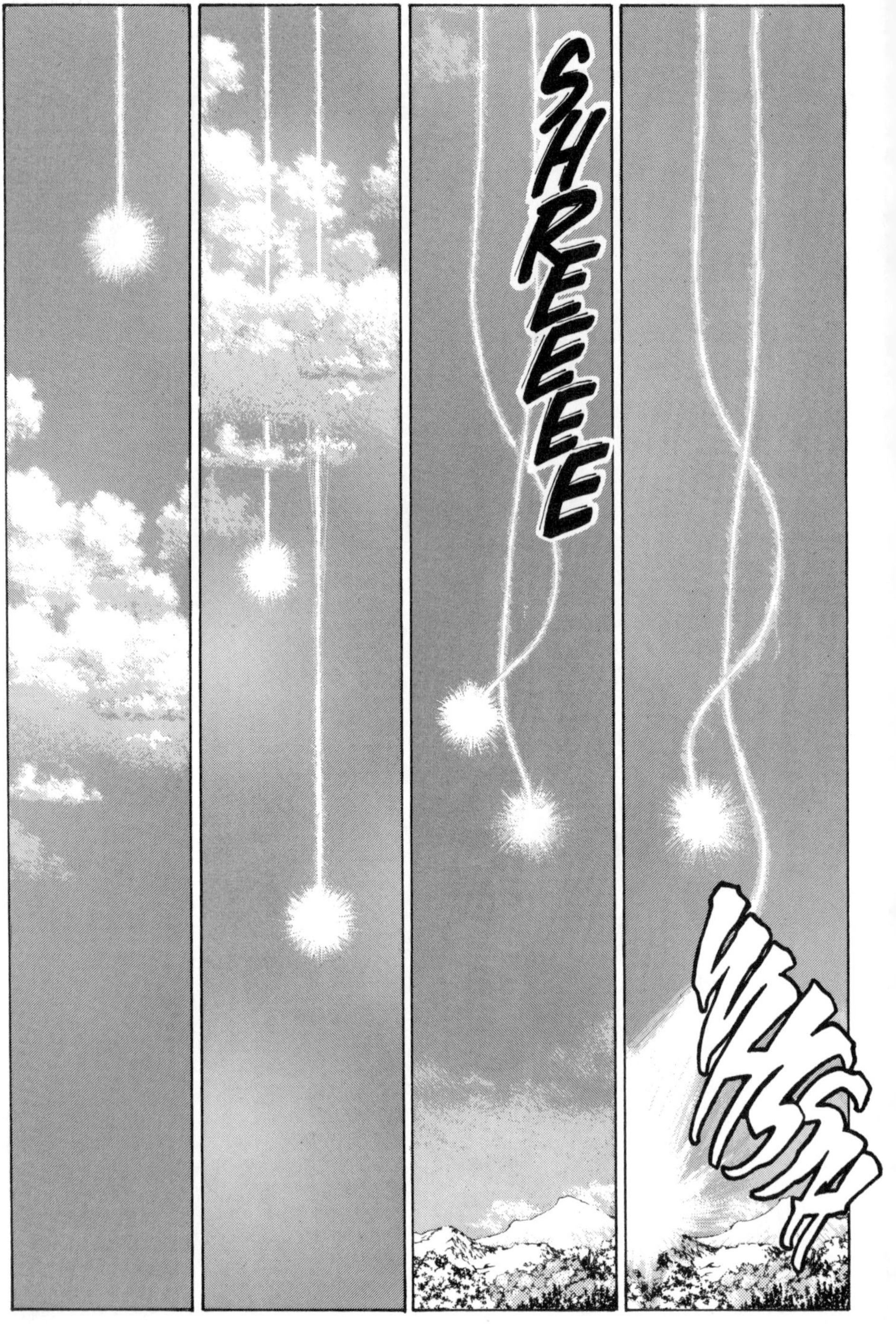
SHREEEE

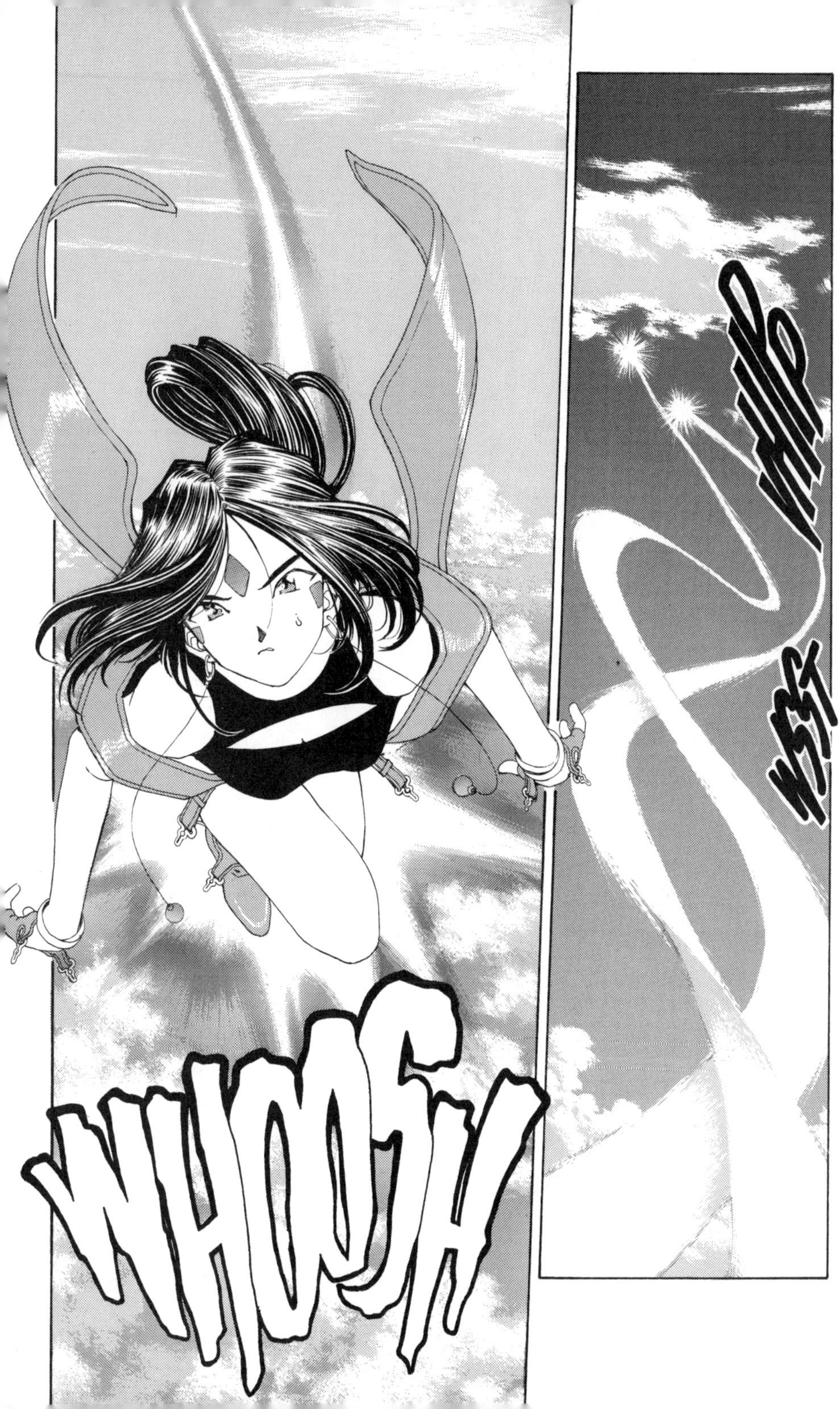
WHOOSH
WHIP
WSST

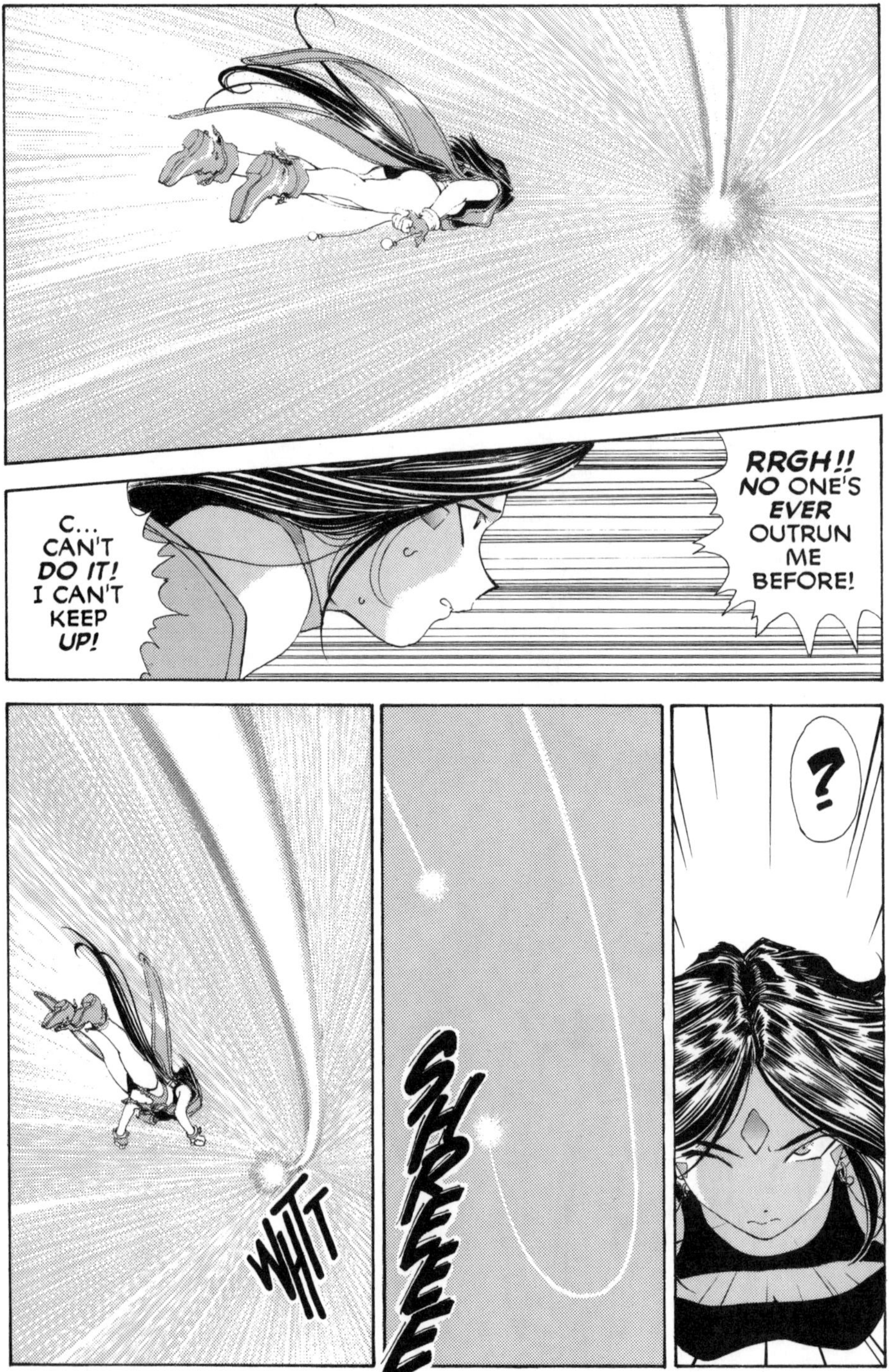
C... CAN'T DO IT! I CAN'T KEEP UP!
RRGH!! NO ONE'S EVER OUTRUN ME BEFORE!
WHIT
SHREEEE
?

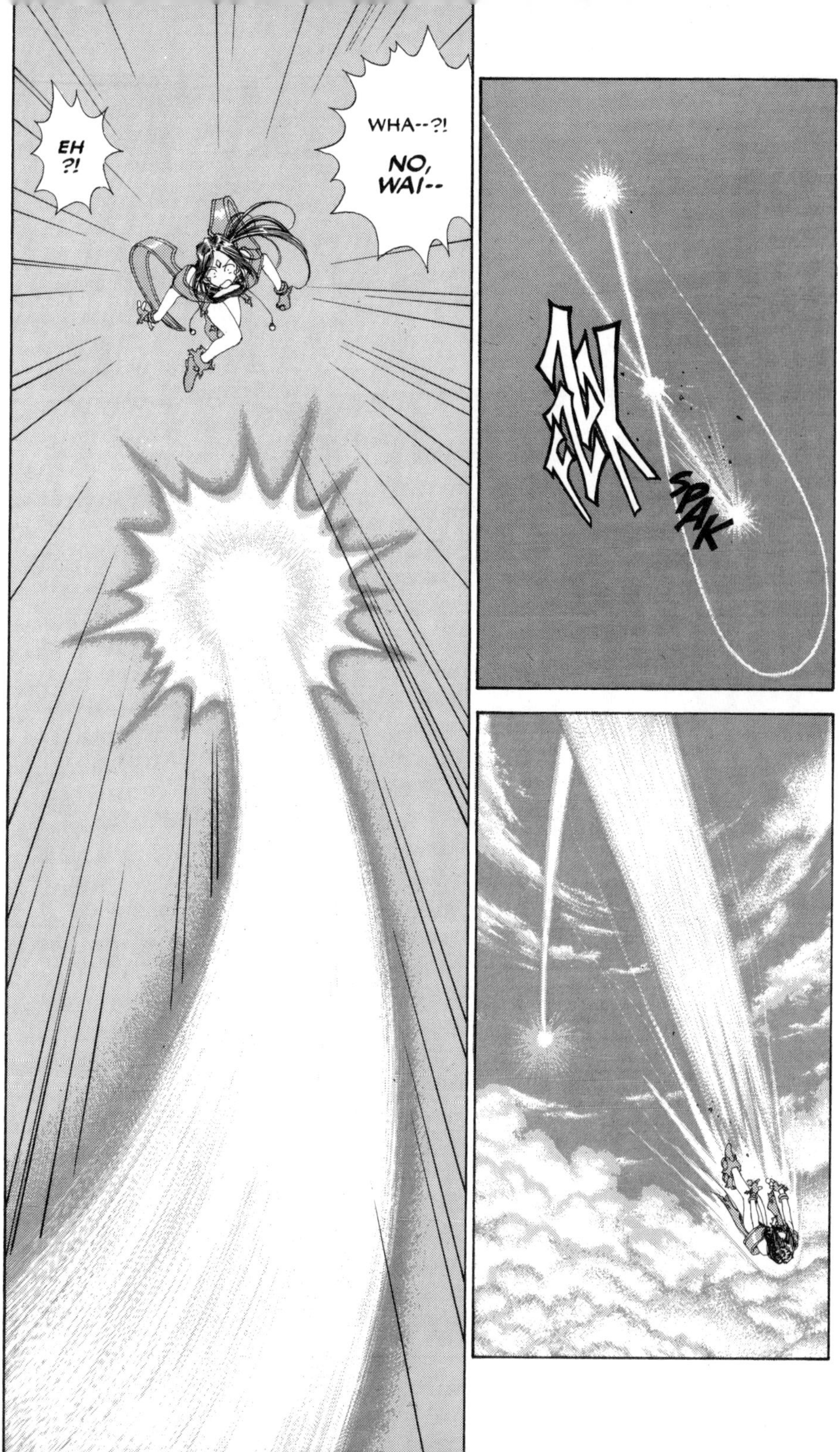
EH ?!
WHA--?!
NO, WAI--
SPAK

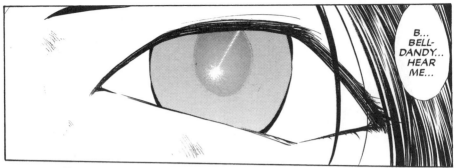

B...
BELL-
DANDY...
HEAR
ME...

THE
WORLD...

....
...IS
IN...
DANGER...

KSSH

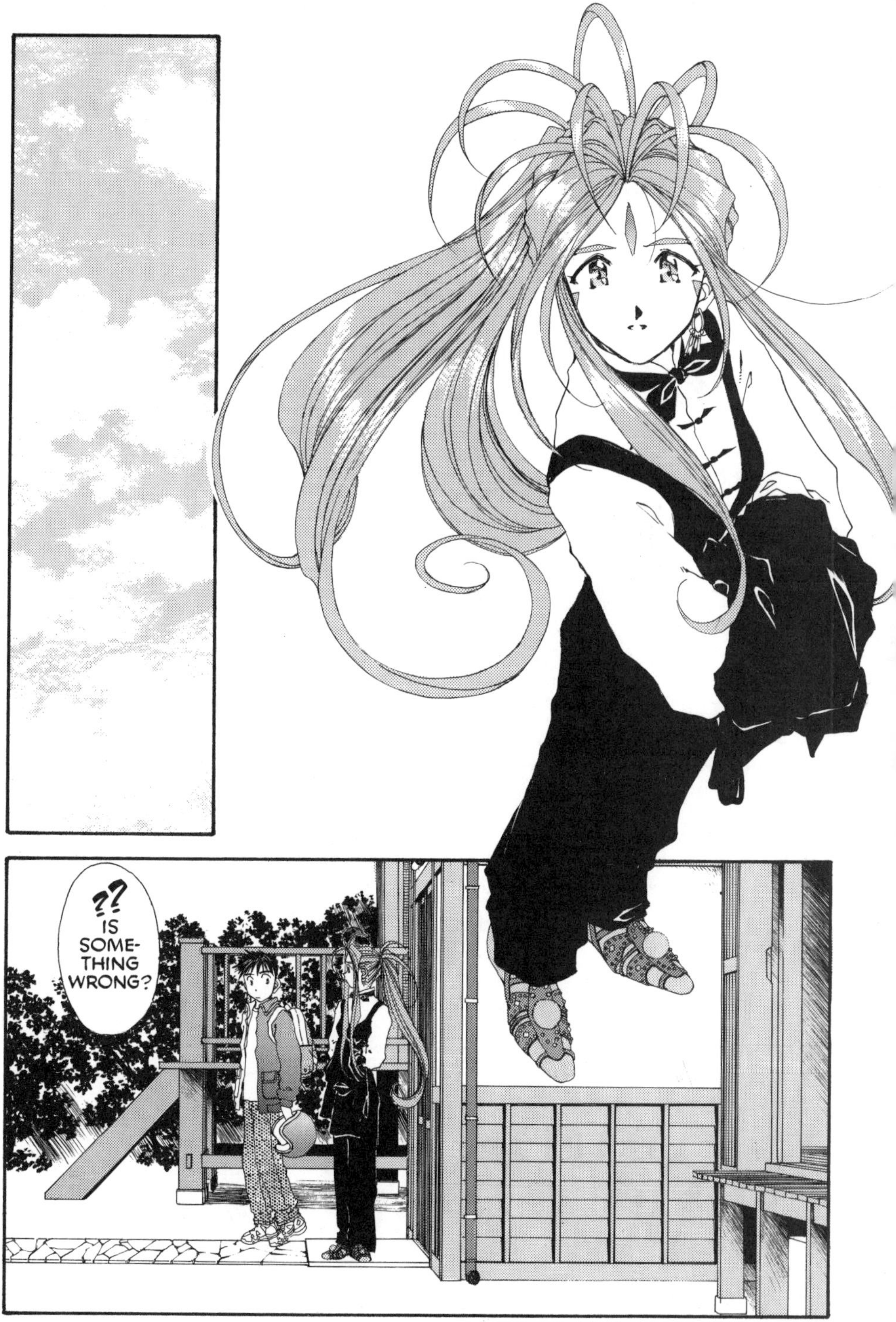
?? IS SOMETHING WRONG?

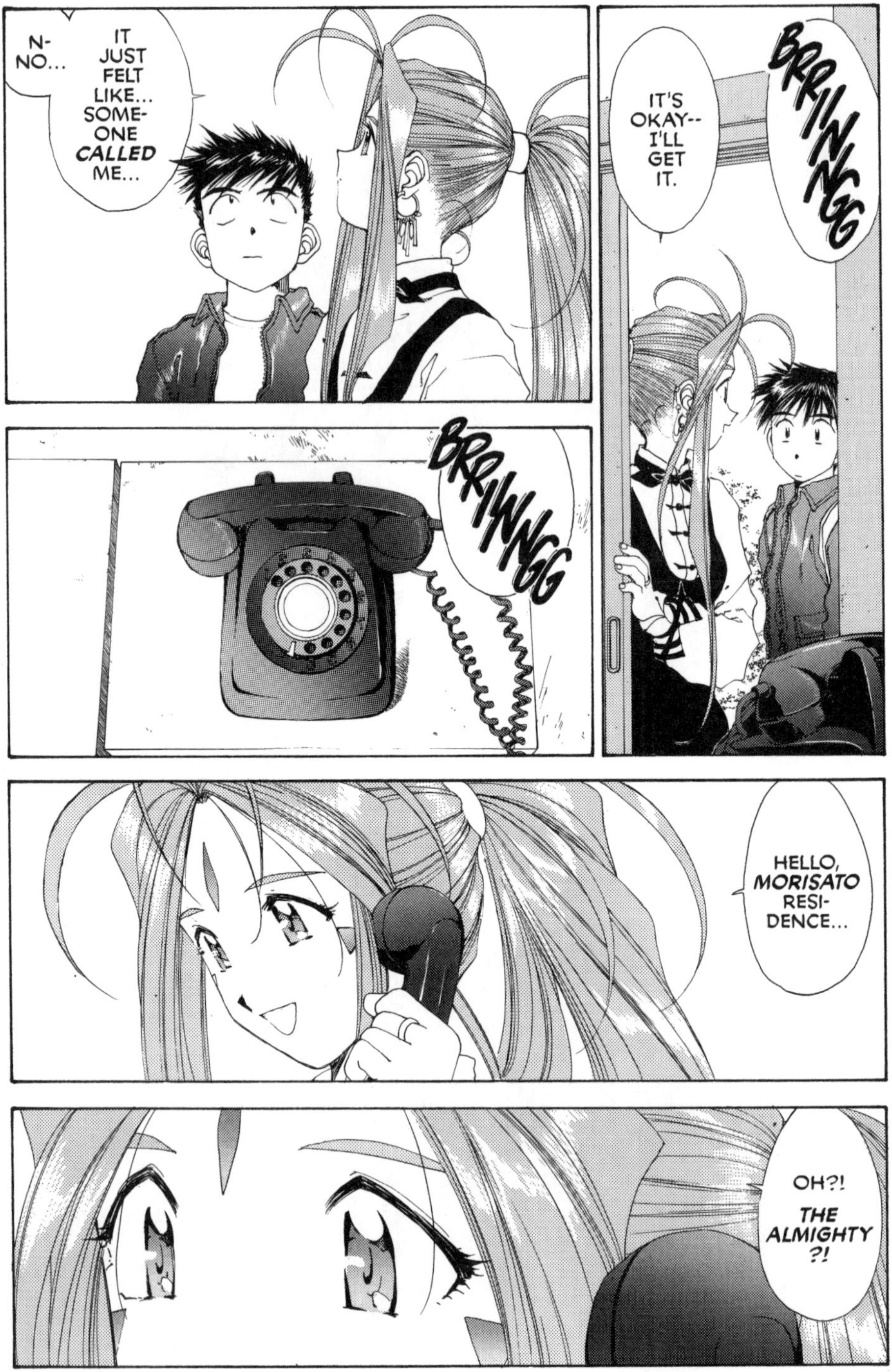
N-NO...
IT JUST FELT LIKE... SOMEONE *CALLED* ME...
BRRINNGG
IT'S OKAY-- I'LL GET IT.
BRRINNGG
HELLO, *MORISATO* RESIDENCE...
OH?! *THE ALMIGHTY* ?!

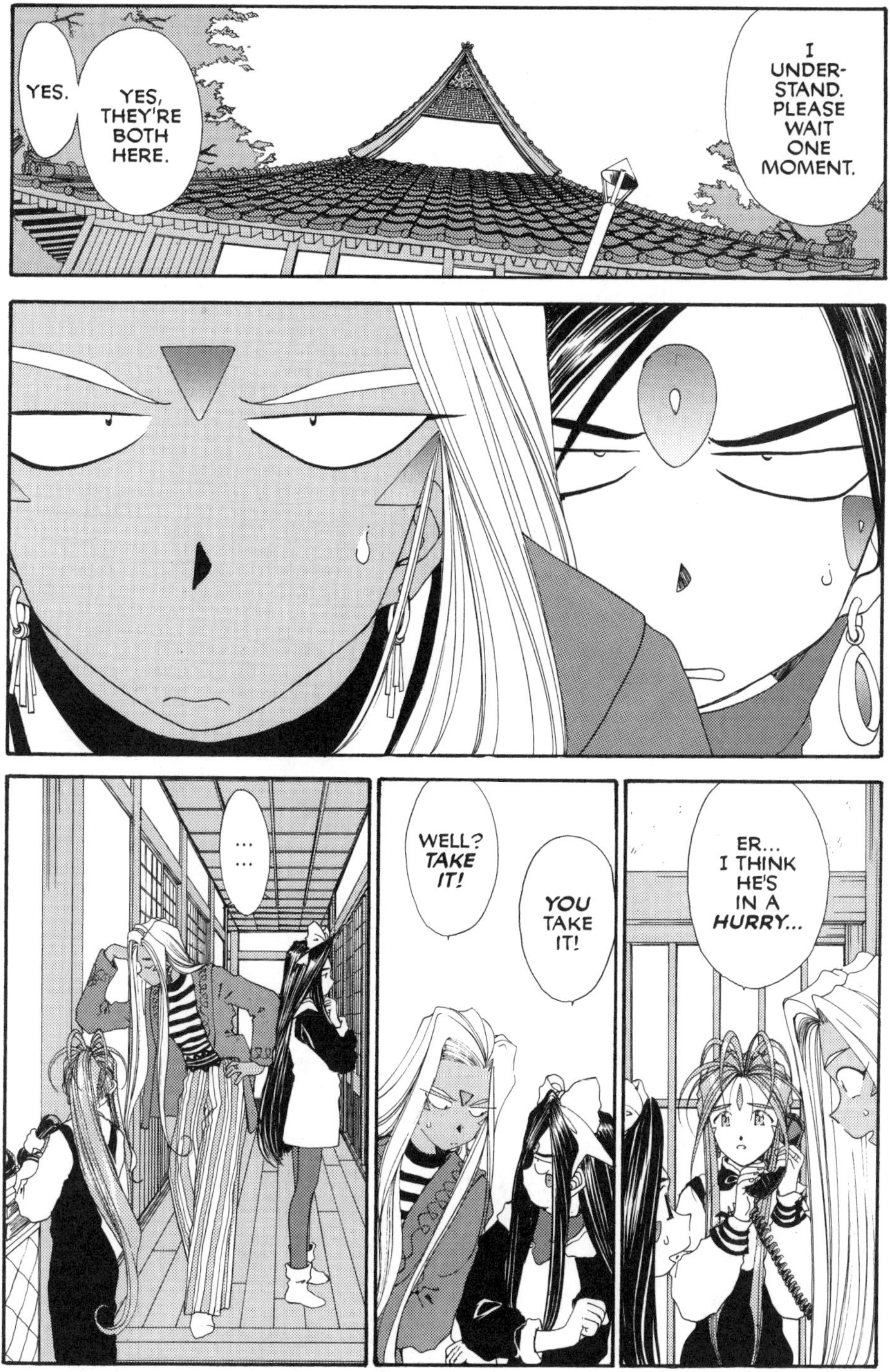
YES.
YES, THEY'RE BOTH HERE.
I UNDER-STAND. PLEASE WAIT ONE MOMENT.
......
WELL? *TAKE IT!*
YOU TAKE IT!
ER... I THINK HE'S IN A *HURRY...*

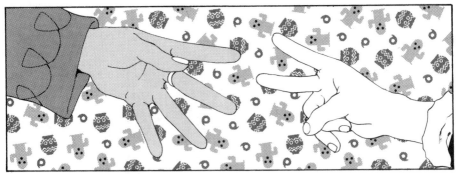

GRR...

WHAT ?!

Hello! ♥ Who is it...? ♥

Oh, ♥ Goodness! Daddy?! ♥ It's been ages!

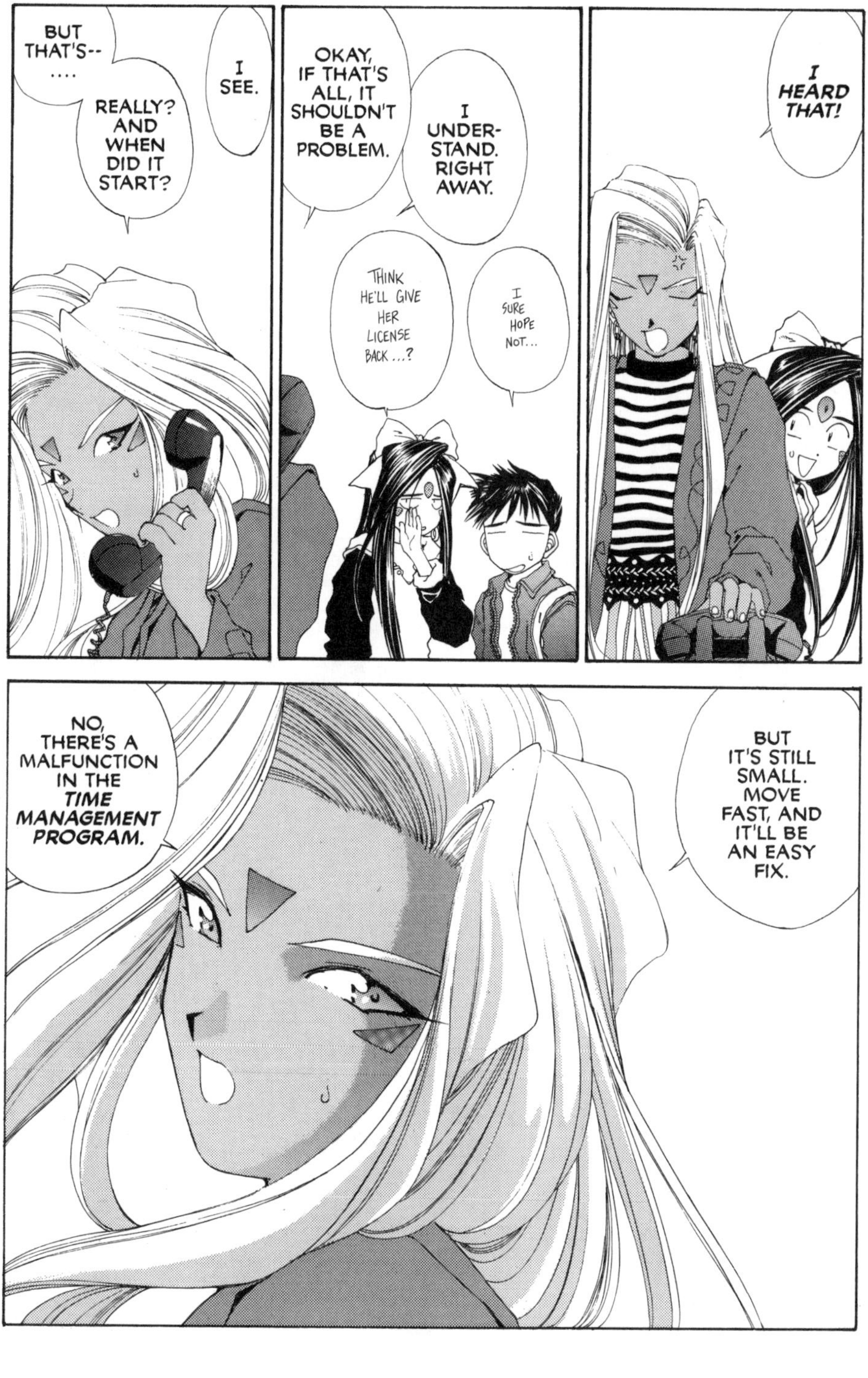
BUT THAT'S-- ....
REALLY? AND WHEN DID IT START?
I SEE.
OKAY, IF THAT'S ALL, IT SHOULDN'T BE A PROBLEM.
I UNDER-STAND. RIGHT AWAY.
THINK HE'LL GIVE HER LICENSE BACK ...?
I SURE HOPE NOT...
I HEARD THAT!
NO, THERE'S A MALFUNCTION IN THE *TIME MANAGEMENT PROGRAM.*
BUT IT'S STILL SMALL. MOVE FAST, AND IT'LL BE AN EASY FIX.

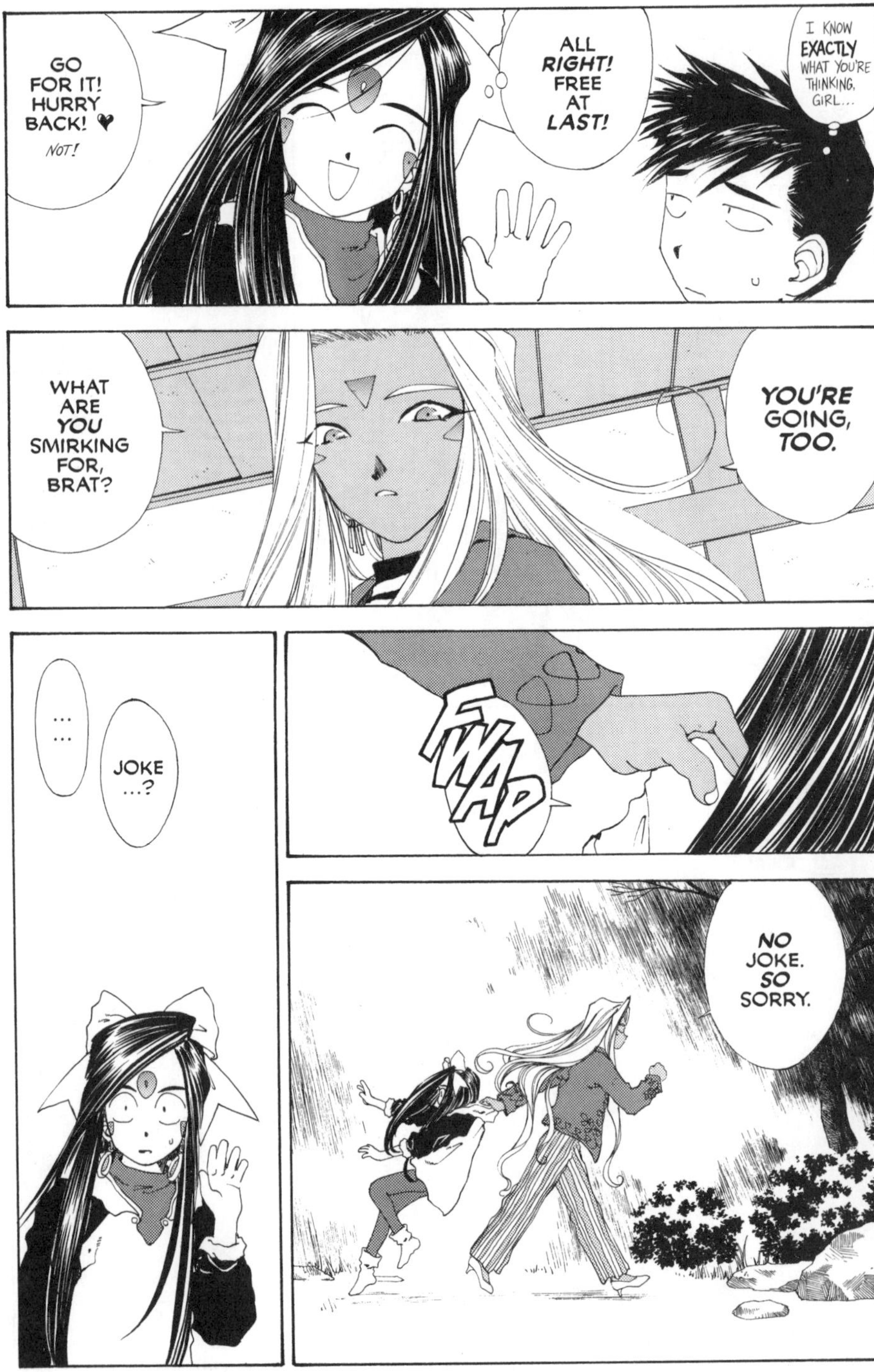
GO FOR IT! HURRY BACK! ♥
NOT!
ALL RIGHT! FREE AT LAST!
I KNOW EXACTLY WHAT YOU'RE THINKING, GIRL...
WHAT ARE YOU SMIRKING FOR, BRAT?
YOU'RE GOING, TOO.
......
JOKE ...?
FWAP
NO JOKE. SO SORRY.

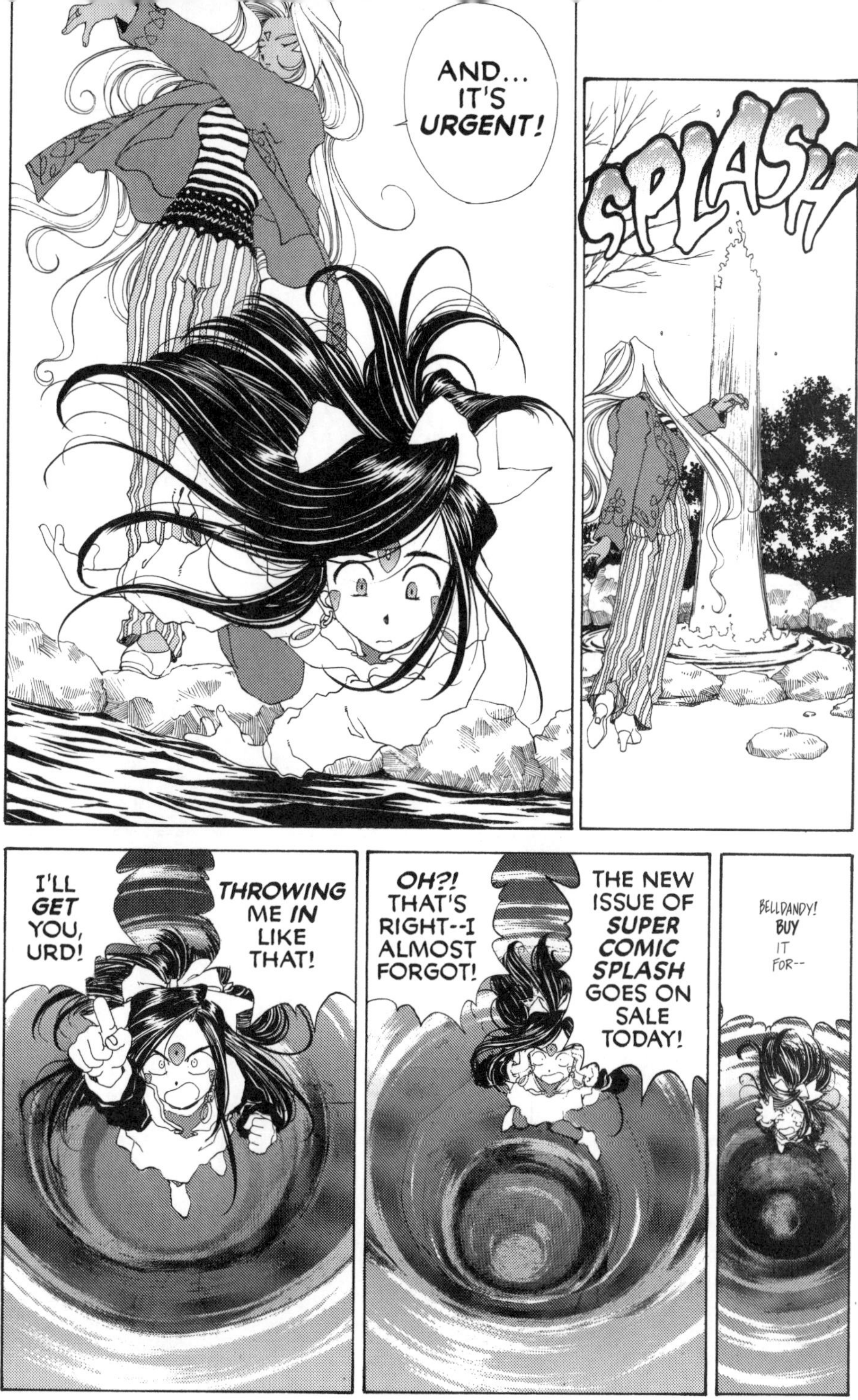
AND... IT'S URGENT!
SPLASH
I'LL GET YOU, URD!
THROWING ME IN LIKE THAT!
OH?! THAT'S RIGHT--I ALMOST FORGOT!
THE NEW ISSUE OF SUPER COMIC SPLASH GOES ON SALE TODAY!
BELLDANDY! BUY IT FOR--

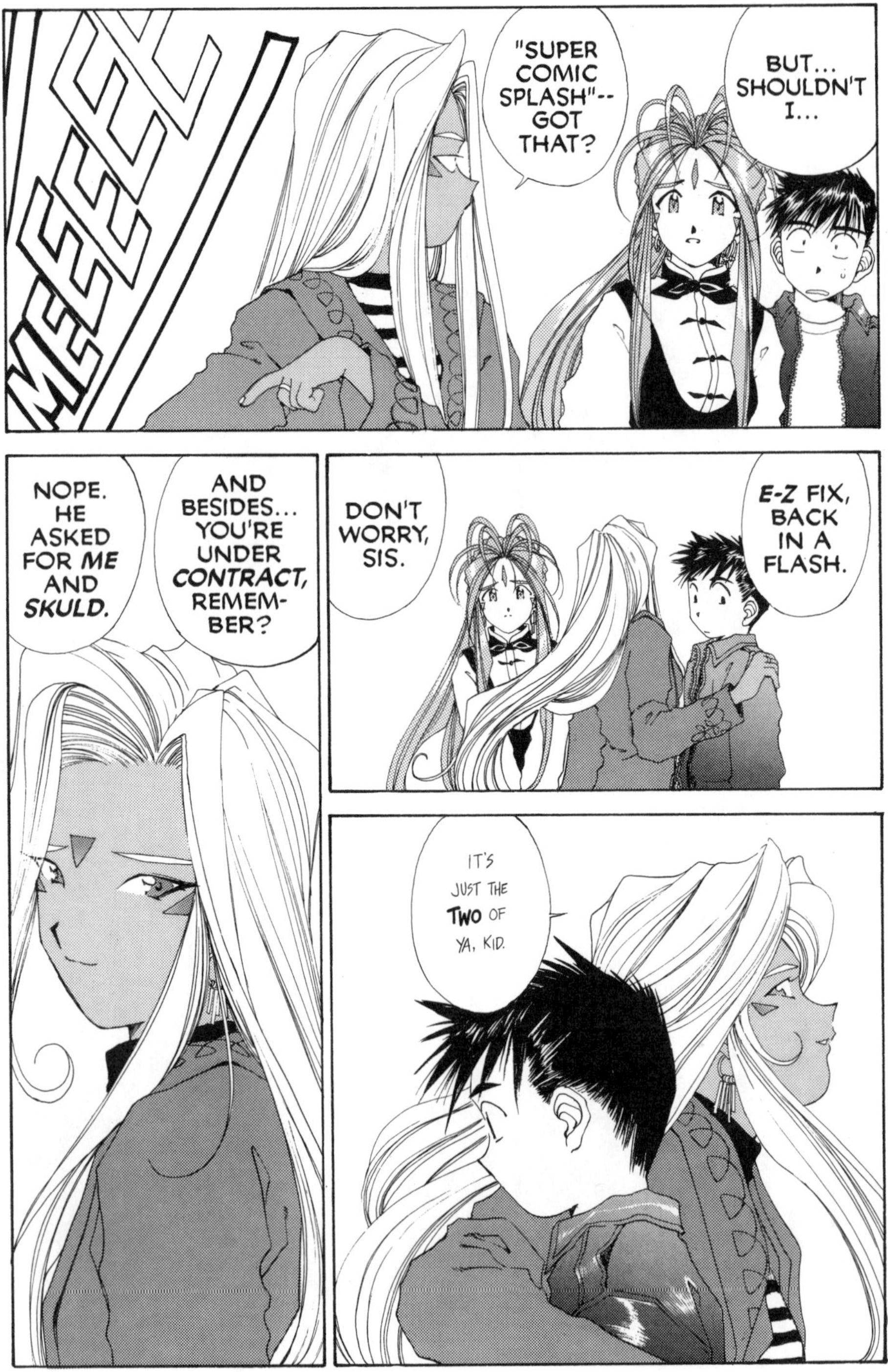
MEEEEEE
"SUPER COMIC SPLASH"-- GOT THAT?
BUT... SHOULDN'T I...
NOPE. HE ASKED FOR *ME* AND *SKULD.*
AND BESIDES... YOU'RE UNDER *CONTRACT,* REMEM-BER?
DON'T WORRY, SIS.
E-Z FIX, BACK IN A FLASH.
IT'S JUST THE **TWO** OF YA, KID.

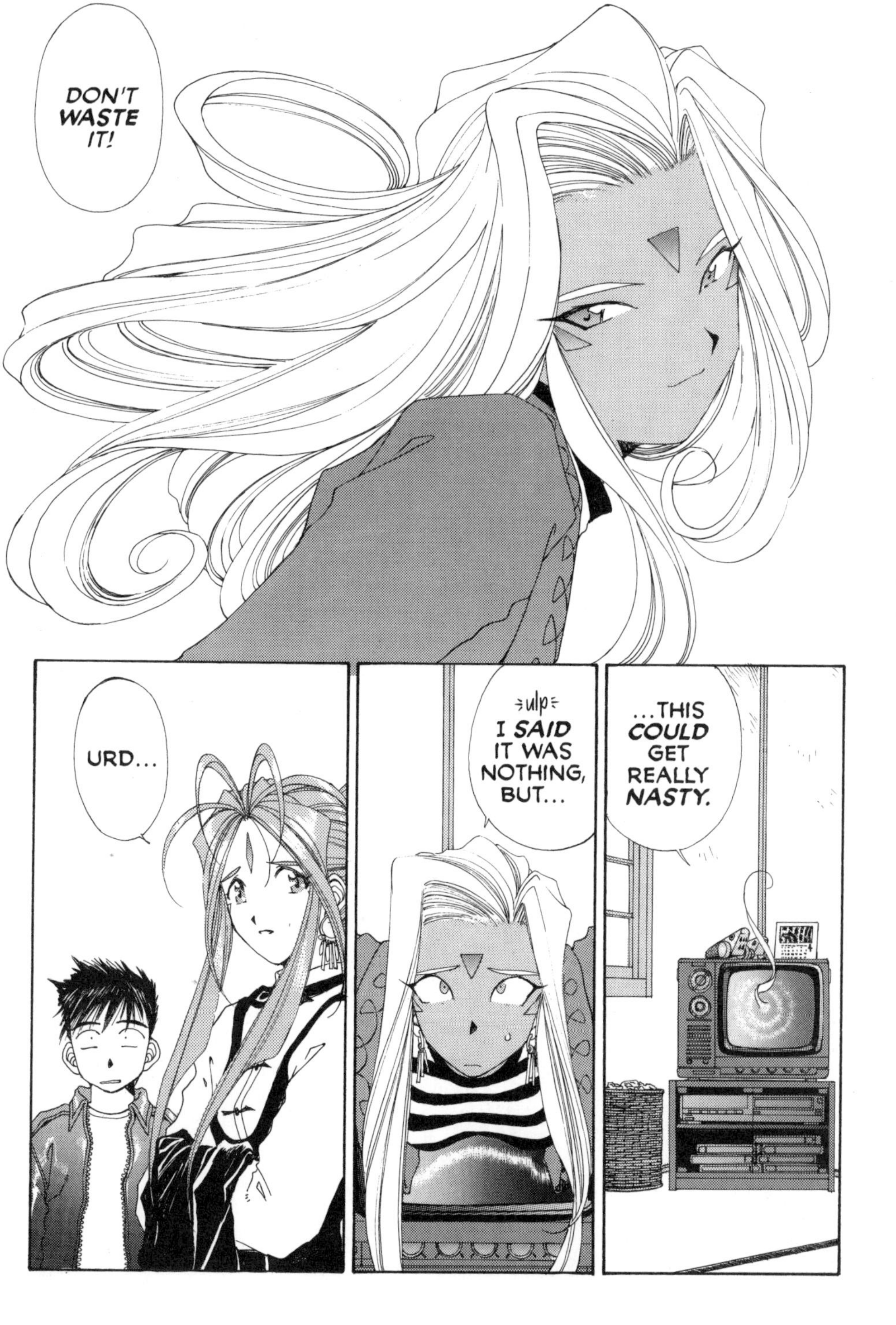
DON'T WASTE IT!
URD...
ulp
I SAID IT WAS NOTHING, BUT...
...THIS COULD GET REALLY NASTY.

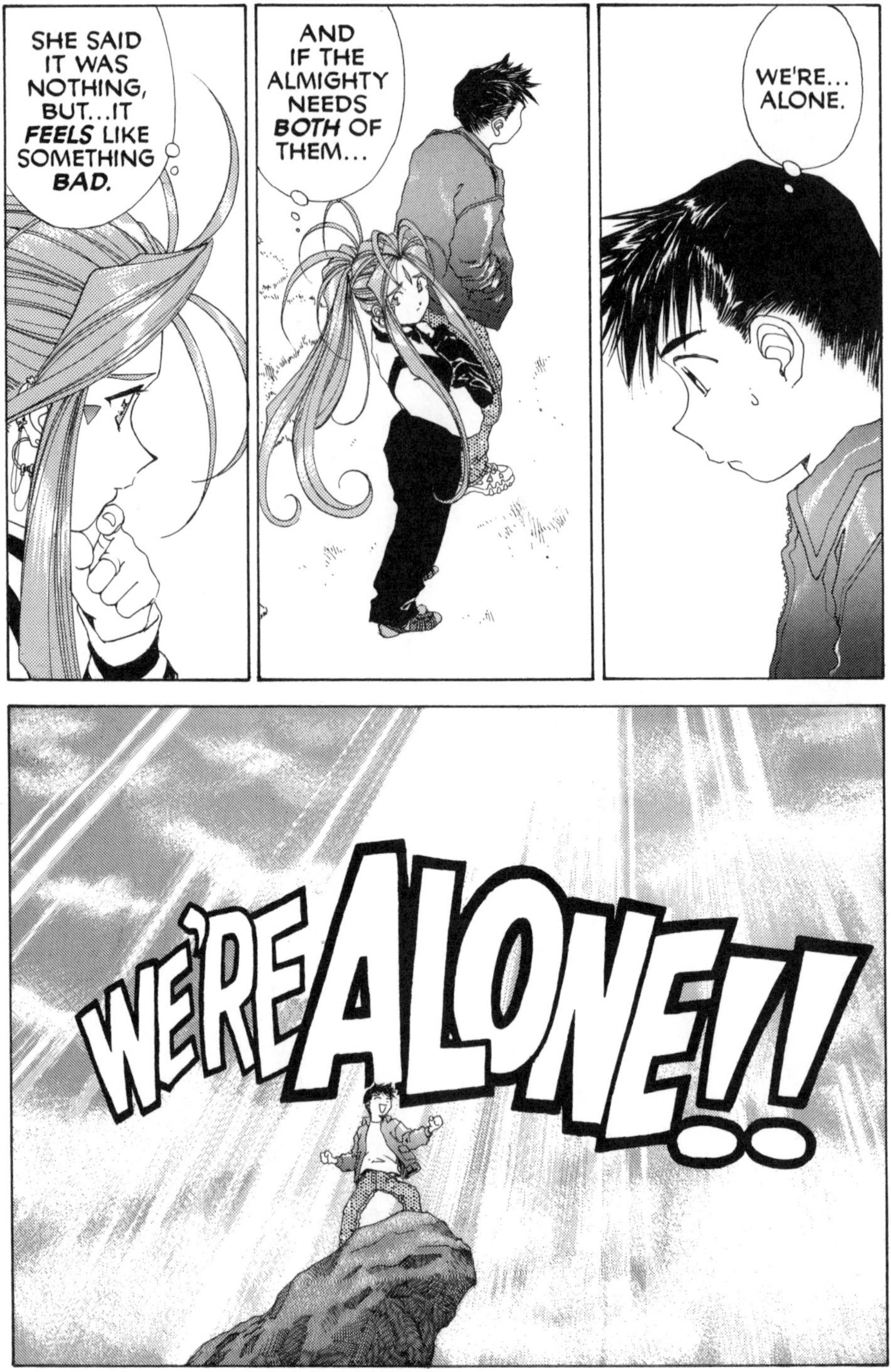
SHE SAID IT WAS NOTHING, BUT...IT *FEELS* LIKE SOMETHING *BAD.*
AND IF THE ALMIGHTY NEEDS *BOTH* OF THEM...
WE'RE... ALONE.
WE'RE ALONE!!

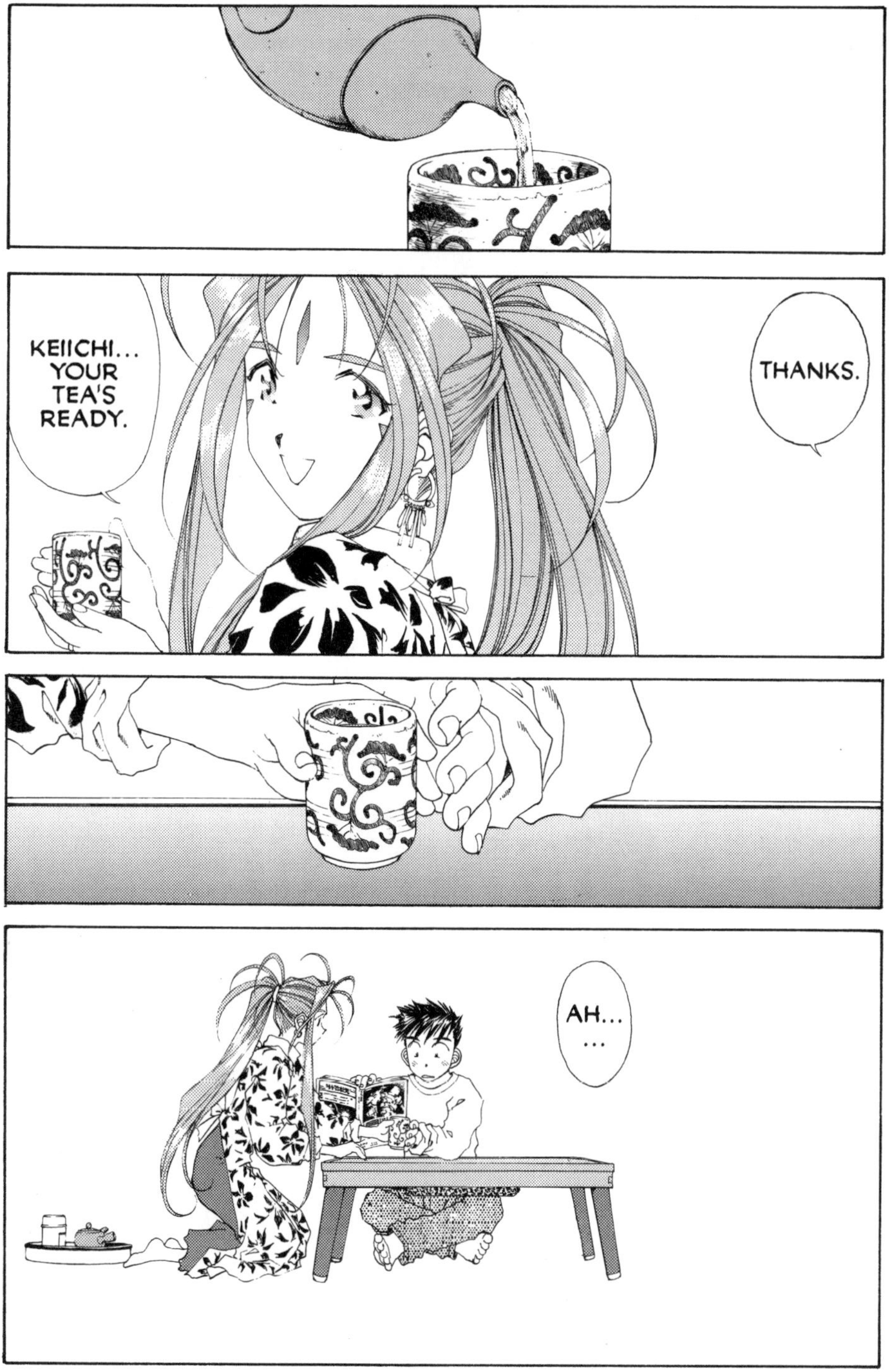
KEIICHI... YOUR TEA'S READY.
THANKS.
AH... ...

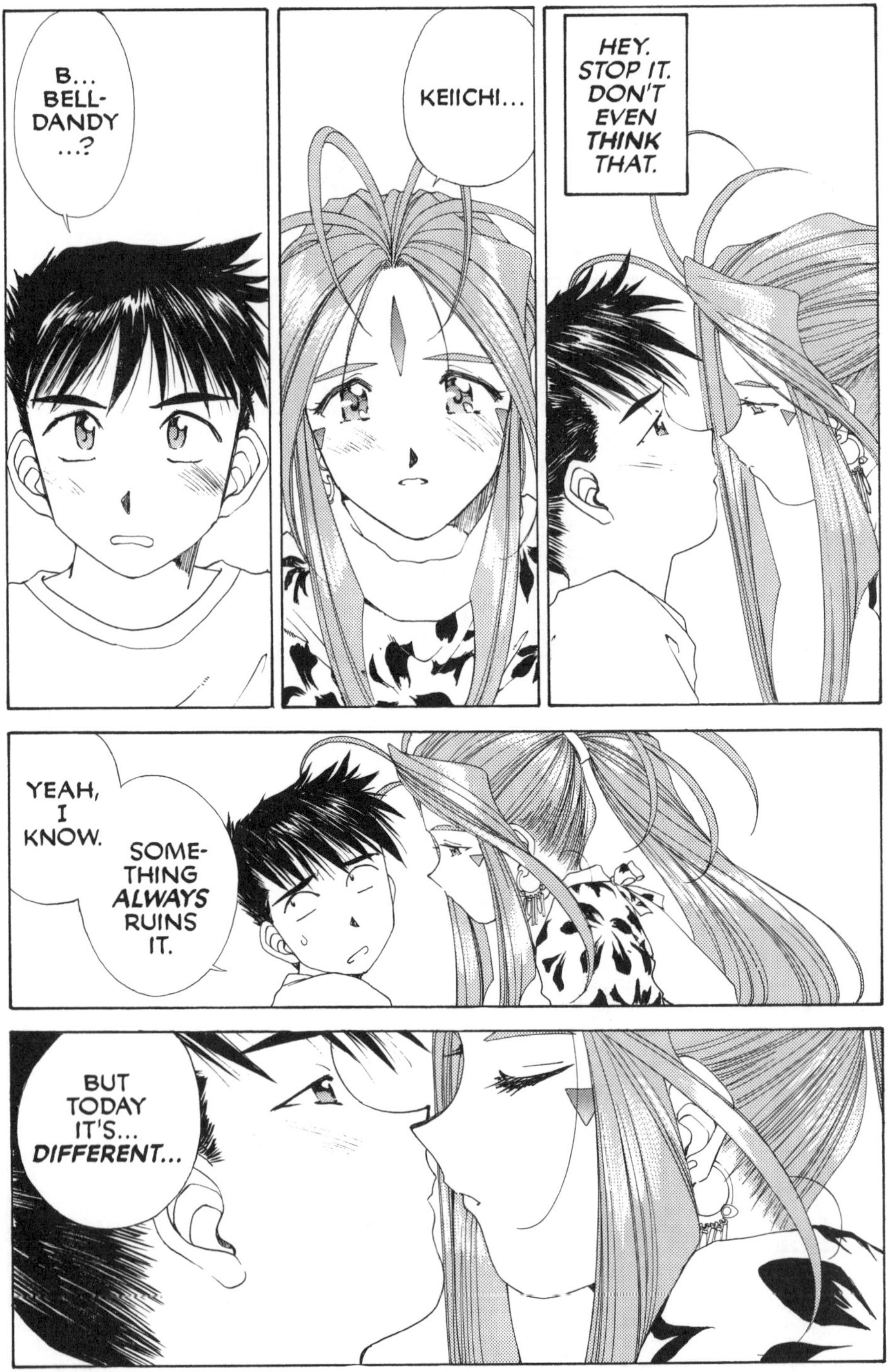
B... BELL-DANDY ...?
KEIICHI...
HEY. STOP IT. DON'T EVEN THINK THAT.
YEAH, I KNOW.
SOME-THING *ALWAYS* RUINS IT.
BUT TODAY IT'S... ***DIFFERENT...***

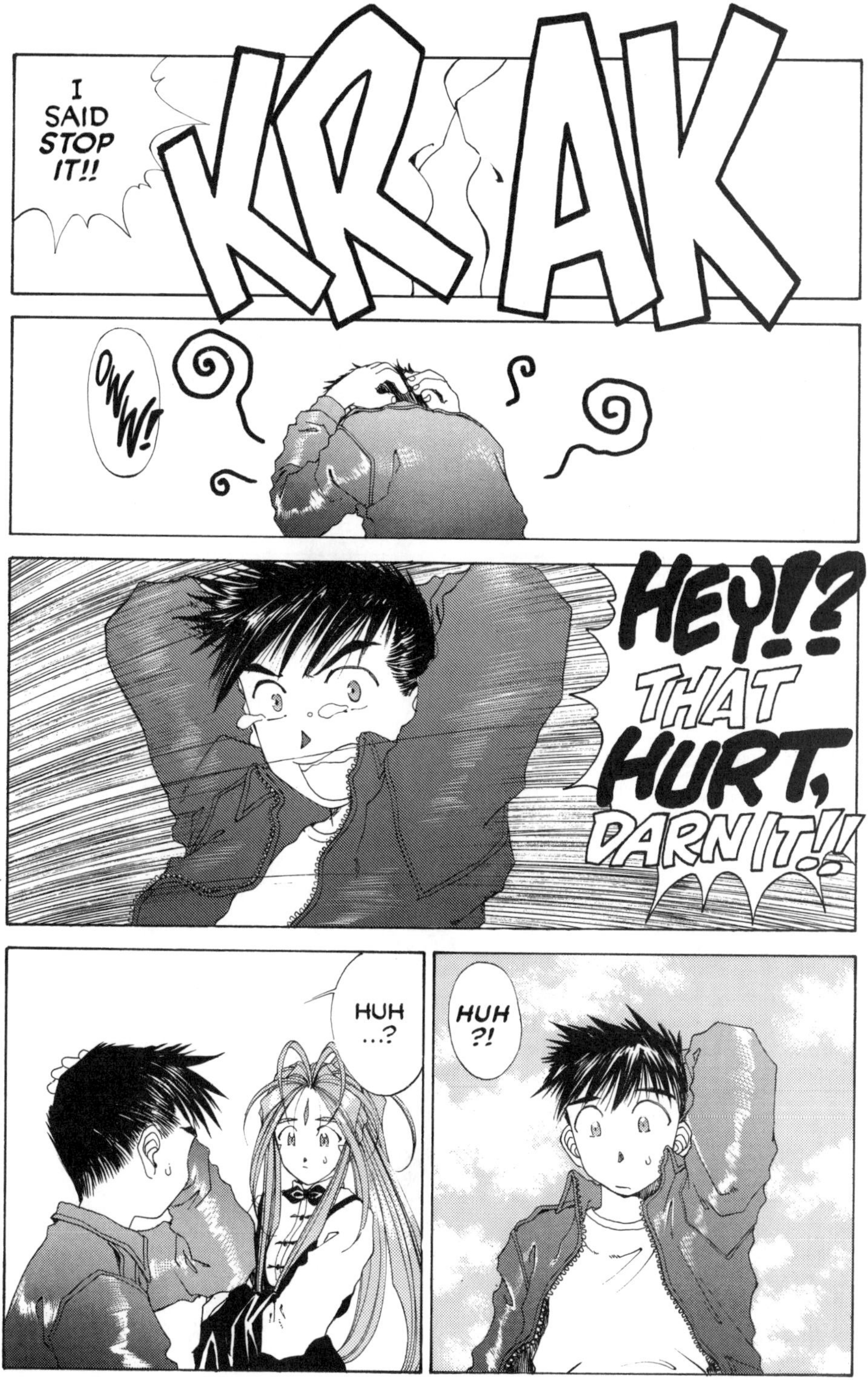
I SAID STOP IT!!
KRAK
OWW!
HEY!?
THAT HURT, DARN IT!!
HUH ...?
HUH ?!

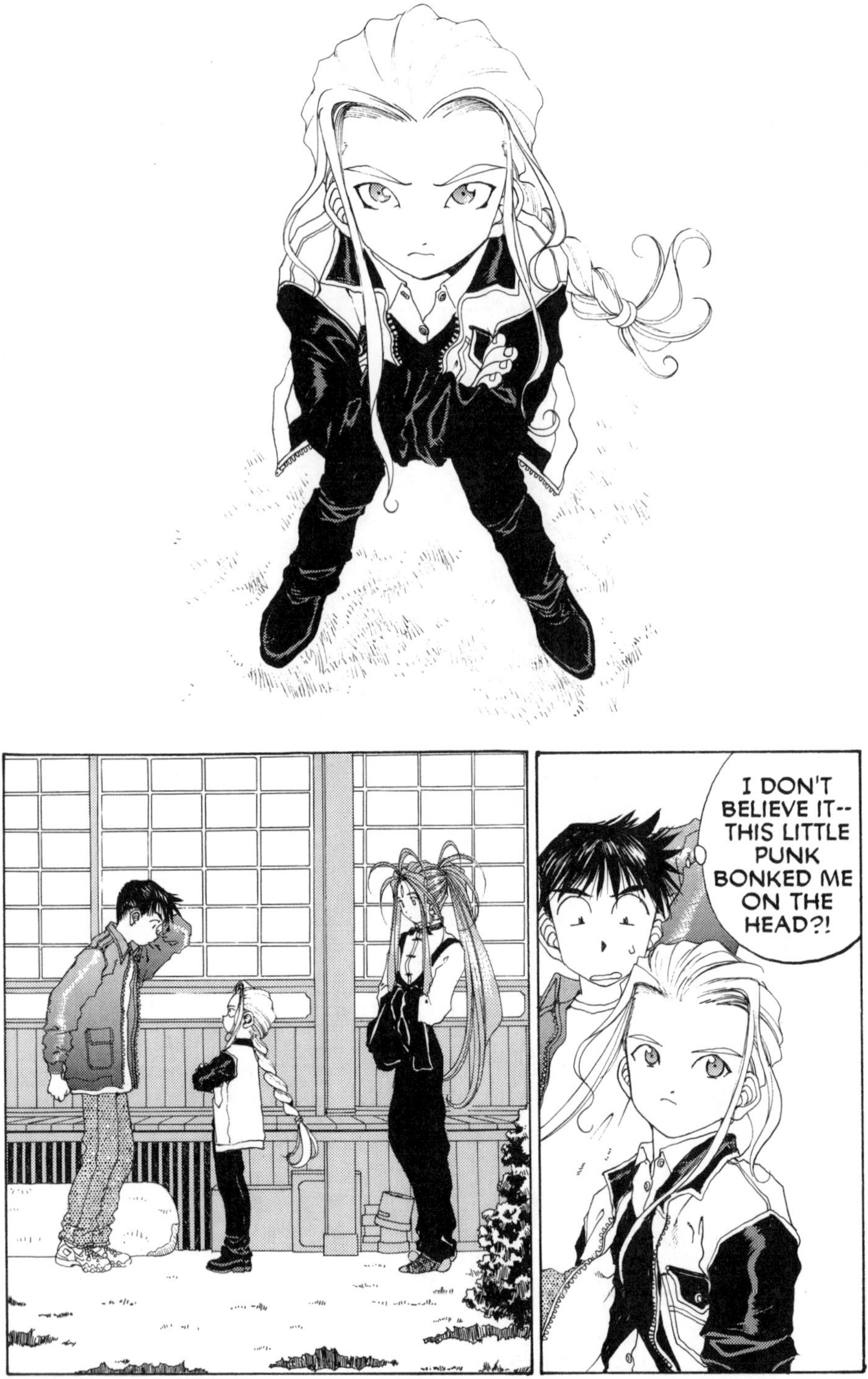
I DON'T BELIEVE IT-- THIS LITTLE PUNK BONKED ME ON THE HEAD?!

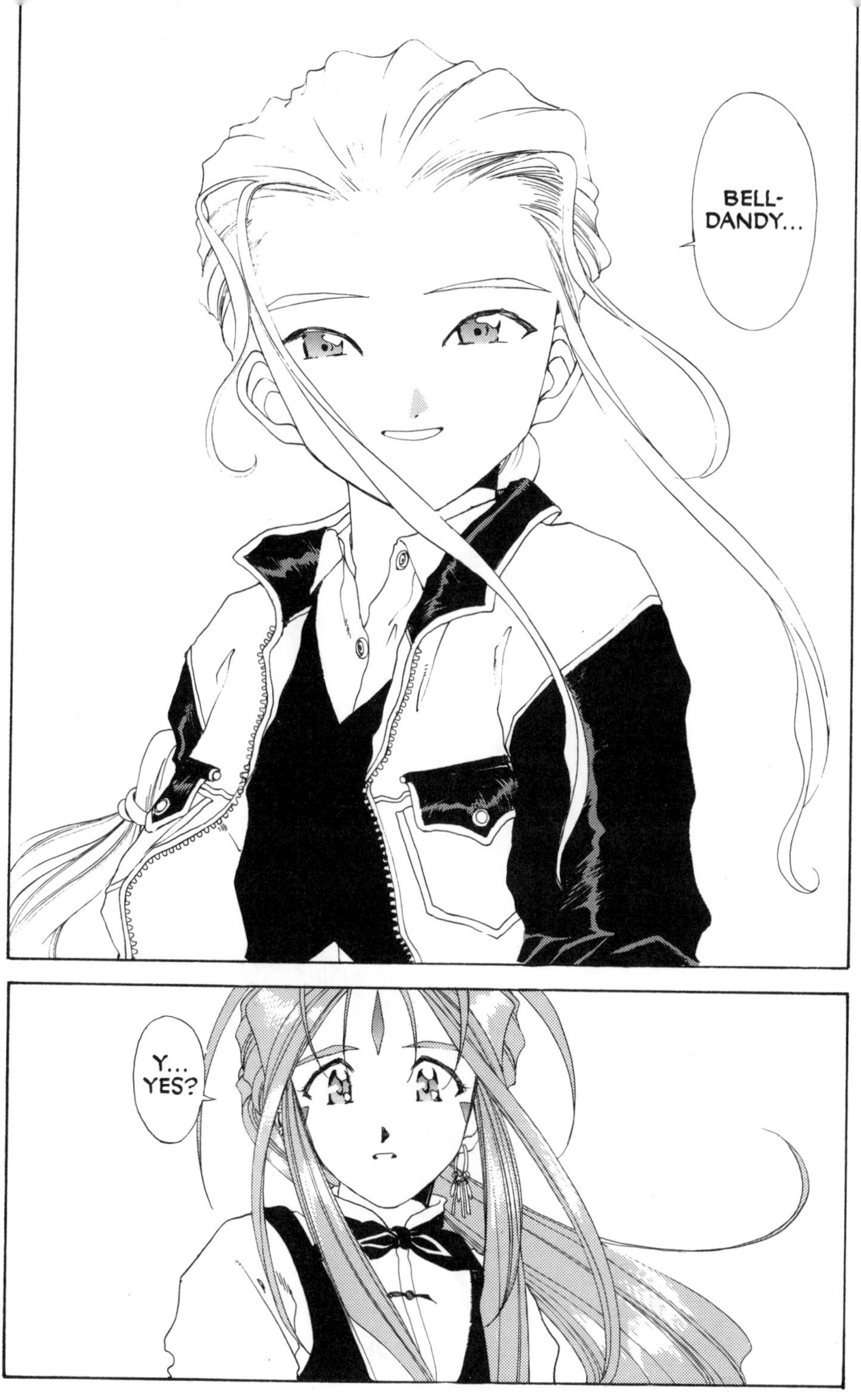
BELL-DANDY...
Y... YES?

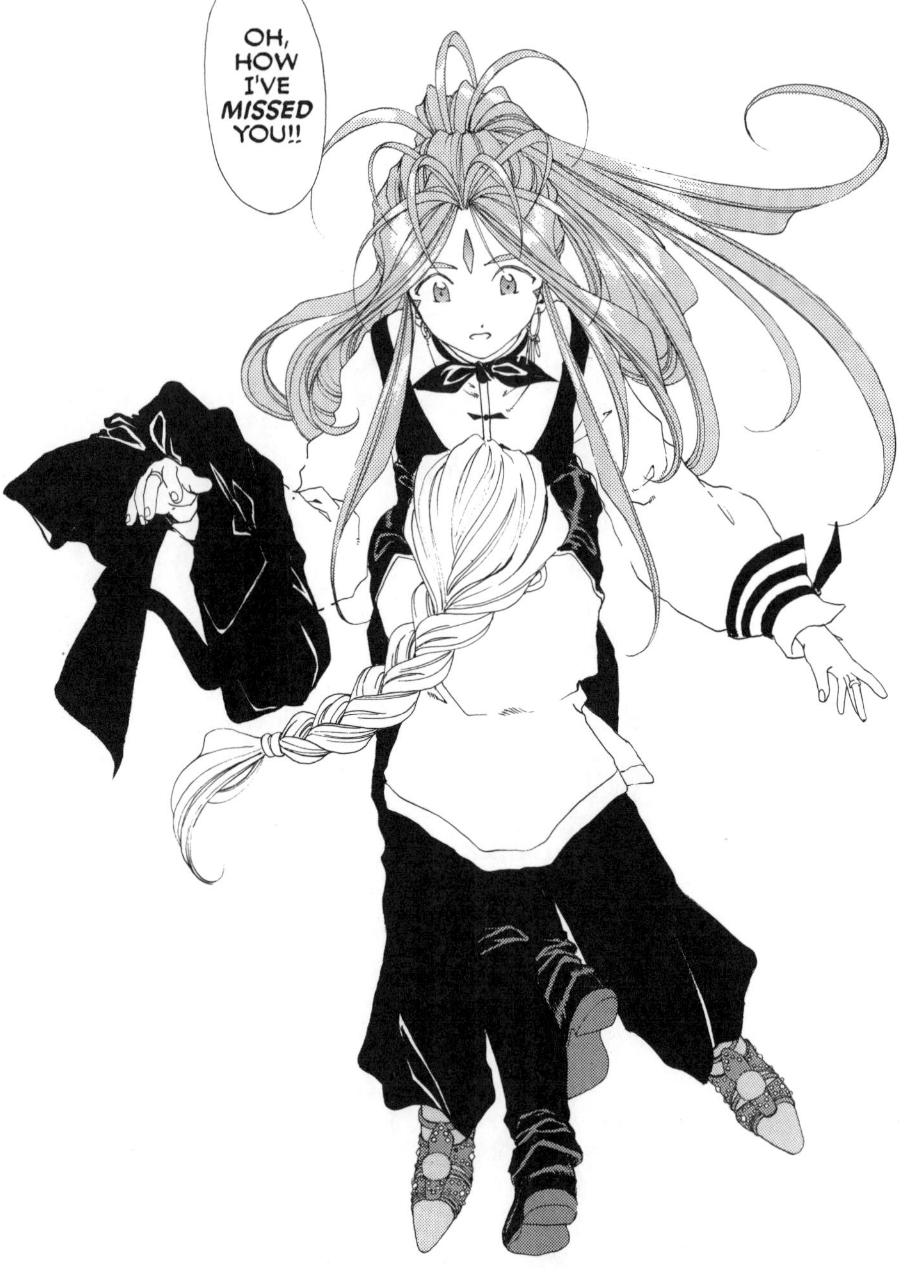
OH, HOW I'VE *MISSED* YOU!!

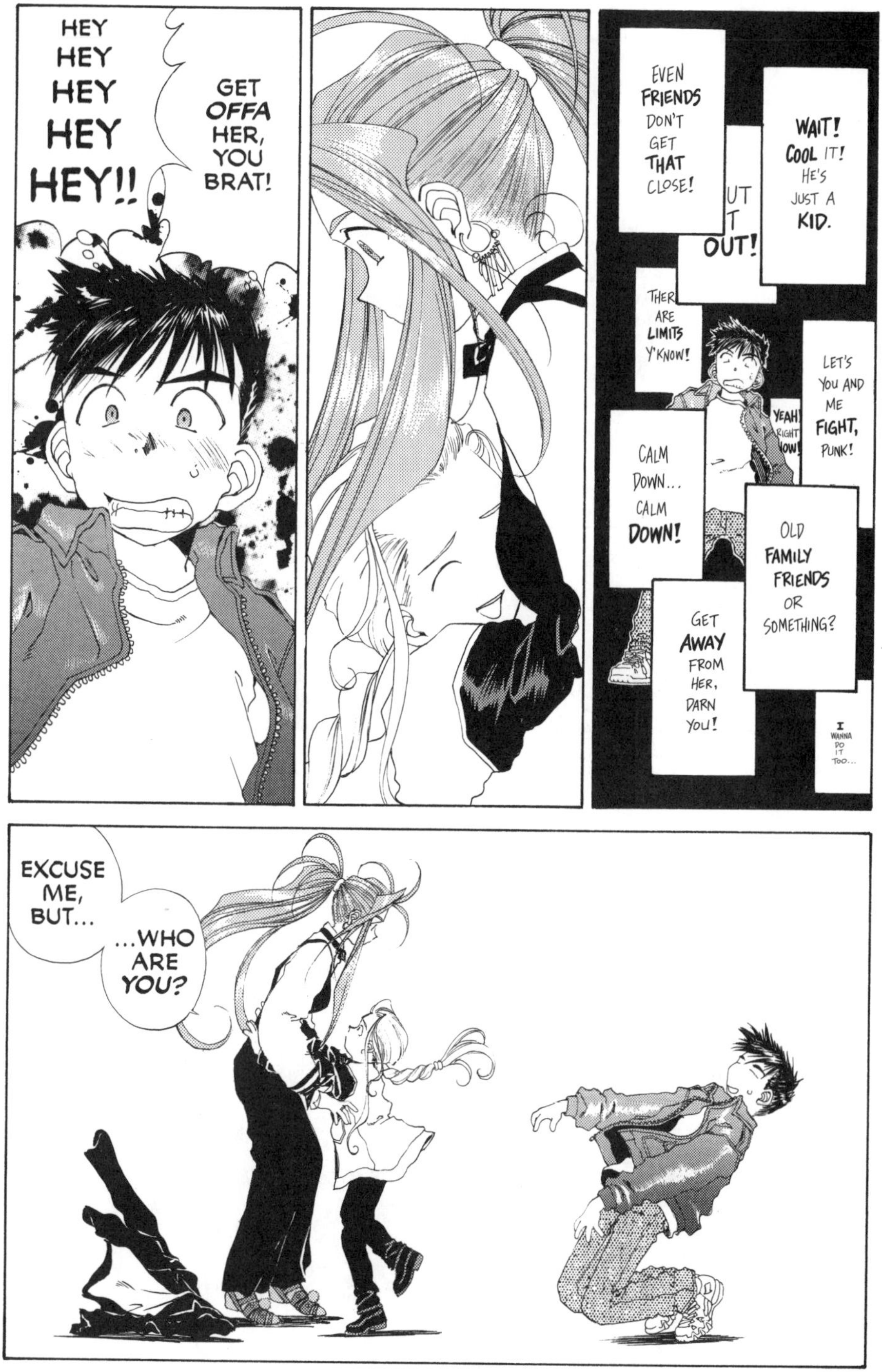
HEY HEY HEY HEY HEY!!
GET OFFA HER, YOU BRAT!
EVEN FRIENDS DON'T GET THAT CLOSE!
UT T OUT!
WAIT! COOL IT! HE'S JUST A KID.
THER ARE LIMITS Y'KNOW!
LET'S YOU AND ME FIGHT, PUNK!
YEAH RIGHT NOW!
CALM DOWN... CALM DOWN!
OLD FAMILY FRIENDS OR SOMETHING?
GET AWAY FROM HER, DARN YOU!
I WANNA DO IT TOO...
EXCUSE ME, BUT...
...WHO ARE YOU?

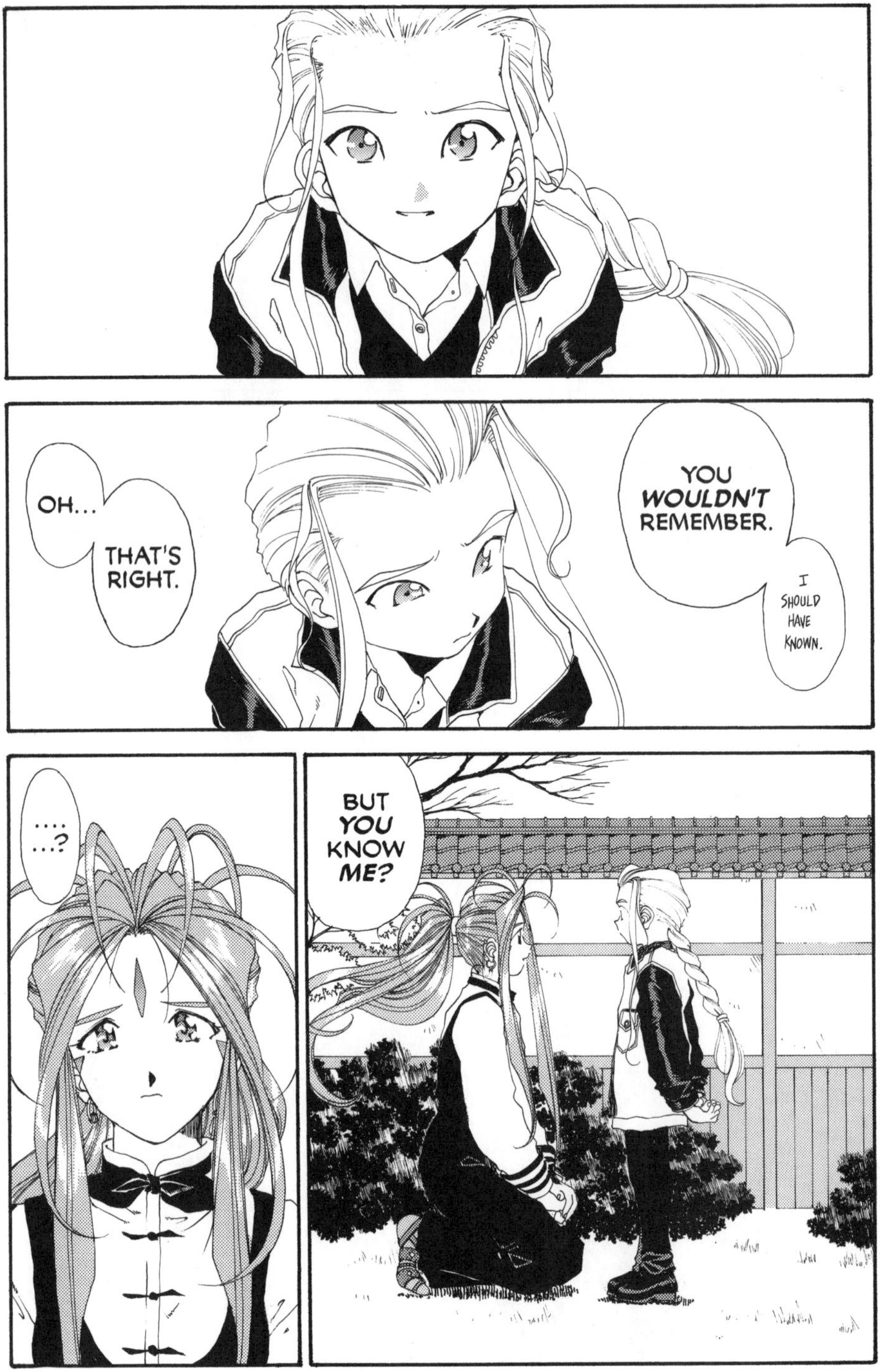

OH...
THAT'S RIGHT.
YOU *WOULDN'T* REMEMBER.
I SHOULD HAVE KNOWN.
....
...?
BUT *YOU* KNOW *ME?*

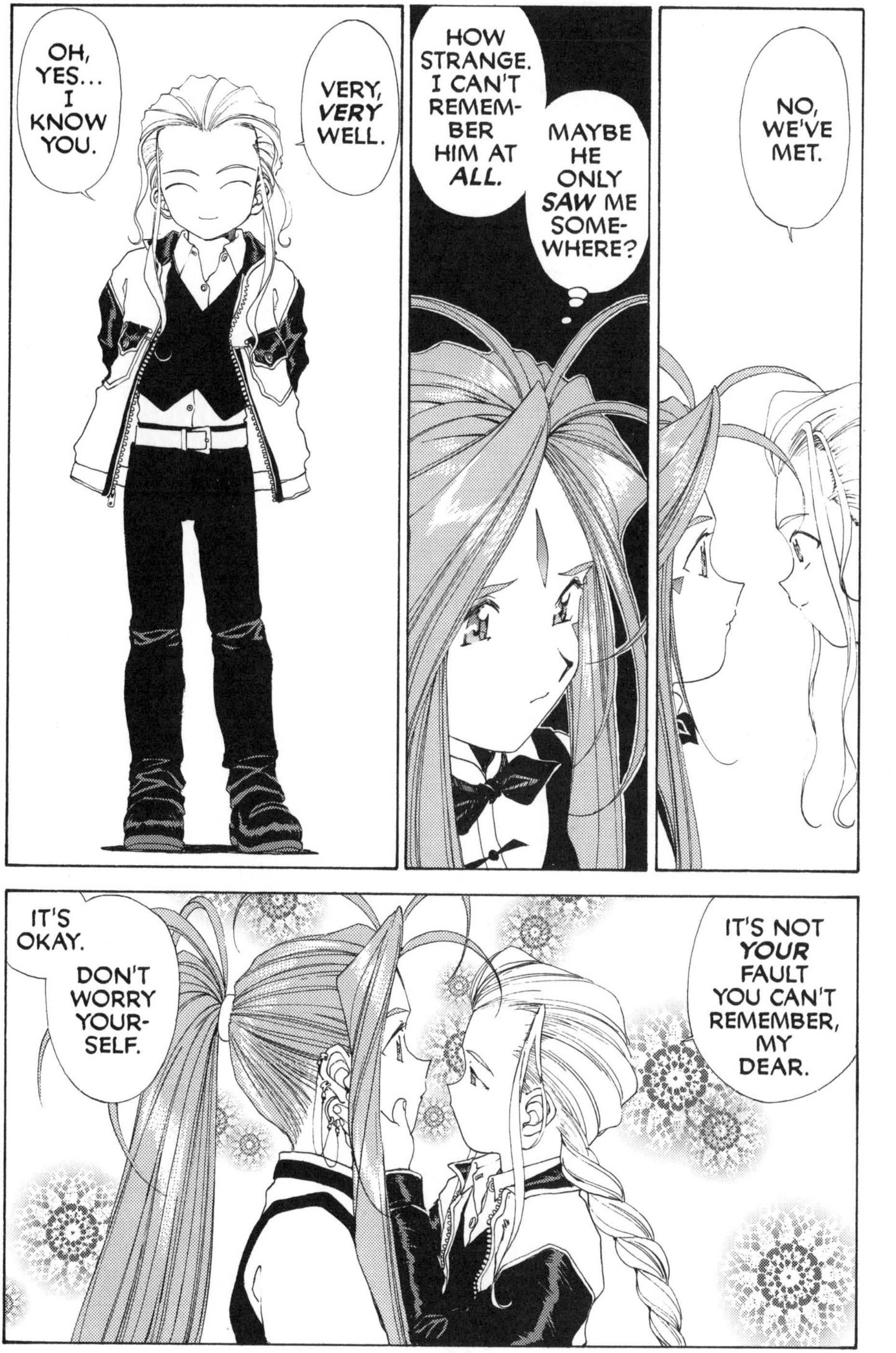
OH, YES... I KNOW YOU.
VERY, VERY WELL.
HOW STRANGE. I CAN'T REMEMBER HIM AT ALL.
MAYBE HE ONLY SAW ME SOMEWHERE?
NO, WE'VE MET.
IT'S OKAY.
DON'T WORRY YOURSELF.
IT'S NOT YOUR FAULT YOU CAN'T REMEMBER, MY DEAR.

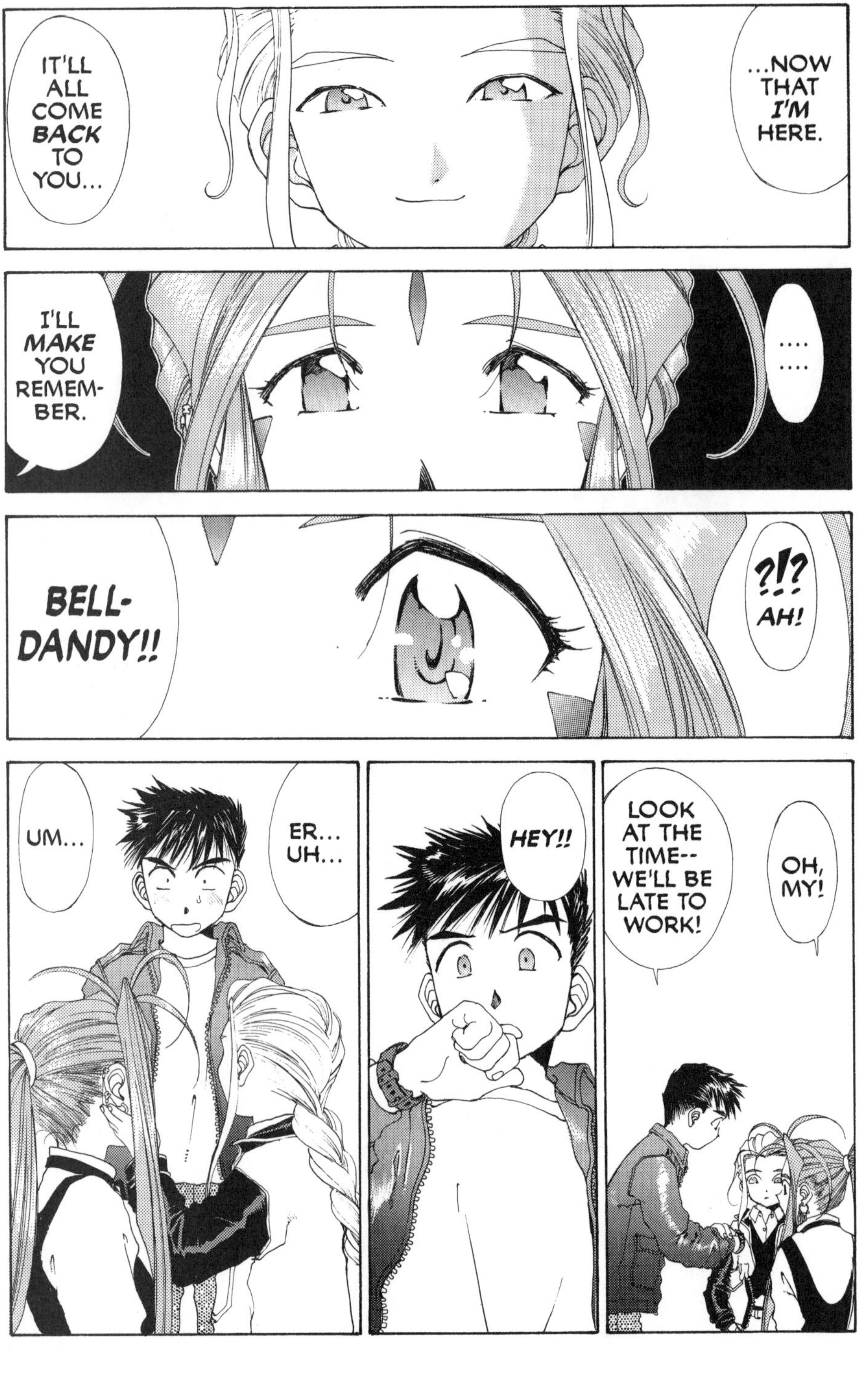
IT'LL ALL COME *BACK* TO YOU...
...NOW THAT *I'M* HERE.
I'LL *MAKE* YOU REMEMBER.
....
BELL-DANDY!!
?!? *AH!*
UM...
ER... UH...
HEY!!
LOOK AT THE TIME-- WE'LL BE LATE TO WORK!
OH, MY!

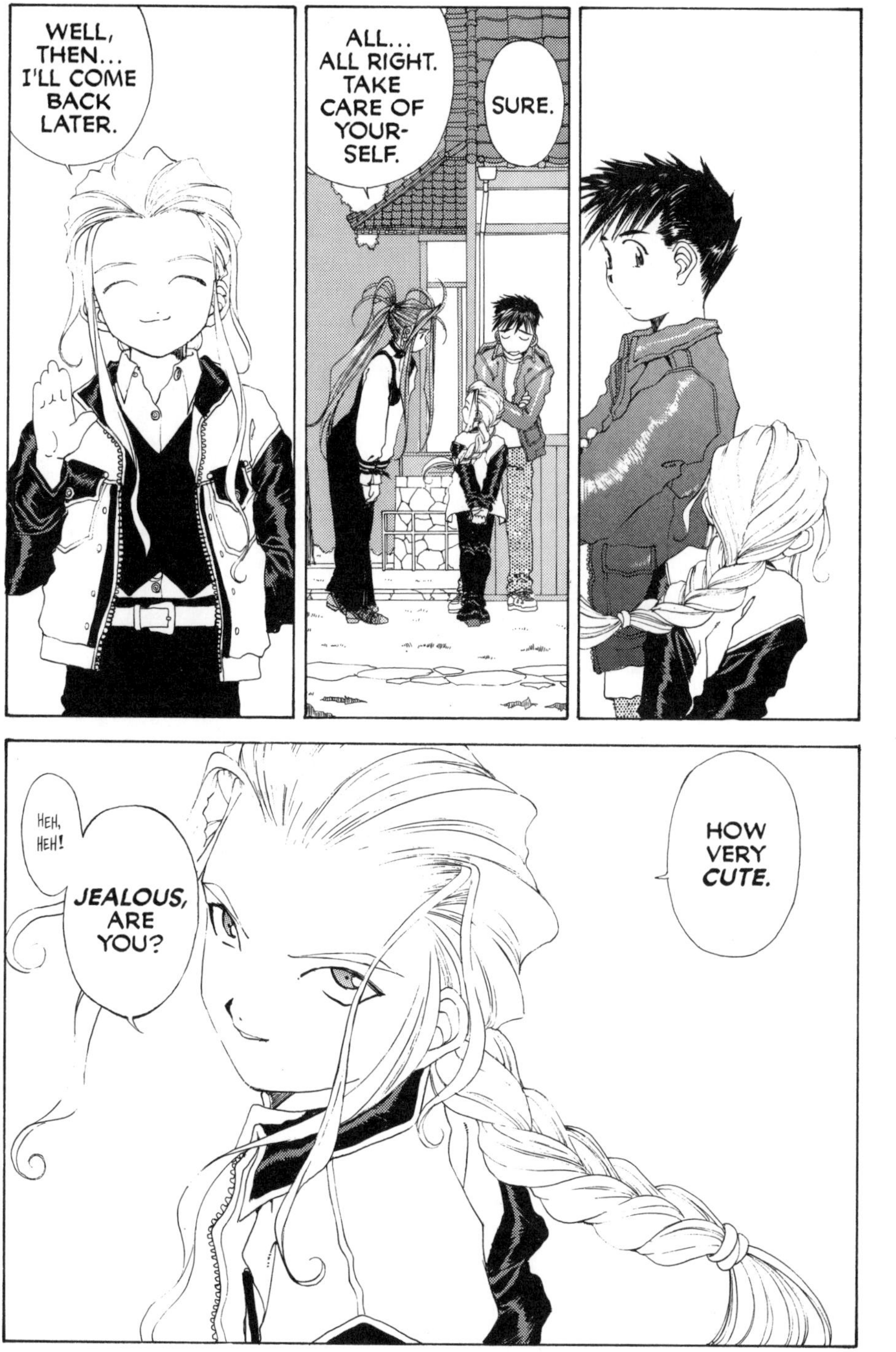
WELL, THEN... I'LL COME BACK LATER.
ALL... ALL RIGHT. TAKE CARE OF YOUR-SELF.
SURE.
HEH, HEH!
JEALOUS, ARE YOU?
HOW VERY CUTE.

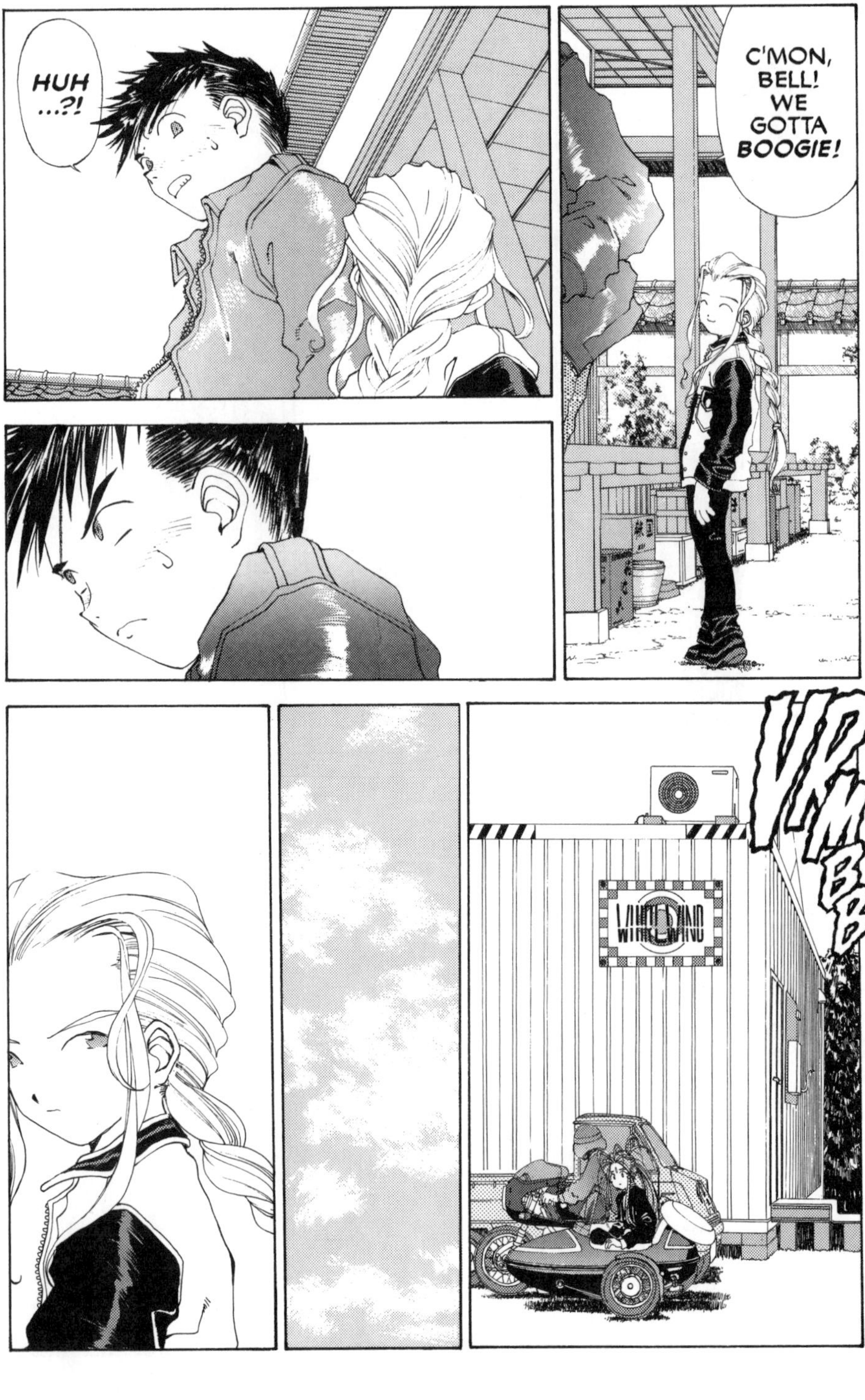
HUH ...?!
C'MON, BELL! WE GOTTA BOOGIE!
WHIRLWIND
VROMBB

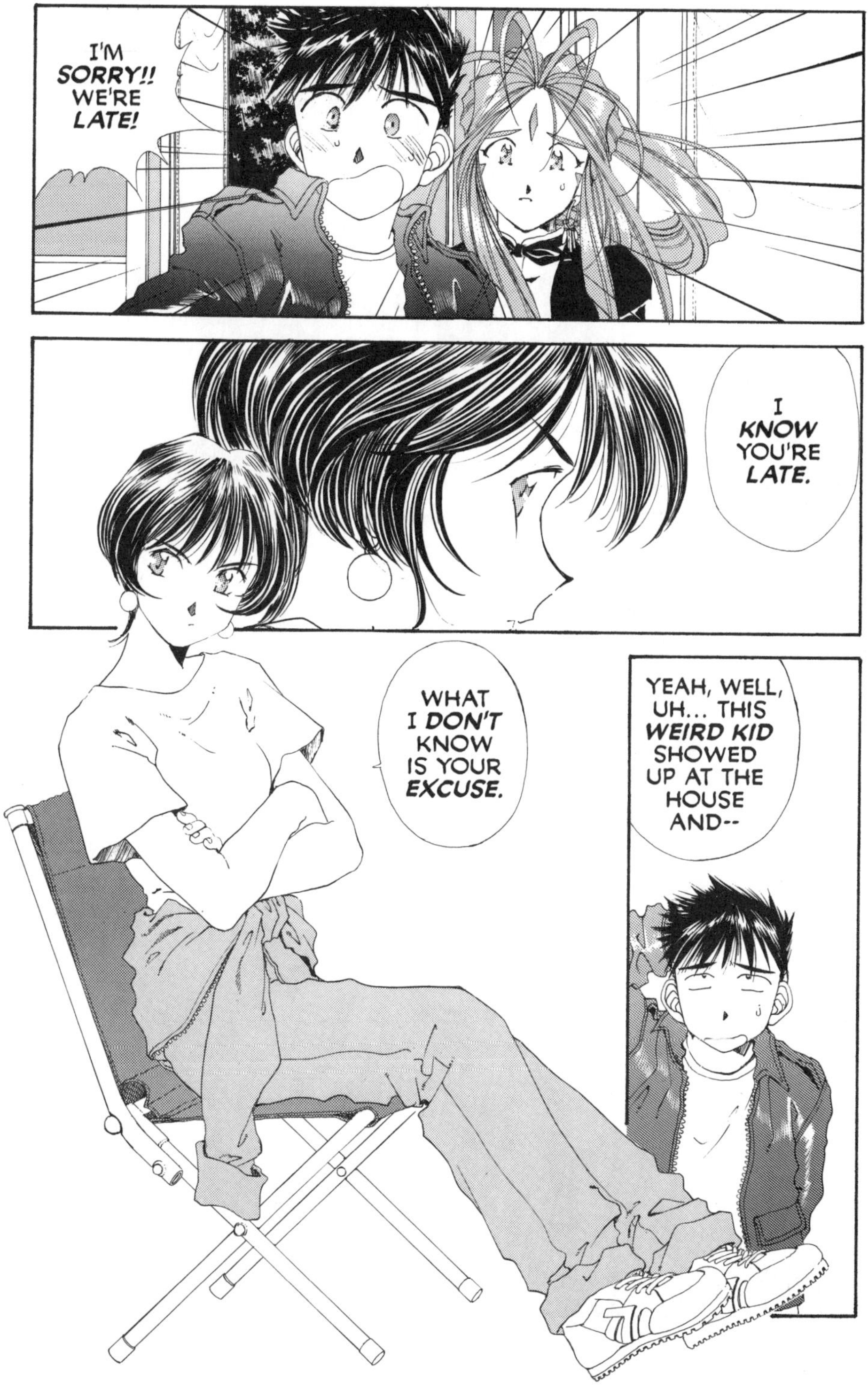
I'M *SORRY!!* WE'RE *LATE!*
I *KNOW* YOU'RE *LATE.*
WHAT I *DON'T* KNOW IS YOUR *EXCUSE.*
YEAH, WELL, UH... THIS *WEIRD KID* SHOWED UP AT THE HOUSE AND--

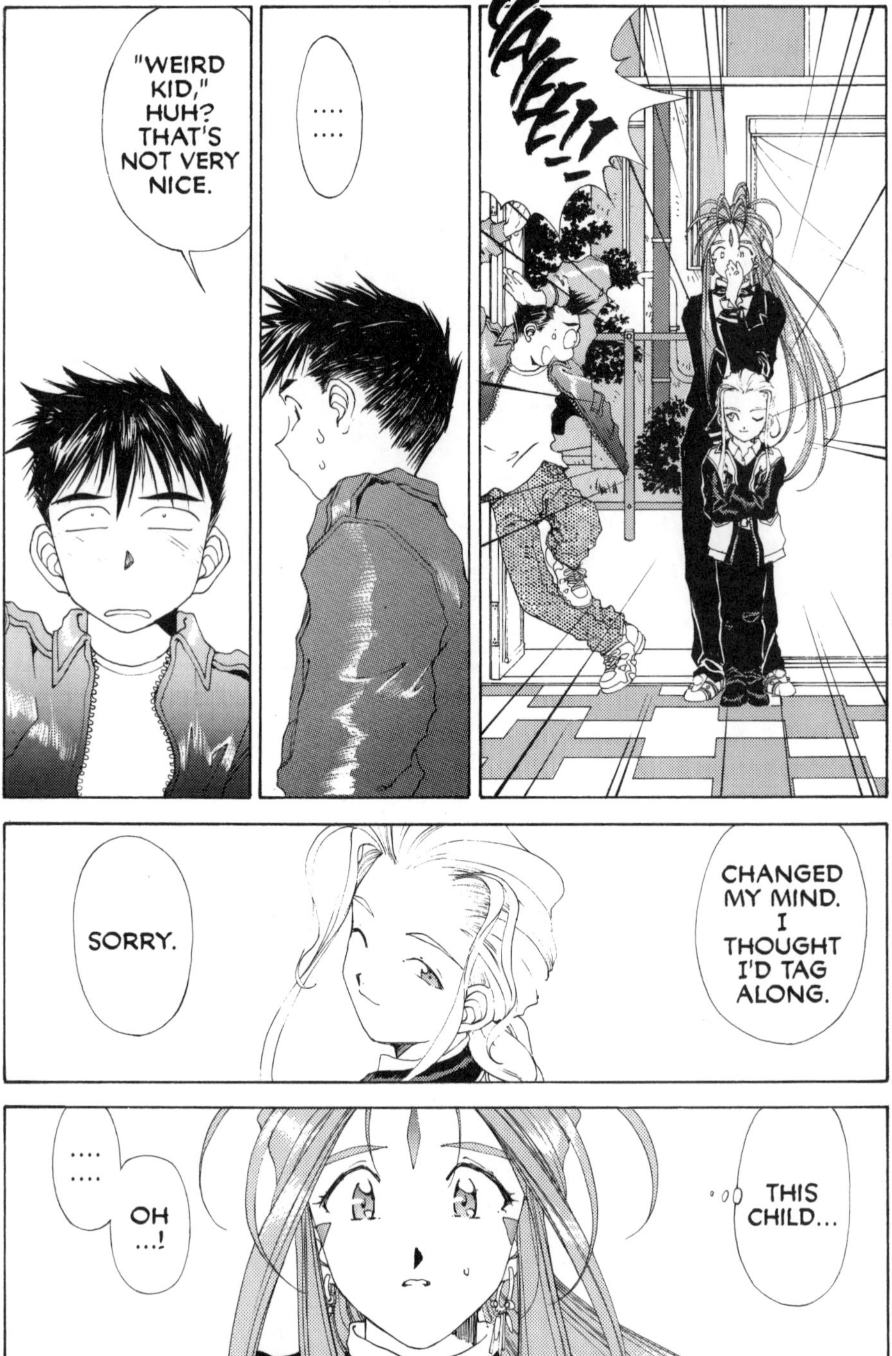
"WEIRD KID," HUH? THAT'S NOT VERY NICE.
....
SORRY.
CHANGED MY MIND. I THOUGHT I'D TAG ALONG.
.... OH ...!
THIS CHILD...

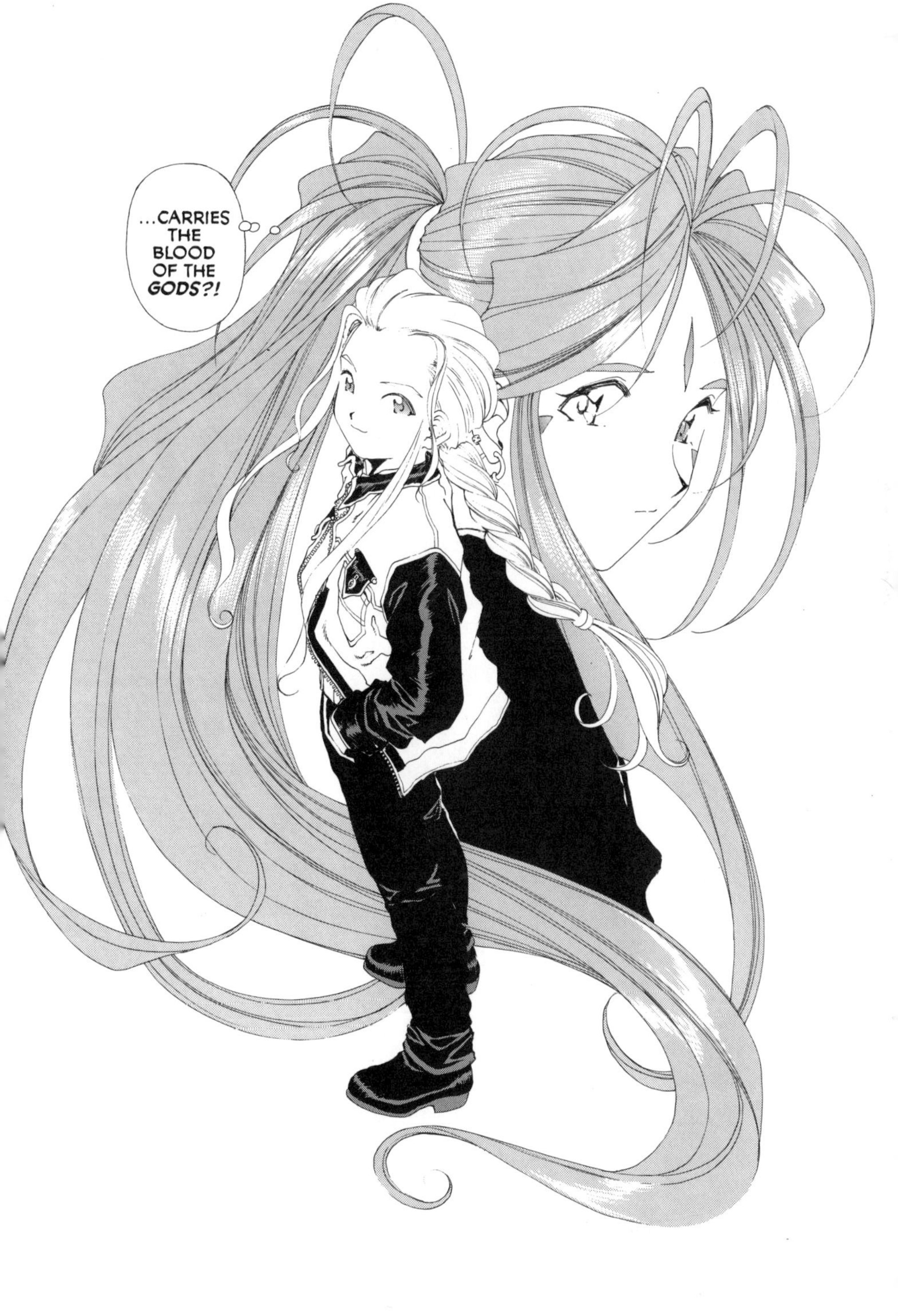
...CARRIES THE BLOOD OF THE *GODS?!*

THE
TIME
I MET
YOU
IT
BEGAN...

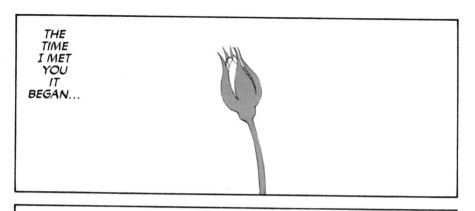

THE TIME
YOU
FORGOT
ME, IT
CAME
TO
BLOOM...

AND
IF YOU
DON'T
REMEMBER
ME
NOW...

THE BEGINNING OF THE END

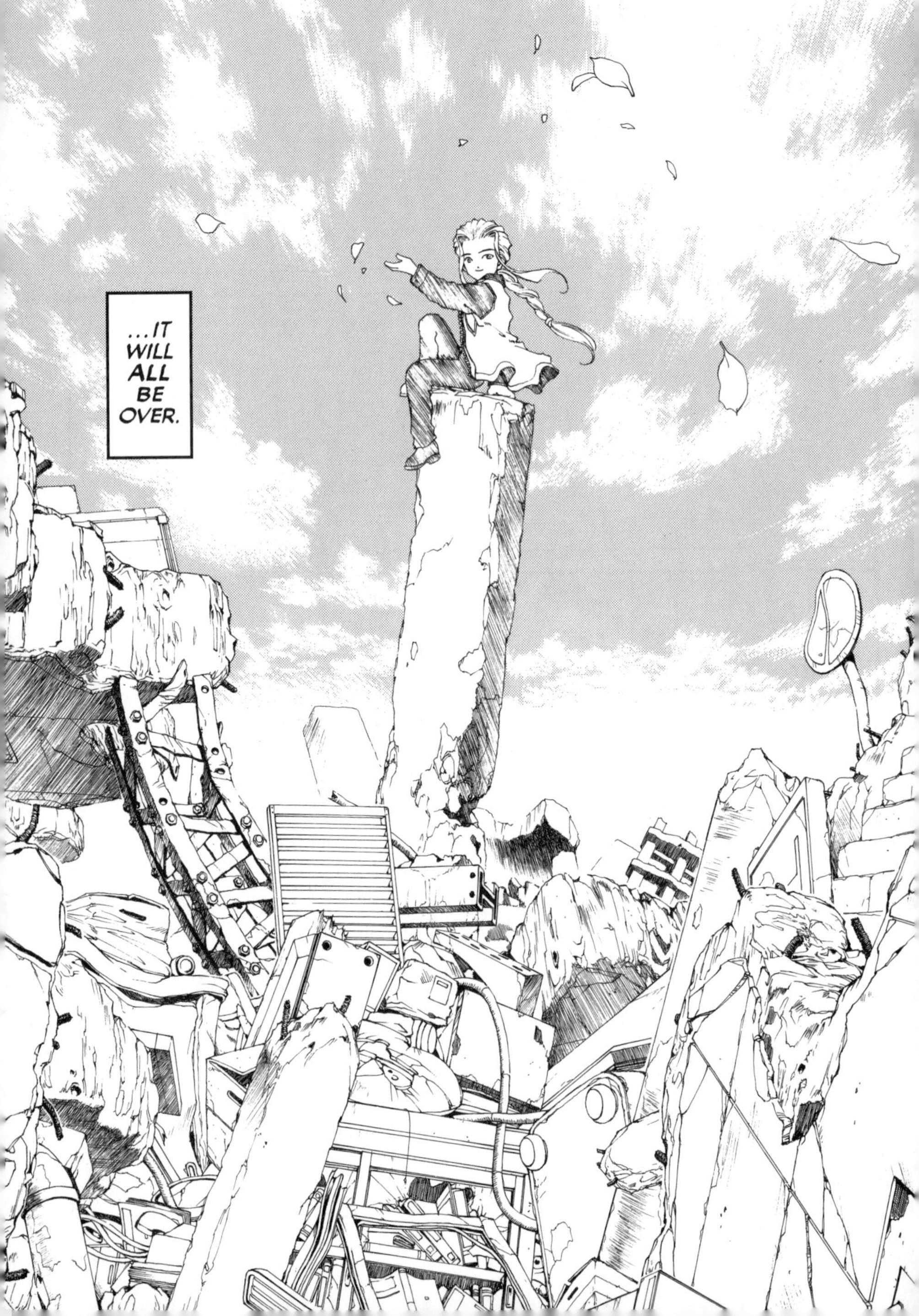
...IT WILL ALL BE OVER.

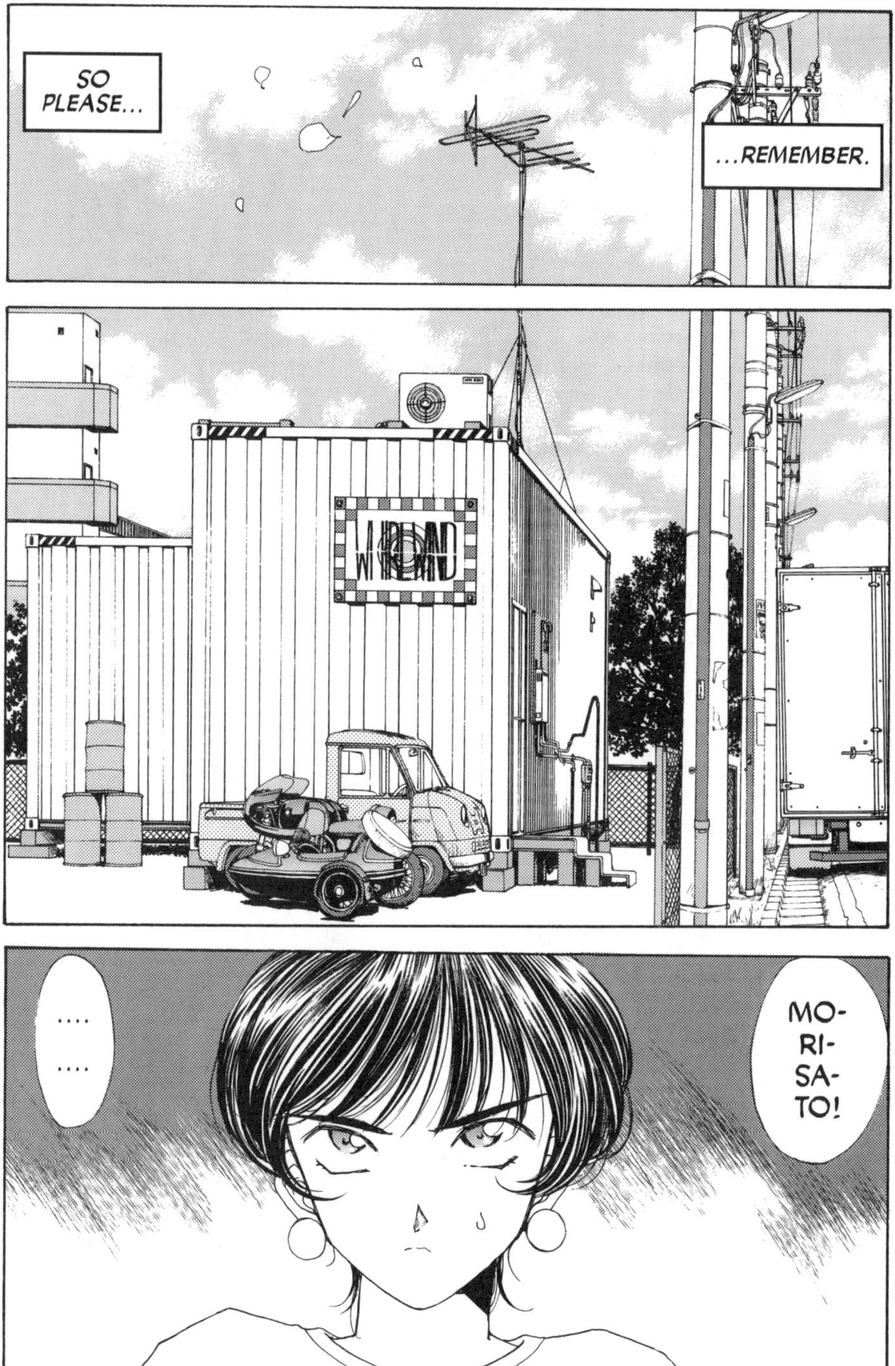
SO PLEASE...
...REMEMBER.
....
....
MO-RI-SA-TO!

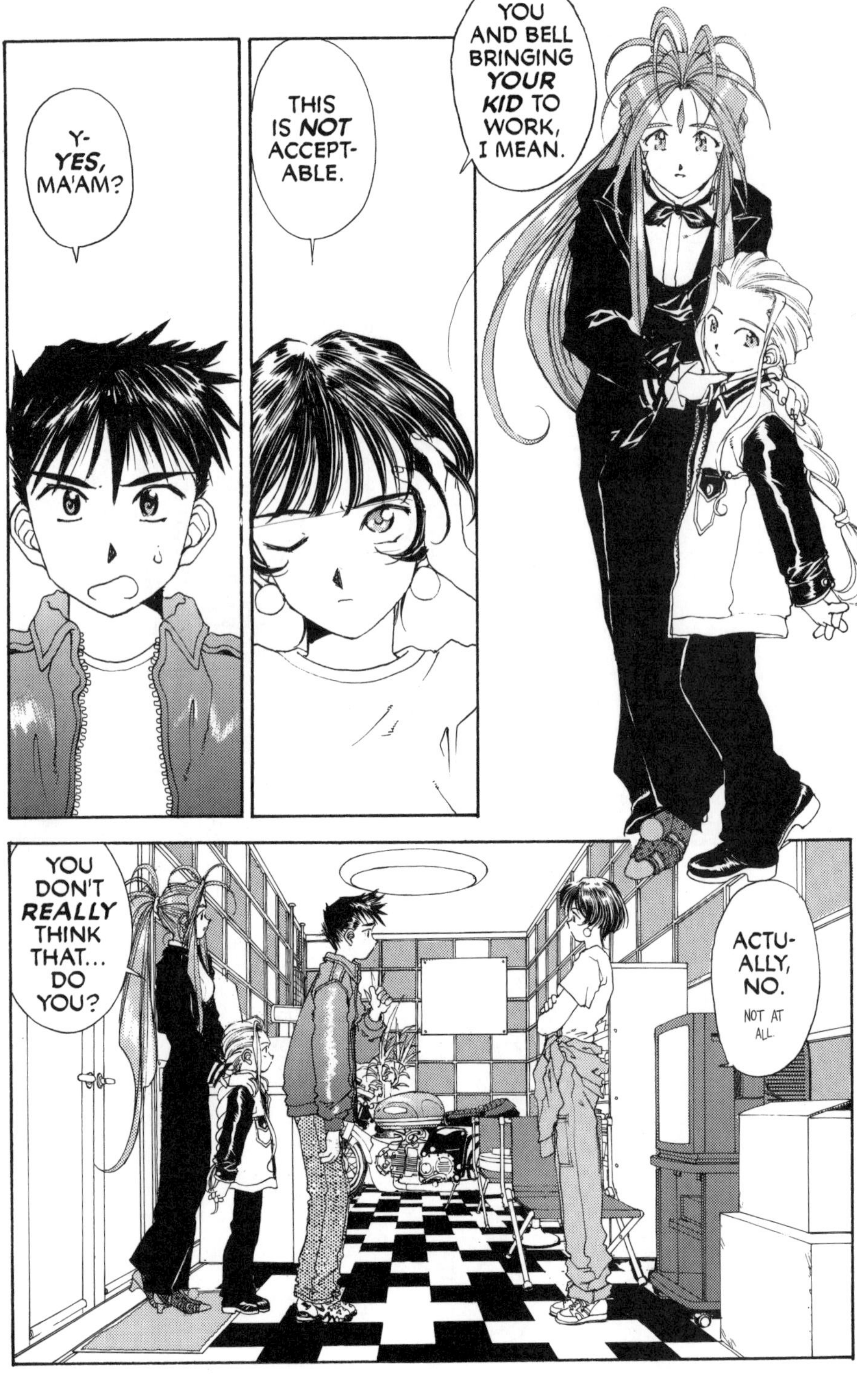
Y-
YES,
MA'AM?
THIS IS NOT ACCEPTABLE.
YOU AND BELL BRINGING YOUR KID TO WORK, I MEAN.
YOU DON'T REALLY THINK THAT... DO YOU?
ACTUALLY, NO.
NOT AT ALL.

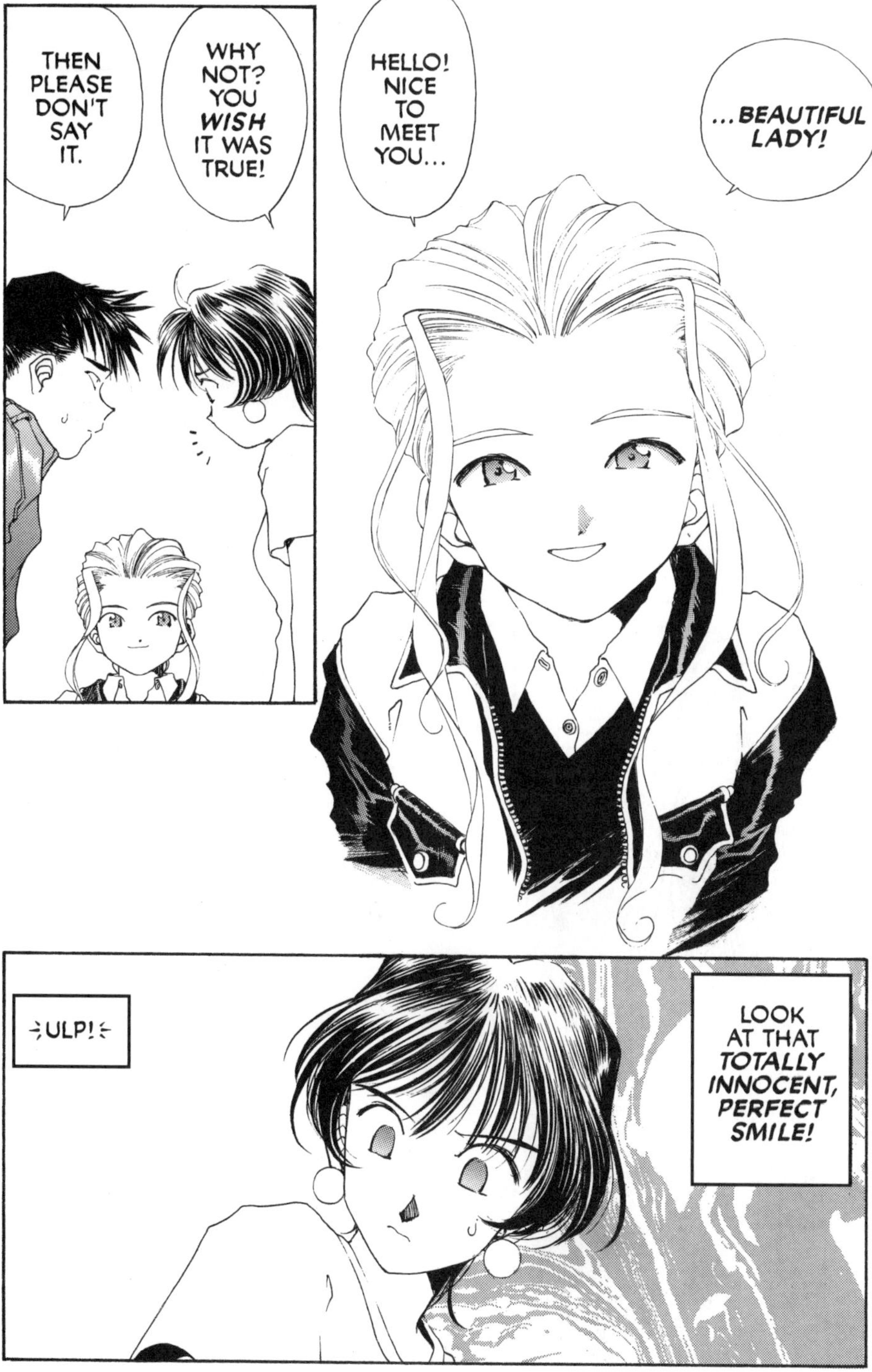
THEN PLEASE DON'T SAY IT.
WHY NOT? YOU *WISH* IT WAS TRUE!
HELLO! NICE TO MEET YOU...
...BEAUTIFUL LADY!
ULP!
LOOK AT THAT *TOTALLY INNOCENT, PERFECT SMILE!*

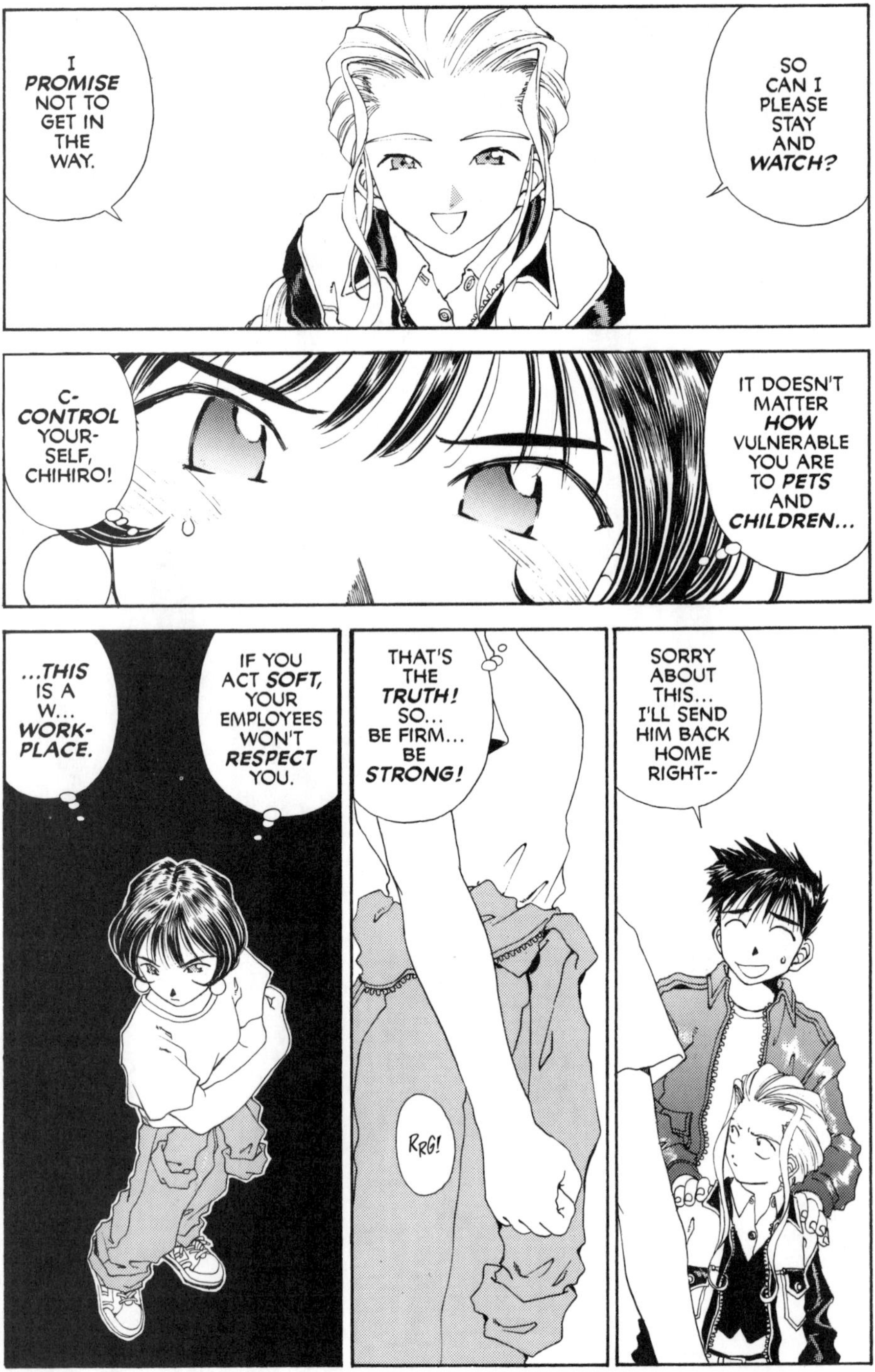
I *PROMISE* NOT TO GET IN THE WAY.
SO CAN I PLEASE STAY AND *WATCH?*
C-*CONTROL* YOUR-SELF, CHIHIRO!
IT DOESN'T MATTER *HOW* VULNERABLE YOU ARE TO *PETS* AND *CHILDREN...*
...*THIS* IS A W... *WORK-PLACE.*
IF YOU ACT *SOFT,* YOUR EMPLOYEES WON'T *RESPECT* YOU.
THAT'S THE *TRUTH!* SO... BE FIRM... BE *STRONG!*
RRG!
SORRY ABOUT THIS... I'LL SEND HIM BACK HOME RIGHT--

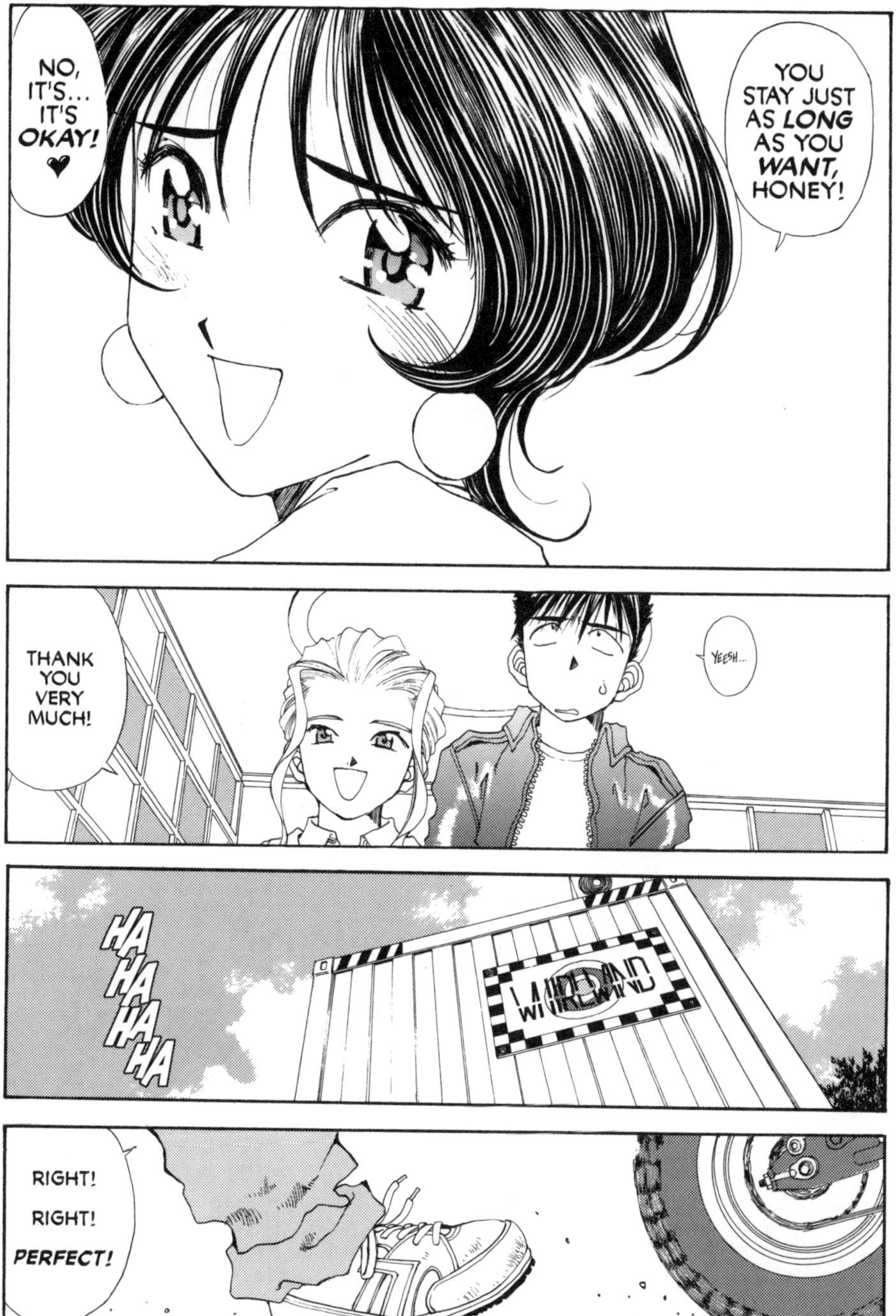
NO, IT'S... IT'S **OKAY!** ♥
YOU STAY JUST AS **LONG** AS YOU **WANT,** HONEY!
THANK YOU VERY MUCH!
YEESH...
HA HA HA HA HA HA
RIGHT!
RIGHT!
PERFECT!

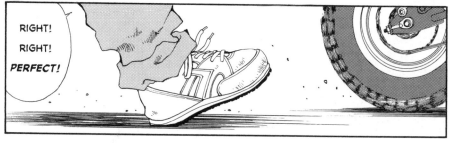

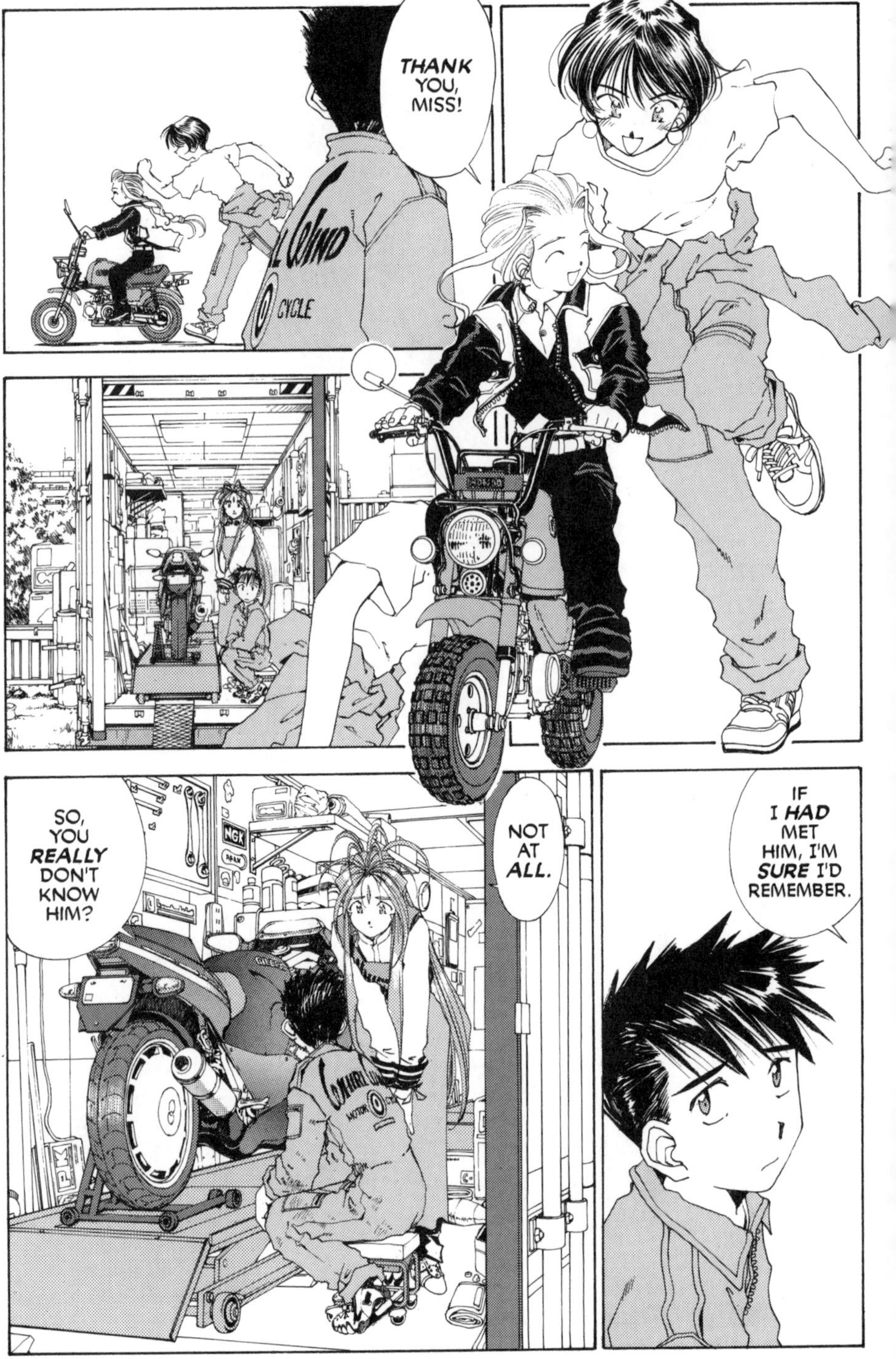
THANK YOU, MISS!
SO, YOU REALLY DON'T KNOW HIM?
NOT AT ALL.
IF I HAD MET HIM, I'M SURE I'D REMEMBER.

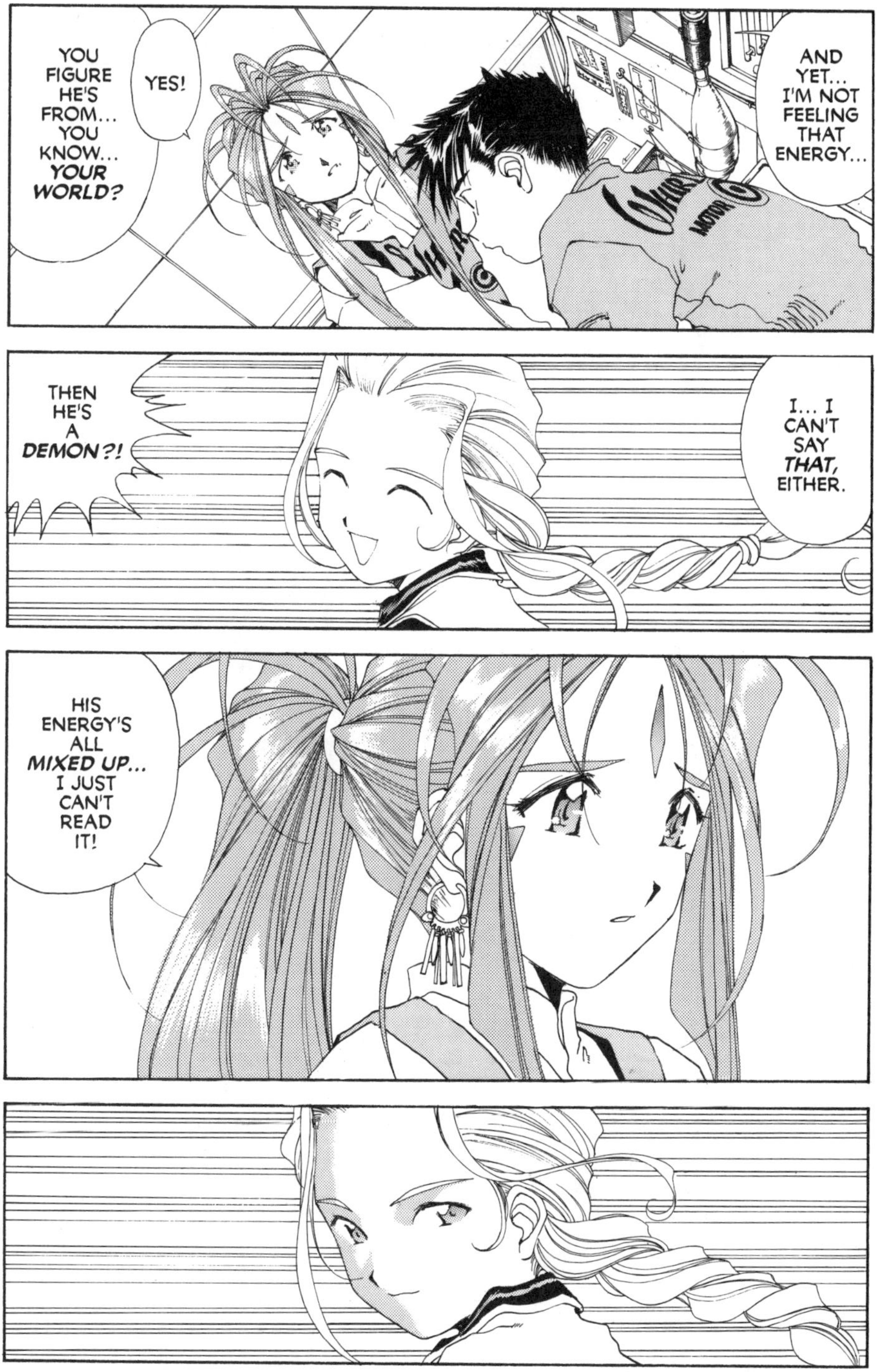
YOU FIGURE HE'S FROM... YOU KNOW... *YOUR WORLD?*
YES!
AND YET... I'M NOT FEELING THAT ENERGY...
THEN HE'S A *DEMON?!*
I... I CAN'T SAY *THAT,* EITHER.
HIS ENERGY'S ALL *MIXED UP...* I JUST CAN'T READ IT!

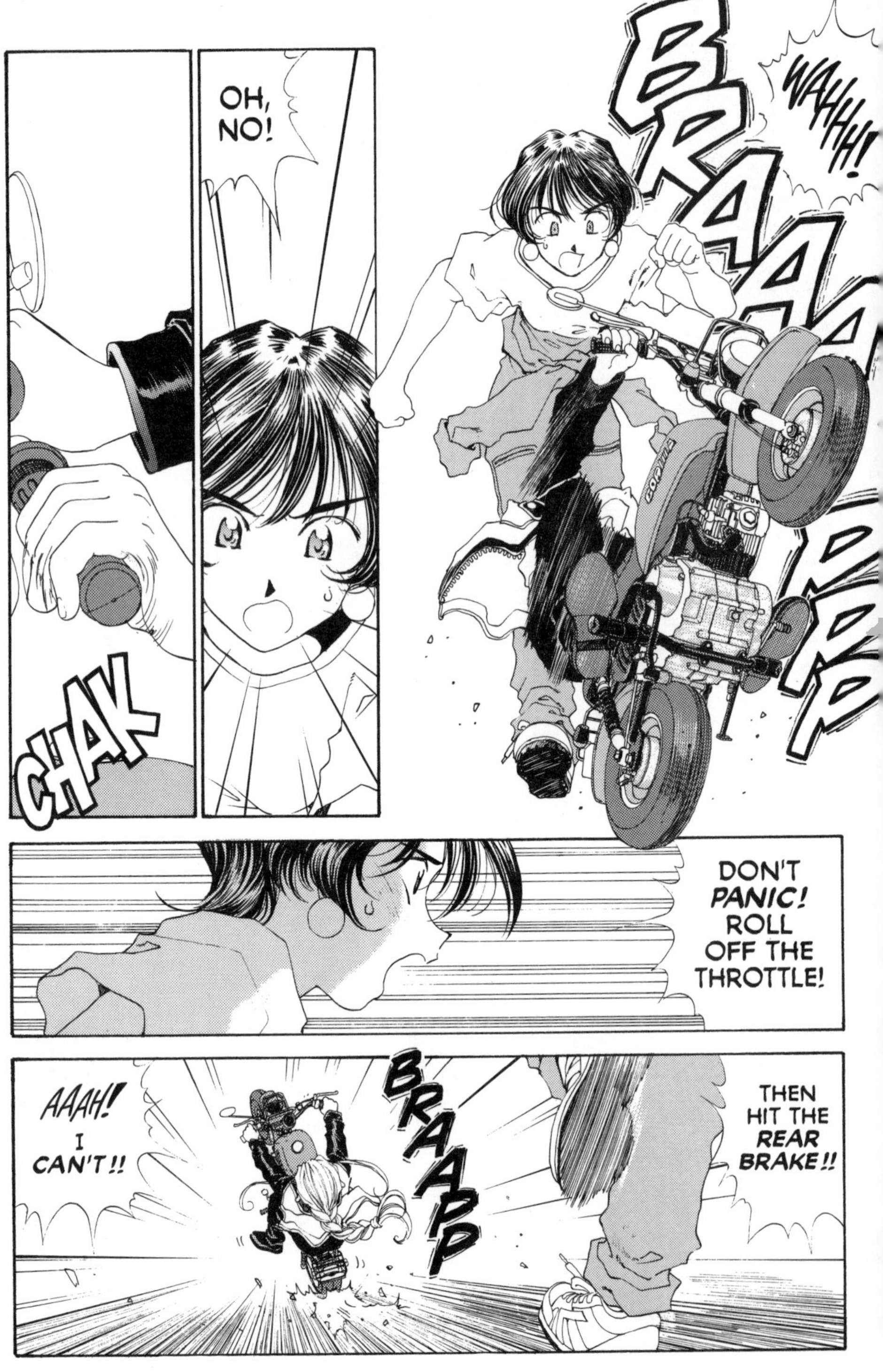
CHAK
OH, NO!
BRAAAAPPPP
WAHHH!
DON'T *PANIC!* ROLL OFF THE THROTTLE!
AAAH!
I CAN'T!!
BRAAPP
THEN HIT THE *REAR BRAKE!!*

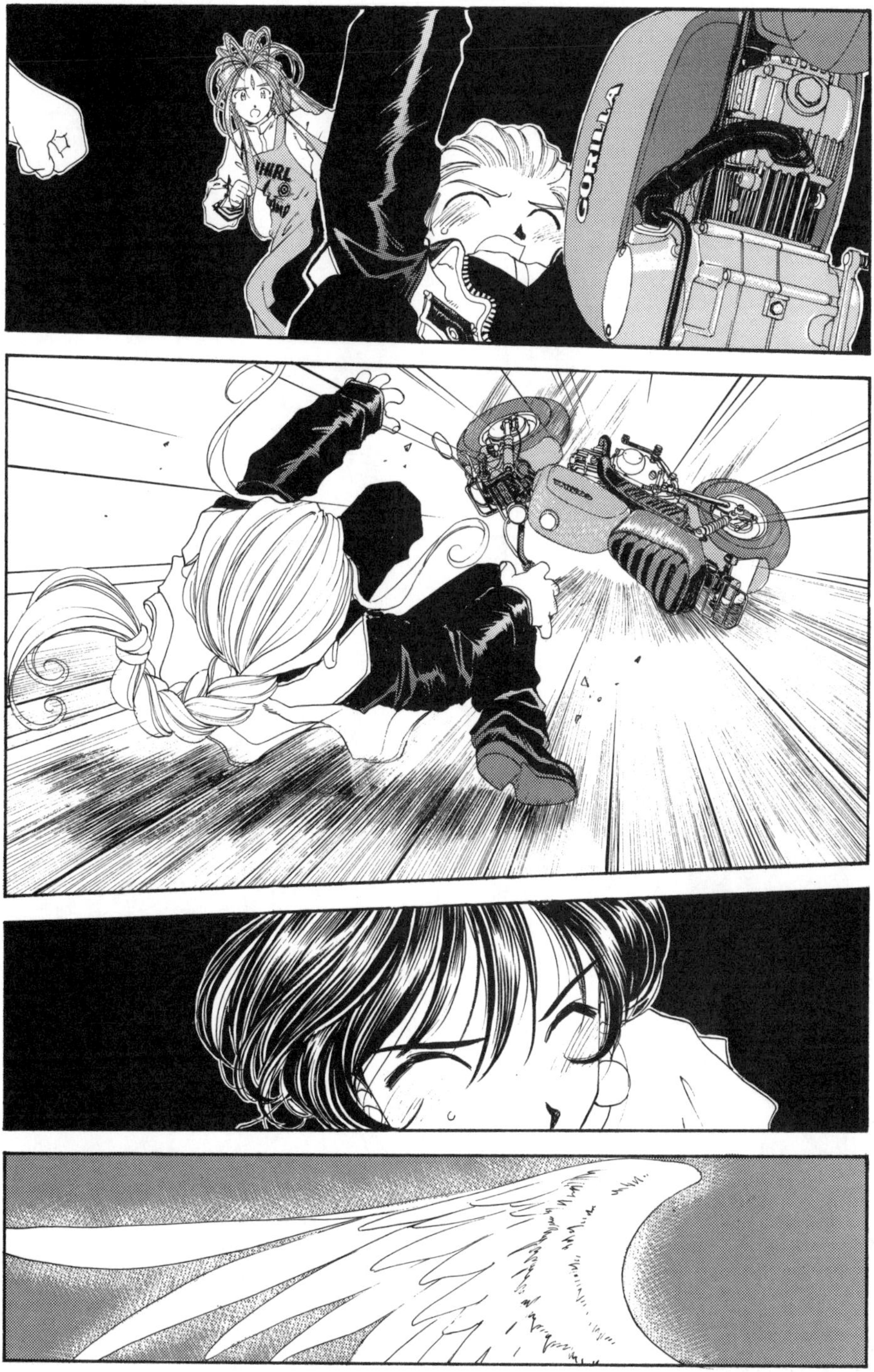
GORILLA

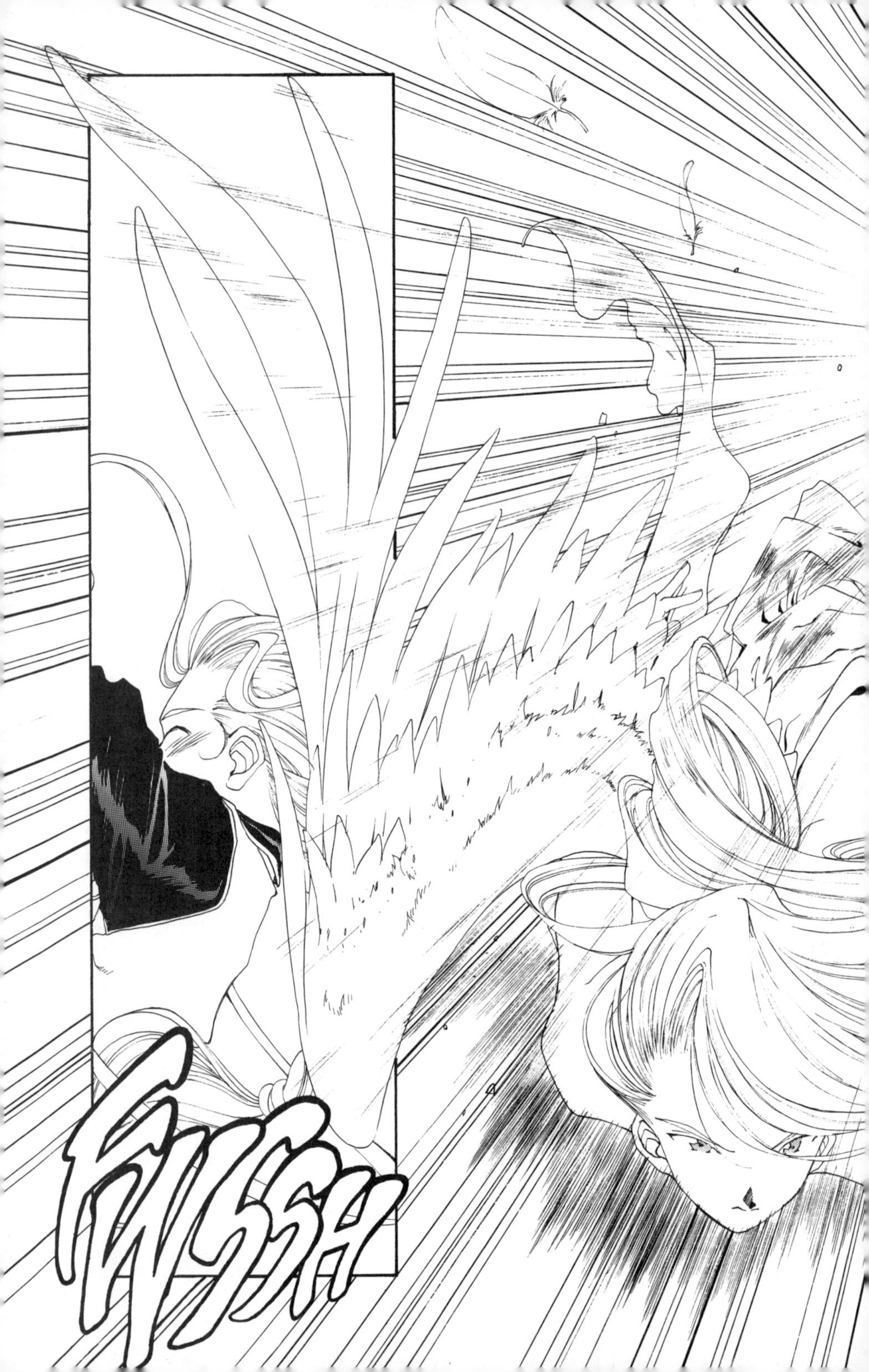
FWSSA

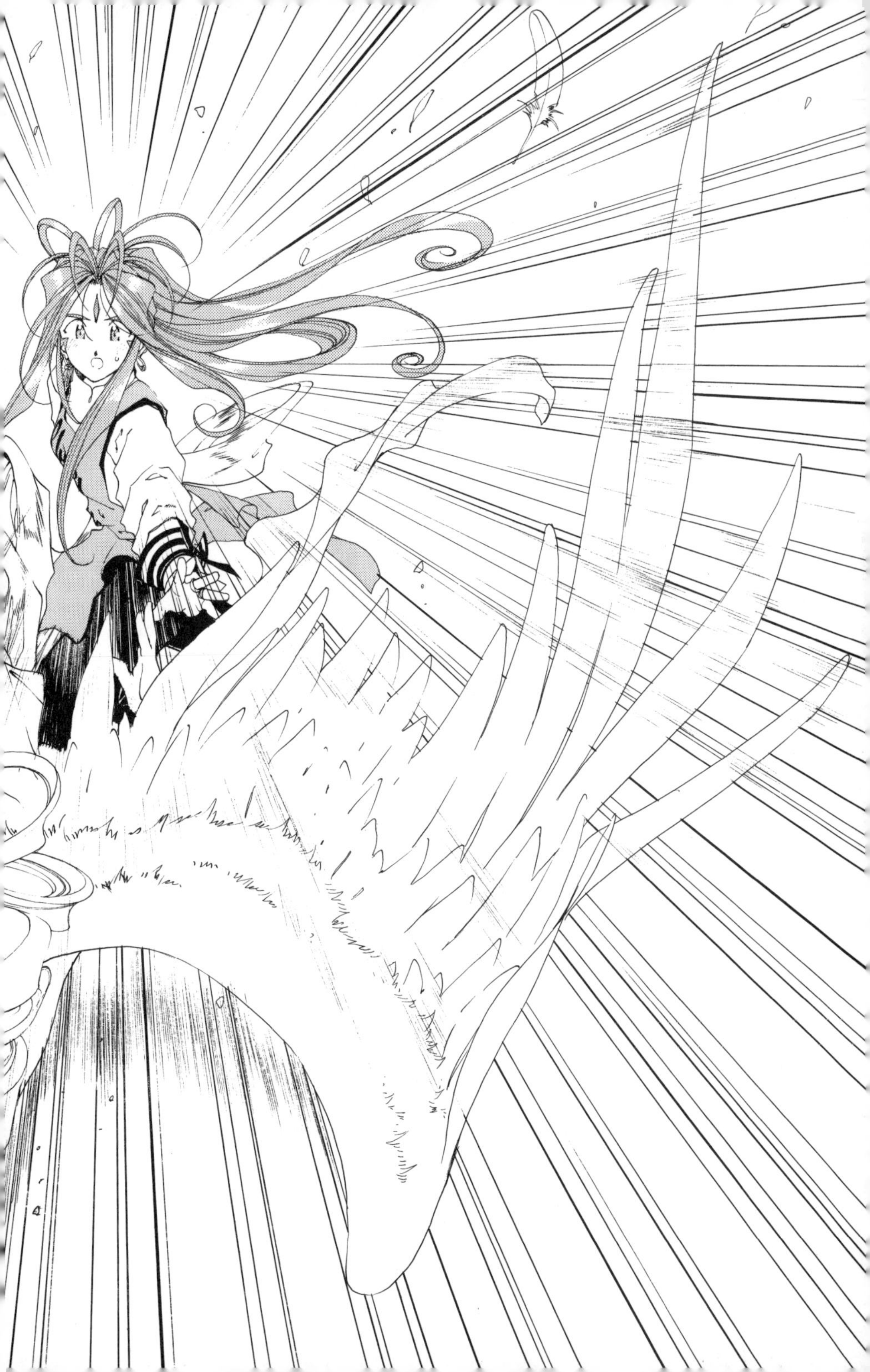

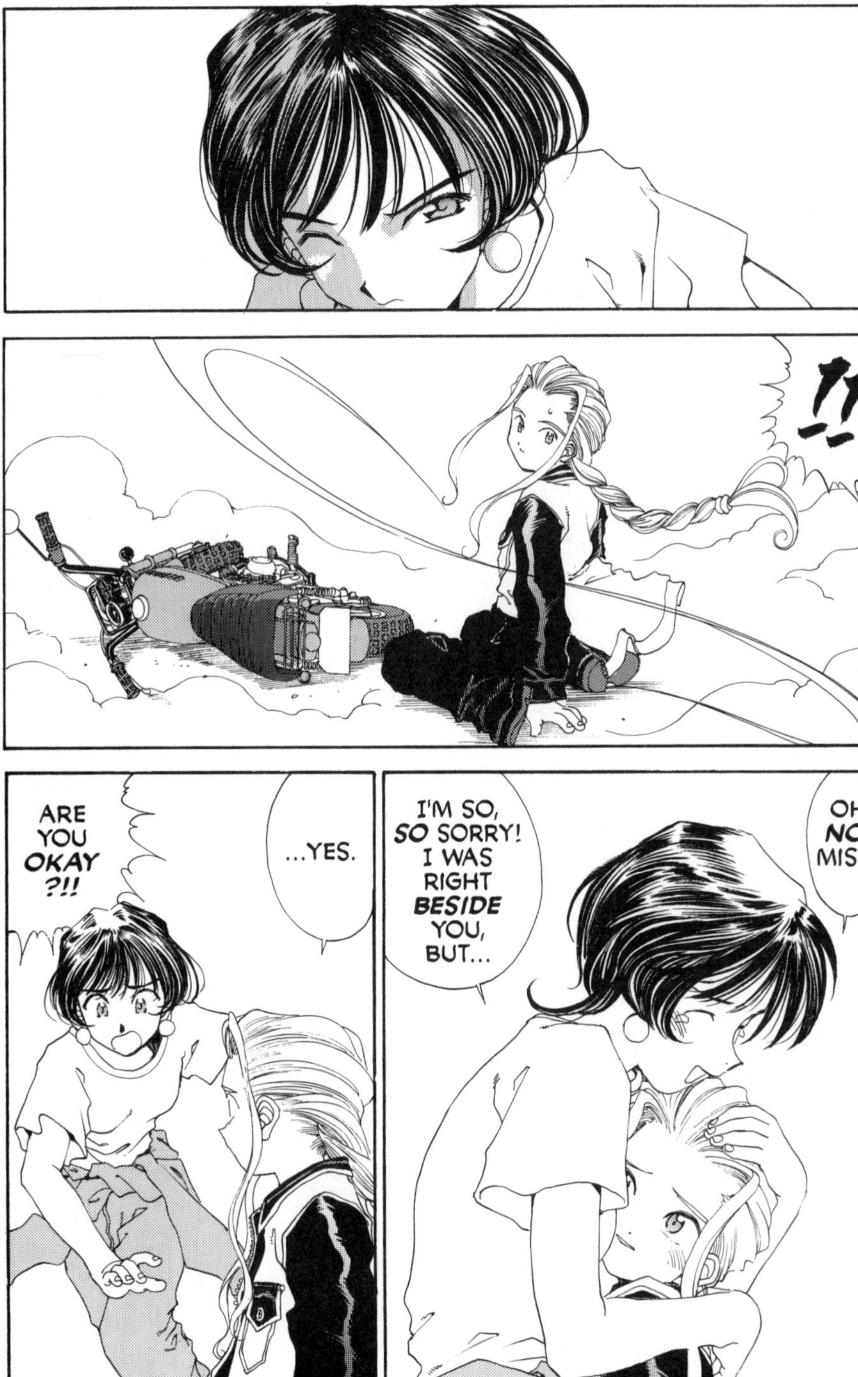
!!
ARE YOU OKAY ?!!
...YES.
I'M SO, SO SORRY! I WAS RIGHT BESIDE YOU, BUT...
OH NO, MISS!

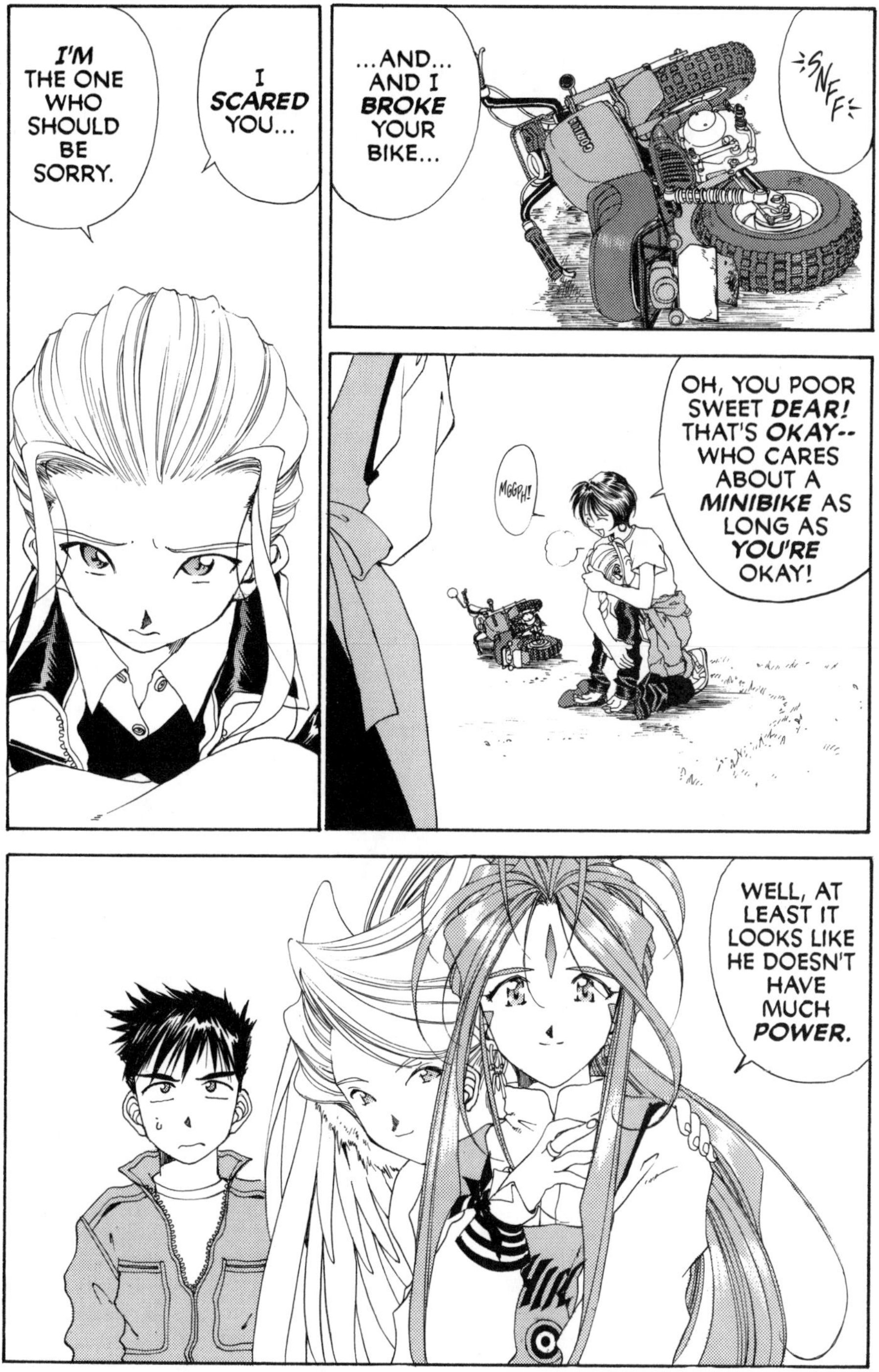
I'M THE ONE WHO SHOULD BE SORRY.
I SCARED YOU...
...AND... AND I BROKE YOUR BIKE...
SNFF
OH, YOU POOR SWEET DEAR! THAT'S OKAY-- WHO CARES ABOUT A MINIBIKE AS LONG AS YOU'RE OKAY!
MGGPH!
WELL, AT LEAST IT LOOKS LIKE HE DOESN'T HAVE MUCH POWER.

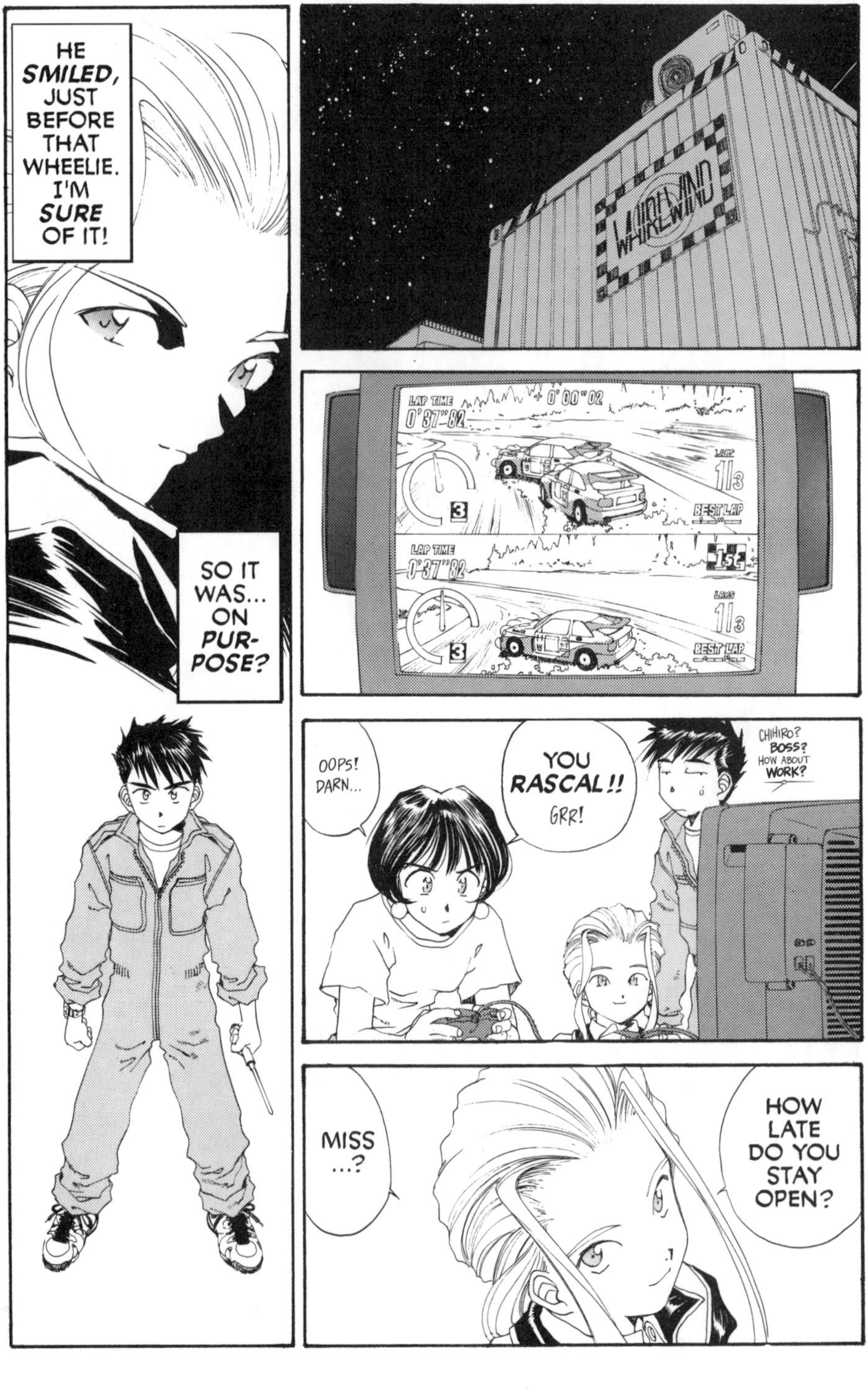
HE SMILED, JUST BEFORE THAT WHEELIE. I'M SURE OF IT!
SO IT WAS... ON PURPOSE?
WHIRLWIND
LAP TIME
0'37"82
+0'00"02
BEST LAP
LAP TIME
0'37"82
1st
BEST LAP
OOPS! DARN...
YOU RASCAL!! GRR!
CHIHIRO? BOSS? HOW ABOUT WORK?
MISS ...?
HOW LATE DO YOU STAY OPEN?

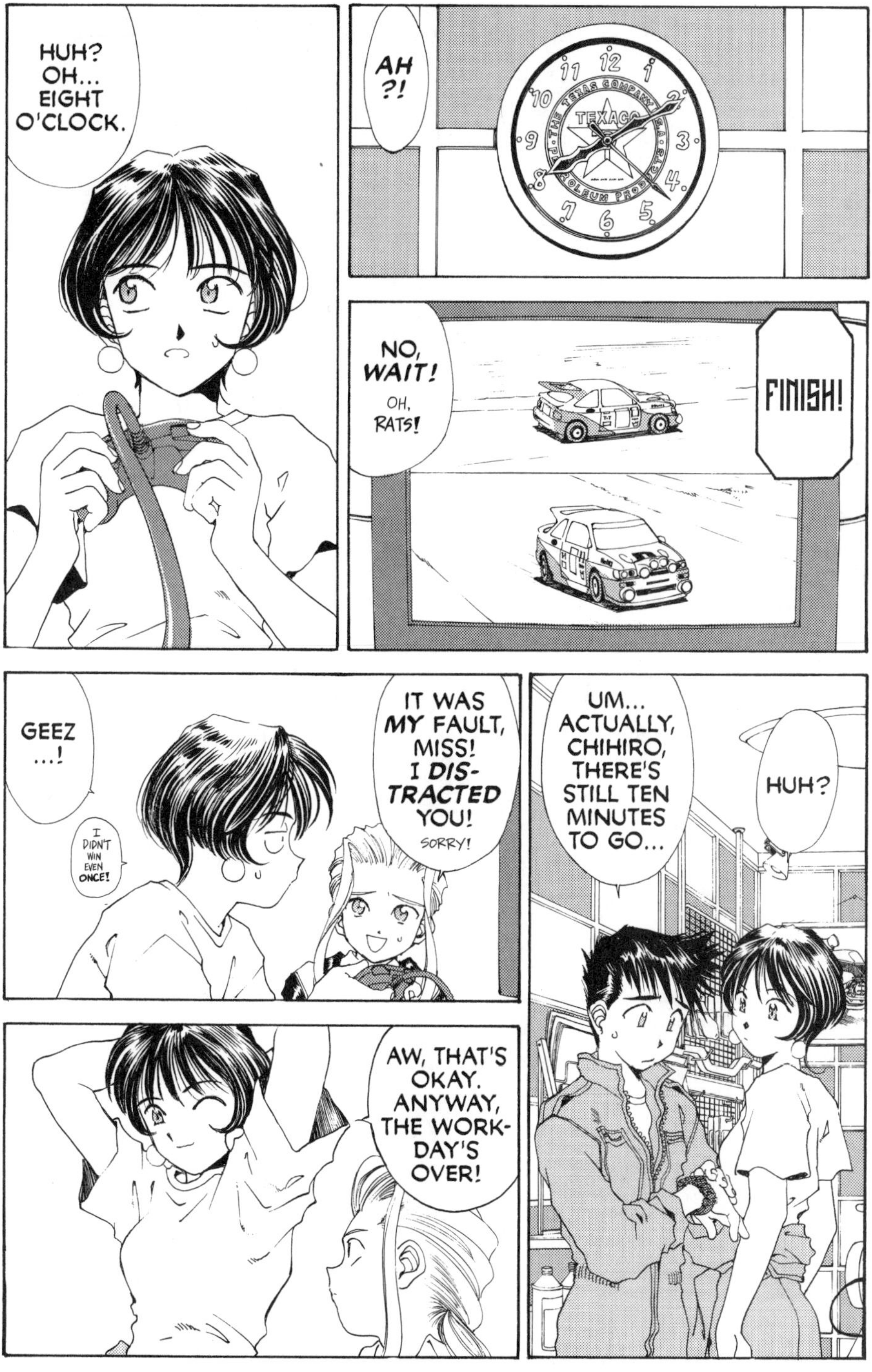
HUH? OH... EIGHT O'CLOCK.
AH ?!
NO, WAIT! OH, RATS!
FINISH!
GEEZ ...!
I DIDN'T WIN EVEN ONCE!
IT WAS MY FAULT, MISS! I DISTRACTED YOU! SORRY!
AW, THAT'S OKAY. ANYWAY, THE WORK-DAY'S OVER!
UM... ACTUALLY, CHIHIRO, THERE'S STILL TEN MINUTES TO GO...
HUH?

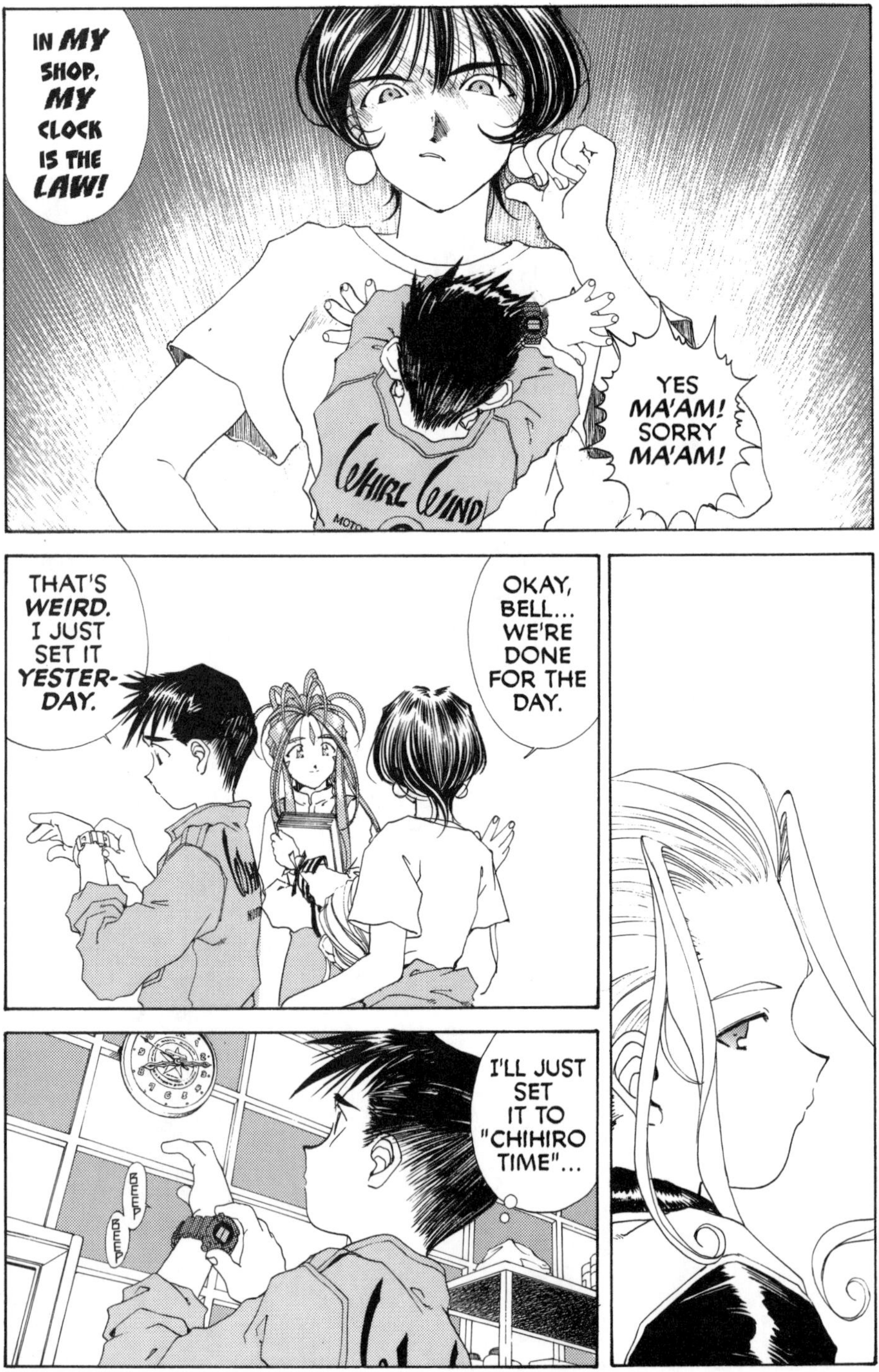
IN MY SHOP, MY CLOCK IS THE LAW!
YES MA'AM! SORRY MA'AM!
THAT'S WEIRD. I JUST SET IT YESTER-DAY.
OKAY, BELL... WE'RE DONE FOR THE DAY.
I'LL JUST SET IT TO "CHIHIRO TIME"...
BEEP BEEP

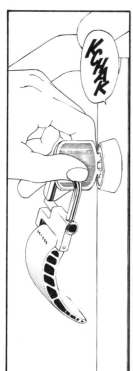

KCHAK

AND NOW, YOUNG MAN... LET'S GET YOU SOMETHING TO *EAT*, OKAY?

EH? ?!?

HE WAS *HERE* JUST A SECOND AGO!

DID HE GO ON AHEAD ...?

LOOKS THAT WAY.

BRING HIM WITH YOU AGAIN *TOMOR-ROW*.

Y-YES, BOSS!

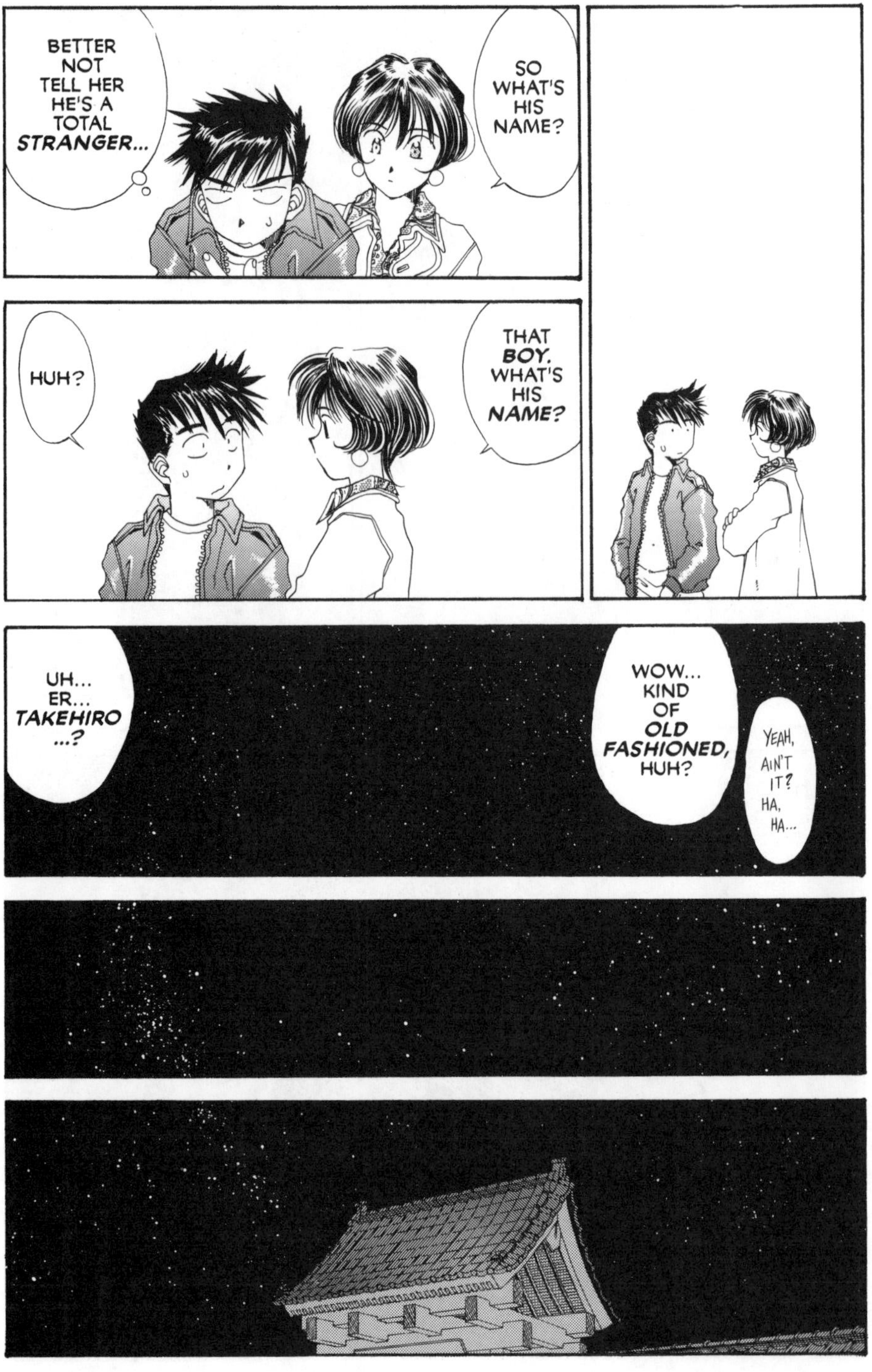
BETTER NOT TELL HER HE'S A TOTAL **STRANGER...**
SO WHAT'S HIS NAME?
THAT **BOY.** WHAT'S HIS **NAME?**
HUH?
UH... ER... **TAKEHIRO ...?**
WOW... KIND OF **OLD FASHIONED,** HUH?
YEAH, AIN'T IT? HA, HA...

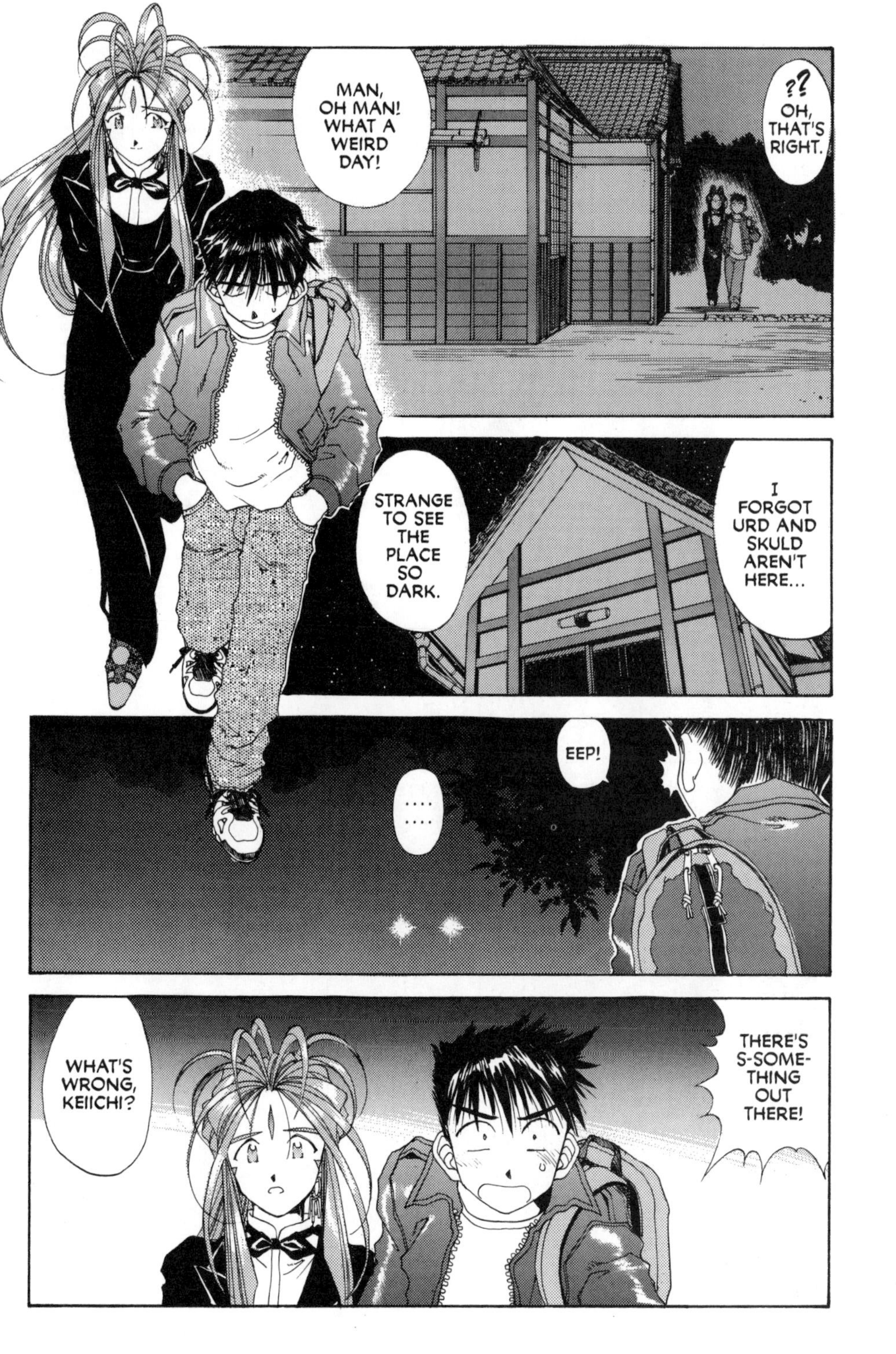
MAN, OH MAN! WHAT A WEIRD DAY!
?? OH, THAT'S RIGHT.
STRANGE TO SEE THE PLACE SO DARK.
I FORGOT URD AND SKULD AREN'T HERE...
....
....
EEP!
WHAT'S WRONG, KEIICHI?
THERE'S S-SOMETHING OUT THERE!

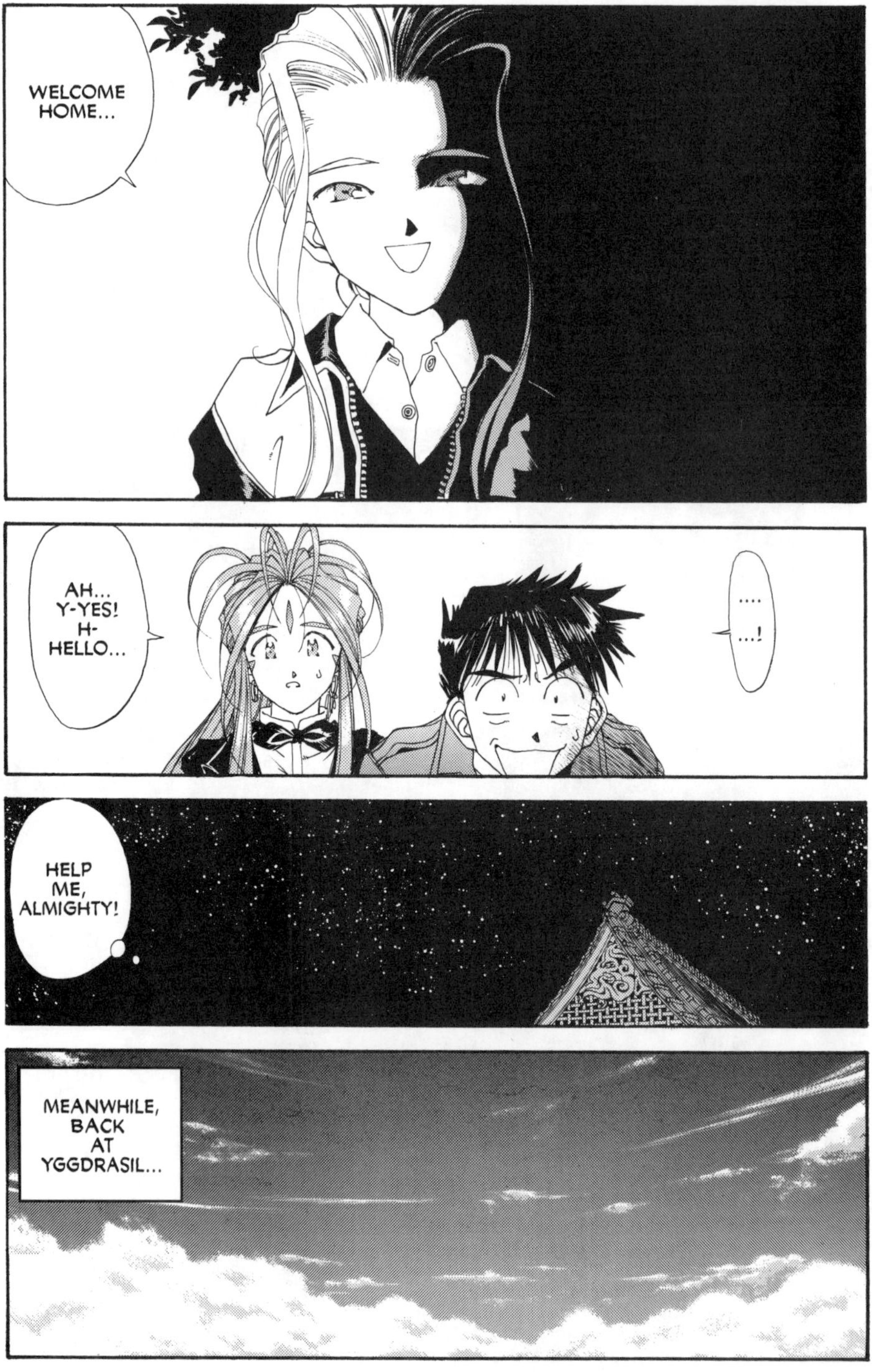
WELCOME HOME...
AH... Y-YES! H-HELLO...
....!
HELP ME, ALMIGHTY!
MEANWHILE, BACK AT YGGDRASIL...

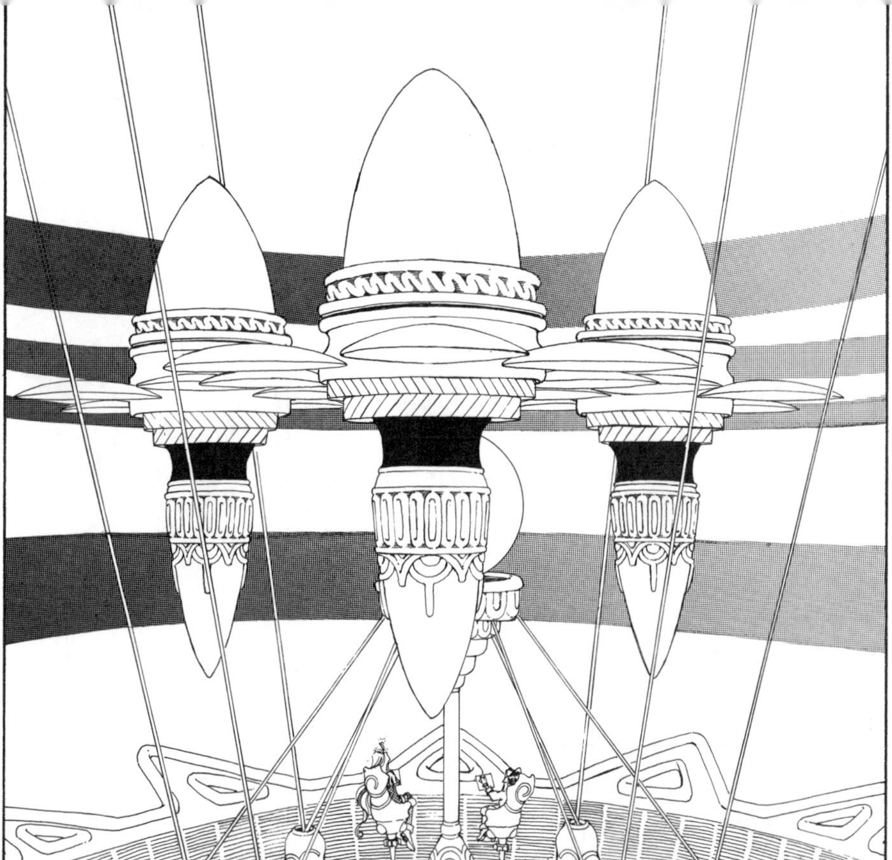

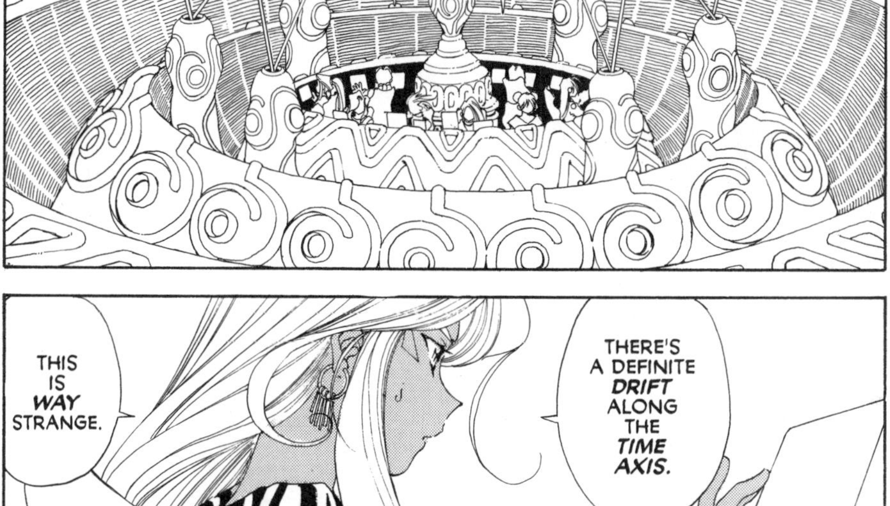
THIS IS WAY STRANGE.
THERE'S A DEFINITE DRIFT ALONG THE TIME AXIS.

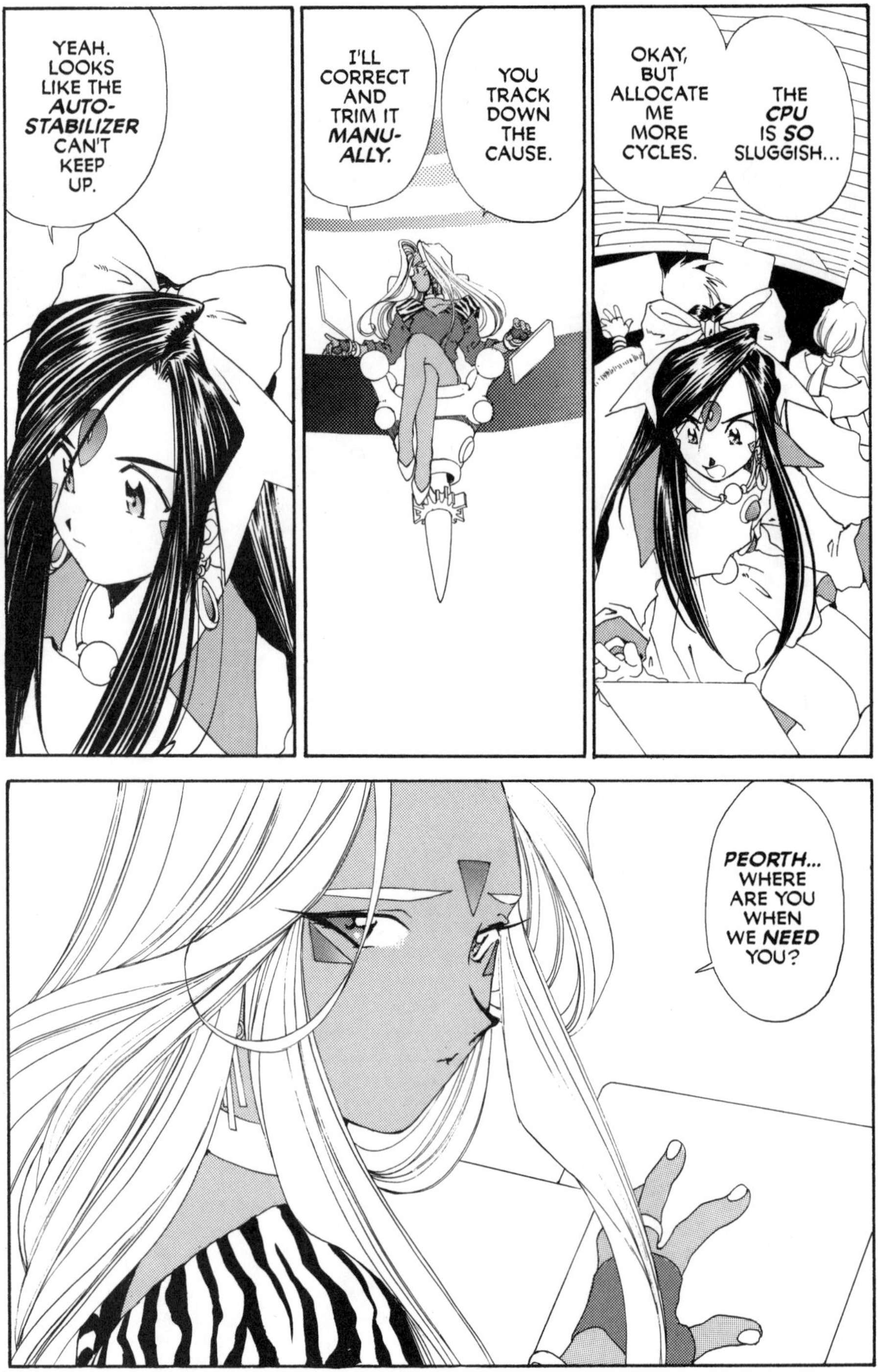
YEAH. LOOKS LIKE THE AUTO-STABILIZER CAN'T KEEP UP.
I'LL CORRECT AND TRIM IT MANU-ALLY.
YOU TRACK DOWN THE CAUSE.
OKAY, BUT ALLOCATE ME MORE CYCLES.
THE CPU IS SO SLUGGISH...
PEORTH... WHERE ARE YOU WHEN WE NEED YOU?

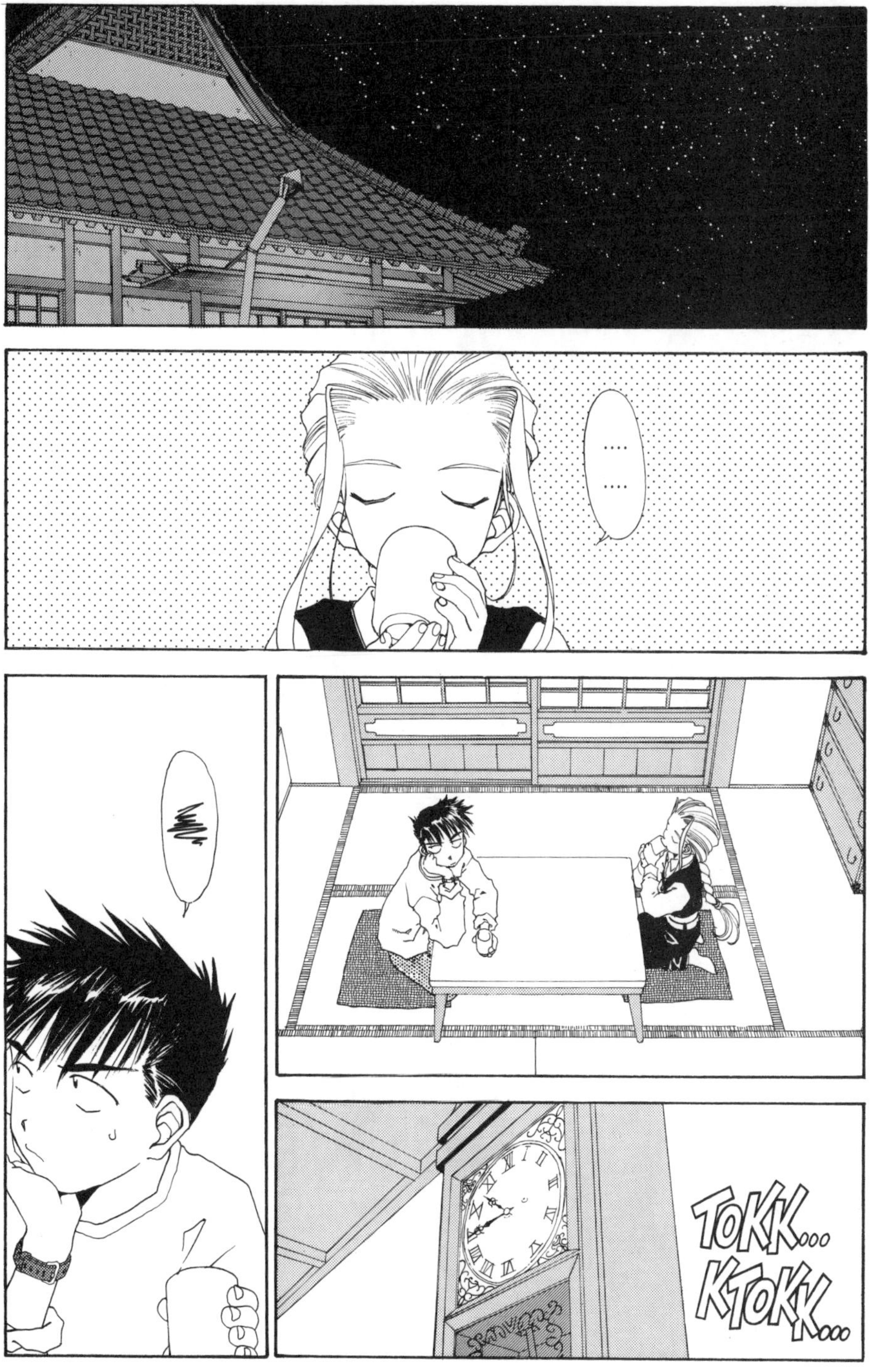
....
....
TOKK...
KTOKK...

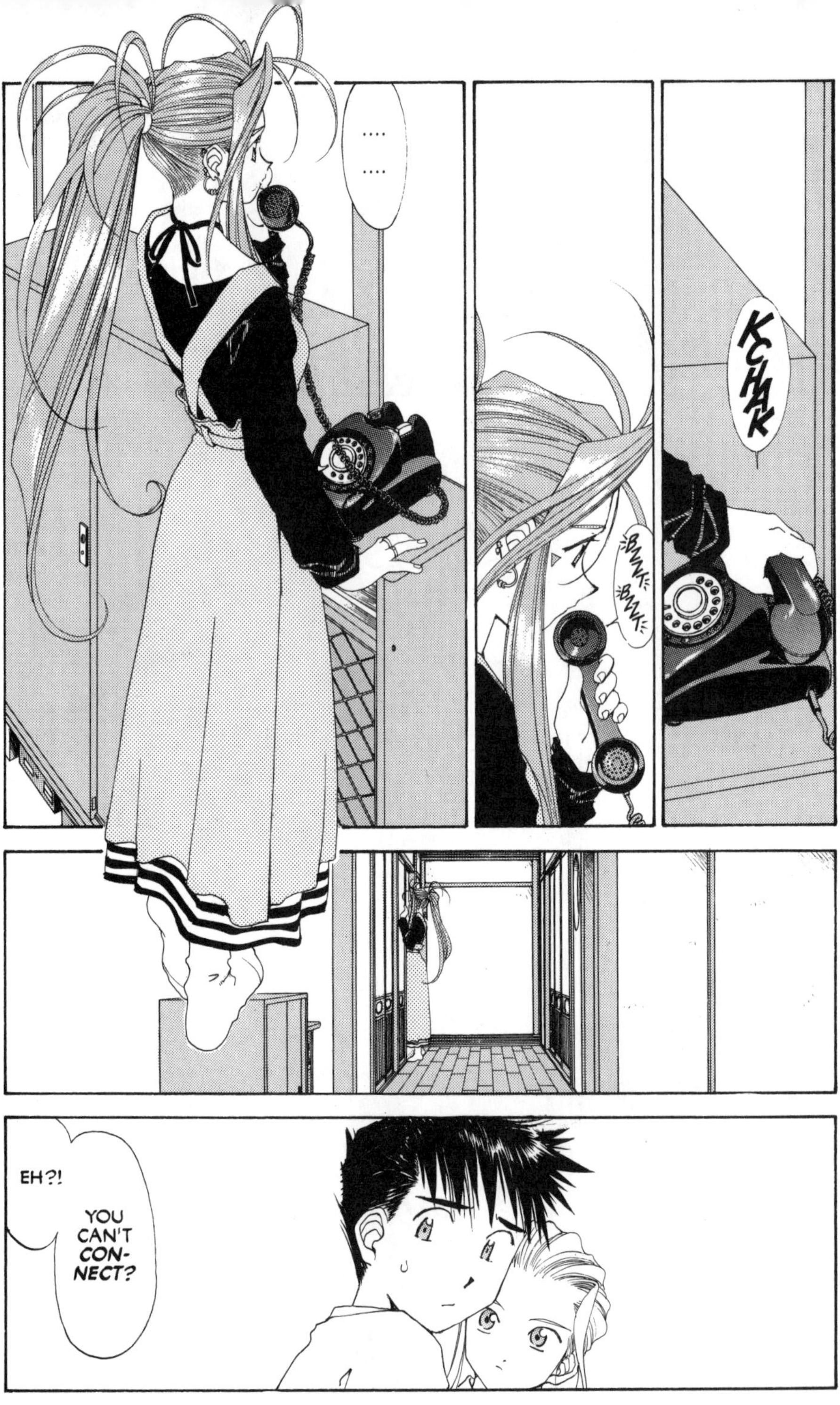
....
....
KCHAK
BZZZT BZZZT
EH?!
YOU CAN'T CON-NECT?

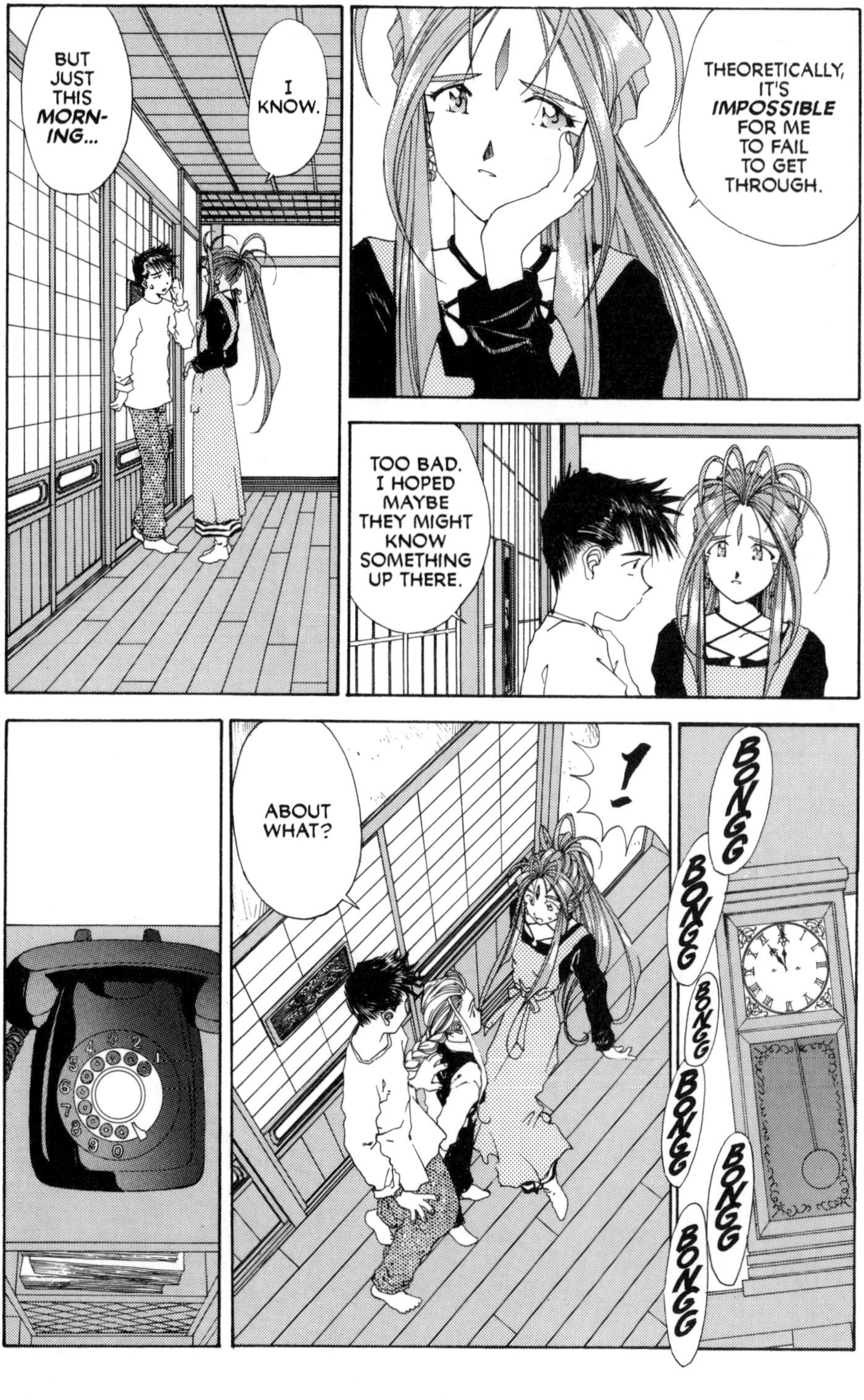
BUT JUST THIS *MORNING*...
I KNOW.
THEORETICALLY, IT'S *IMPOSSIBLE* FOR ME TO FAIL TO GET THROUGH.
TOO BAD. I HOPED MAYBE THEY MIGHT KNOW SOMETHING UP THERE.
ABOUT WHAT?
!
BONGG BONGG BONGG BONGG BONGG BONGG BONGG

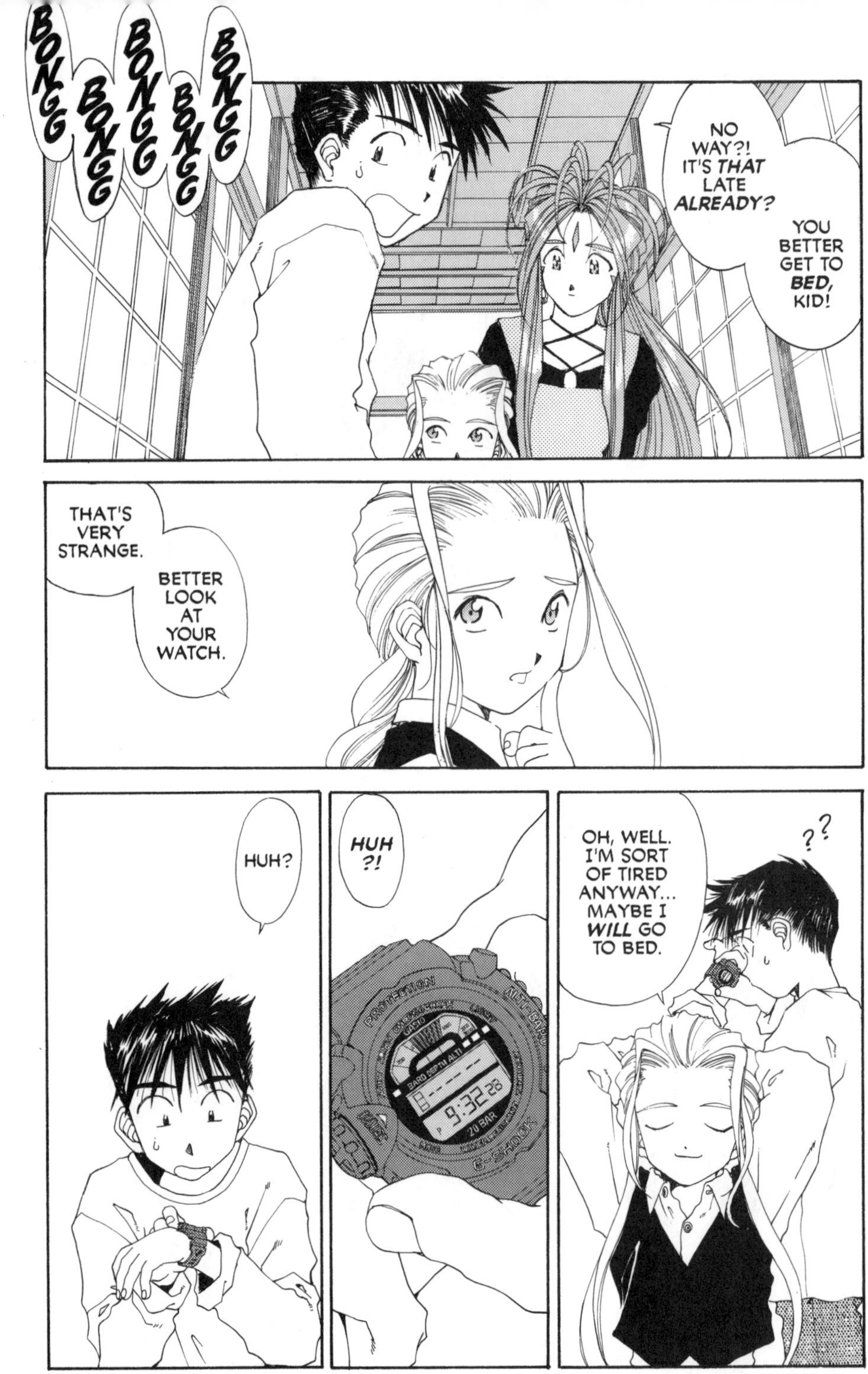
BONGG
BONGG
BONGG
BONGG
BONGG
NO WAY?! IT'S *THAT* LATE *ALREADY?*
YOU BETTER GET TO ***BED,*** KID!
THAT'S VERY STRANGE.
BETTER LOOK AT YOUR WATCH.
HUH?
HUH ?!
OH, WELL. I'M SORT OF TIRED ANYWAY... MAYBE I ***WILL*** GO TO BED.
??

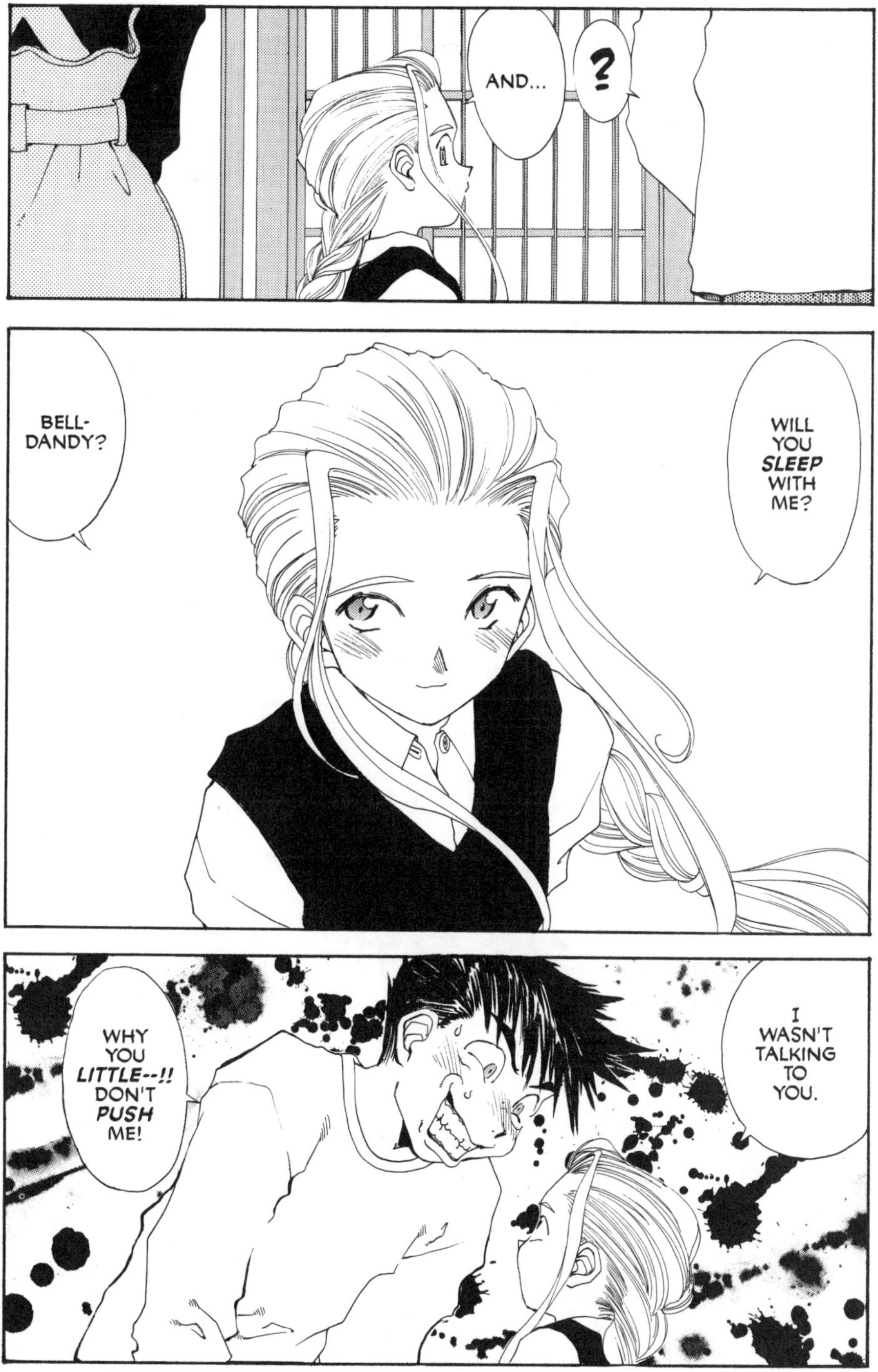
AND...
?
BELL-DANDY?
WILL YOU *SLEEP* WITH ME?
WHY YOU *LITTLE--!!* DON'T *PUSH* ME!
I WASN'T TALKING TO YOU.

WELL, BELL-DANDY? IS THAT OKAY?

OF COURSE! THAT IS... UNTIL YOU FALL ASLEEP, ANYWAY.

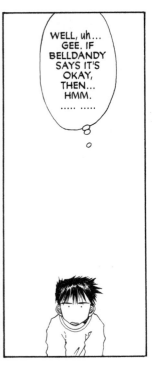

WELL, uh... GEE. IF BELLDANDY SAYS IT'S OKAY, THEN... HMM. ....

YES...

UNTIL SLEEP COMES...

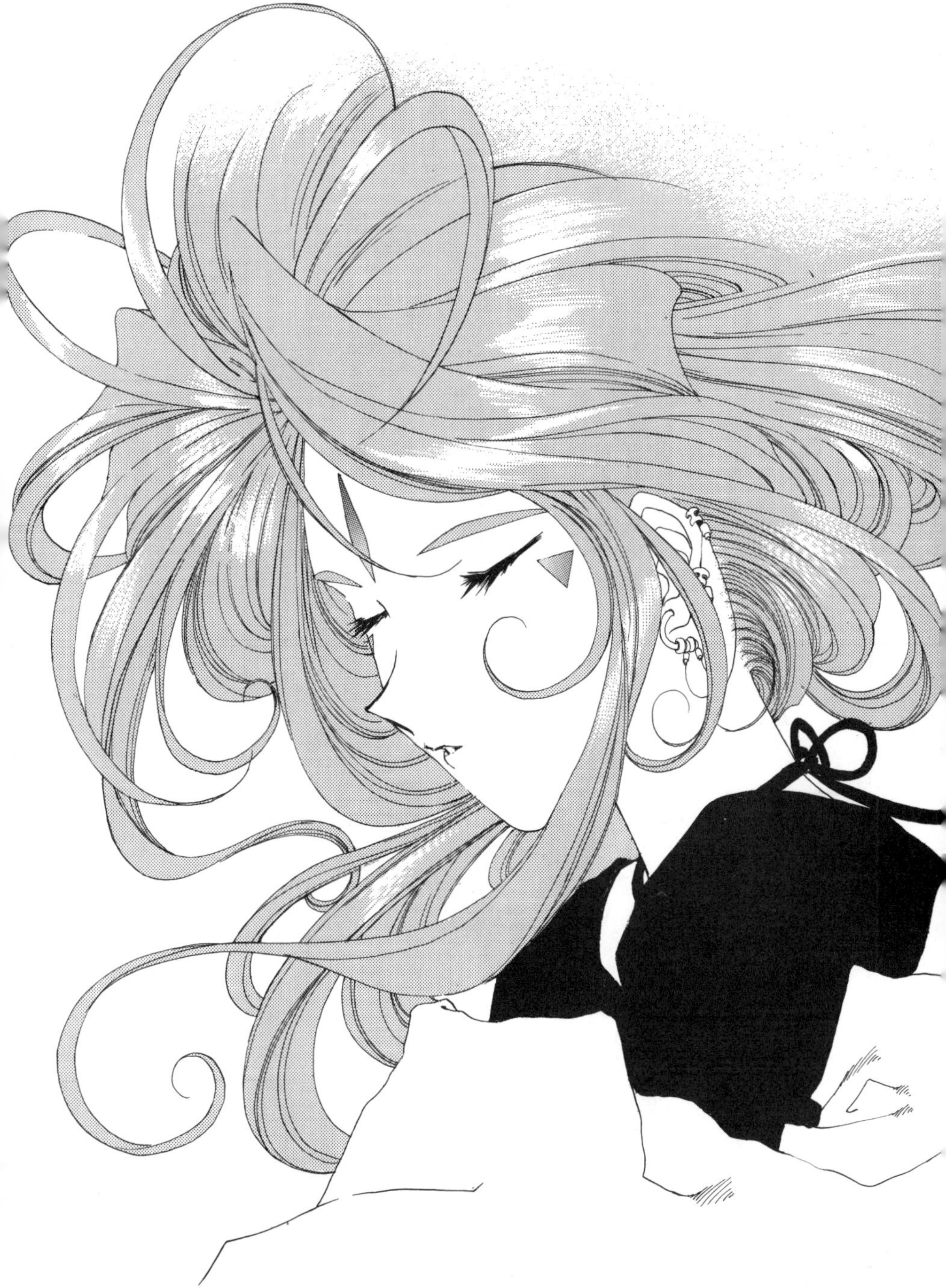

MEMORIES OF A YOUTH

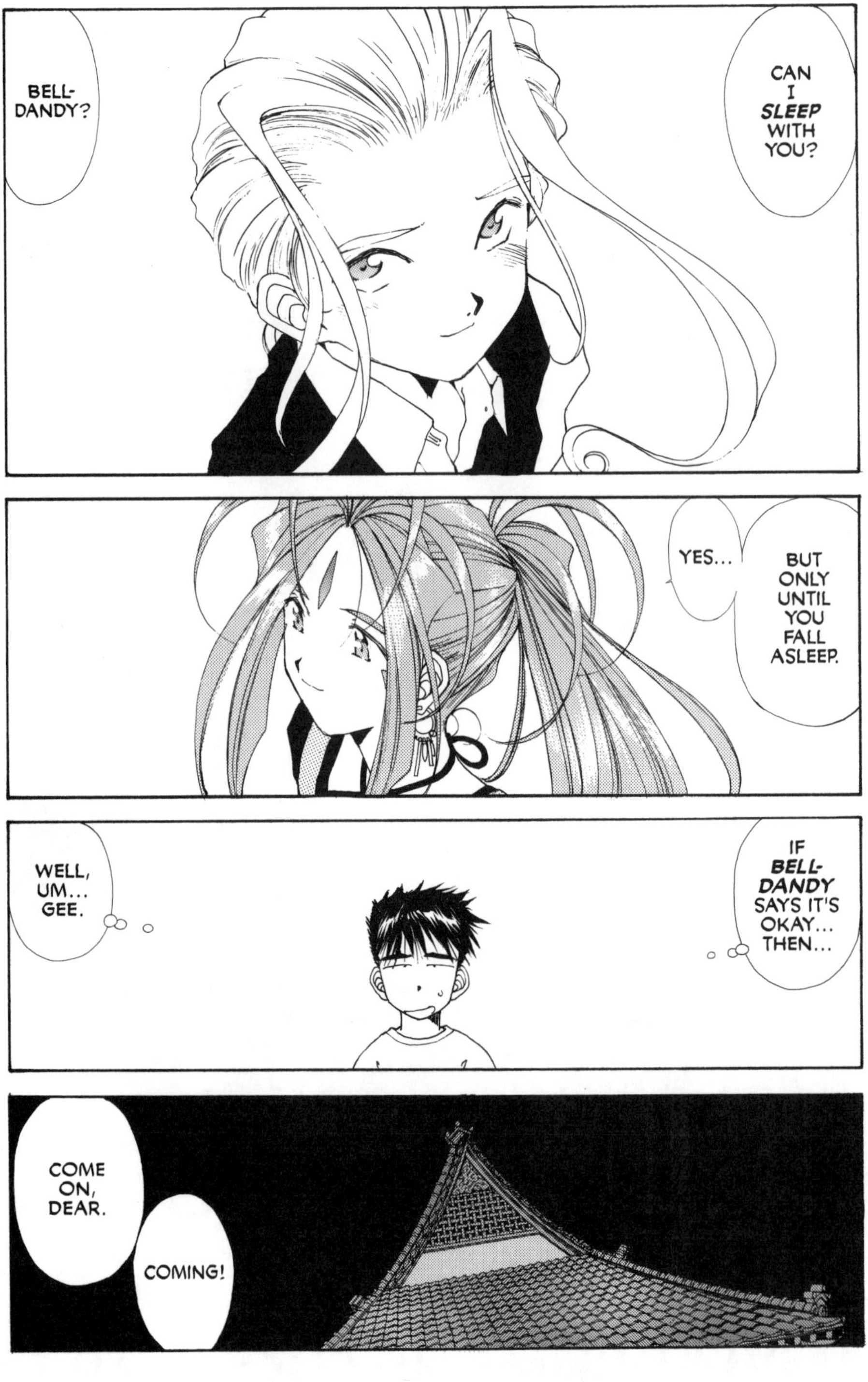
BELL-DANDY?
CAN I *SLEEP* WITH YOU?
YES...
BUT ONLY UNTIL YOU FALL ASLEEP.
WELL, UM... GEE.
IF *BELL-DANDY* SAYS IT'S OKAY... THEN...
COME ON, DEAR.
COMING!

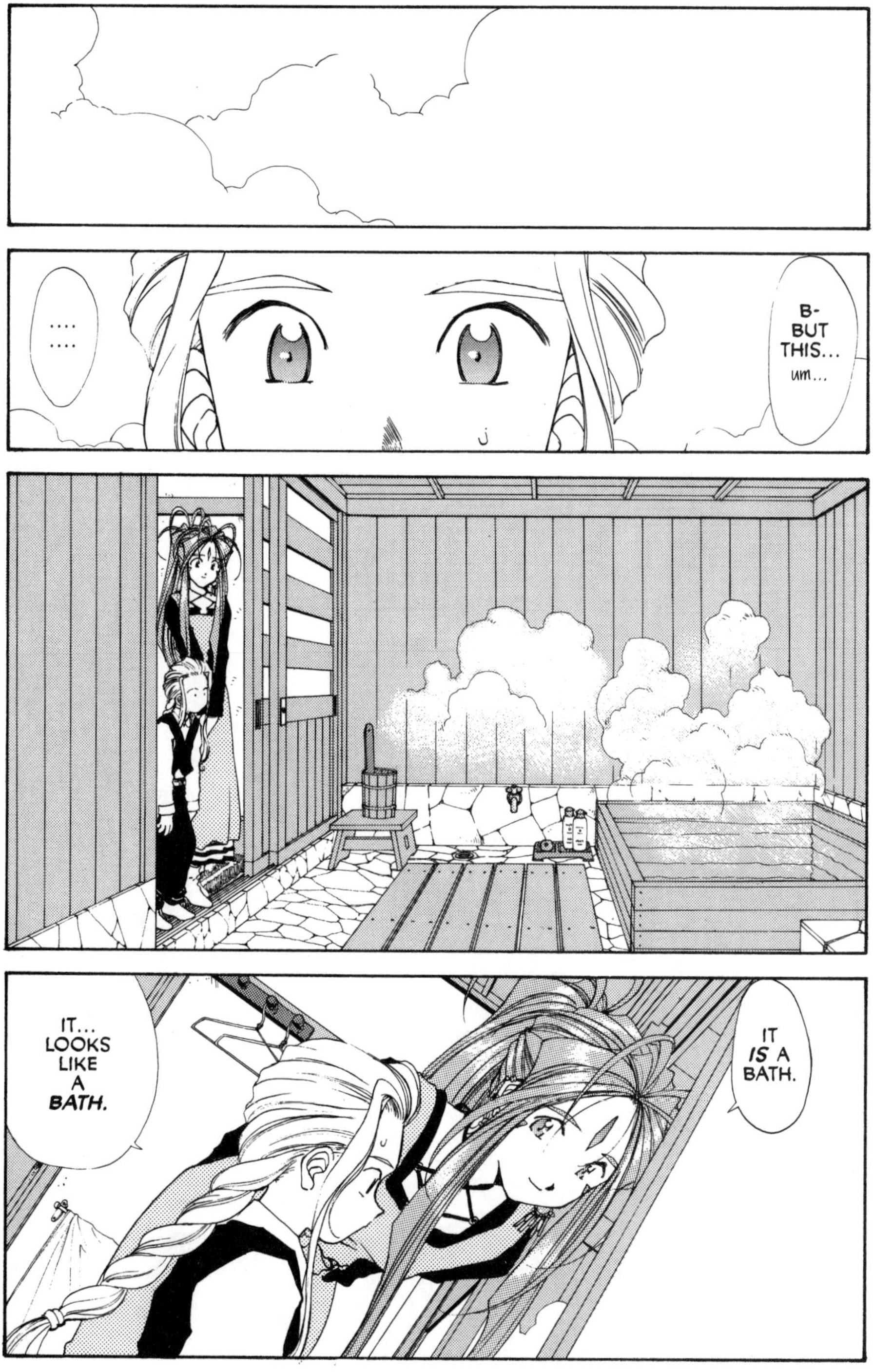
....
B- BUT THIS... um...
IT... LOOKS LIKE A *BATH.*
IT *IS* A BATH.

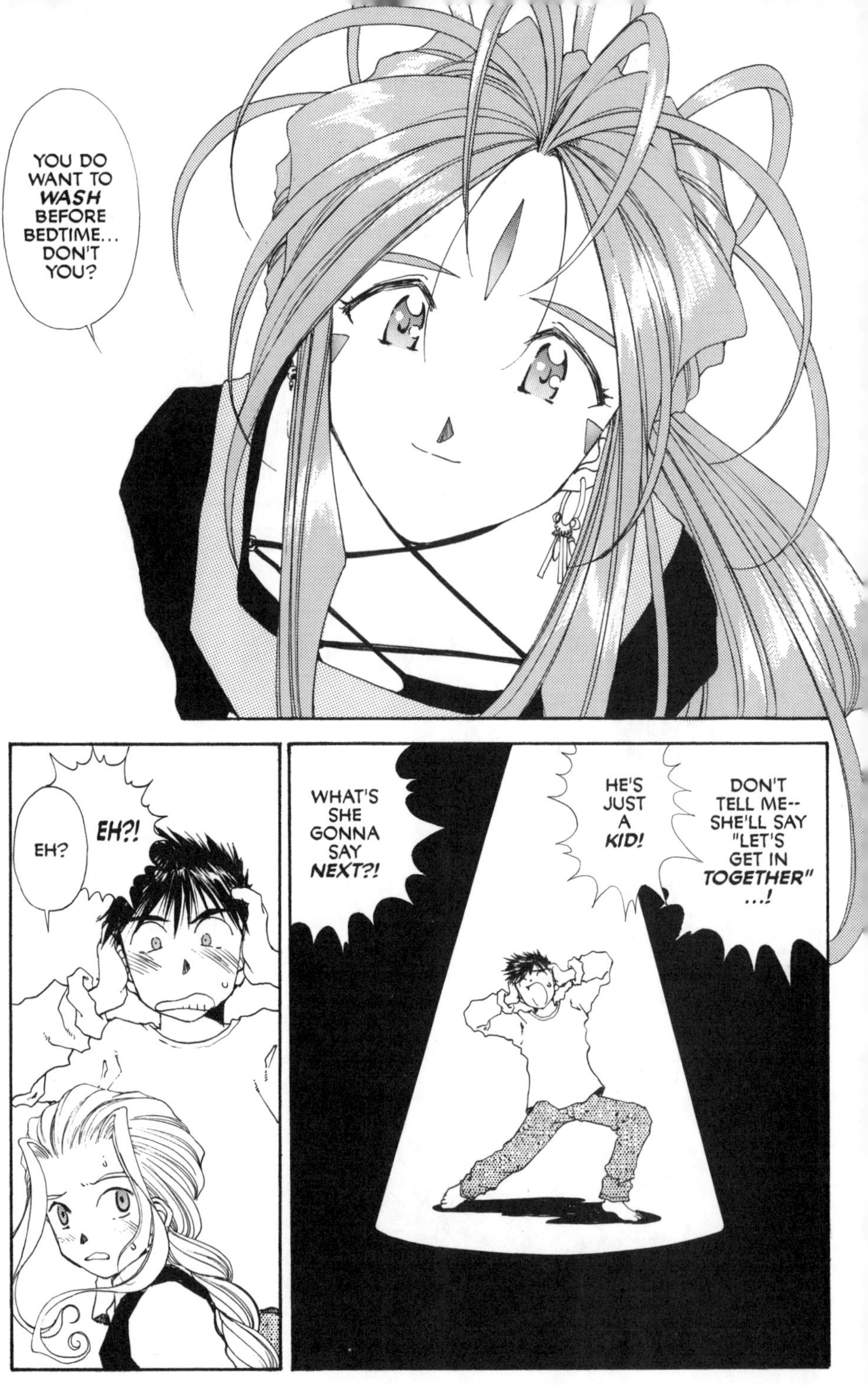
YOU DO WANT TO WASH BEFORE BEDTIME... DON'T YOU?
EH?
EH?!
WHAT'S SHE GONNA SAY NEXT?!
HE'S JUST A KID!
DON'T TELL ME-- SHE'LL SAY "LET'S GET IN TOGETHER" ...!

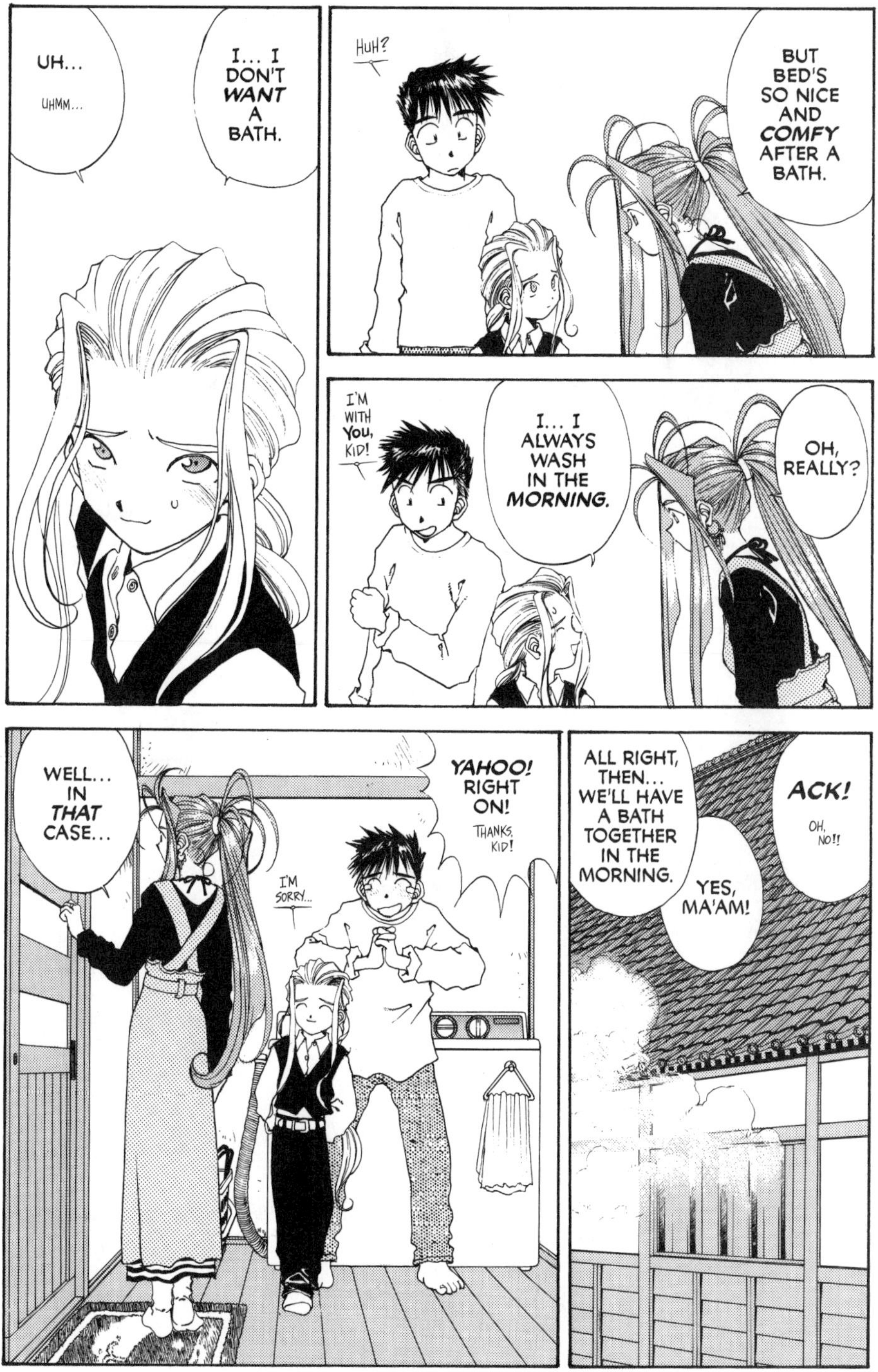
UH...
UHMM...
I... I DON'T WANT A BATH.
HUH?
BUT BED'S SO NICE AND COMFY AFTER A BATH.
I'M WITH YOU, KID!
I... I ALWAYS WASH IN THE MORNING.
OH, REALLY?
WELL... IN THAT CASE...
YAHOO! RIGHT ON!
THANKS, KID!
I'M SORRY...
ALL RIGHT, THEN... WE'LL HAVE A BATH TOGETHER IN THE MORNING.
ACK!
OH, NO!!
YES, MA'AM!

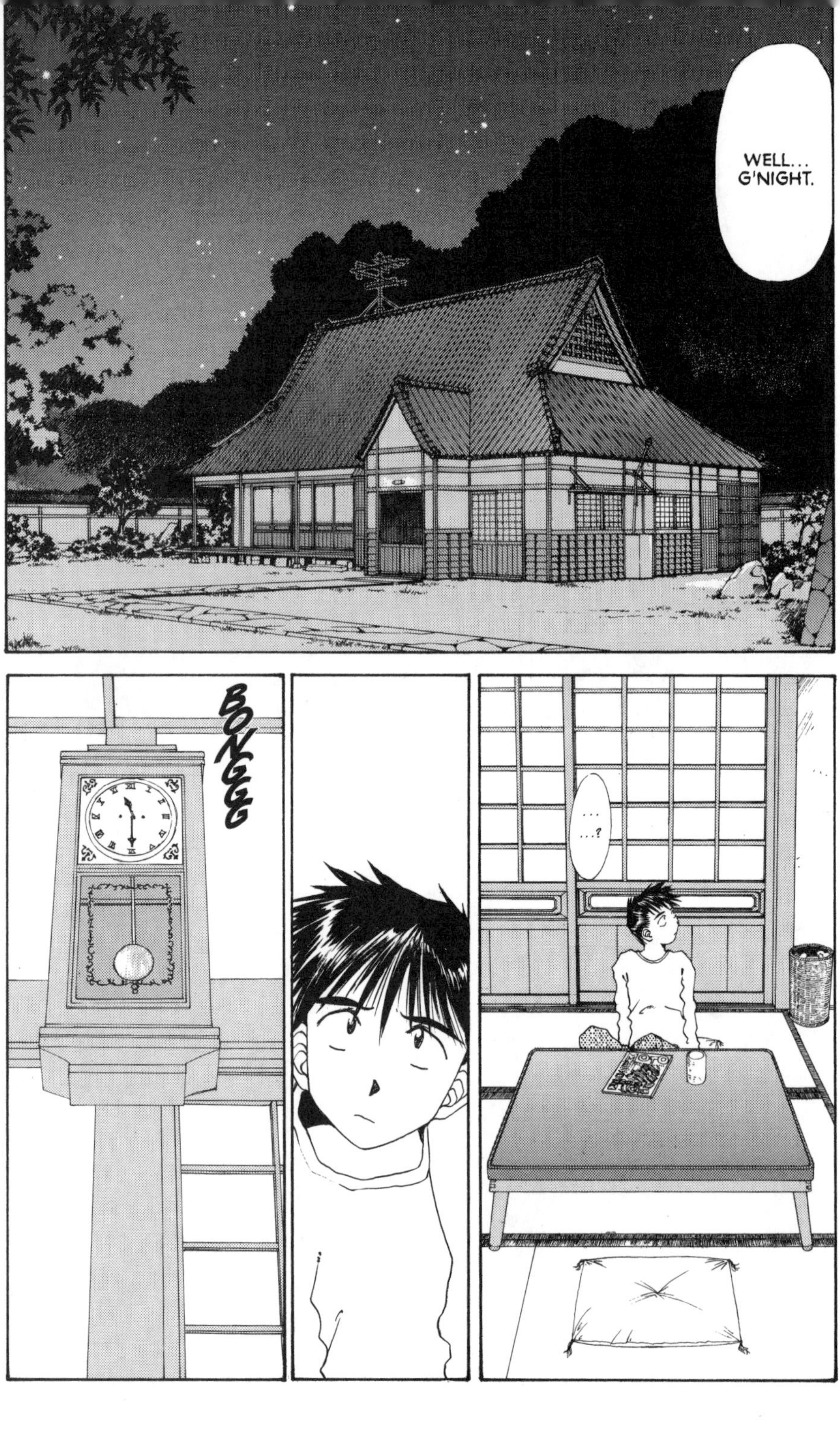
WELL...
G'NIGHT.
BONGGG
...
...?

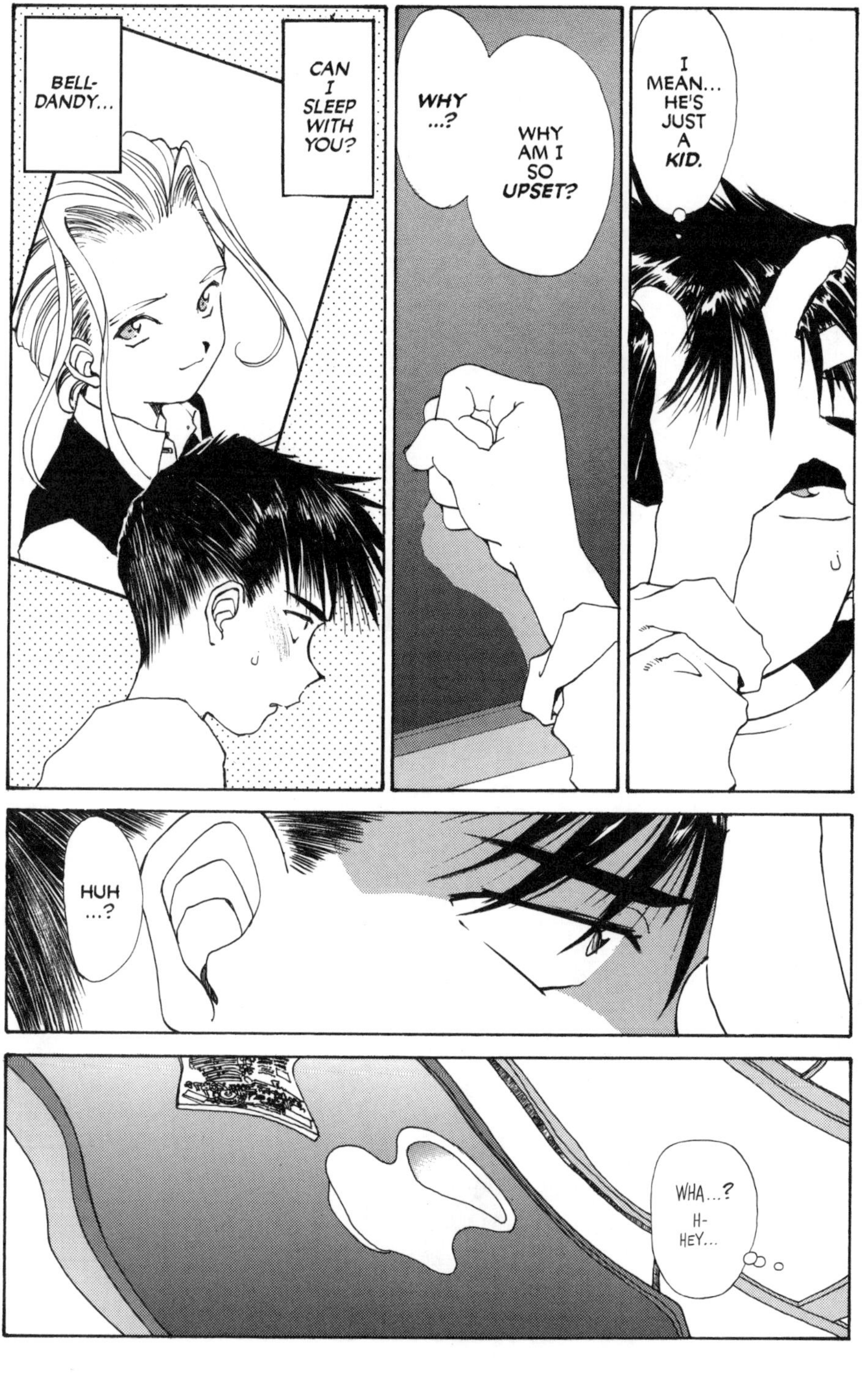
BELL-DANDY...
CAN I SLEEP WITH YOU?
WHY ...?
WHY AM I SO *UPSET?*
I MEAN... HE'S JUST A *KID.*
HUH ...?
WHA...?
H-HEY...

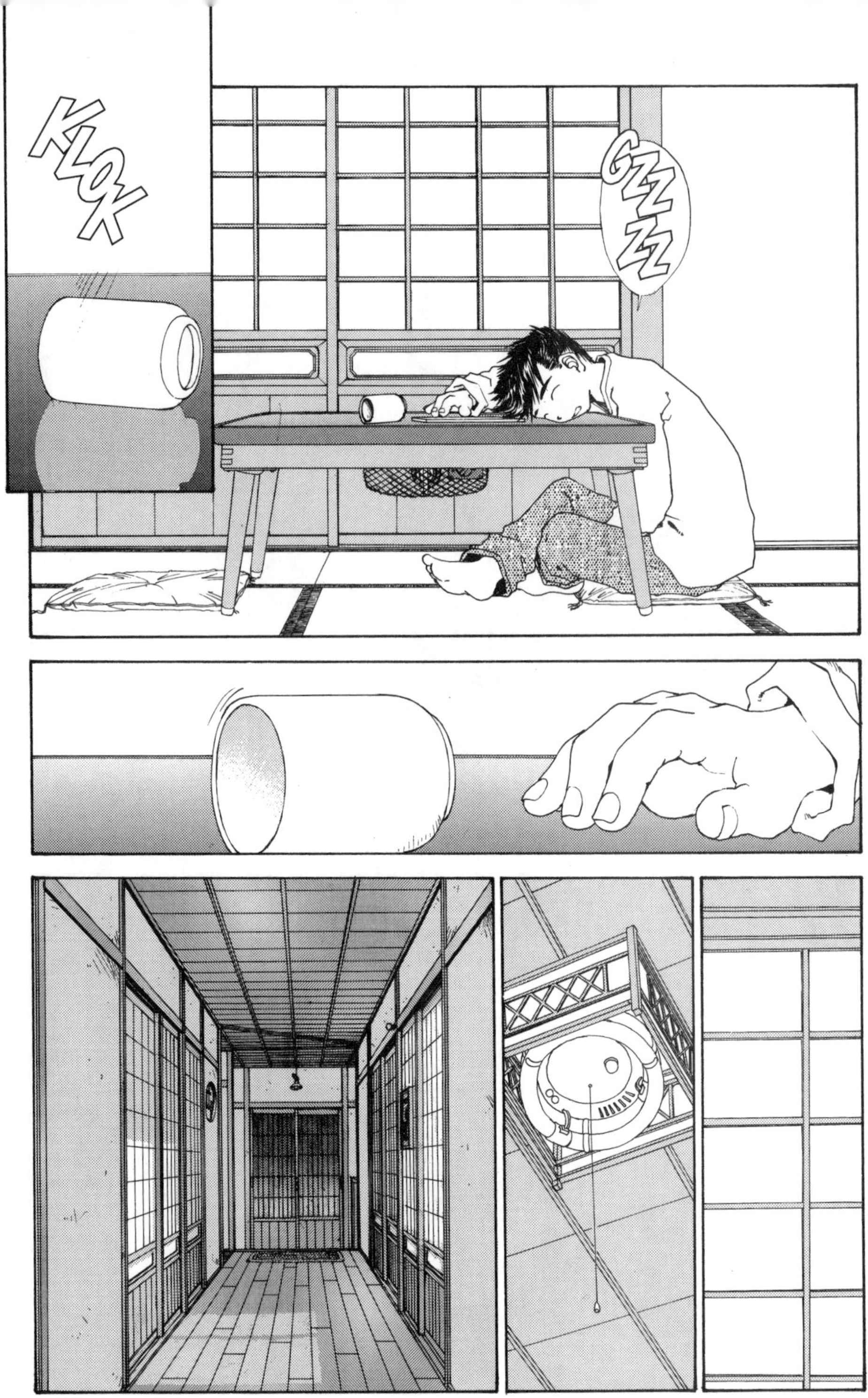
KLOK
GZZZZ

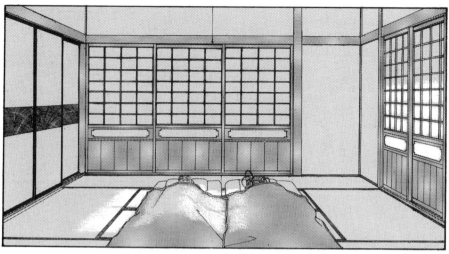

UM...
ARE YOU ASLEEP YET?

NO.

CAN YOU TELL ME ABOUT THE ME **YOU** REMEMBER...?

WELL... HMM... LET ME SEE...

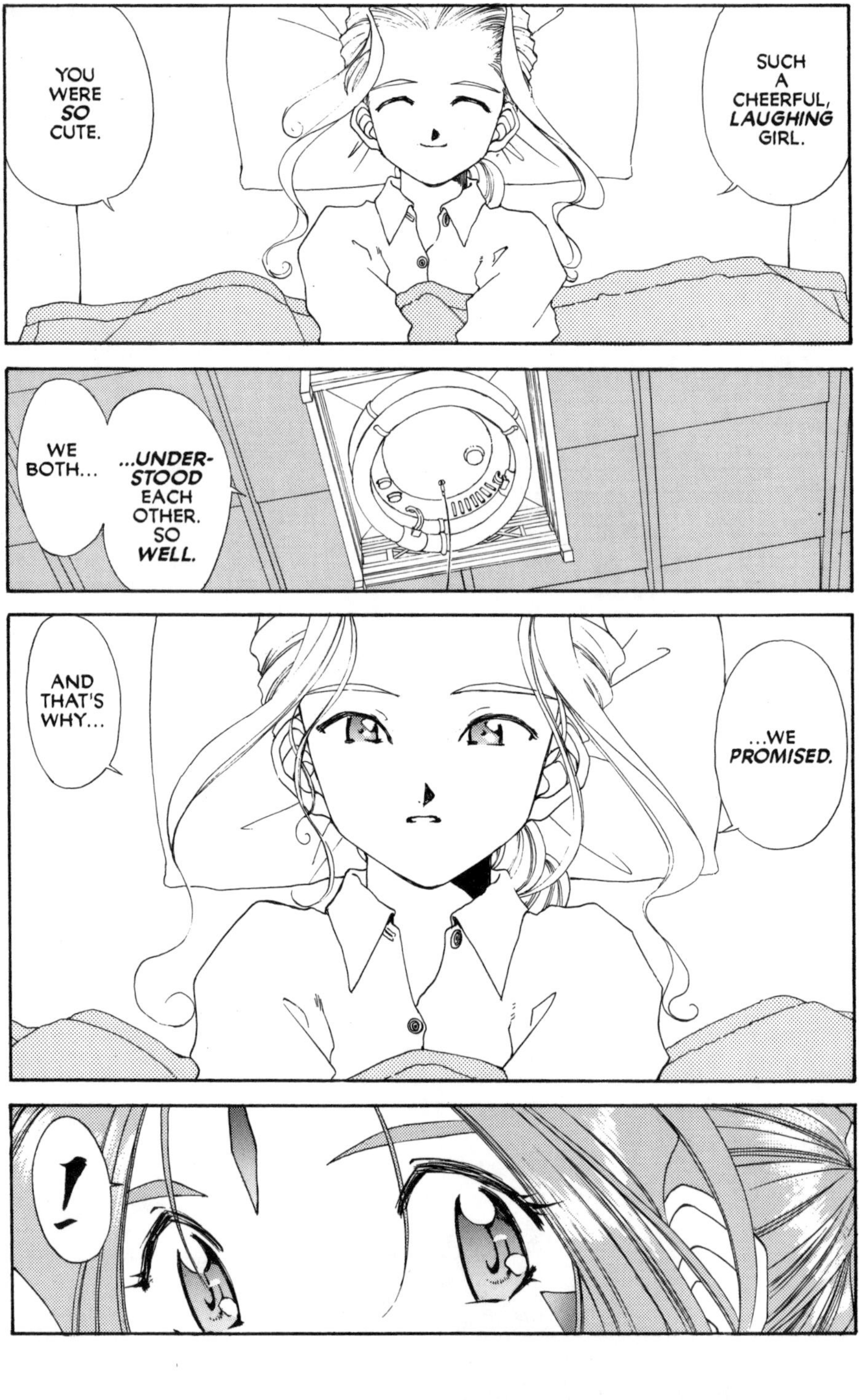
YOU WERE SO CUTE.
SUCH A CHEERFUL, LAUGHING GIRL.
WE BOTH...
...UNDERSTOOD EACH OTHER. SO WELL.
AND THAT'S WHY...
...WE PROMISED.
!

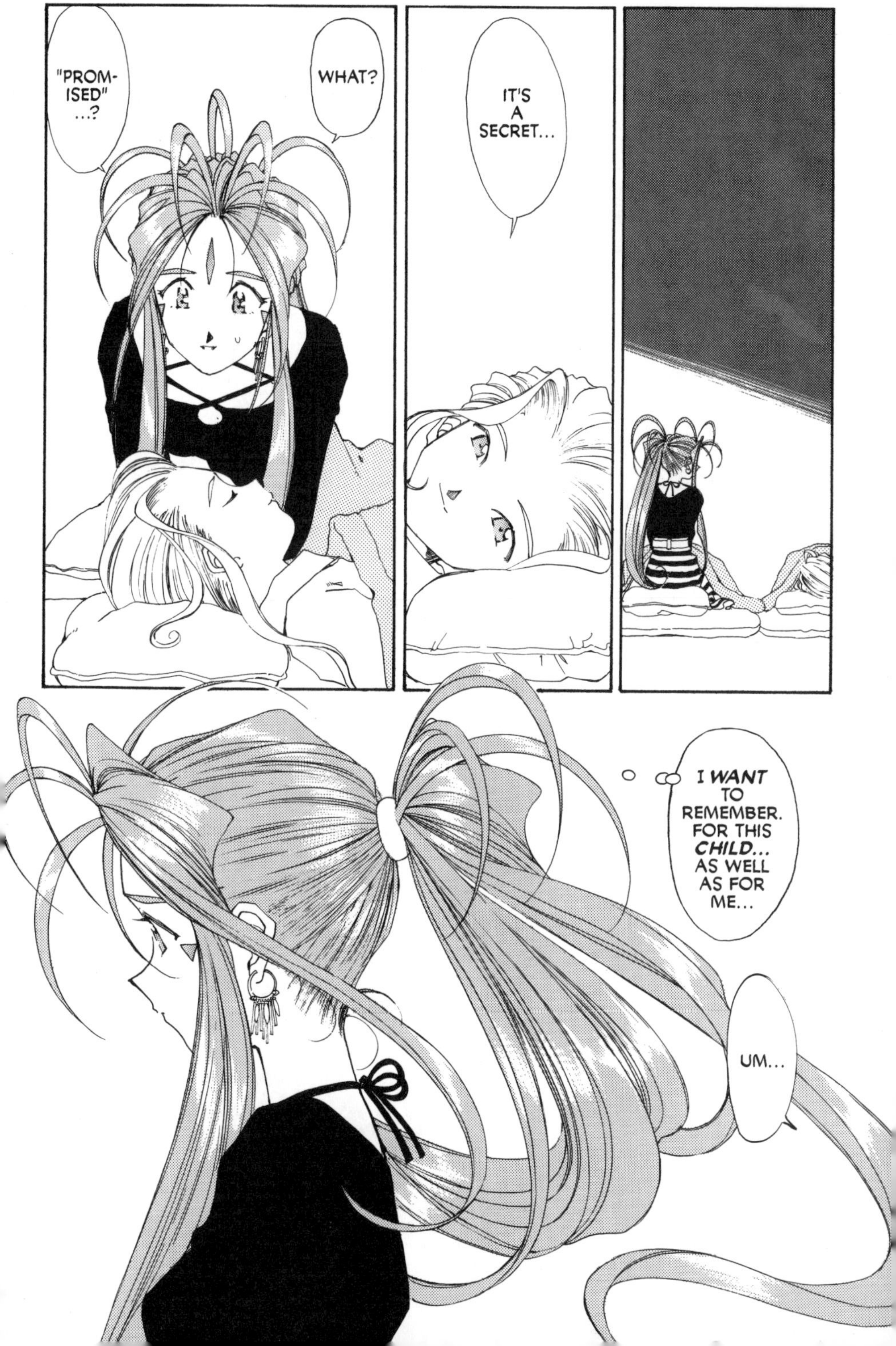

"PROM-ISED" ...?
WHAT?
IT'S A SECRET...
I *WANT* TO REMEMBER. FOR THIS ***CHILD...*** AS WELL AS FOR ME...
UM...

CAN I SLEEP ON *YOUR* SIDE?

YES?

....
....

ALL RIGHT.

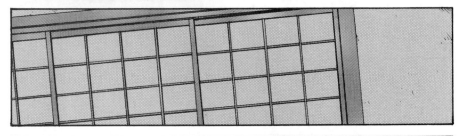

SO *WARM*... JUST LIKE BEFORE.

BUT...

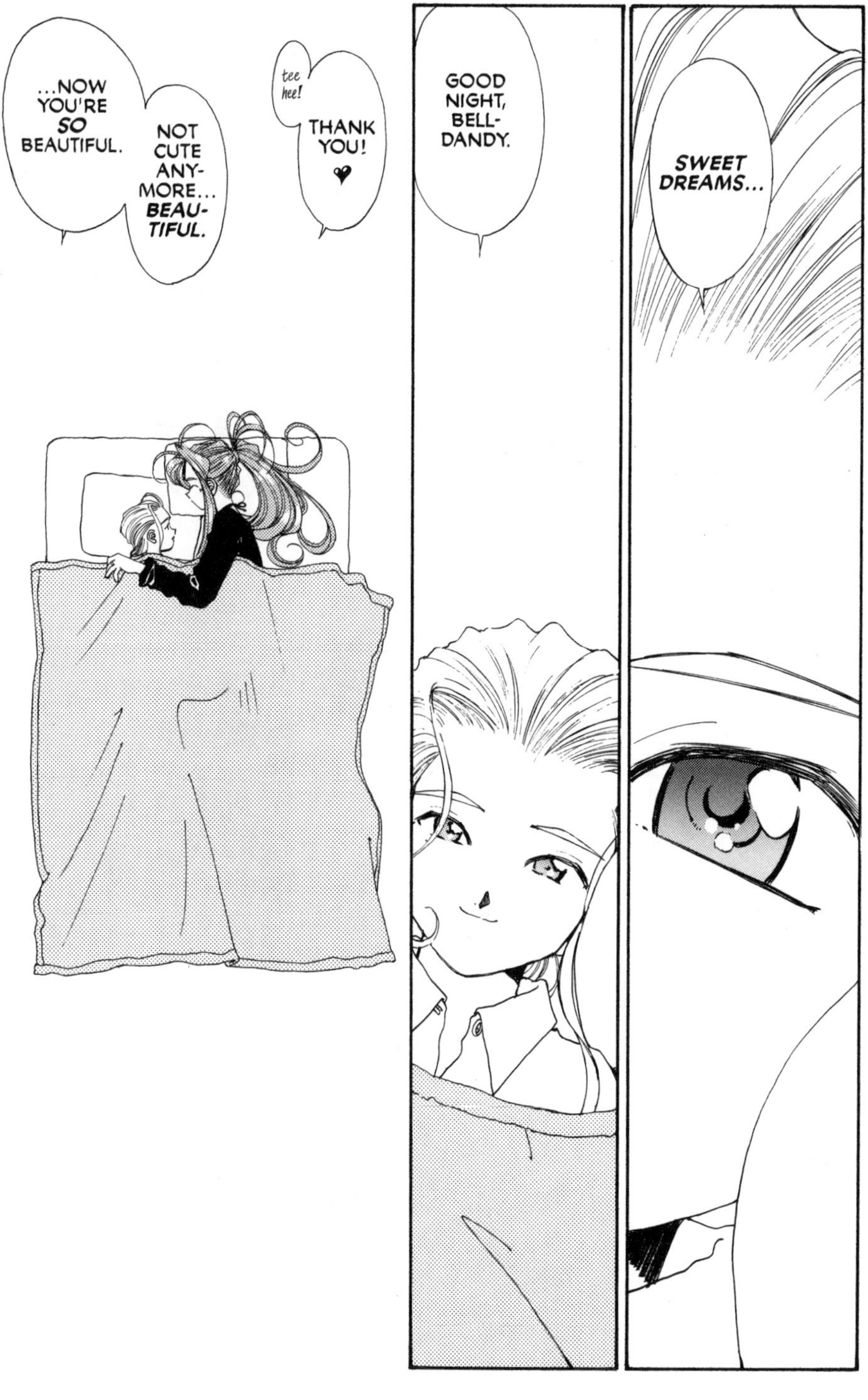
...NOW YOU'RE *SO* BEAUTIFUL.
NOT CUTE ANYMORE... *BEAUTIFUL.*
tee hee!
THANK YOU! ❤
GOOD NIGHT, BELLDANDY.
SWEET DREAMS...

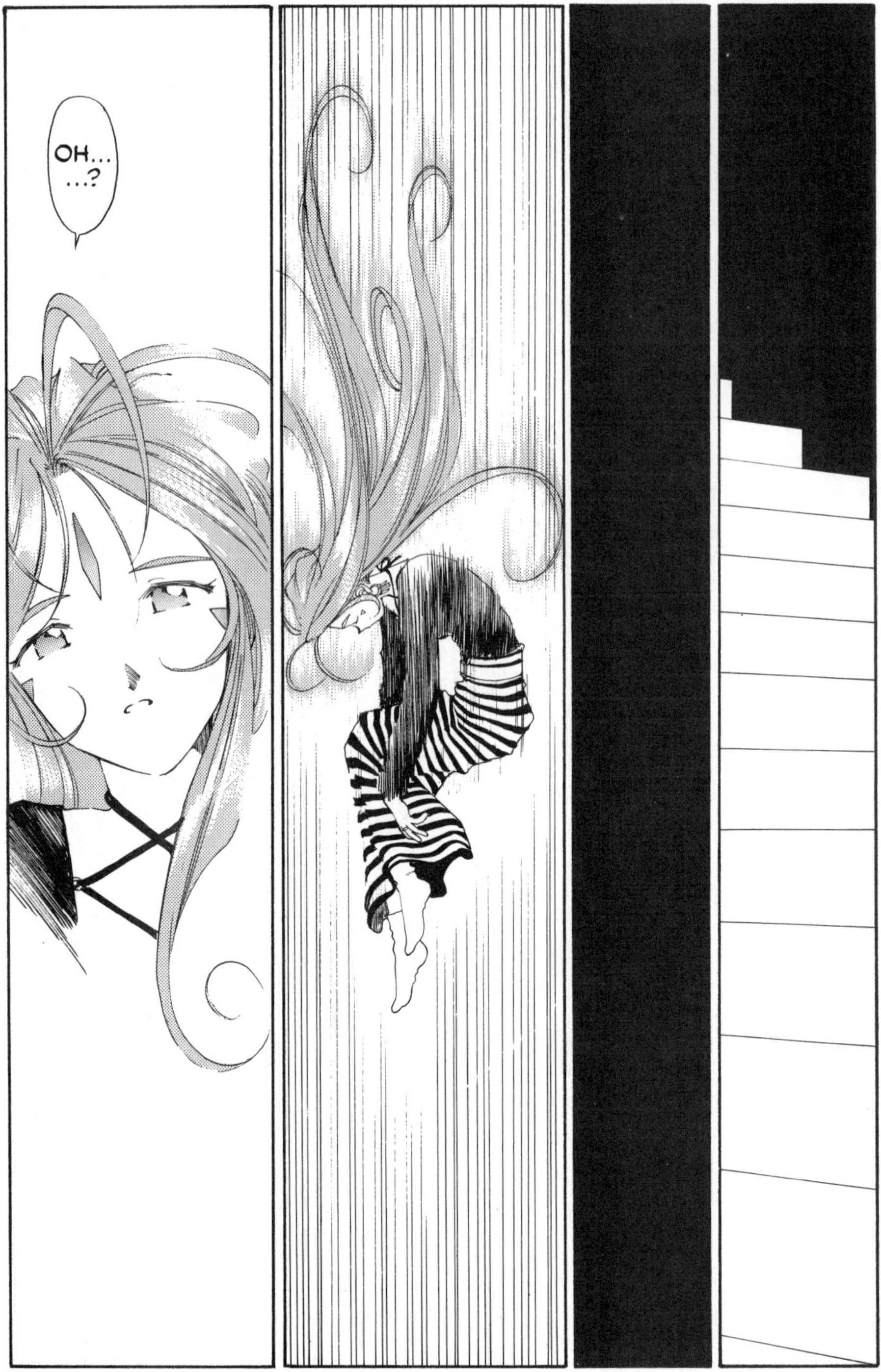
OH... ...?

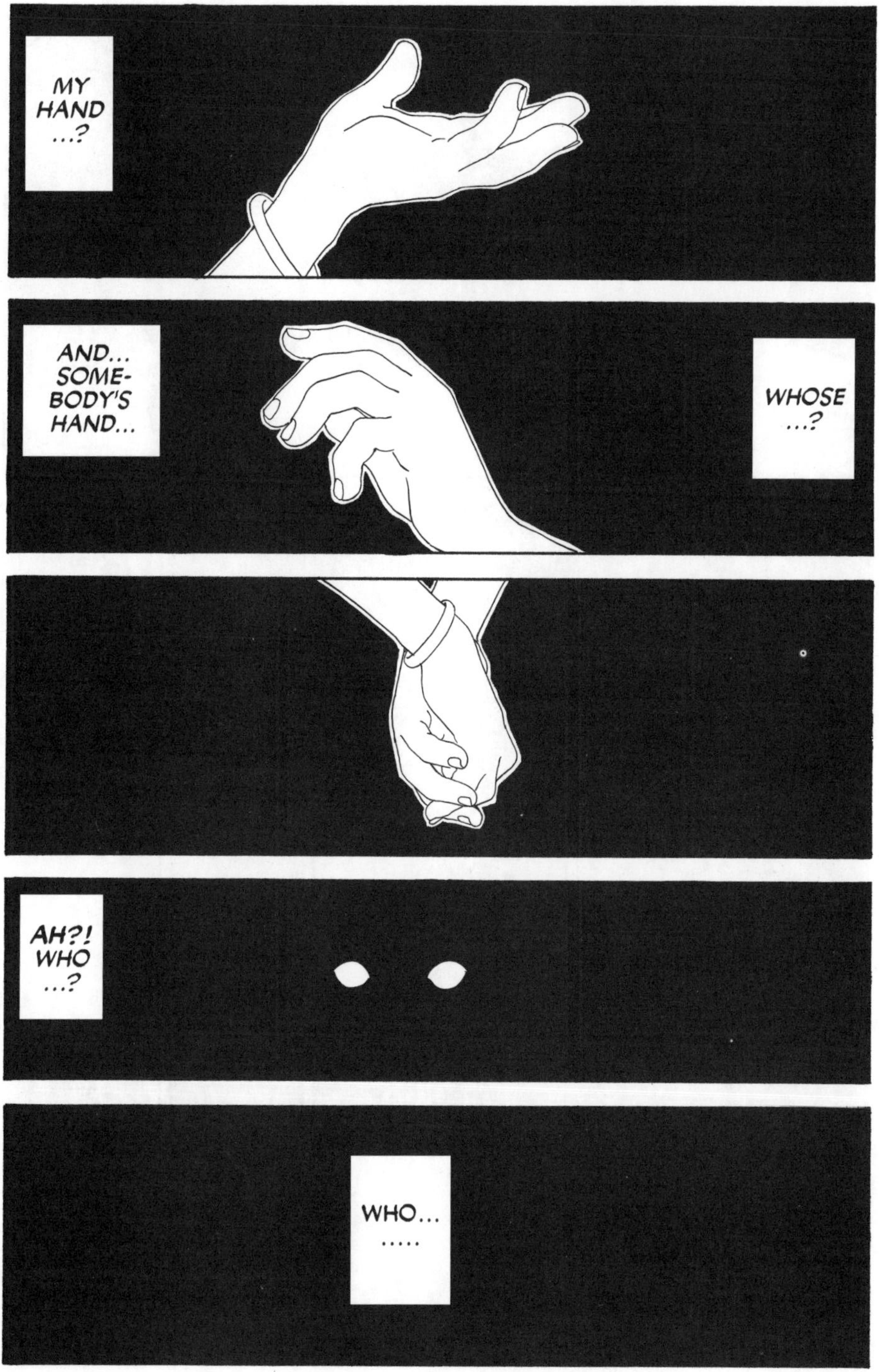
MY HAND ...?
AND... SOME-BODY'S HAND...
WHOSE ...?
AH?! WHO ...?
WHO... .....

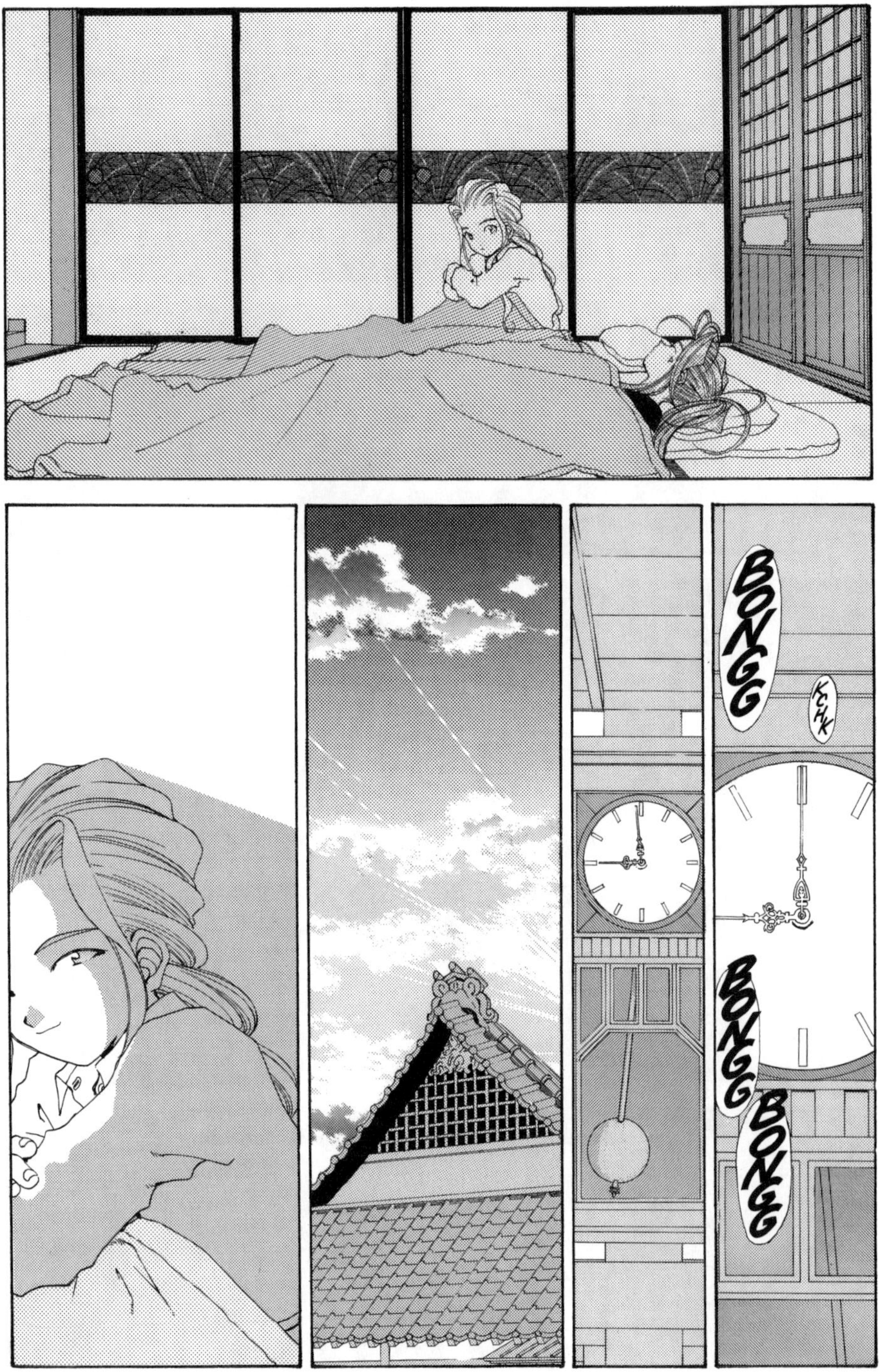
BONGG
KCHK
BONGG
BONGG

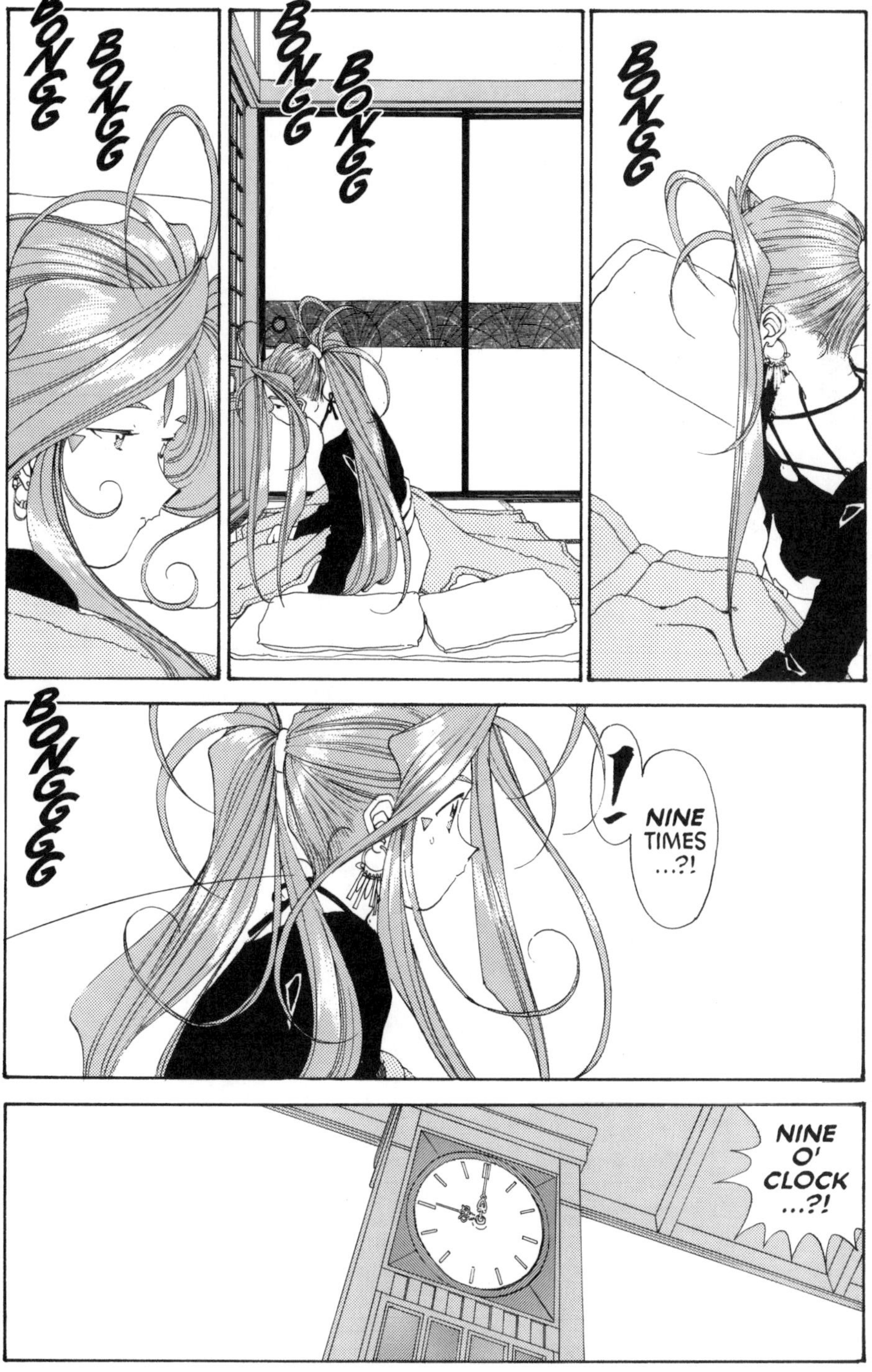
BONGG
BONGG
BONGG
BONGG
BONGG
BONGGGG
!
NINE TIMES ...?!
NINE O' CLOCK ...?!

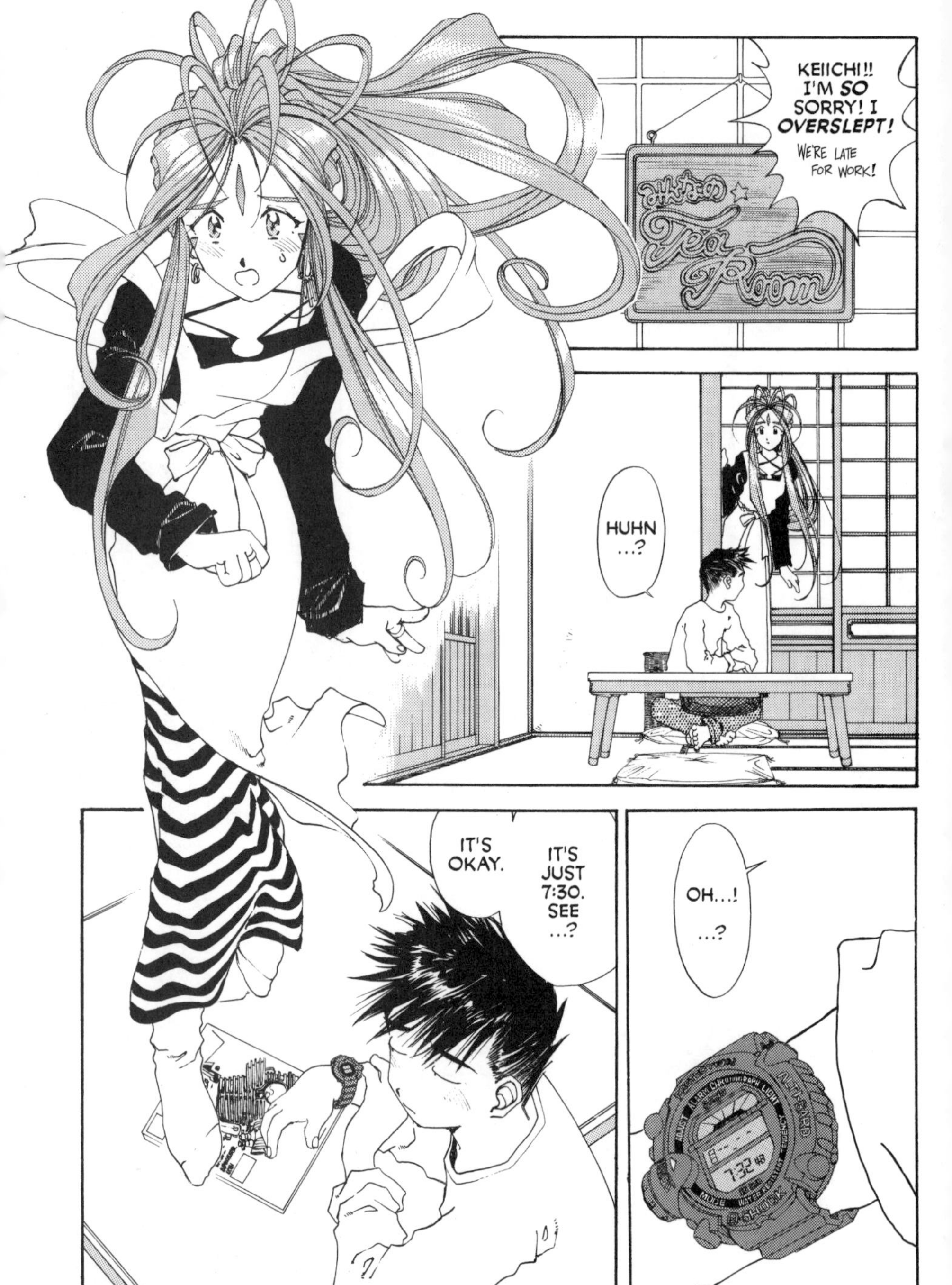

Tea Room
KEIICHI!! I'M SO SORRY! I OVERSLEPT!
WE'RE LATE FOR WORK!
HUHN ...?
IT'S OKAY.
IT'S JUST 7:30. SEE ...?
OH...!
...?

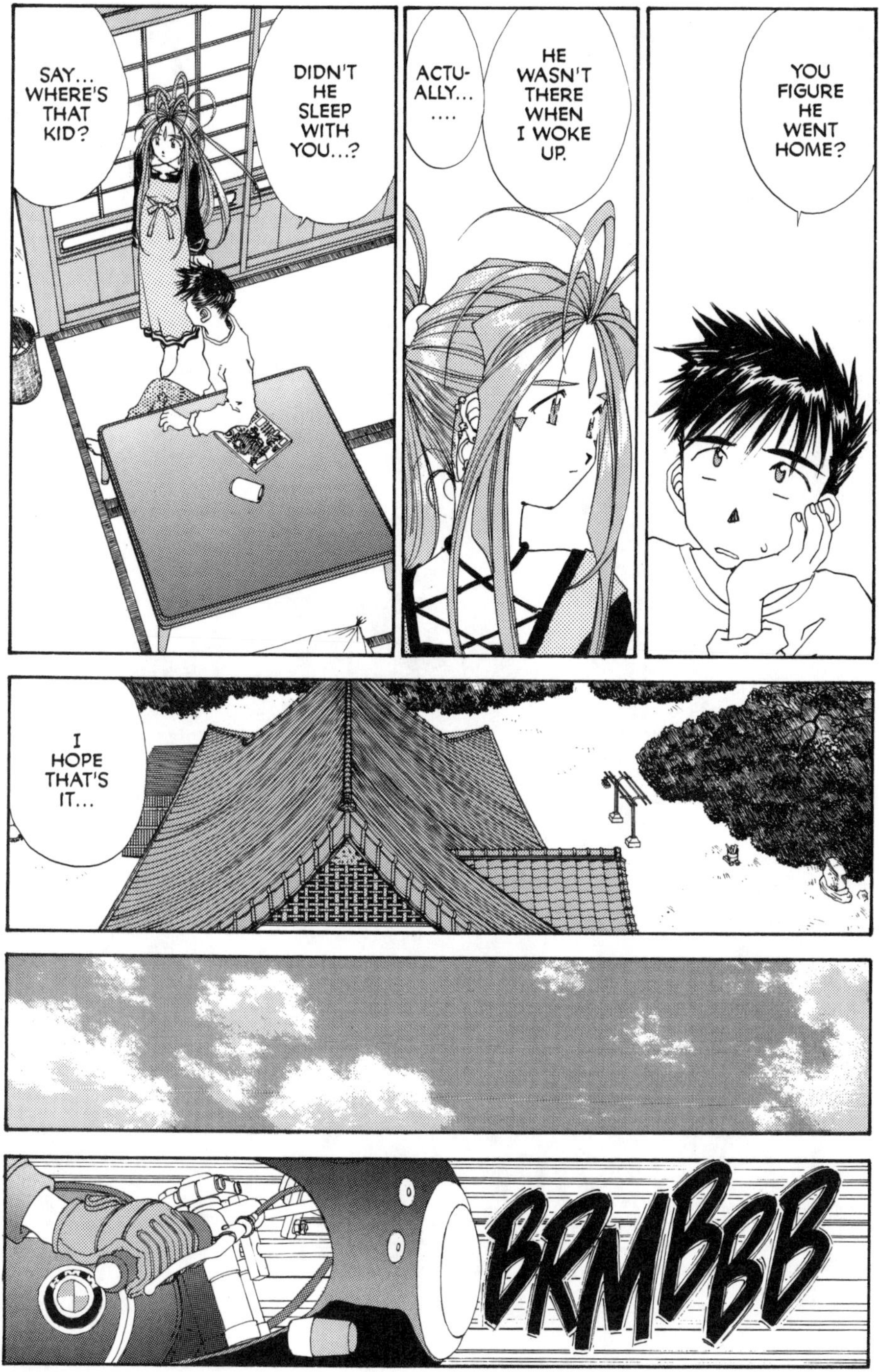
SAY... WHERE'S THAT KID?
DIDN'T HE SLEEP WITH YOU...?
ACTU-ALLY... ....
HE WASN'T THERE WHEN I WOKE UP.
YOU FIGURE HE WENT HOME?
I HOPE THAT'S IT...
BRMBBB

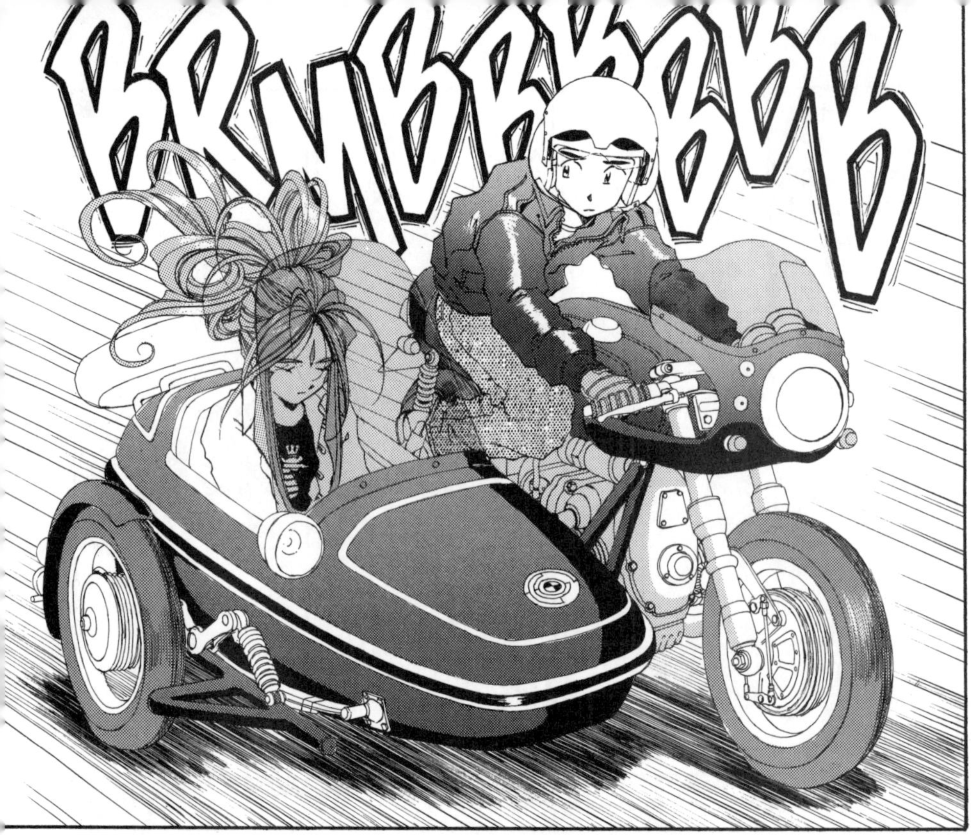
BRMBRRBBB

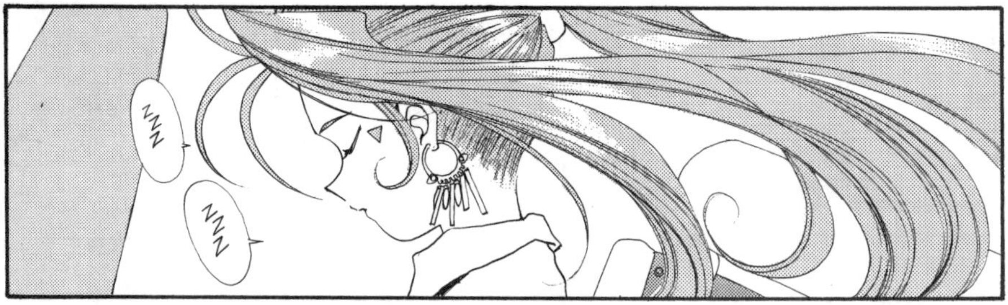
NNN
NNN

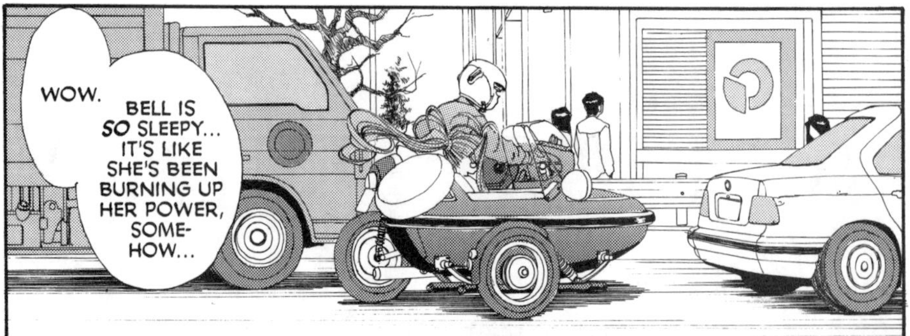
WOW.
BELL IS *SO* SLEEPY... IT'S LIKE SHE'S BEEN BURNING UP HER POWER, SOME-HOW...

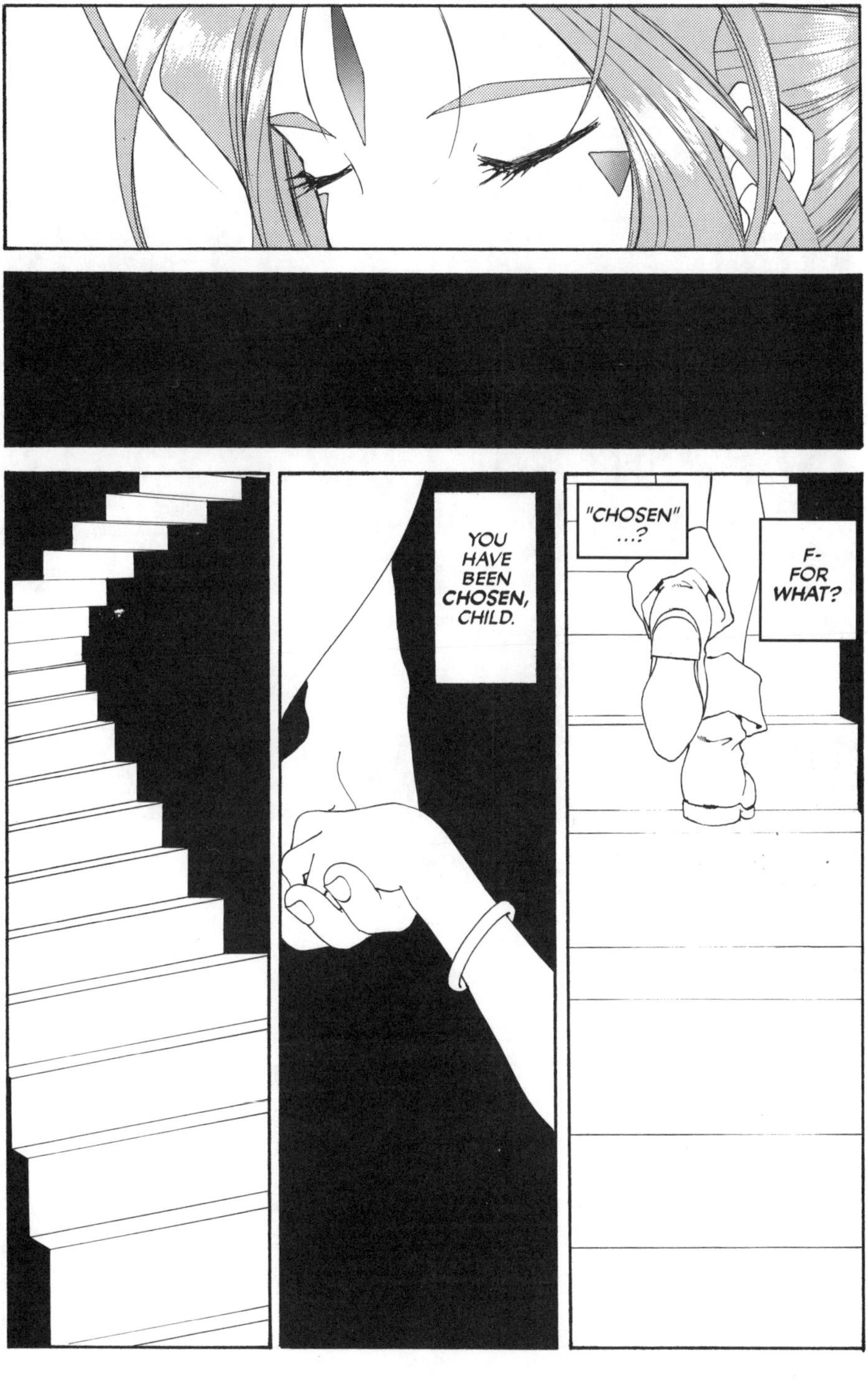
YOU HAVE BEEN CHOSEN, CHILD.
"CHOSEN" ...?
F- FOR WHAT?

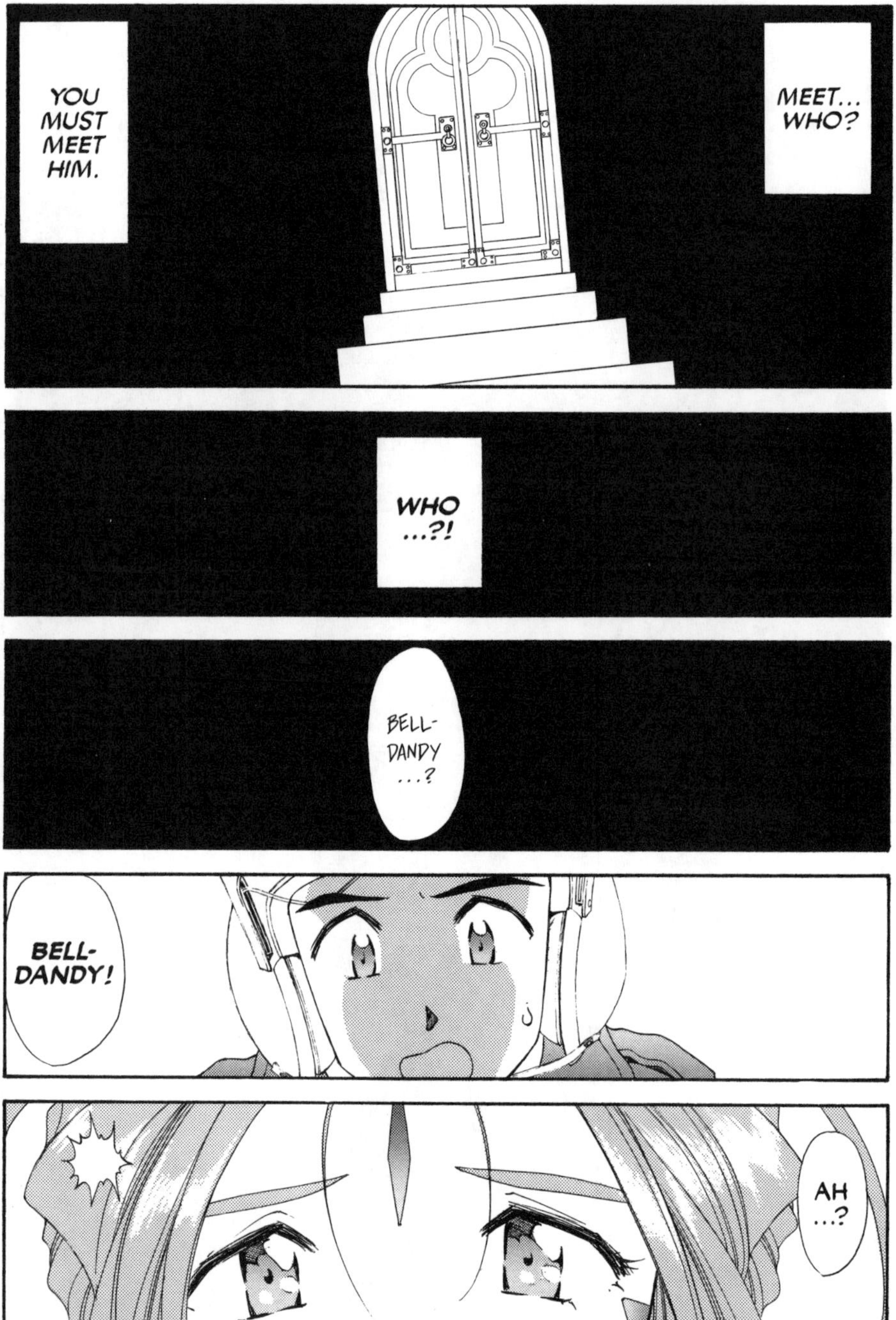
YOU MUST MEET HIM.
MEET... WHO?
WHO ...?!
BELL-DANDY ...?
BELL-DANDY!
AH ...?

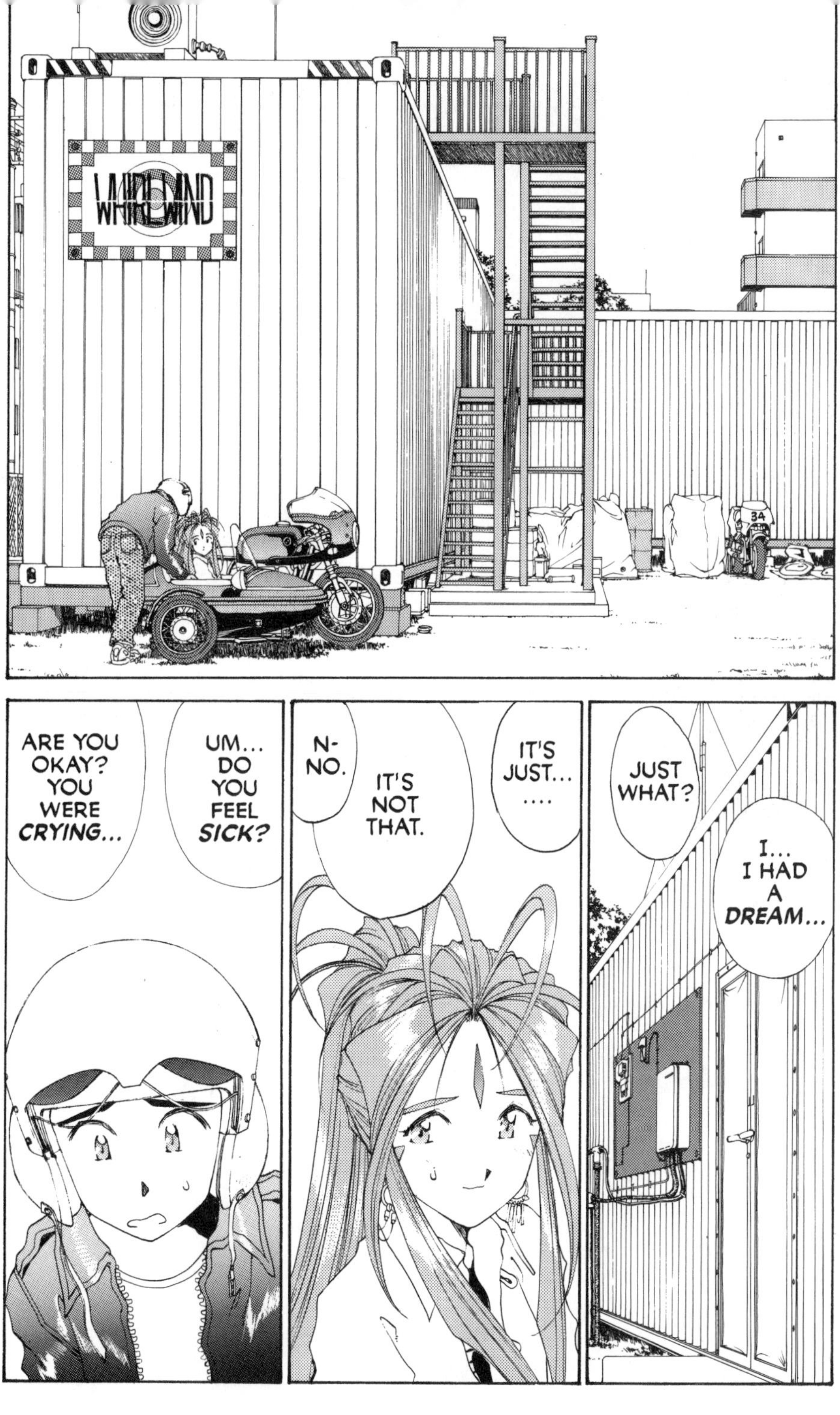
WHIRLWIND
ARE YOU OKAY? YOU WERE *CRYING*...
UM... DO YOU FEEL *SICK?*
N-NO.
IT'S NOT THAT.
IT'S JUST... ....
JUST WHAT?
I... I HAD A *DREAM*...

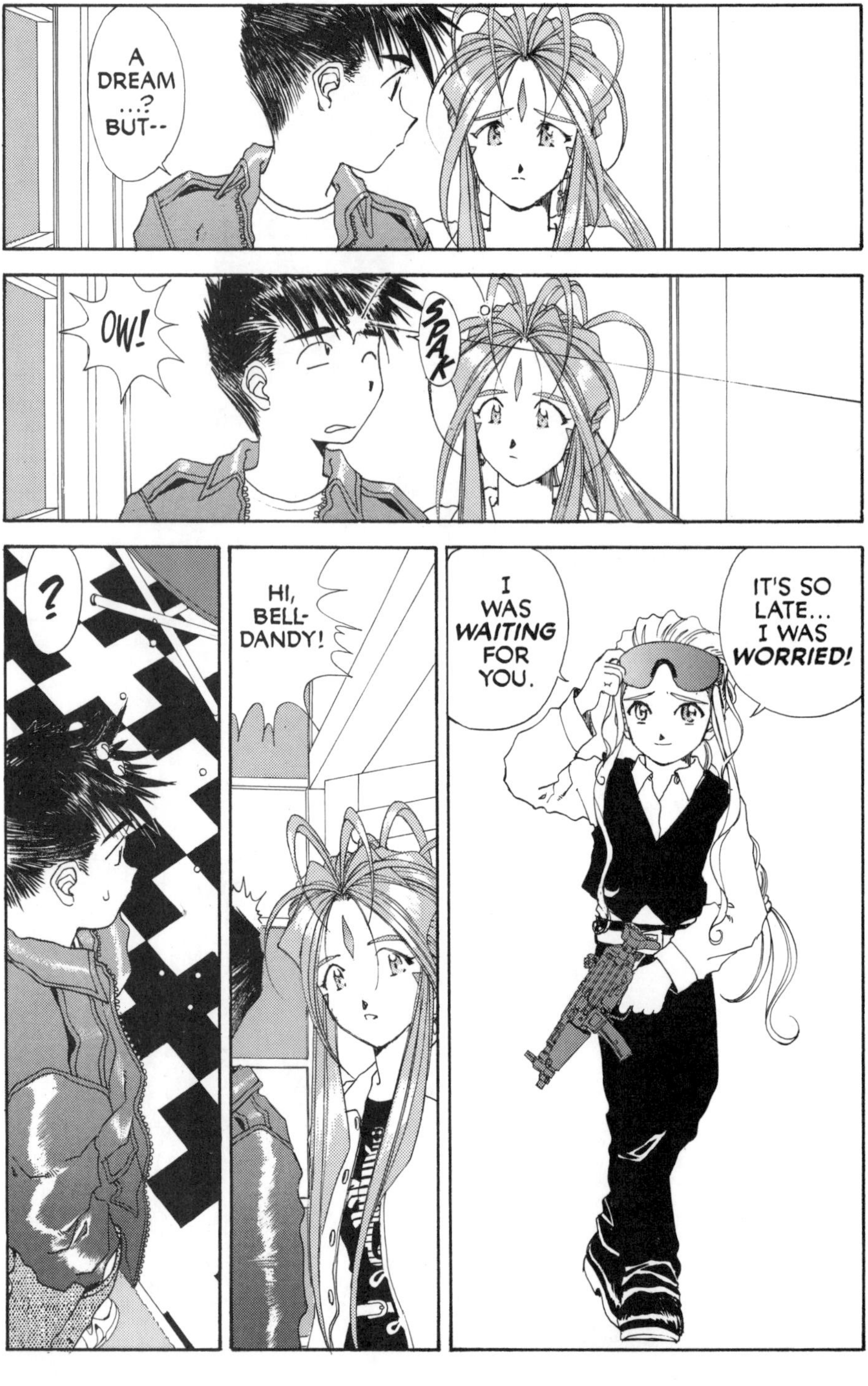
A DREAM ...? BUT--
OW!
SPAK
?
HI, BELL-DANDY!
I WAS *WAITING* FOR YOU.
IT'S SO LATE... I WAS *WORRIED!*

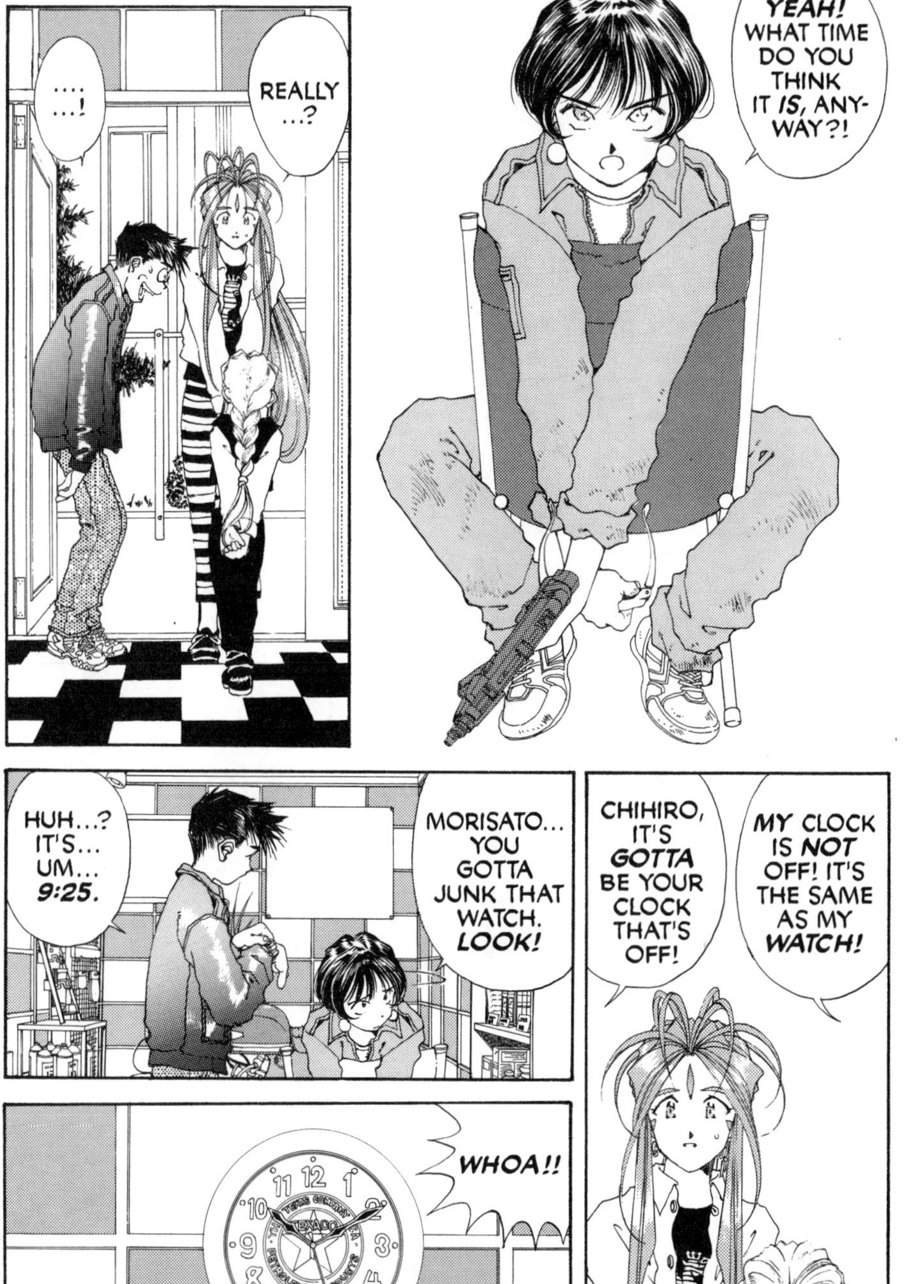

..., ...!
REALLY ...?
YEAH! WHAT TIME DO YOU THINK IT IS, ANYWAY?!
HUH...? IT'S... UM... 9:25.
MORISATO... YOU GOTTA JUNK THAT WATCH. LOOK!
WHOA!!
CHIHIRO, IT'S GOTTA BE YOUR CLOCK THAT'S OFF!
MY CLOCK IS NOT OFF! IT'S THE SAME AS MY WATCH!

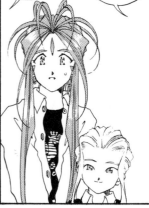

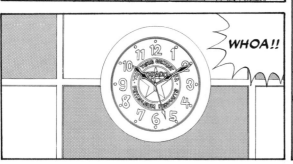

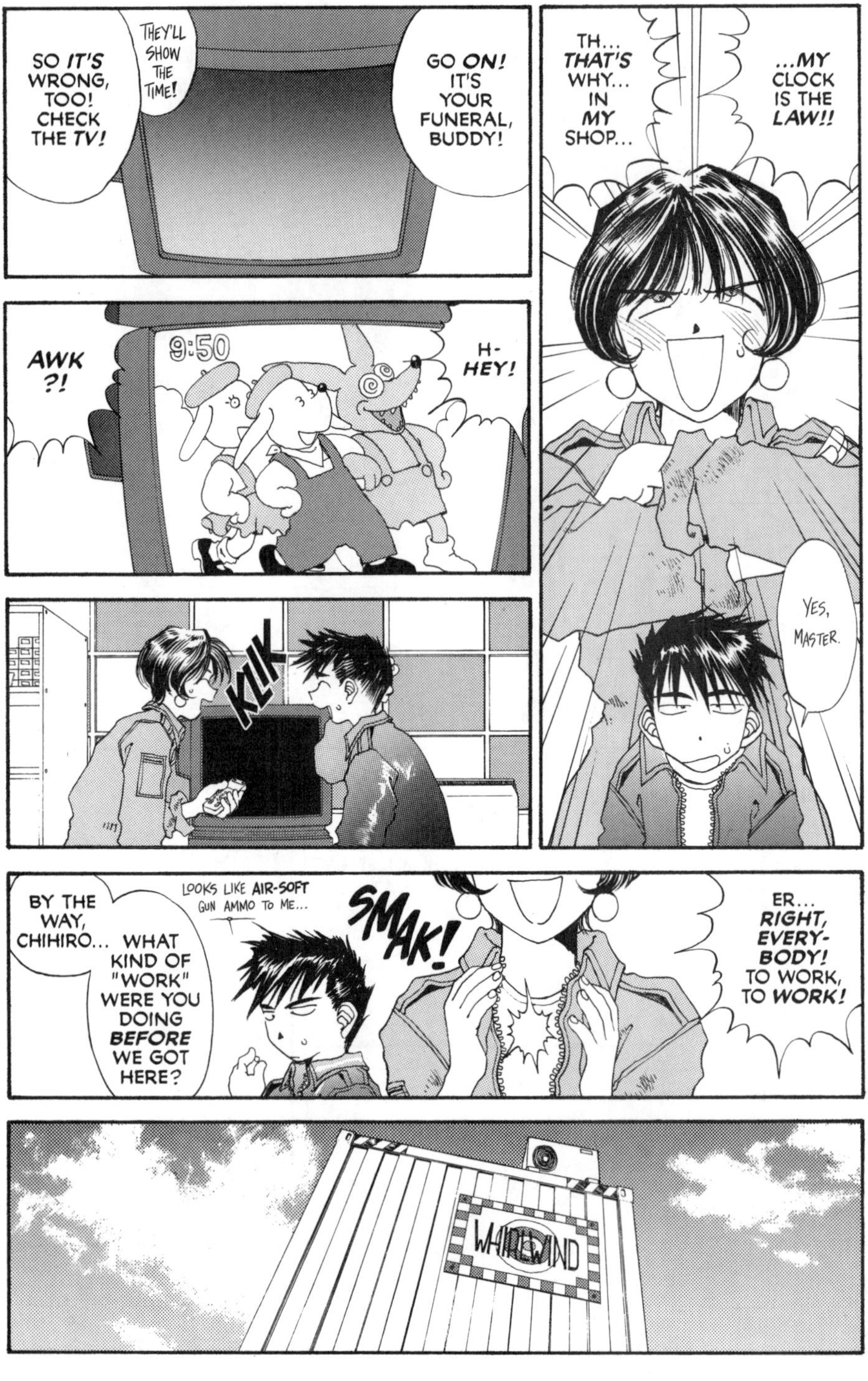
SO IT'S WRONG, TOO! CHECK THE TV!
THEY'LL SHOW THE TIME!
GO ON! IT'S YOUR FUNERAL, BUDDY!
9:50
AWK ?!
H-HEY!
KLIK
TH... THAT'S WHY... IN MY SHOP...
...MY CLOCK IS THE LAW!!
YES, MASTER.
BY THE WAY, CHIHIRO... WHAT KIND OF "WORK" WERE YOU DOING BEFORE WE GOT HERE?
LOOKS LIKE AIR-SOFT GUN AMMO TO ME...
SMAK!
ER... RIGHT, EVERYBODY! TO WORK, TO WORK!
WHIRLWIND

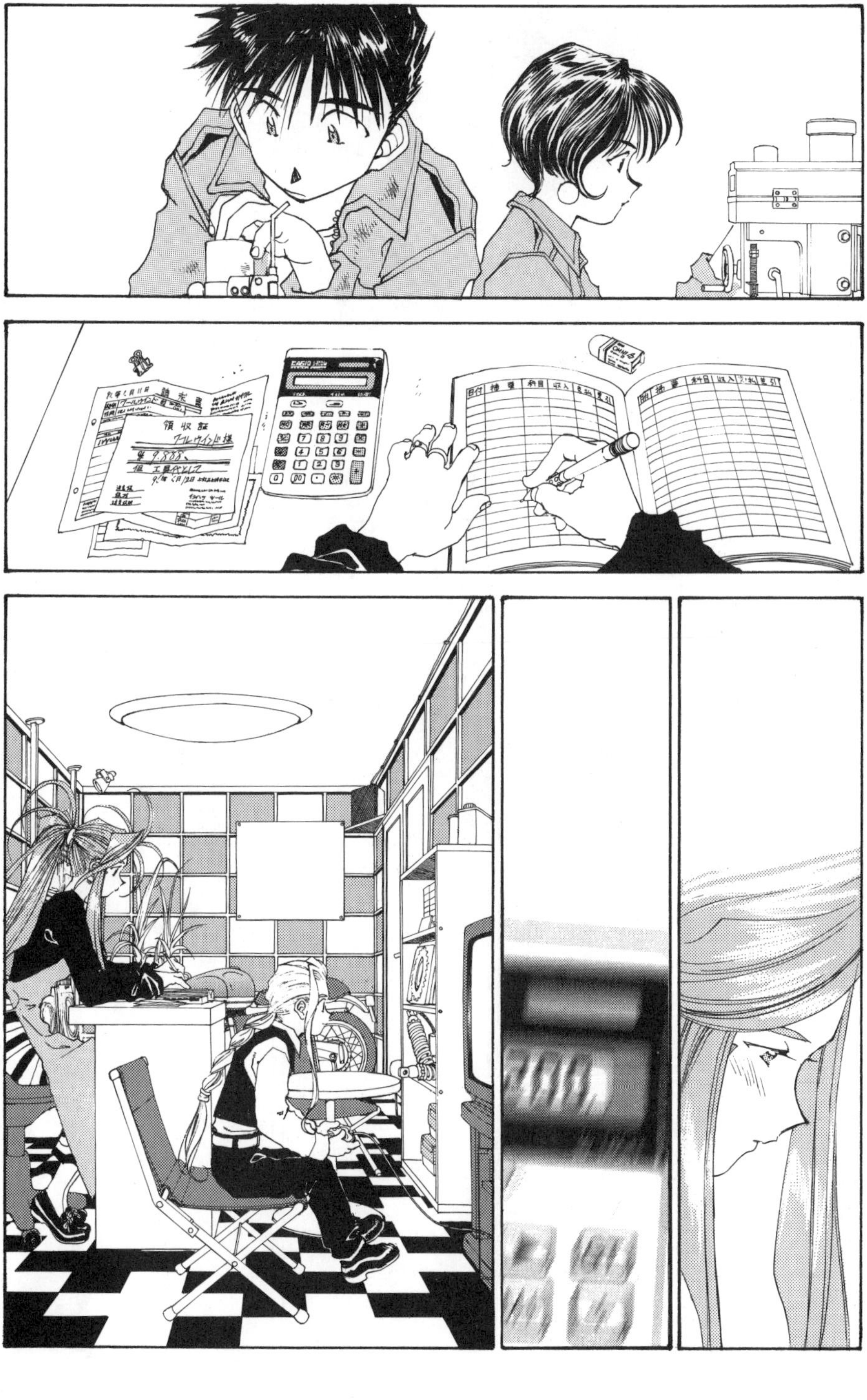
請求書
領収証
ワールウインド様
¥9,888.
但 工具代として
CASIO
日付 摘要 科目 収入 支払 差引
日付 摘要 科目 収入 支払 差引
OMNI

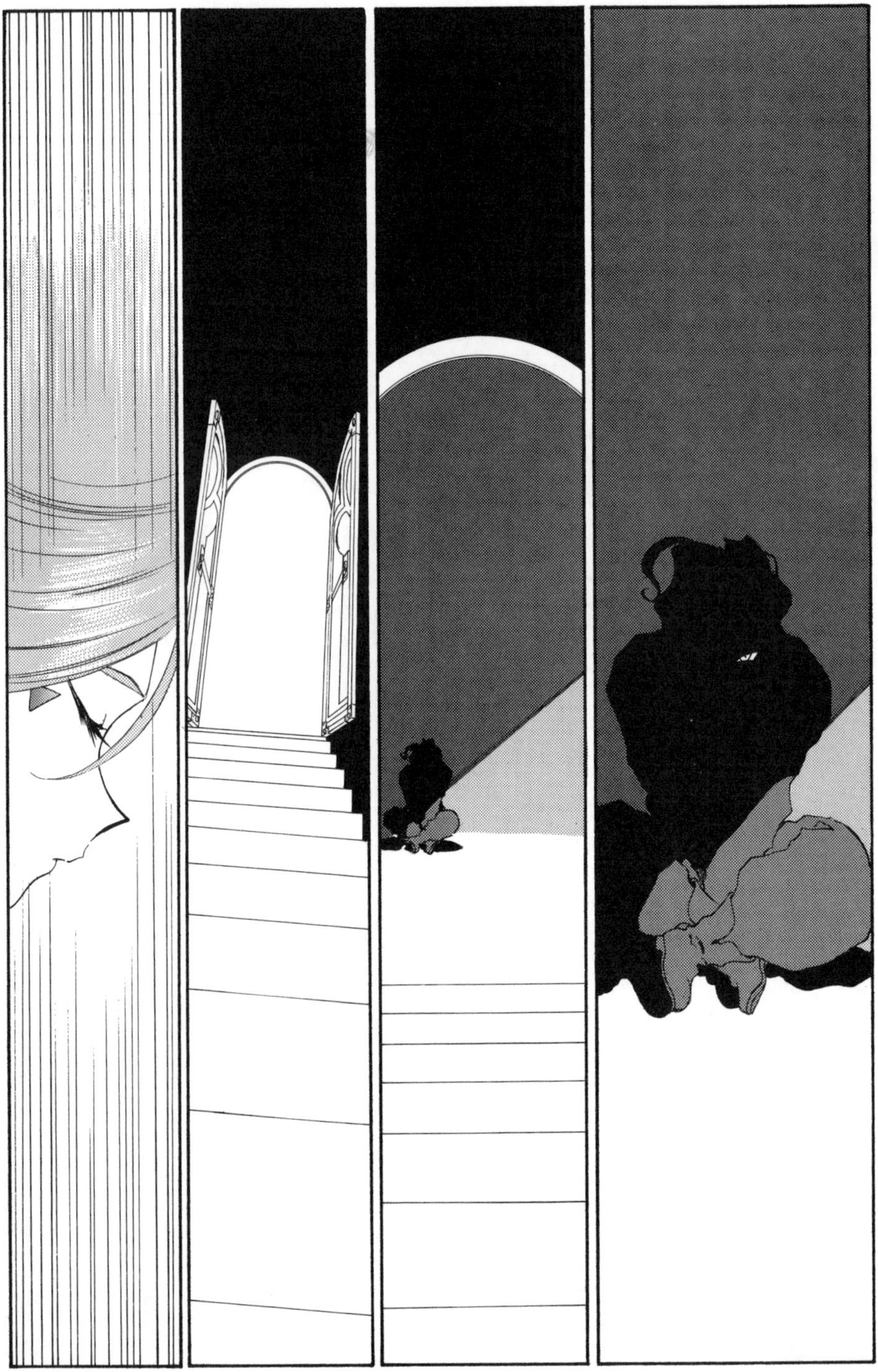

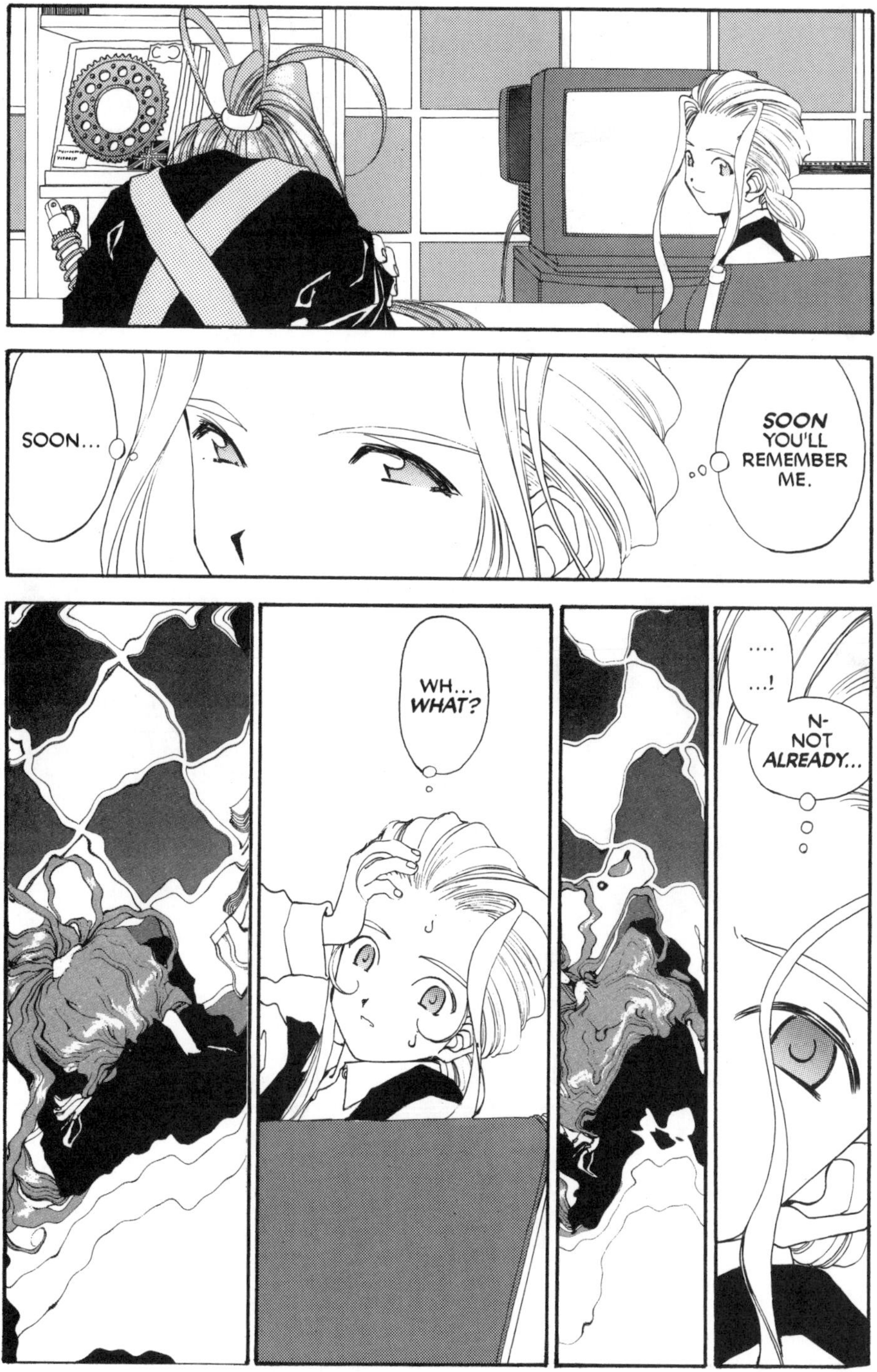
SOON...
SOON YOU'LL REMEMBER ME.
WH... WHAT?
....
...!
N-NOT ALREADY...

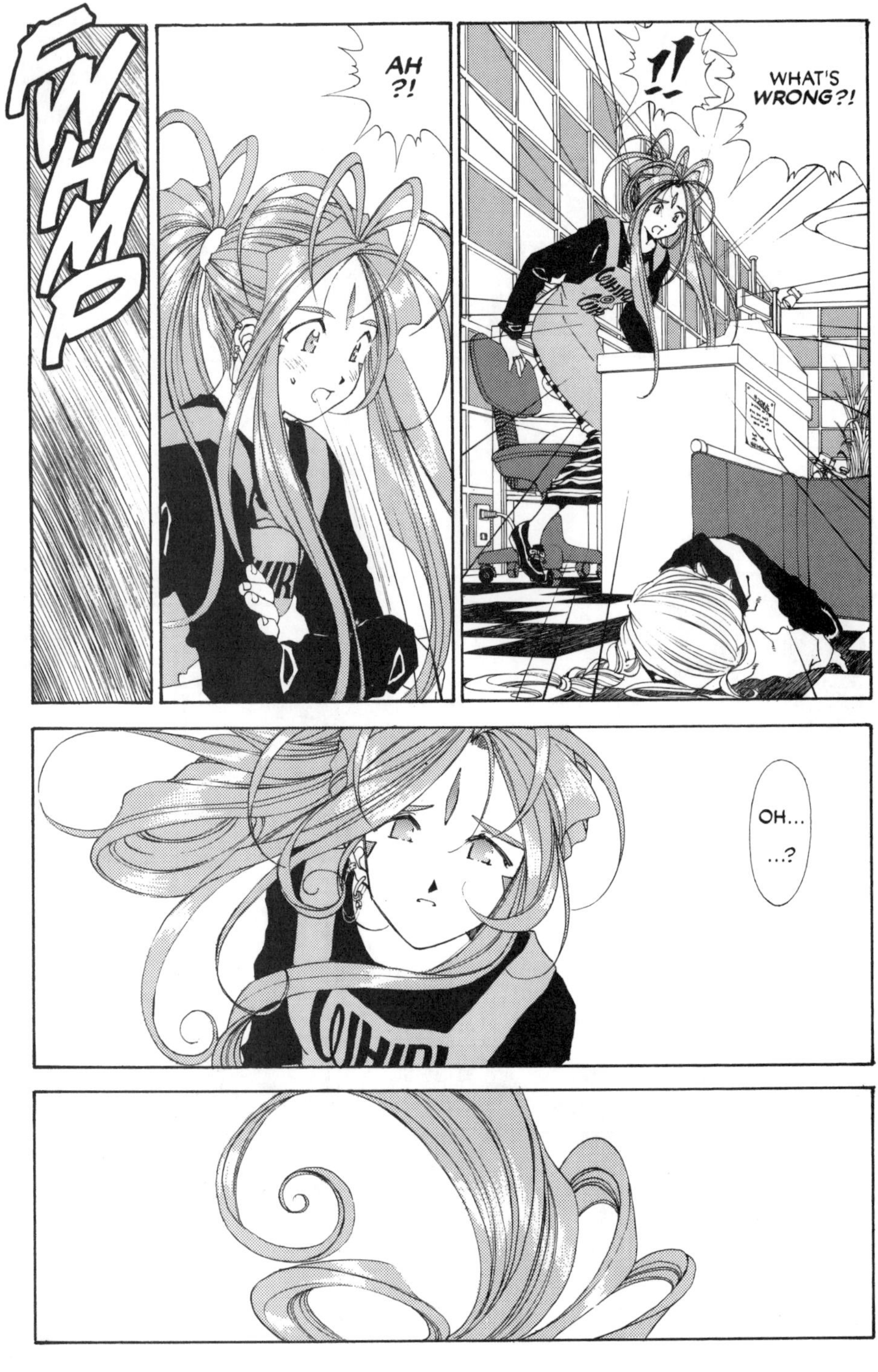
FWHMP
AH ?!
!!
WHAT'S WRONG?!
OH...
...?

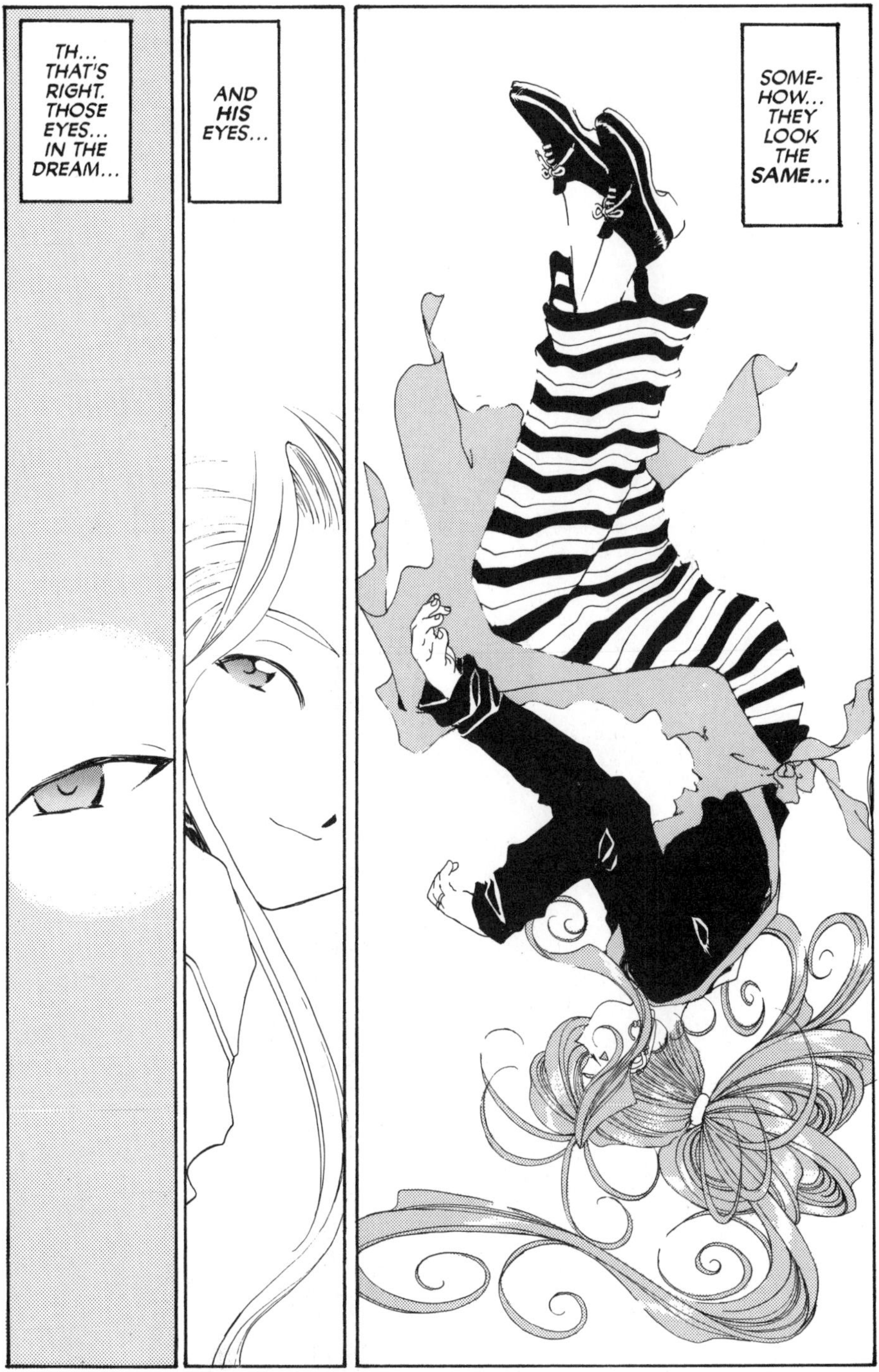
TH... THAT'S RIGHT. THOSE EYES... IN THE DREAM...
AND HIS EYES...
SOME-HOW... THEY LOOK THE SAME...

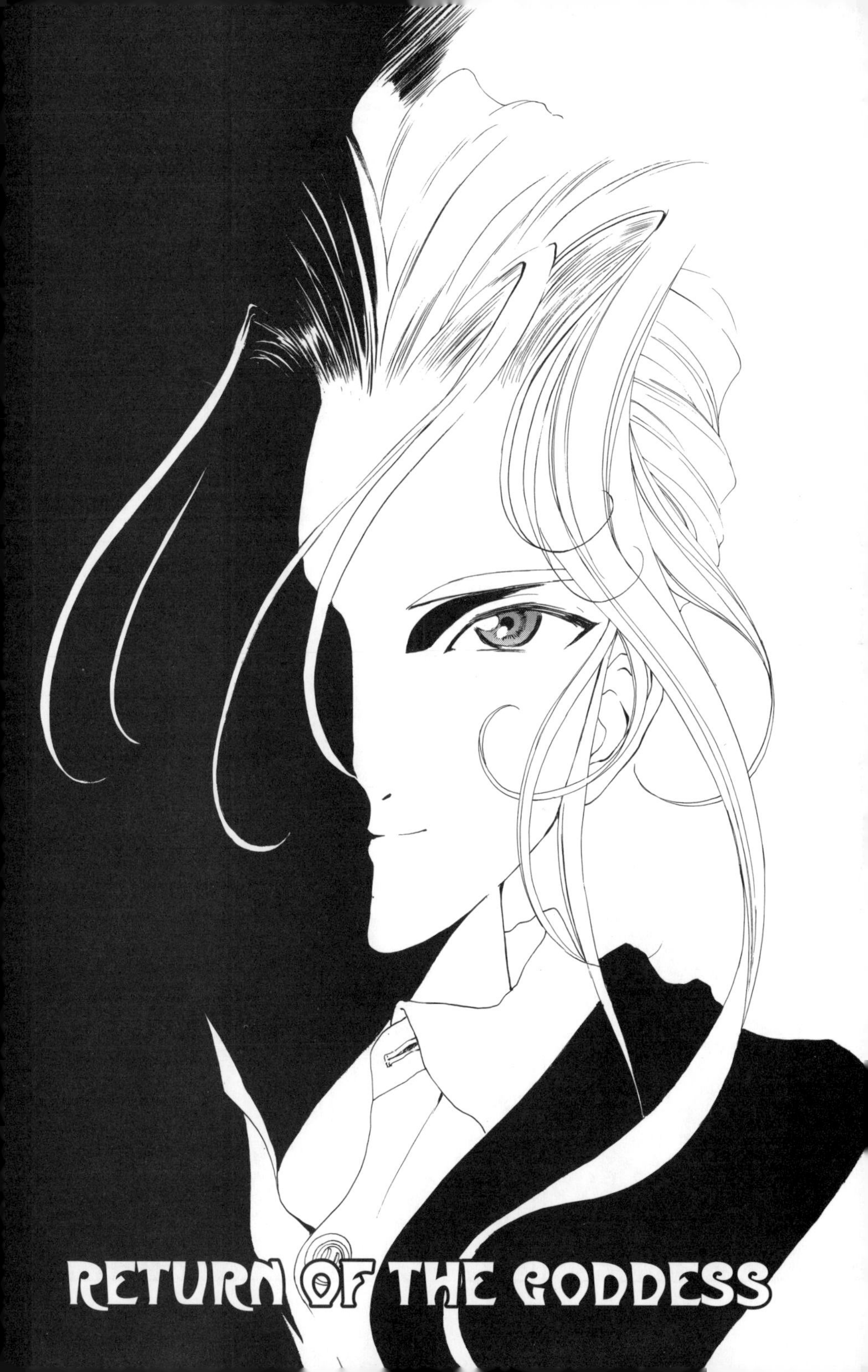
RETURN OF THE GODDESS

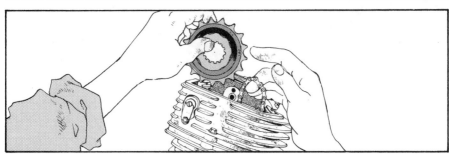

WHAT'S GOT **YOU** ALL UPSET?

...

...

I'M **NOT** UPSET.

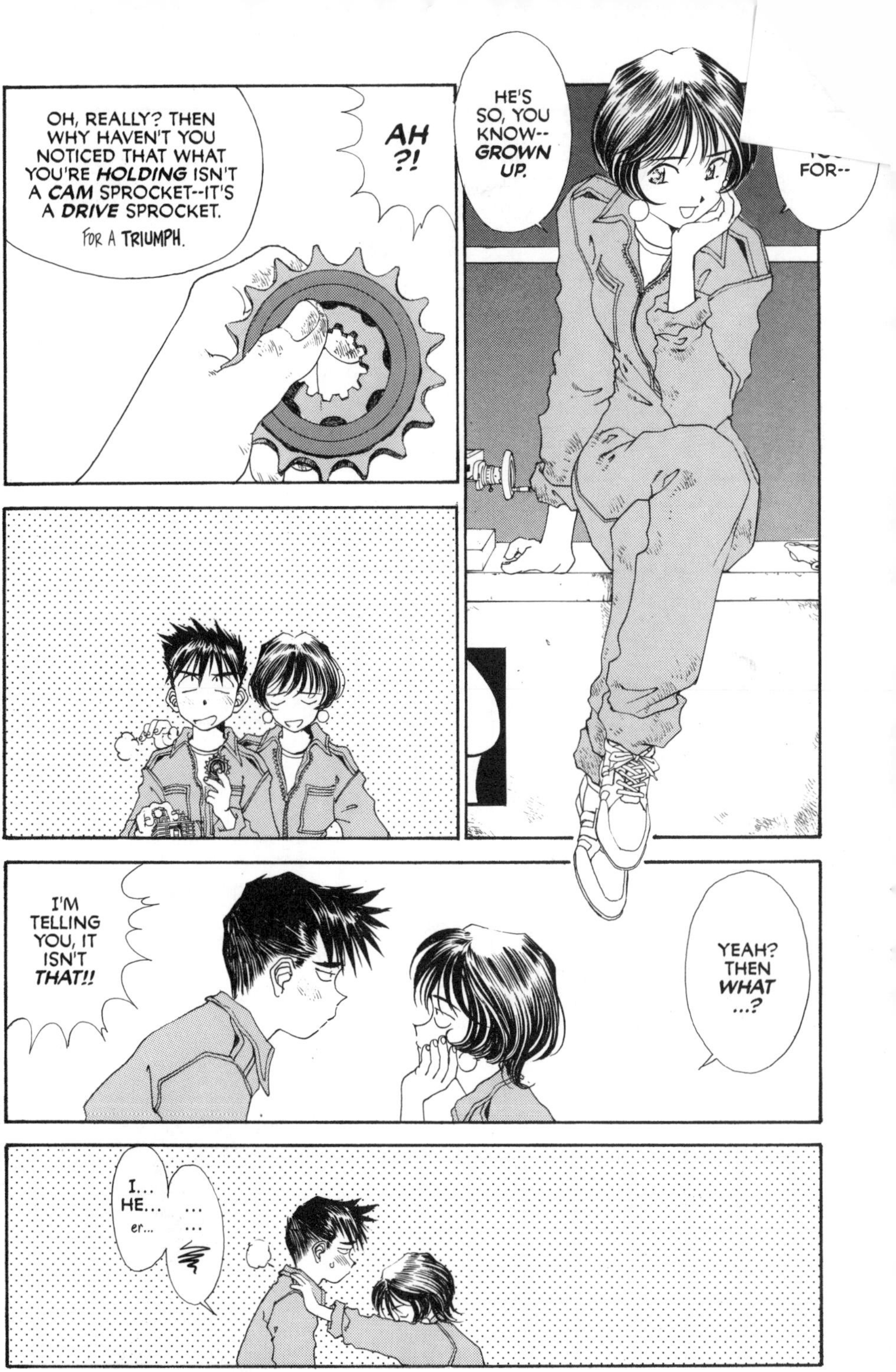
OH, REALLY? THEN WHY HAVEN'T YOU NOTICED THAT WHAT YOU'RE *HOLDING* ISN'T A *CAM* SPROCKET--IT'S A *DRIVE* SPROCKET.
FOR A TRIUMPH.
AH ?!
HE'S SO, YOU KNOW-- *GROWN UP.*
FOR--
I'M TELLING YOU, IT ISN'T *THAT!!*
YEAH? THEN *WHAT* ...?
I... HE... er...
... ...

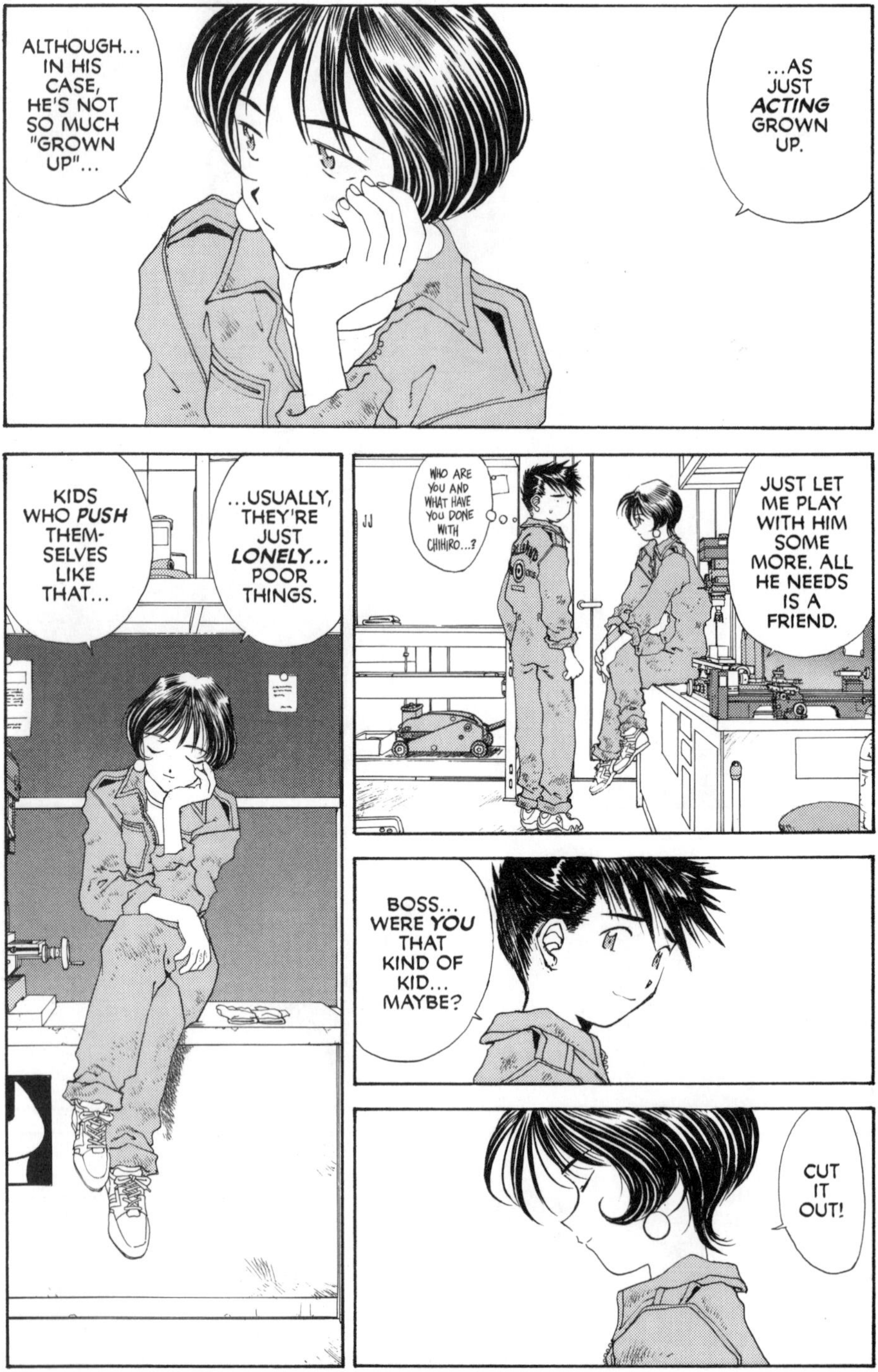
ALTHOUGH... IN HIS CASE, HE'S NOT SO MUCH "GROWN UP"...
...AS JUST ACTING GROWN UP.
KIDS WHO PUSH THEM-SELVES LIKE THAT...
...USUALLY, THEY'RE JUST LONELY... POOR THINGS.
WHO ARE YOU AND WHAT HAVE YOU DONE WITH CHIHIRO...?
JUST LET ME PLAY WITH HIM SOME MORE. ALL HE NEEDS IS A FRIEND.
BOSS... WERE YOU THAT KIND OF KID... MAYBE?
CUT IT OUT!

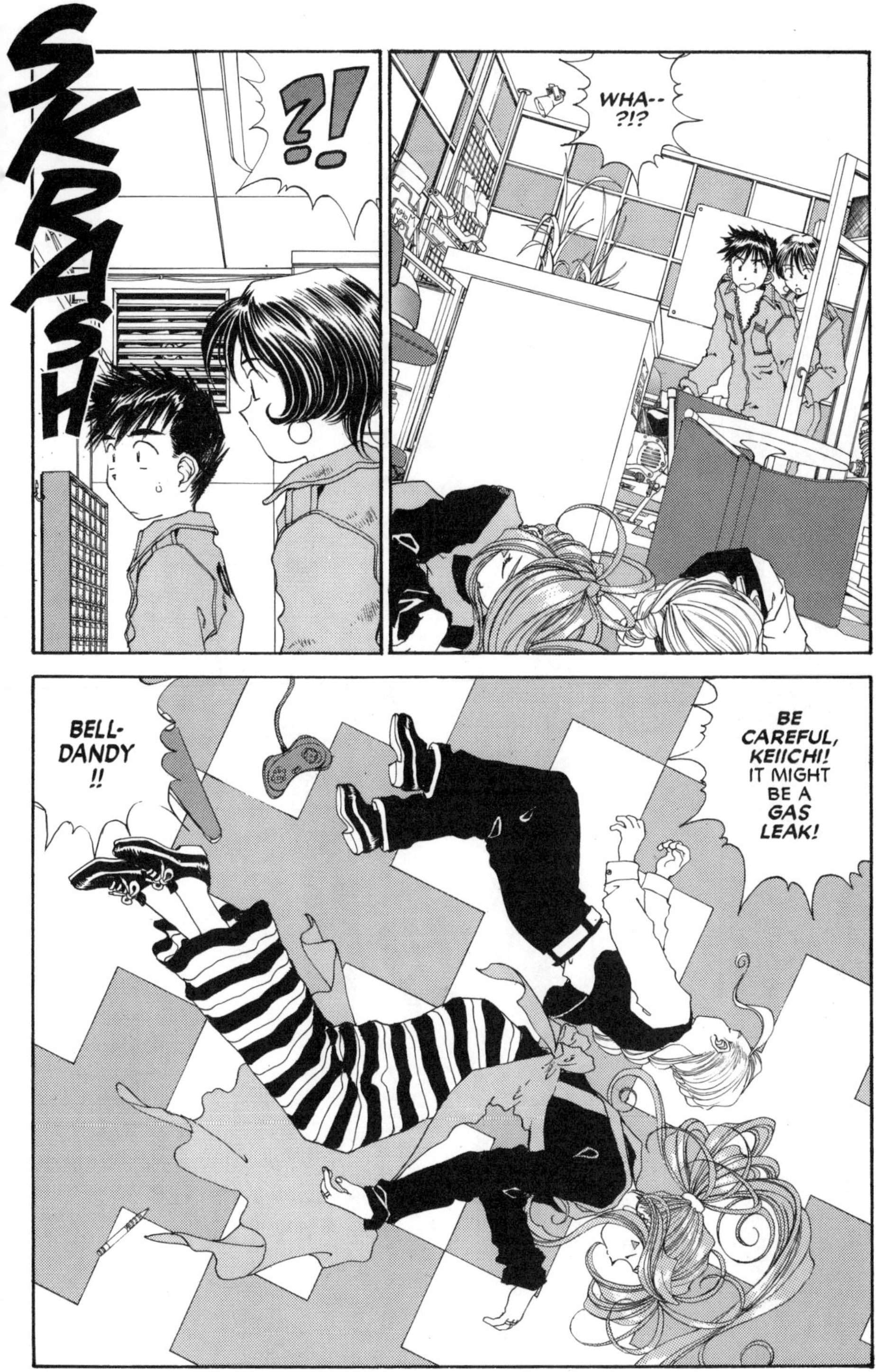
SKRASH
?!
WHA-- ?!?
BELL-DANDY !!
BE CAREFUL, KEIICHI! IT MIGHT BE A GAS LEAK!

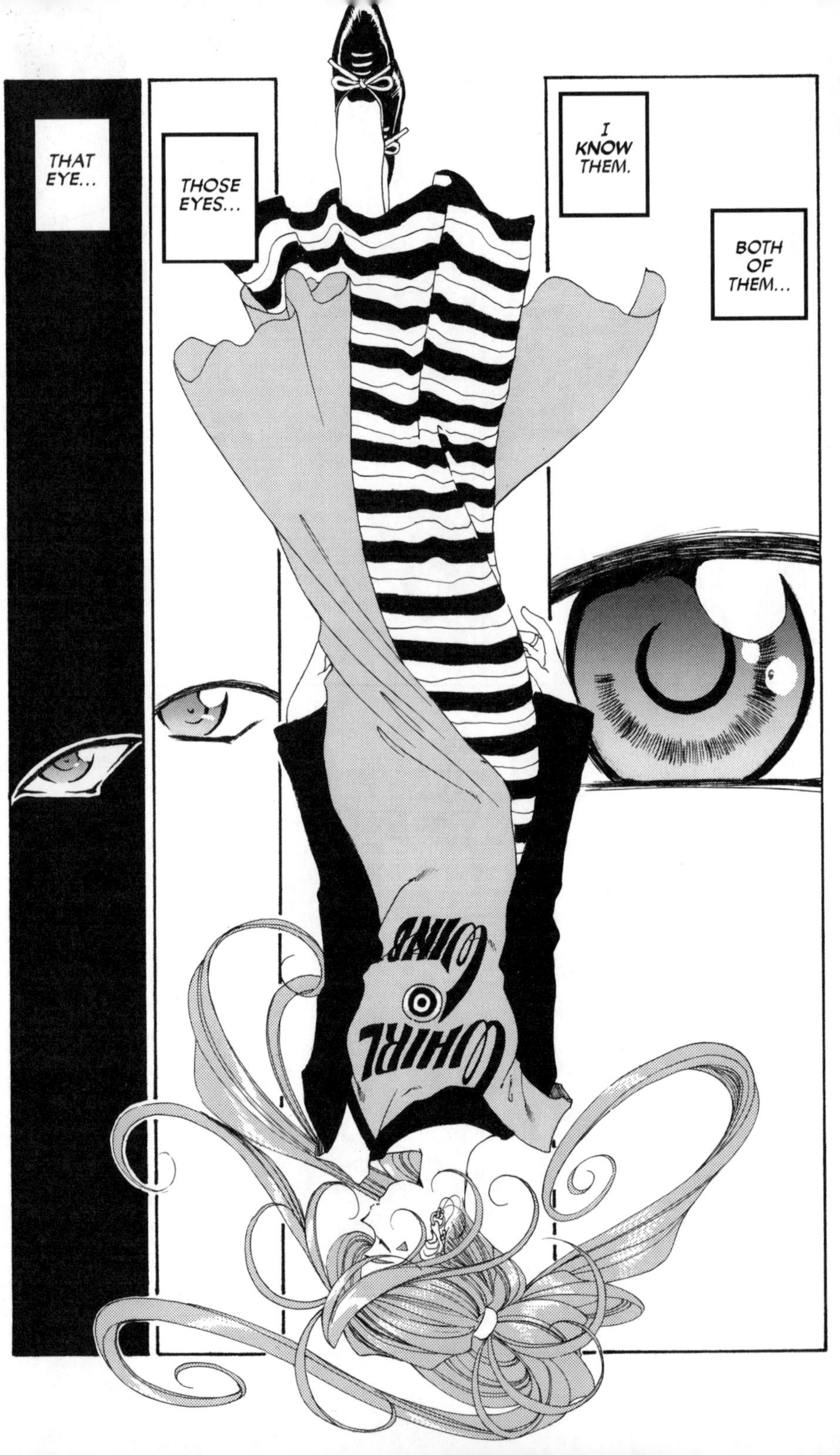
THAT EYE...
THOSE EYES...
I KNOW THEM.
BOTH OF THEM...

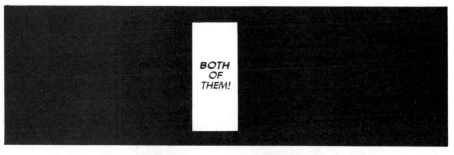

BOTH OF THEM!

AH ...?!

ARE YOU OKAY?

I'M SORRY, KEIICHI. I JUST... GOT A LITTLE *DIZZY*.

I... I'M OKAY, TOO... REALLY...

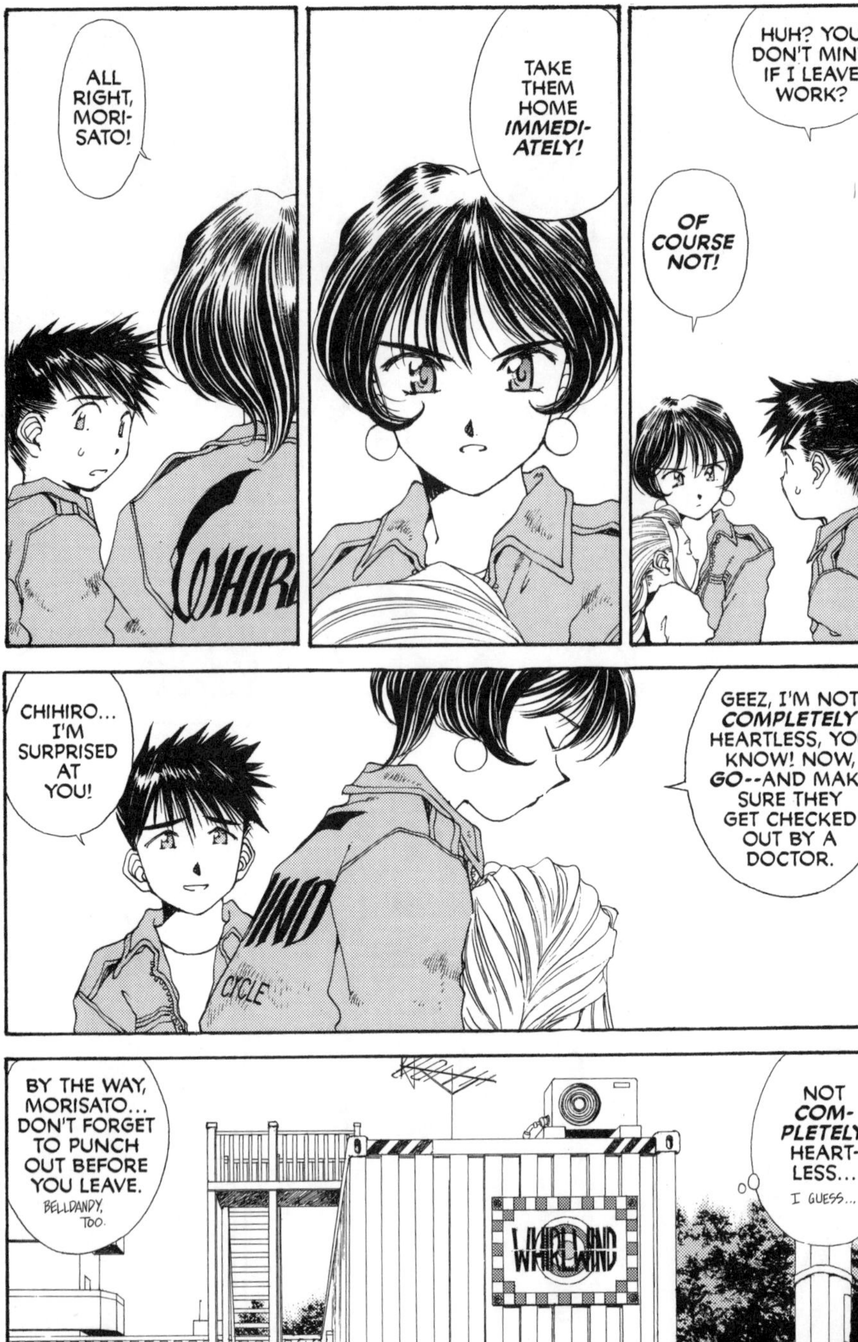
ALL RIGHT, MORI-SATO!
TAKE THEM HOME IMMEDI-ATELY!
HUH? YOU DON'T MIND IF I LEAVE WORK?
OF COURSE NOT!
CHIHIRO... I'M SURPRISED AT YOU!
GEEZ, I'M NOT COMPLETELY HEARTLESS, YOU KNOW! NOW, GO--AND MAKE SURE THEY GET CHECKED OUT BY A DOCTOR.
CYCLE
BY THE WAY, MORISATO... DON'T FORGET TO PUNCH OUT BEFORE YOU LEAVE.
BELLDANDY, TOO.
WHIRLWIND
NOT COM-PLETELY HEART-LESS...
I GUESS...

STRANGE...
WHY
BOTH OF
THEM...?
AT THE
SAME
TIME?

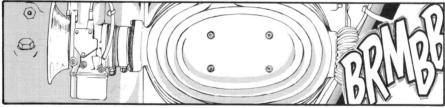

BRMBB

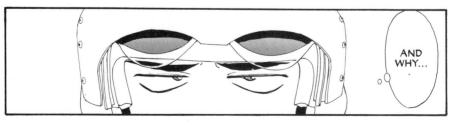

AND
WHY...

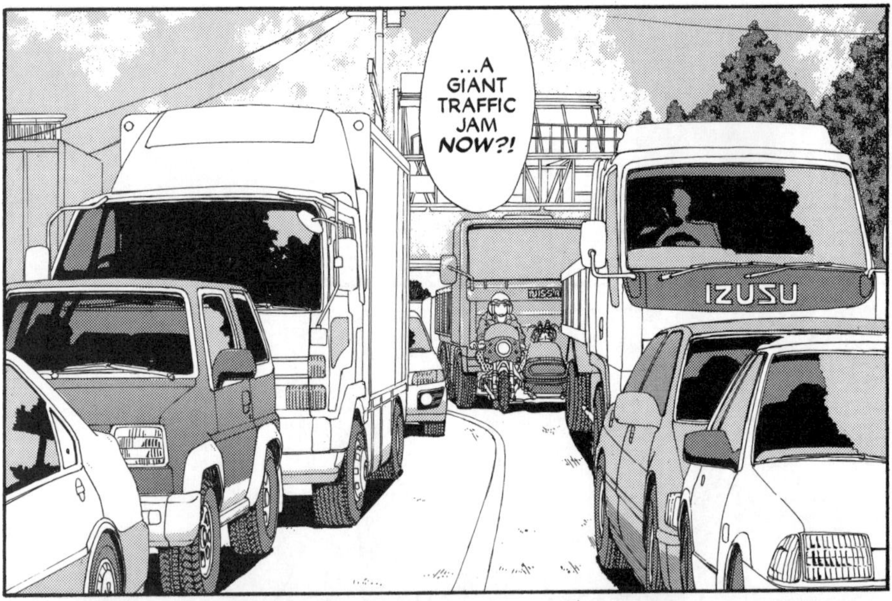
...A GIANT TRAFFIC JAM NOW?!
IZUZU
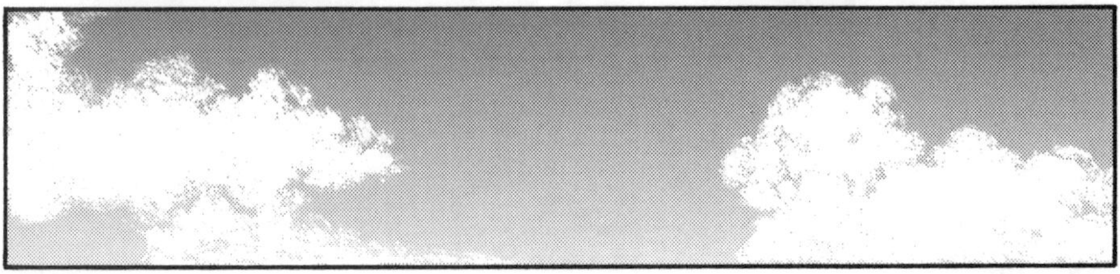
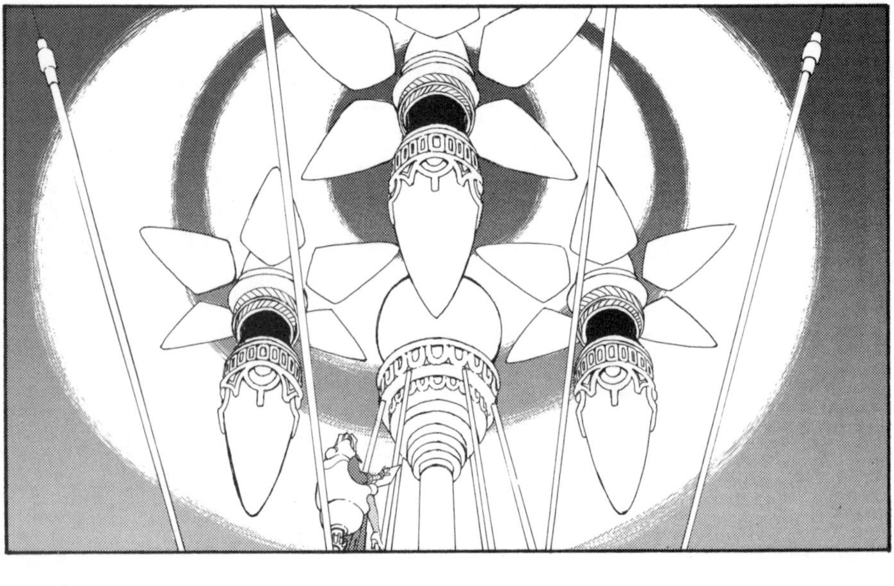

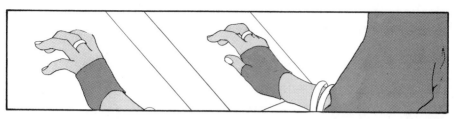

IT'S HOPE-LESS, SKULD!

I CAN'T EVEN KEEP THE TIME AXIS ALIGNED *MANUALLY!*

RIGHT NOW IT'S JUST AFFECTING *CLOCKS*, BUT--

I FOUND IT!

HERE-- LOOK AT *THIS!*

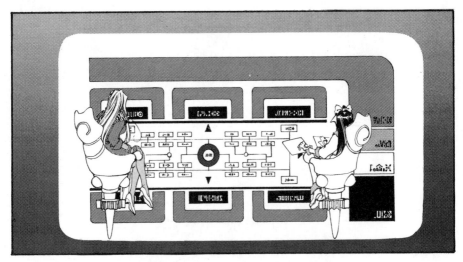

AH?!
NO *WAY!*

SLICK, HUH?

IT *ACTS* LIKE IT'S A SYNCHRONIZATION FILE...

...BUT IT'S *ACTUALLY* LENGTHENING AND DEFORMING THE TIME AXIS VIBRATION CYCLE.

CAN YOU ISOLATE AND DELETE IT?

NOT A CHANCE.

NOT ONLY HAS IT WIPED THE MASTER SYNC FILE AND HOOKED INTO THE *OS* KERNEL, IT'S INFECTED ALL THE PERIPHERAL SUBSYSTEMS AS WELL.

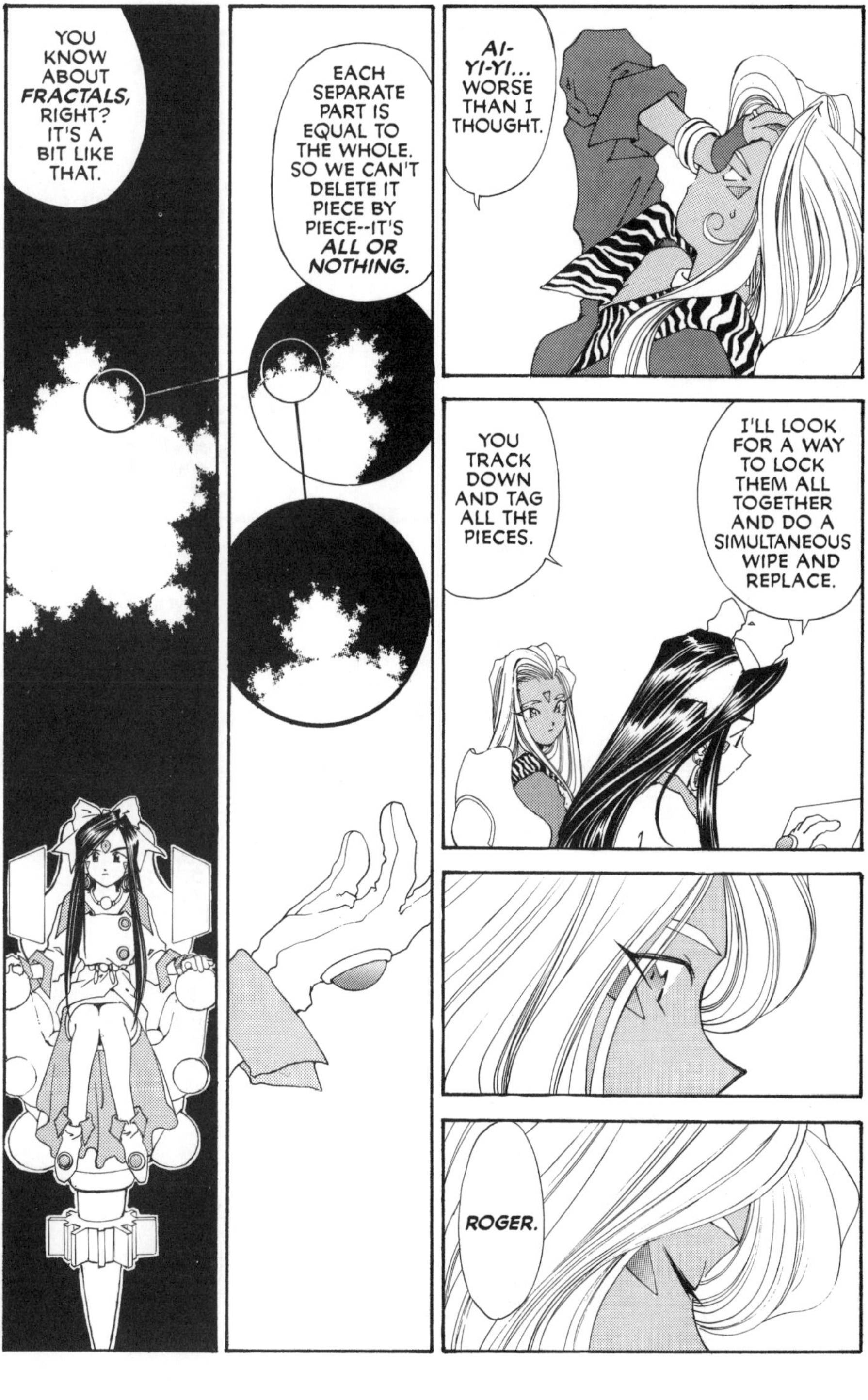
YOU KNOW ABOUT FRACTALS, RIGHT? IT'S A BIT LIKE THAT.
EACH SEPARATE PART IS EQUAL TO THE WHOLE. SO WE CAN'T DELETE IT PIECE BY PIECE--IT'S ALL OR NOTHING.
AI-YI-YI... WORSE THAN I THOUGHT.
YOU TRACK DOWN AND TAG ALL THE PIECES.
I'LL LOOK FOR A WAY TO LOCK THEM ALL TOGETHER AND DO A SIMULTANEOUS WIPE AND REPLACE.
ROGER.

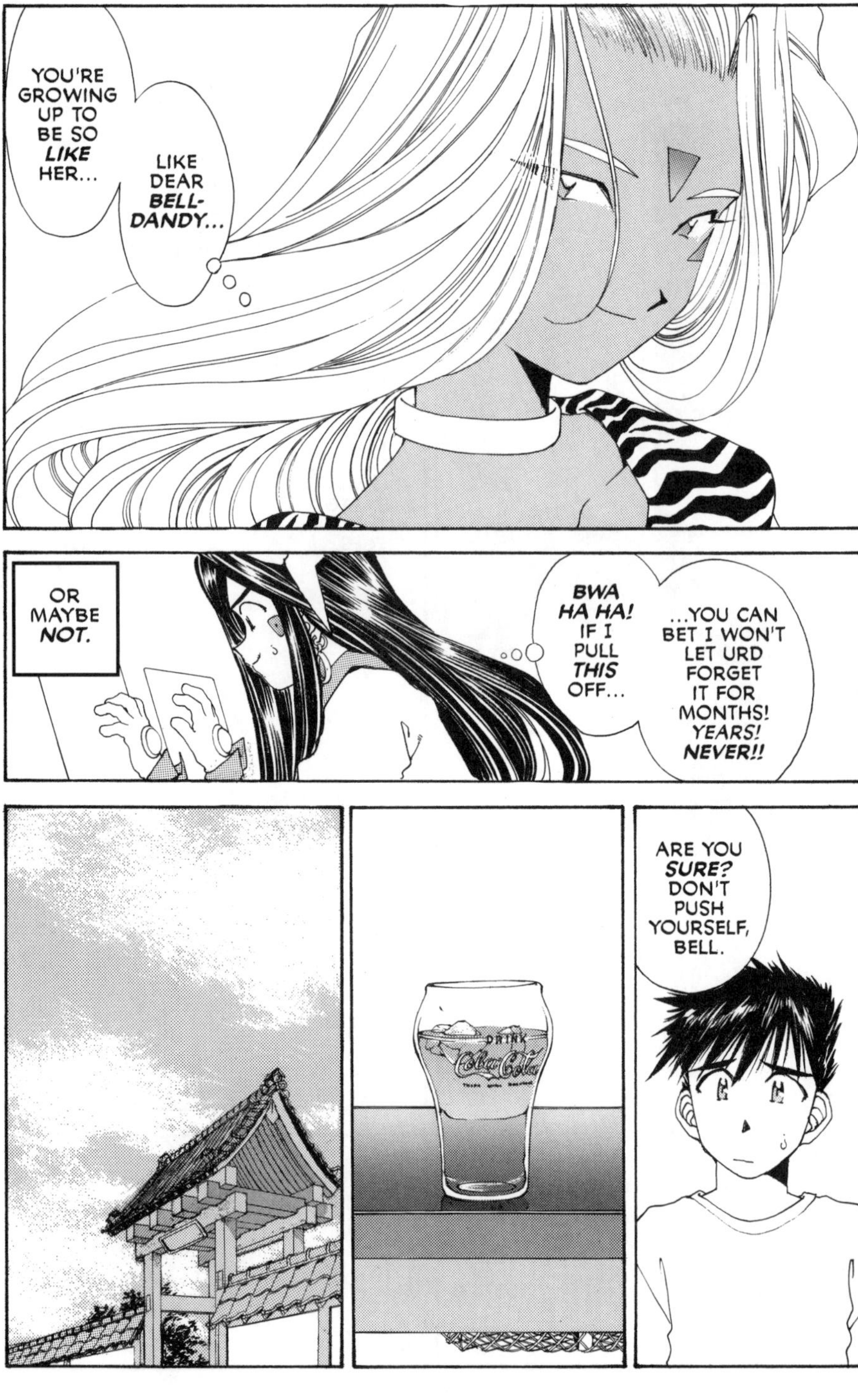
YOU'RE GROWING UP TO BE SO *LIKE* HER...
LIKE DEAR *BELL-DANDY...*
OR MAYBE *NOT.*
BWA HA HA! IF I PULL *THIS* OFF...
...YOU CAN BET I WON'T LET URD FORGET IT FOR MONTHS! *YEARS! NEVER!!*
DRINK Coca-Cola
ARE YOU *SURE?* DON'T PUSH YOURSELF, BELL.

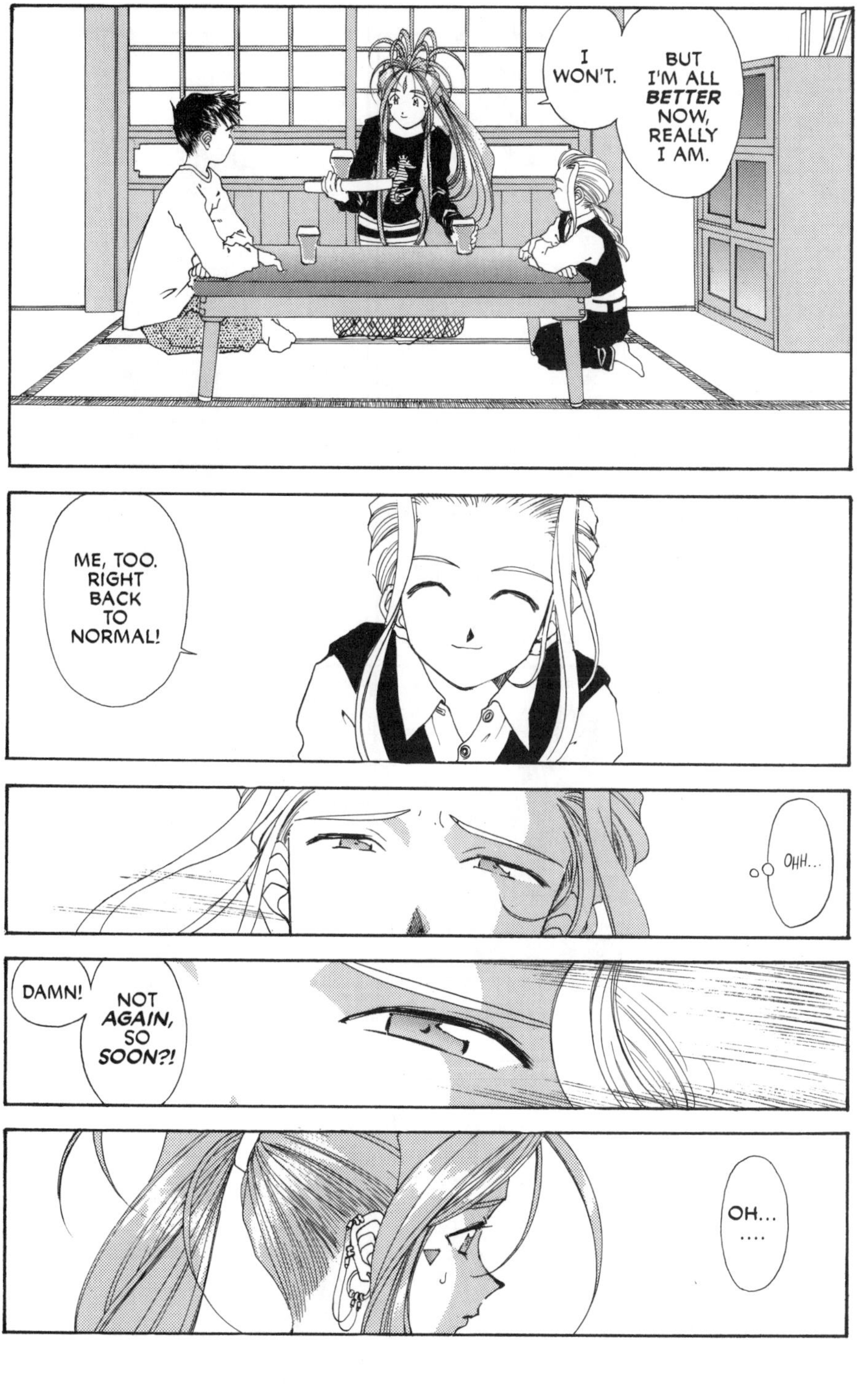

I WON'T.
BUT I'M ALL BETTER NOW, REALLY I AM.
ME, TOO. RIGHT BACK TO NORMAL!
OHH...
DAMN!
NOT AGAIN, SO SOON?!
OH... ....

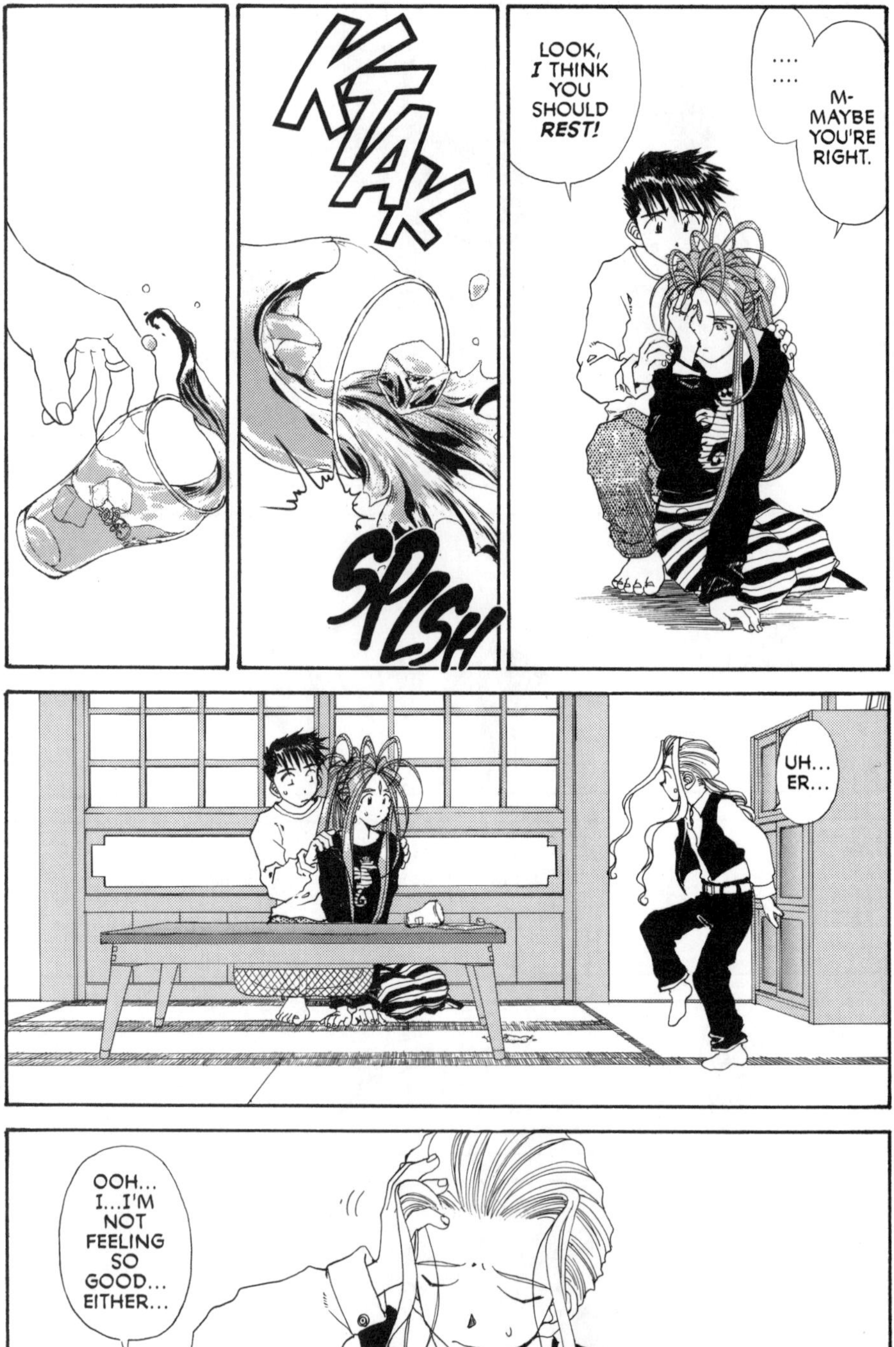

KTAK
SPLSH
LOOK, I THINK YOU SHOULD REST!
....
....
M-MAYBE YOU'RE RIGHT.
UH... ER...
OOH... I...I'M NOT FEELING SO GOOD... EITHER...

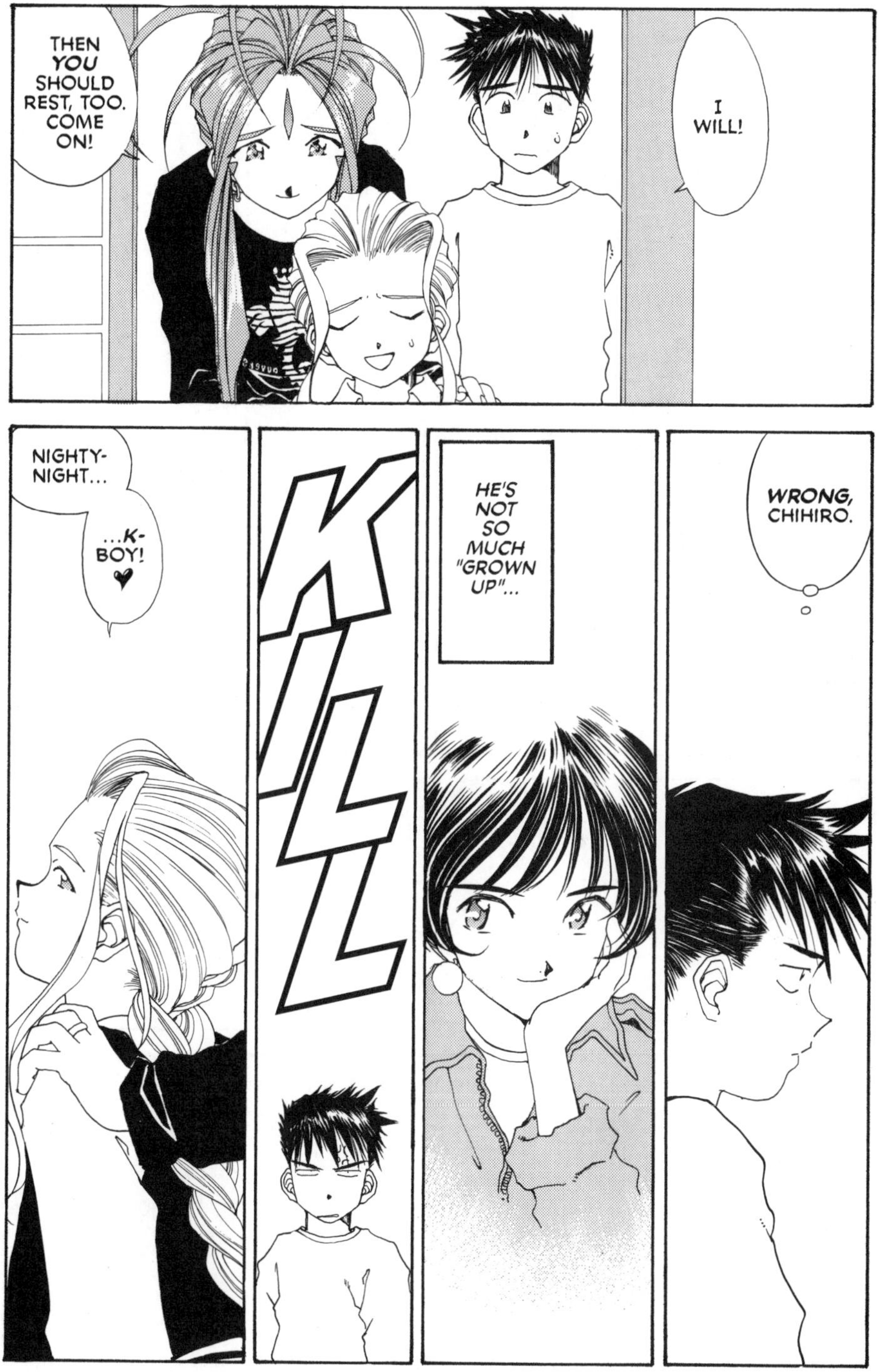
THEN ***YOU*** SHOULD REST, TOO. COME ON!
I WILL!
NIGHTY-NIGHT…
…***K-***BOY! ♥
KILL
HE'S NOT SO MUCH "GROWN UP"…
WRONG, CHIHIRO.

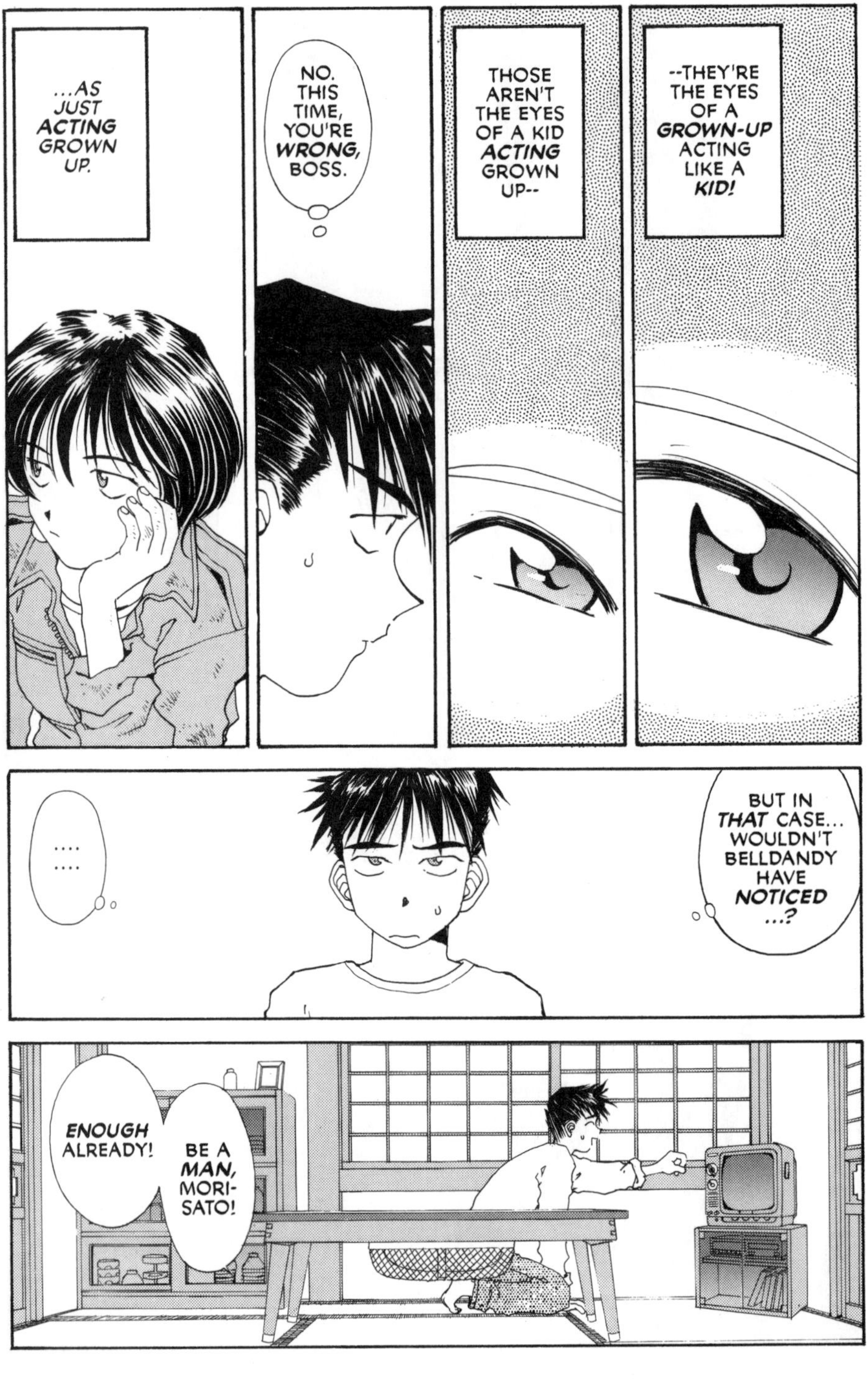

...AS JUST ACTING GROWN UP.
NO. THIS TIME, YOU'RE WRONG, BOSS.
THOSE AREN'T THE EYES OF A KID ACTING GROWN UP--
--THEY'RE THE EYES OF A GROWN-UP ACTING LIKE A KID!
....
BUT IN THAT CASE... WOULDN'T BELLDANDY HAVE NOTICED ...?
ENOUGH ALREADY!
BE A MAN, MORI-SATO!

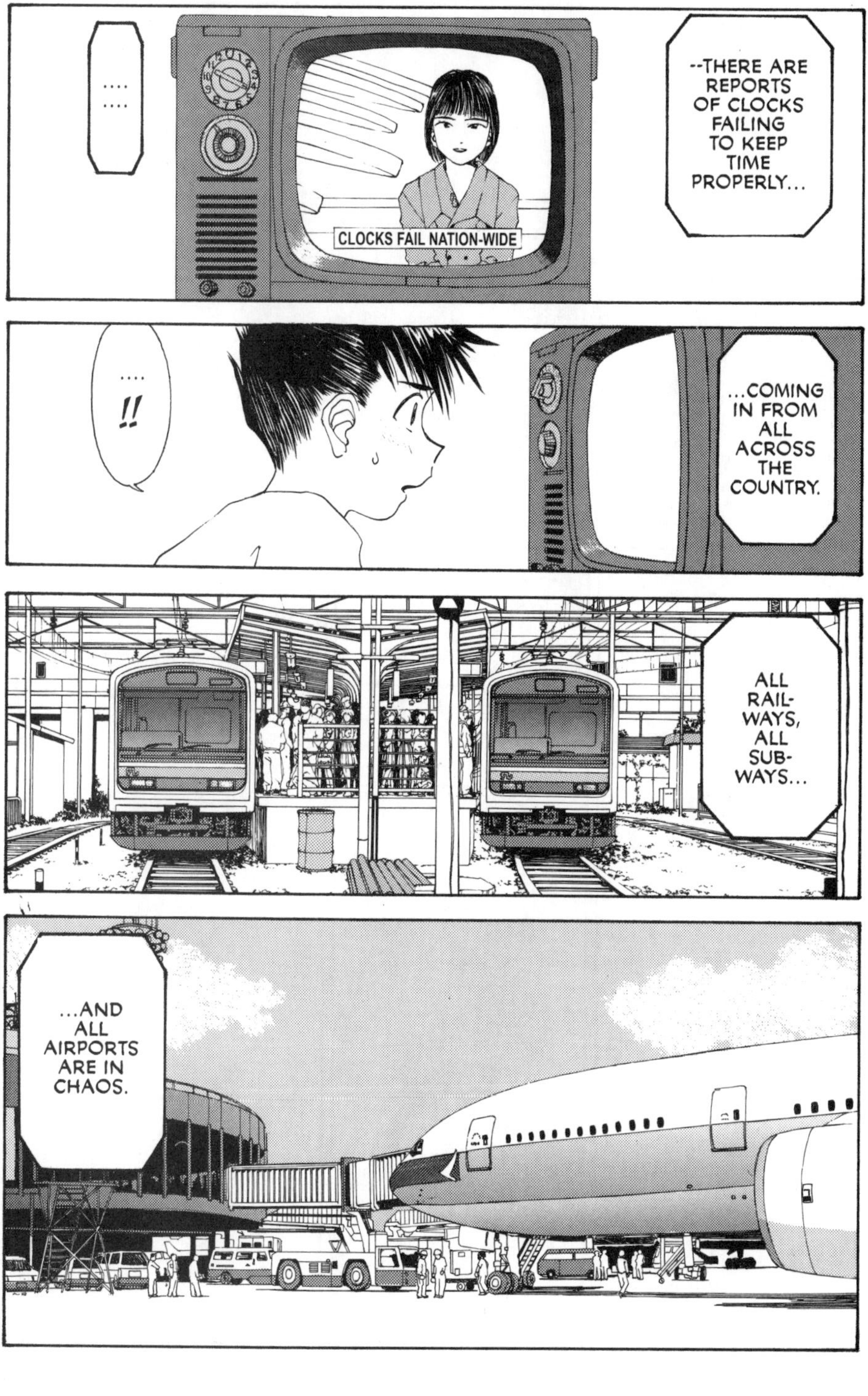
....
....
--THERE ARE REPORTS OF CLOCKS FAILING TO KEEP TIME PROPERLY...
CLOCKS FAIL NATION-WIDE
....
!!
...COMING IN FROM ALL ACROSS THE COUNTRY.
ALL RAIL-WAYS, ALL SUB-WAYS...
...AND ALL AIRPORTS ARE IN CHAOS.

THE PHENOMENON HAS NO KNOWN CAUSE.

THE GOVERNMENT, DEEPLY CONCERNED, HAS ESTABLISHED...

...AN EMERGENCY OFFICE TO COORDINATE--

THAT'S VERY STRANGE.

BETTER LOOK AT YOUR WATCH.

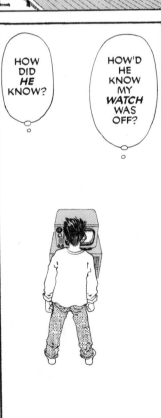

HOW DID *HE* KNOW?

HOW'D HE KNOW MY *WATCH* WAS OFF?

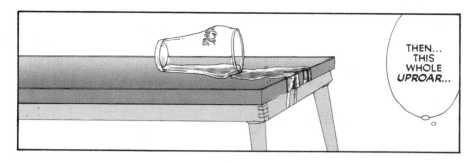

THEN...
THIS
WHOLE
UPROAR...

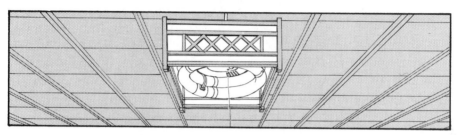

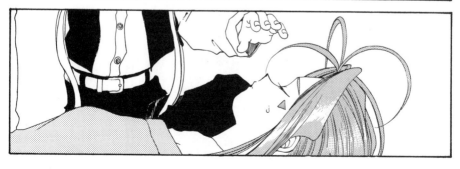

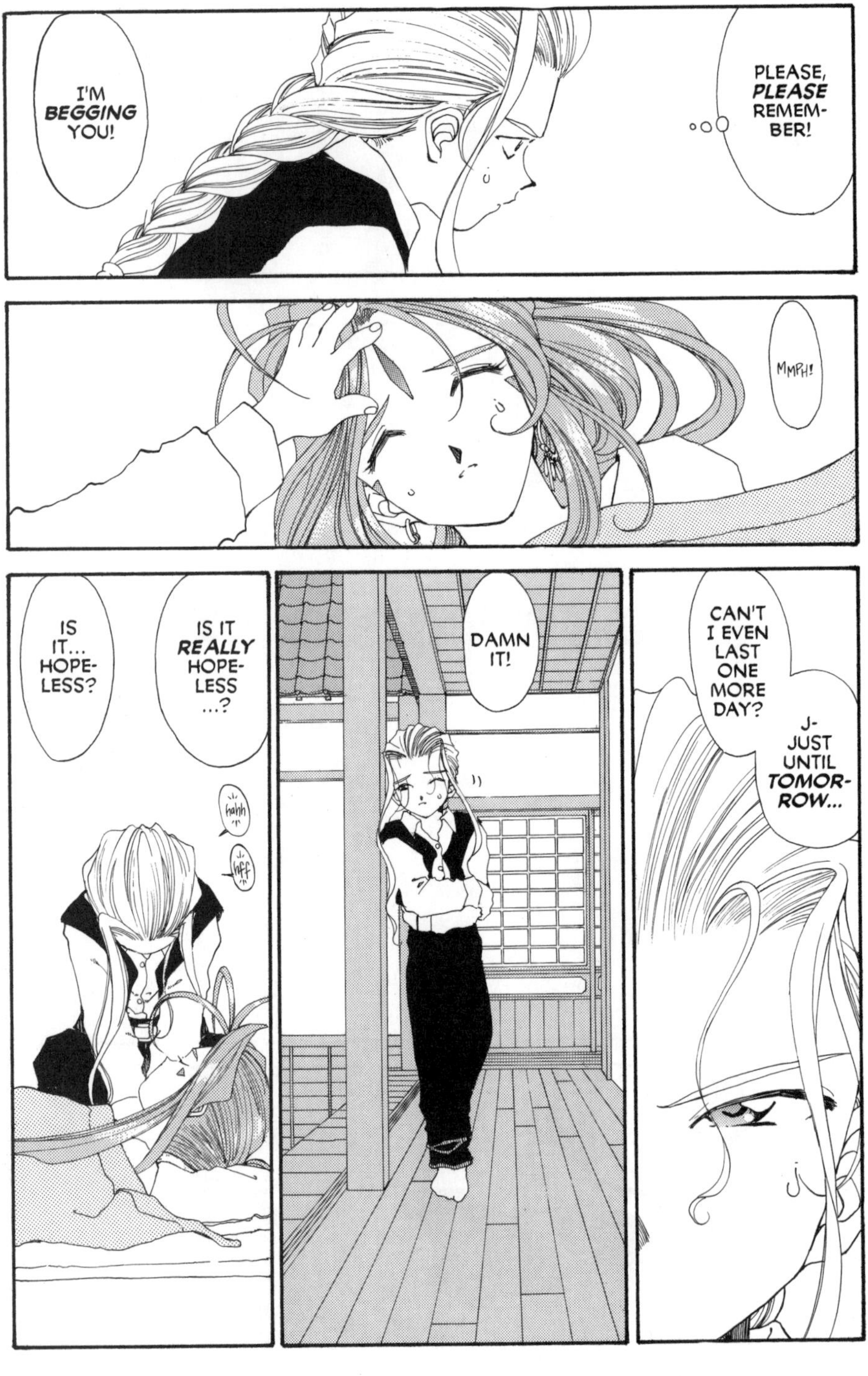
I'M BEGGING YOU!
PLEASE, PLEASE REMEMBER!
MMPH!
IS IT... HOPELESS?
IS IT REALLY HOPELESS ...?
hahh
hff
DAMN IT!
CAN'T I EVEN LAST ONE MORE DAY?
J-JUST UNTIL TOMORROW...

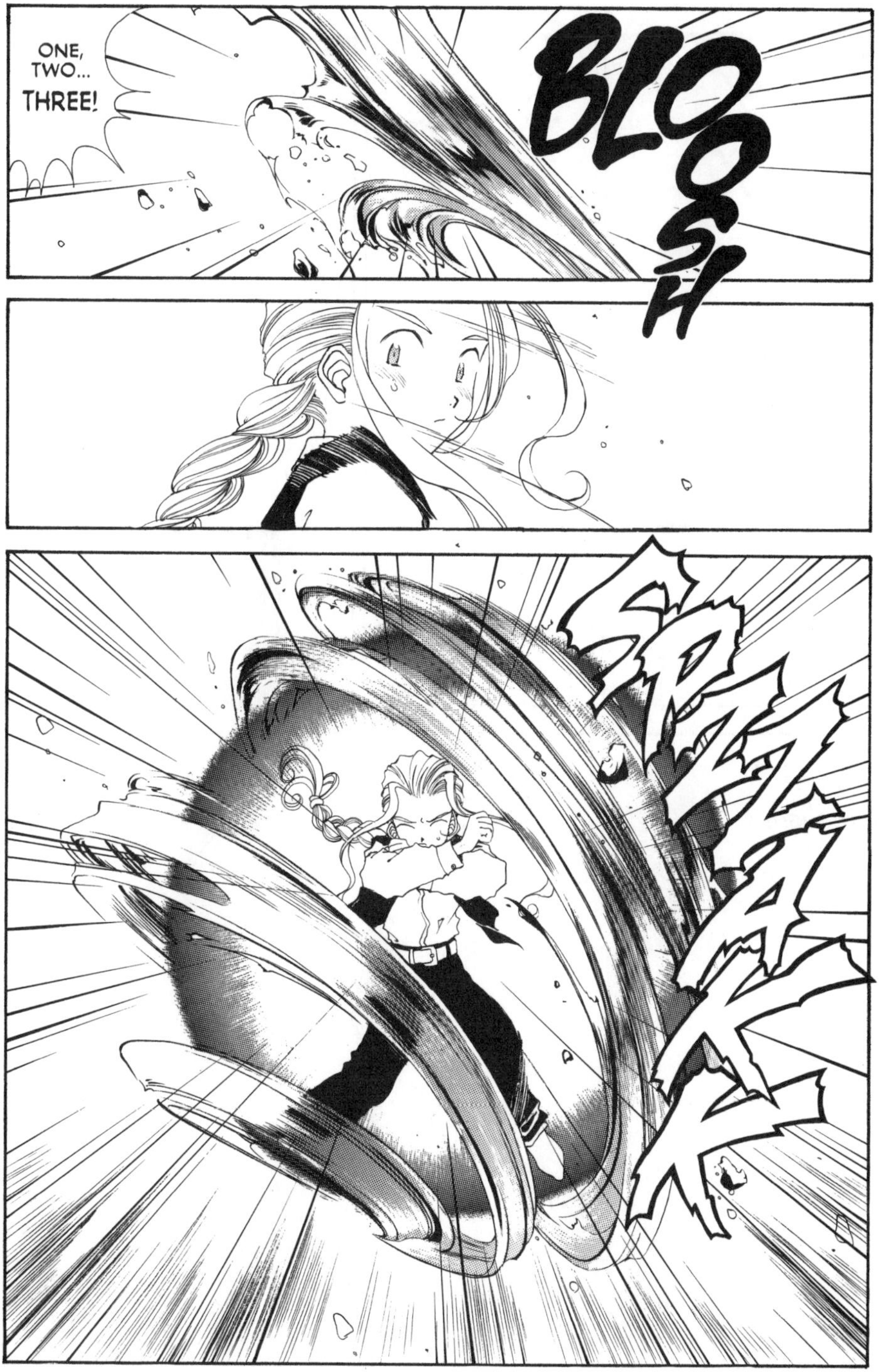
ONE, TWO... THREE!
BLOOSH
SPZZAK

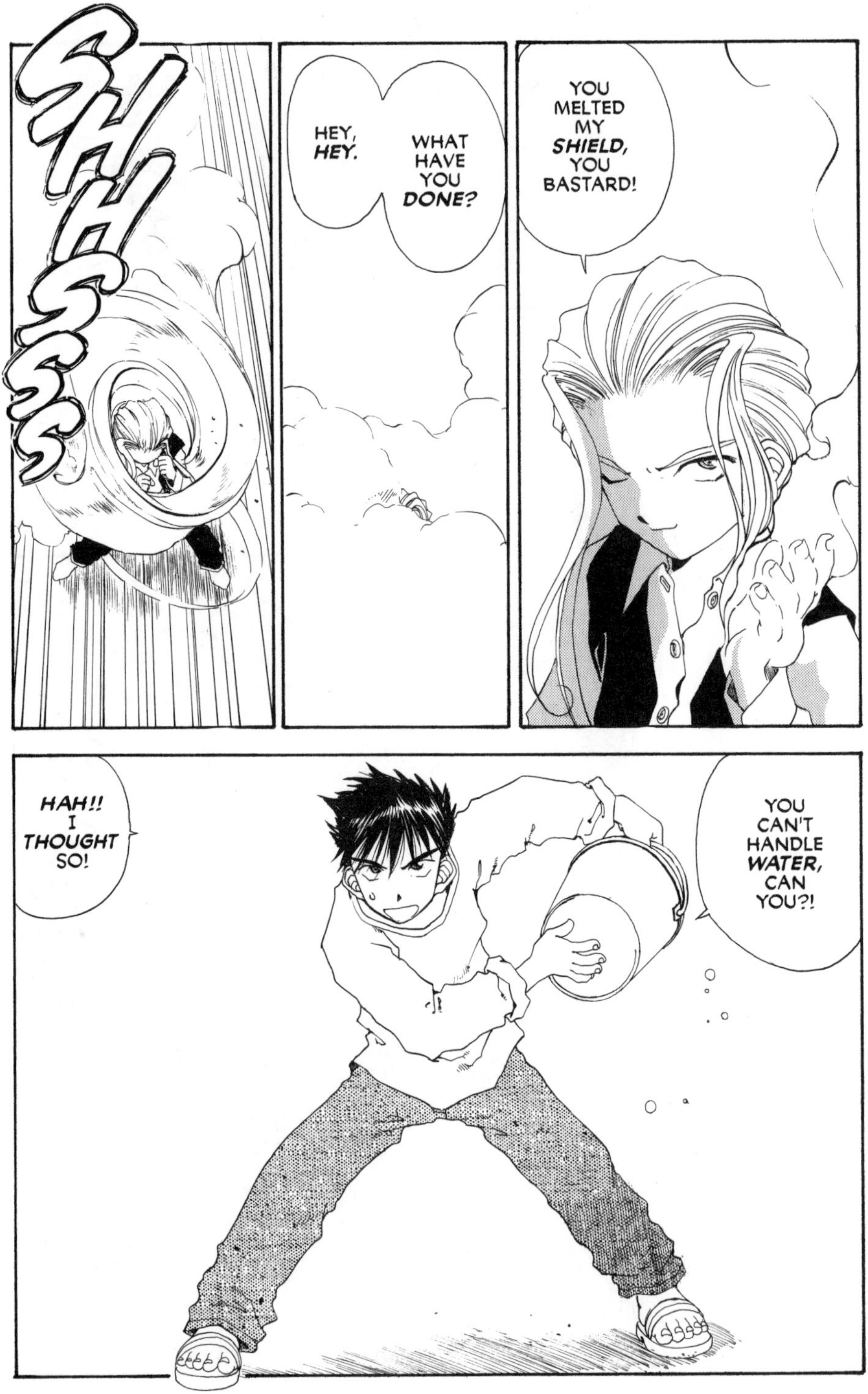
SHHSSSS
HEY, HEY.
WHAT HAVE YOU DONE?
YOU MELTED MY SHIELD, YOU BASTARD!
HAH!! I THOUGHT SO!
YOU CAN'T HANDLE WATER, CAN YOU?!

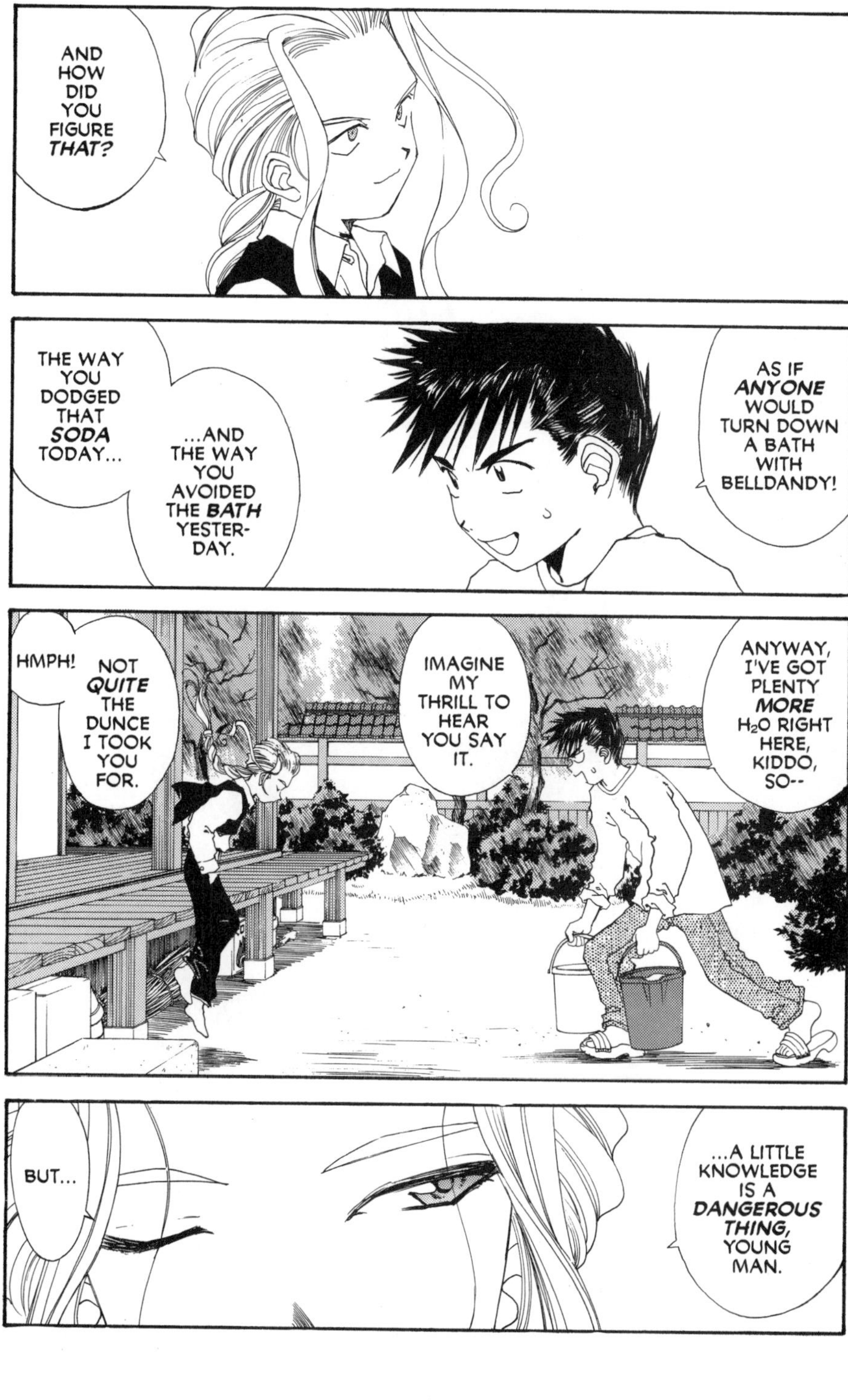
AND HOW DID YOU FIGURE *THAT?*
THE WAY YOU DODGED THAT *SODA* TODAY...
...AND THE WAY YOU AVOIDED THE *BATH* YESTER-DAY.
AS IF *ANYONE* WOULD TURN DOWN A BATH WITH BELLDANDY!
HMPH!
NOT *QUITE* THE DUNCE I TOOK YOU FOR.
IMAGINE MY THRILL TO HEAR YOU SAY IT.
ANYWAY, I'VE GOT PLENTY *MORE* H_2O RIGHT HERE, KIDDO, SO--
BUT...
...A LITTLE KNOWLEDGE IS A *DANGEROUS THING,* YOUNG MAN.

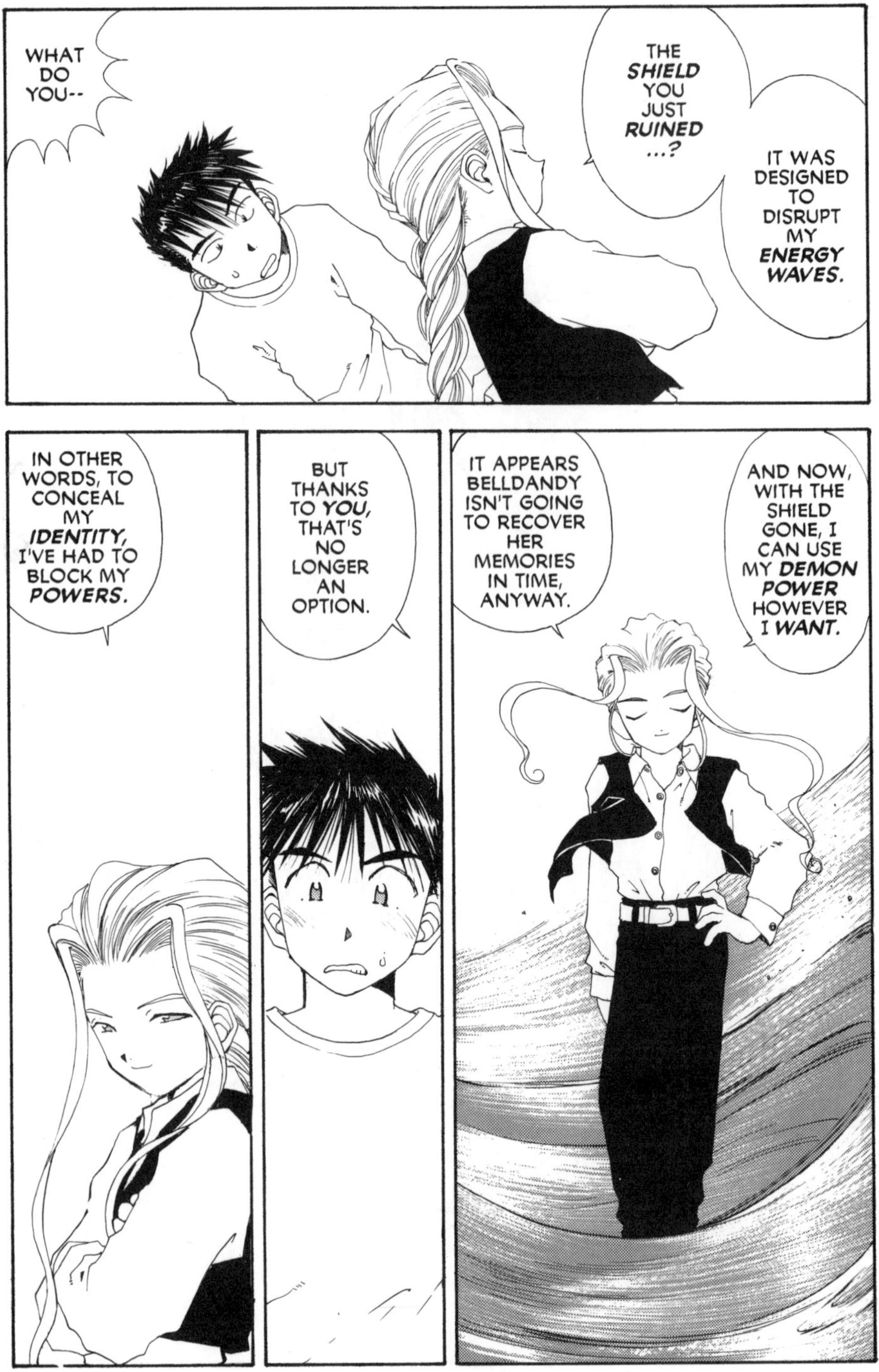
WHAT DO YOU--
THE SHIELD YOU JUST RUINED ...?
IT WAS DESIGNED TO DISRUPT MY ENERGY WAVES.
IN OTHER WORDS, TO CONCEAL MY IDENTITY, I'VE HAD TO BLOCK MY POWERS.
BUT THANKS TO YOU, THAT'S NO LONGER AN OPTION.
IT APPEARS BELLDANDY ISN'T GOING TO RECOVER HER MEMORIES IN TIME, ANYWAY.
AND NOW, WITH THE SHIELD GONE, I CAN USE MY DEMON POWER HOWEVER I WANT.

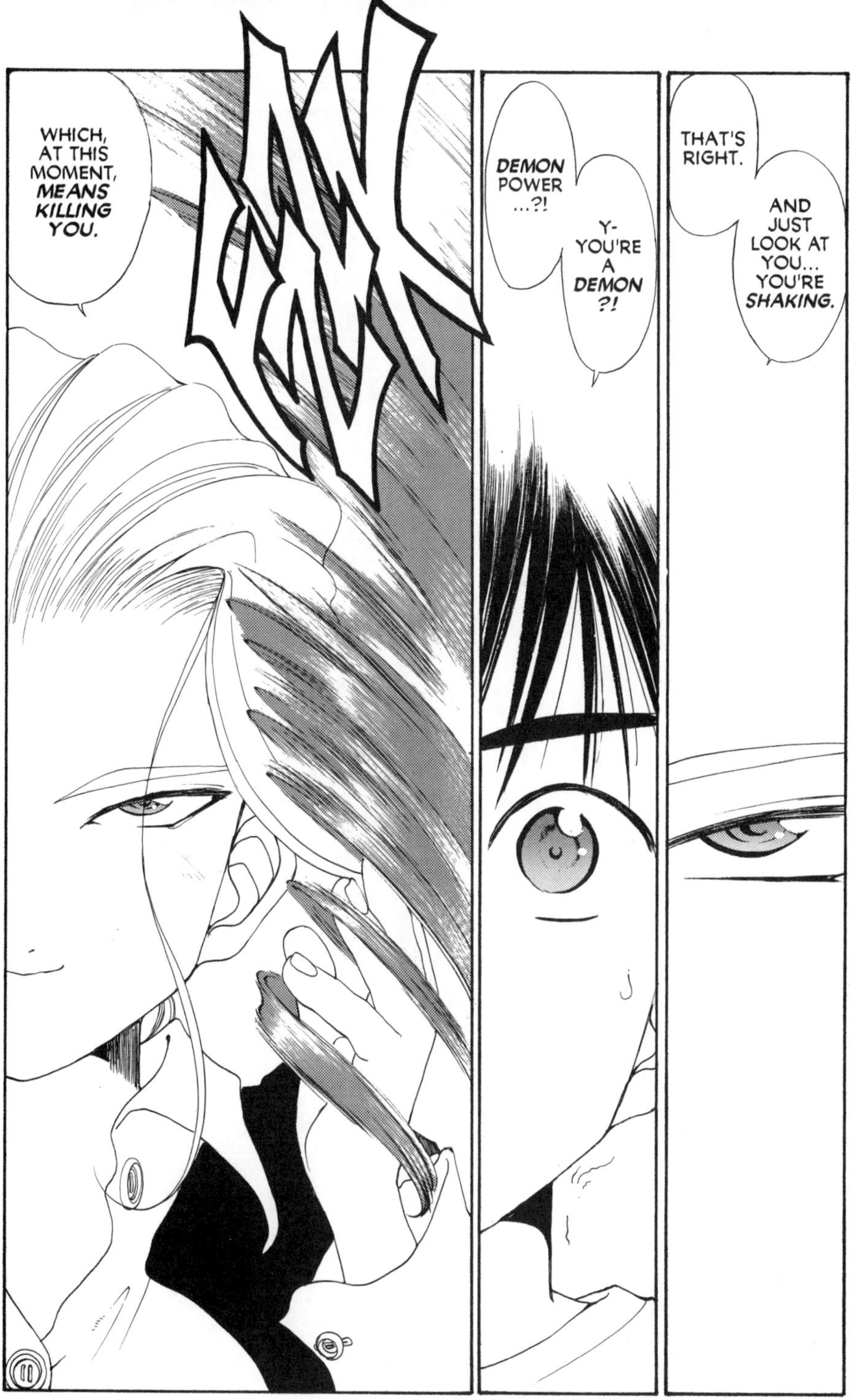
WHICH, AT THIS MOMENT, *MEANS KILLING YOU.*
DEMON POWER ...?!
Y- YOU'RE A *DEMON* ?!
THAT'S RIGHT.
AND JUST LOOK AT YOU... YOU'RE *SHAKING.*

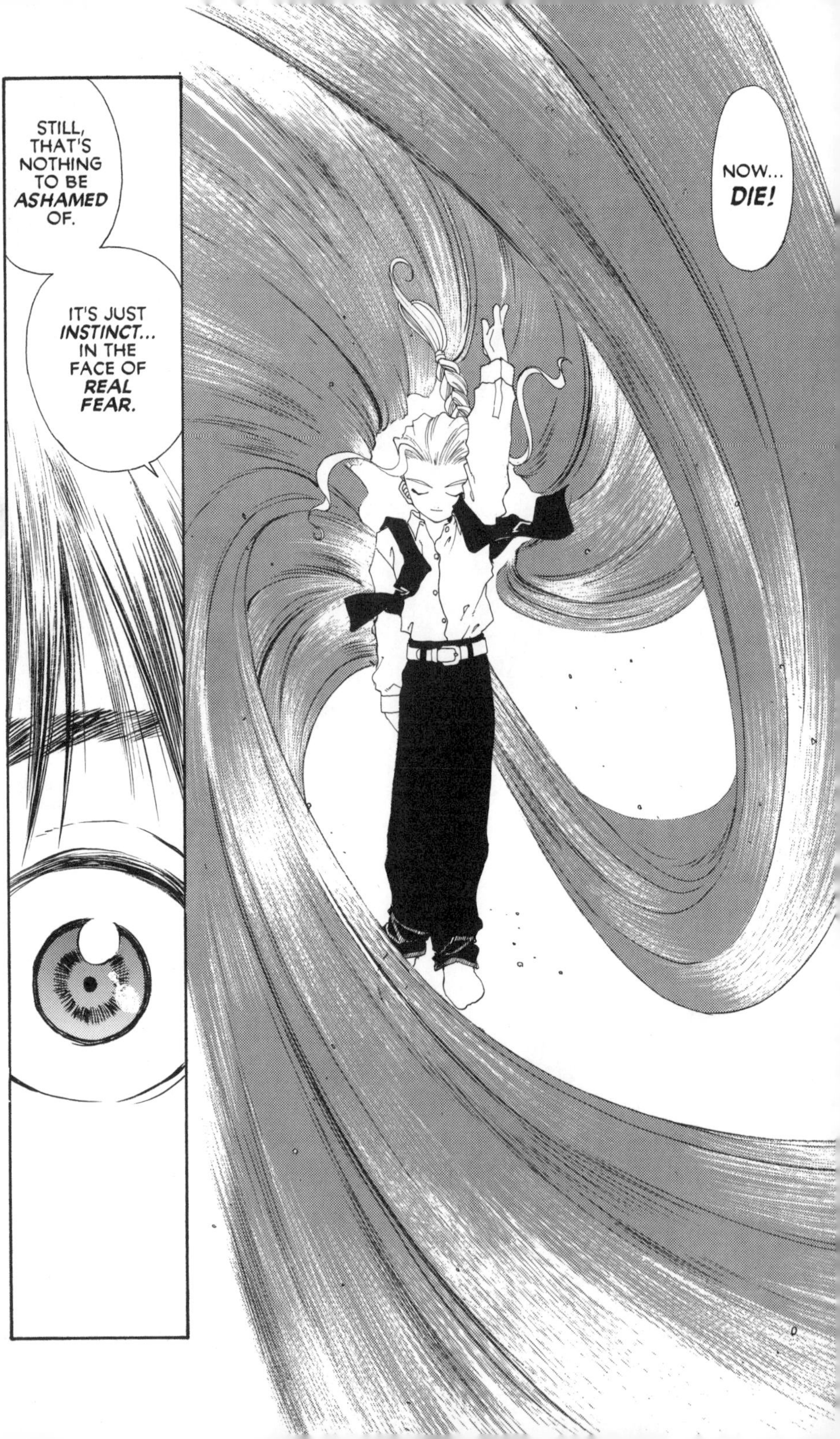
STILL, THAT'S NOTHING TO BE *ASHAMED* OF.
IT'S JUST *INSTINCT*... IN THE FACE OF *REAL FEAR.*
NOW... ***DIE!***

IT'S BEEN *SO* LONG, N'EST PAS?

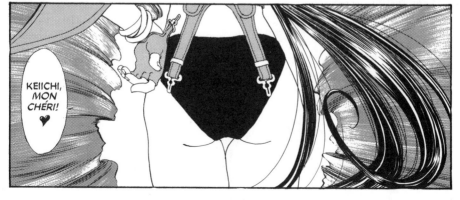

KEIICHI, MON CHÉRI! ♥

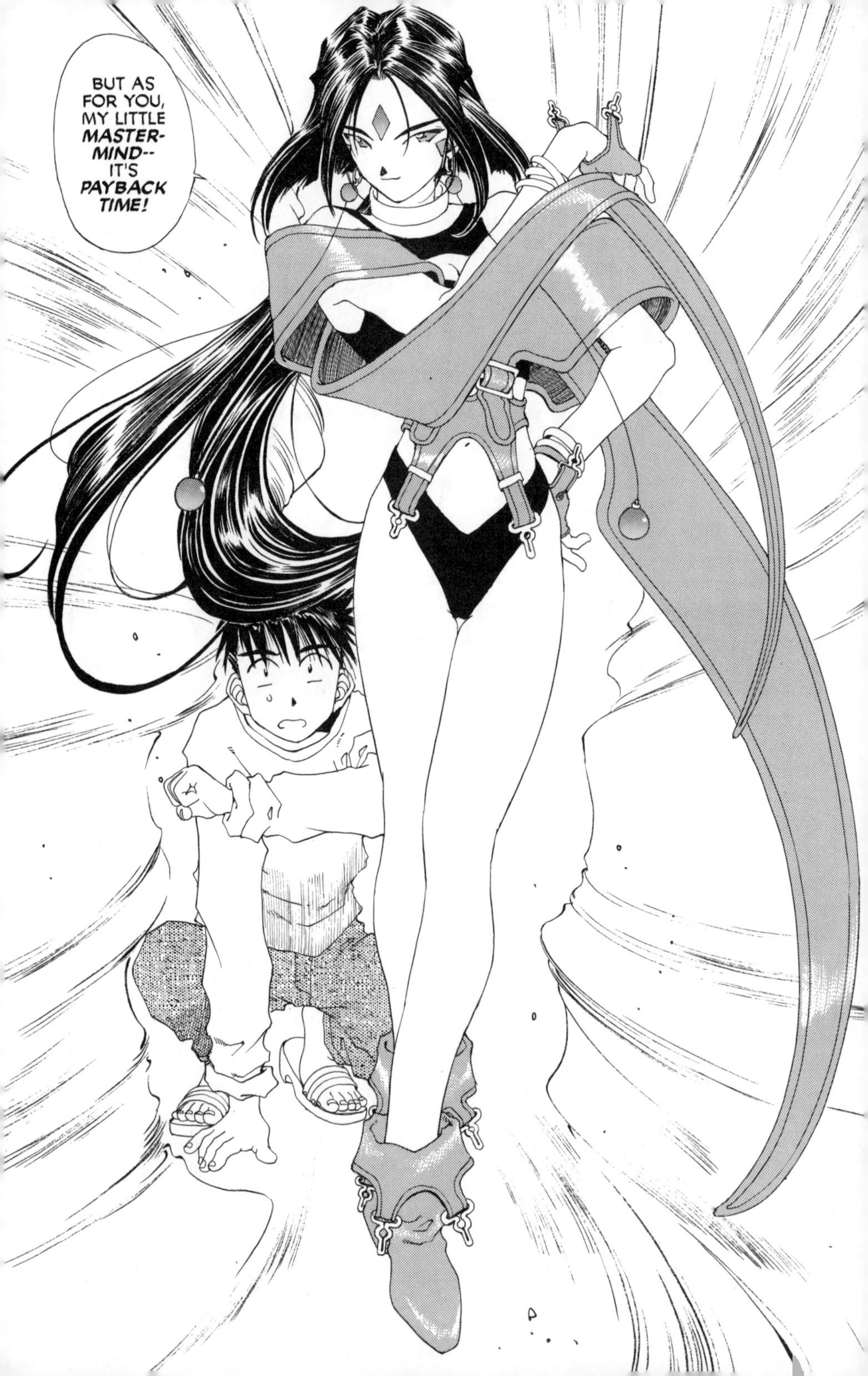
BUT AS FOR YOU, MY LITTLE ***MASTER-MIND***-- IT'S ***PAYBACK TIME!***

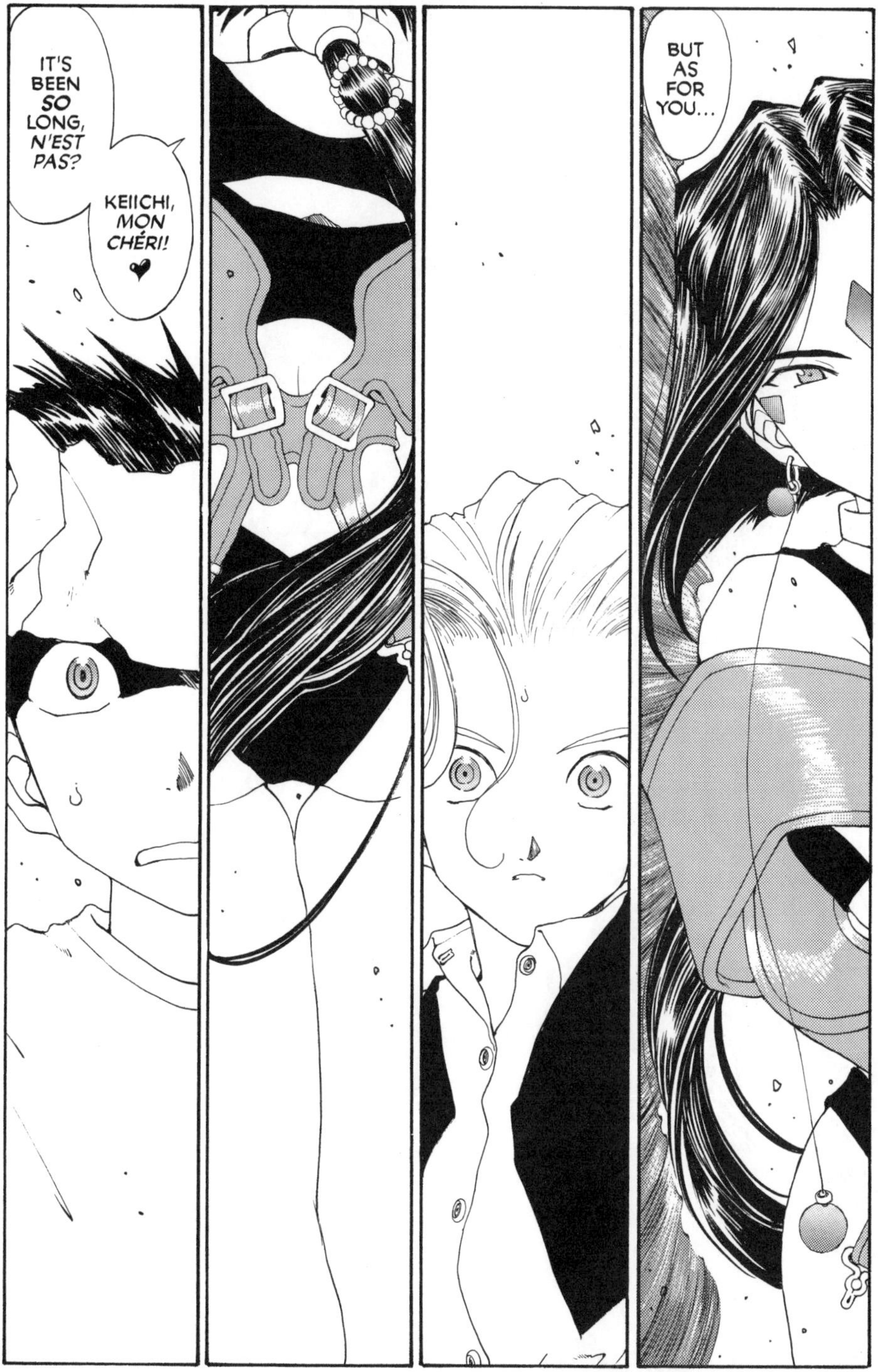
IT'S BEEN SO LONG, N'EST PAS?
KEIICHI, MON CHÉRI! ♥
BUT AS FOR YOU...

LIGHT AND SHADOW

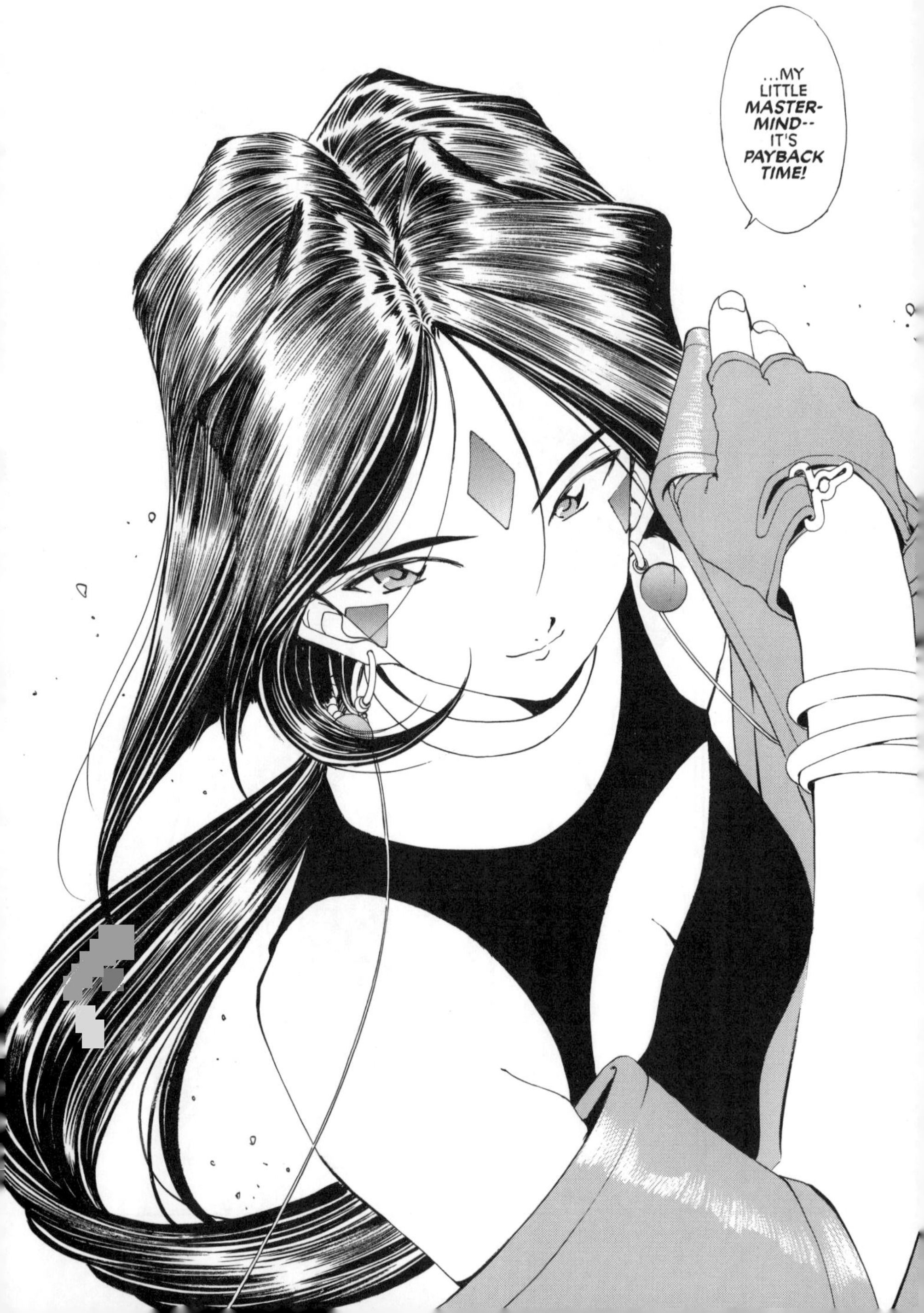
...MY LITTLE MASTER-MIND-- IT'S PAYBACK TIME!

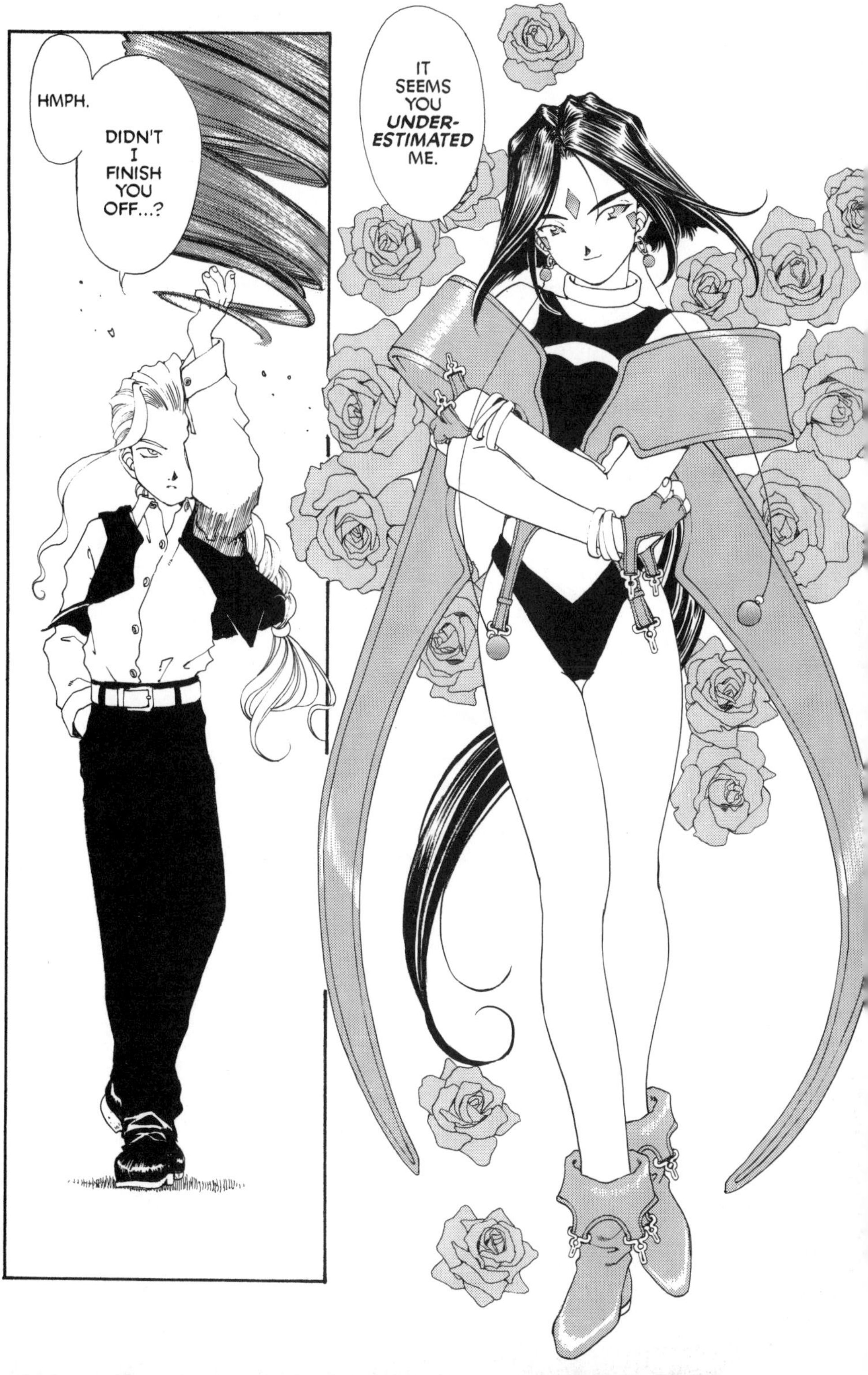
HMPH.
DIDN'T I FINISH YOU OFF...?
IT SEEMS YOU *UNDER-ESTIMATED* ME.

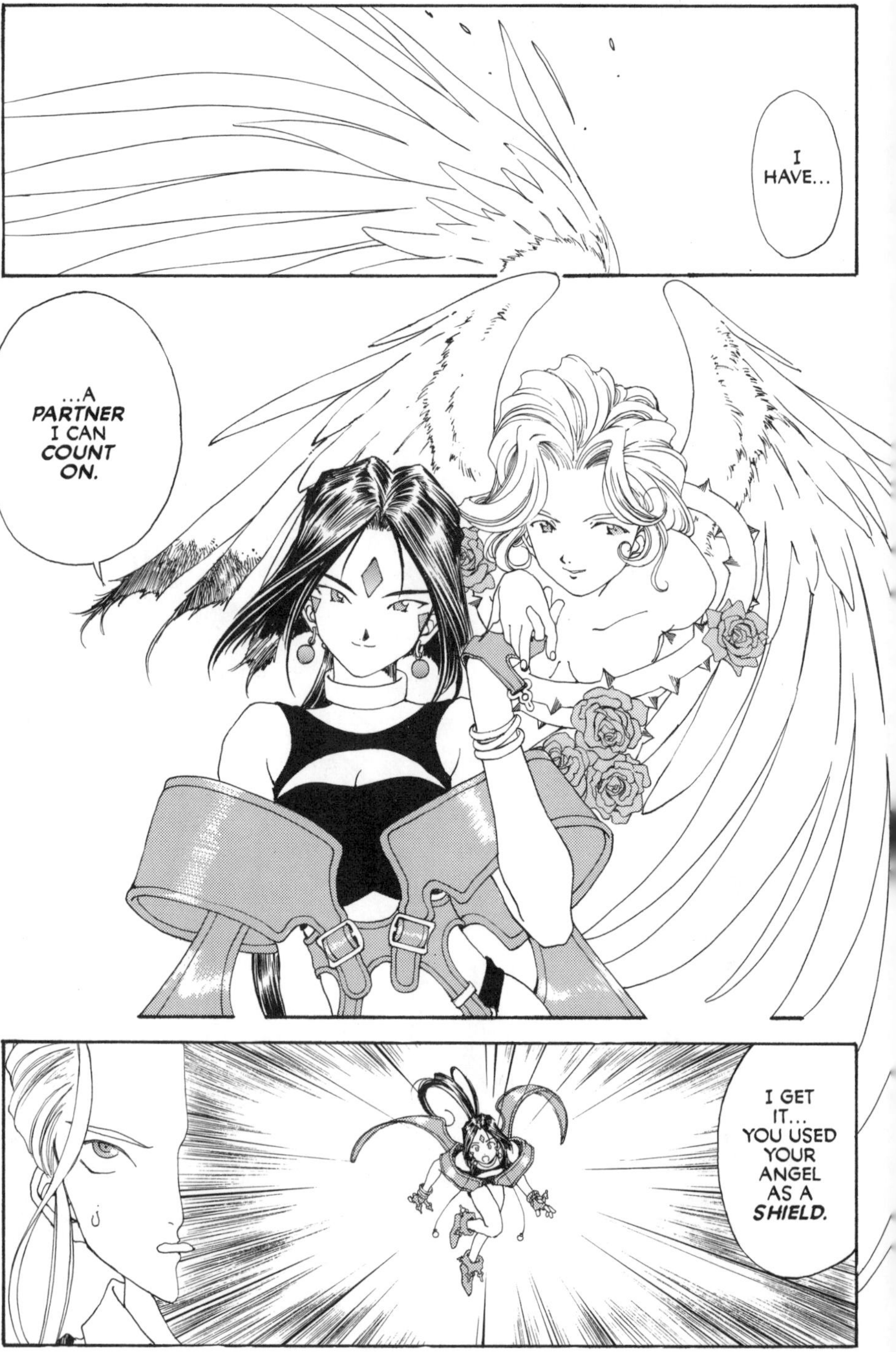
I HAVE...
...A PARTNER I CAN COUNT ON.
I GET IT... YOU USED YOUR ANGEL AS A SHIELD.

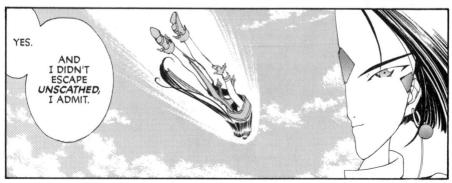

YES.

AND I DIDN'T ESCAPE *UNSCATHED,* I ADMIT.

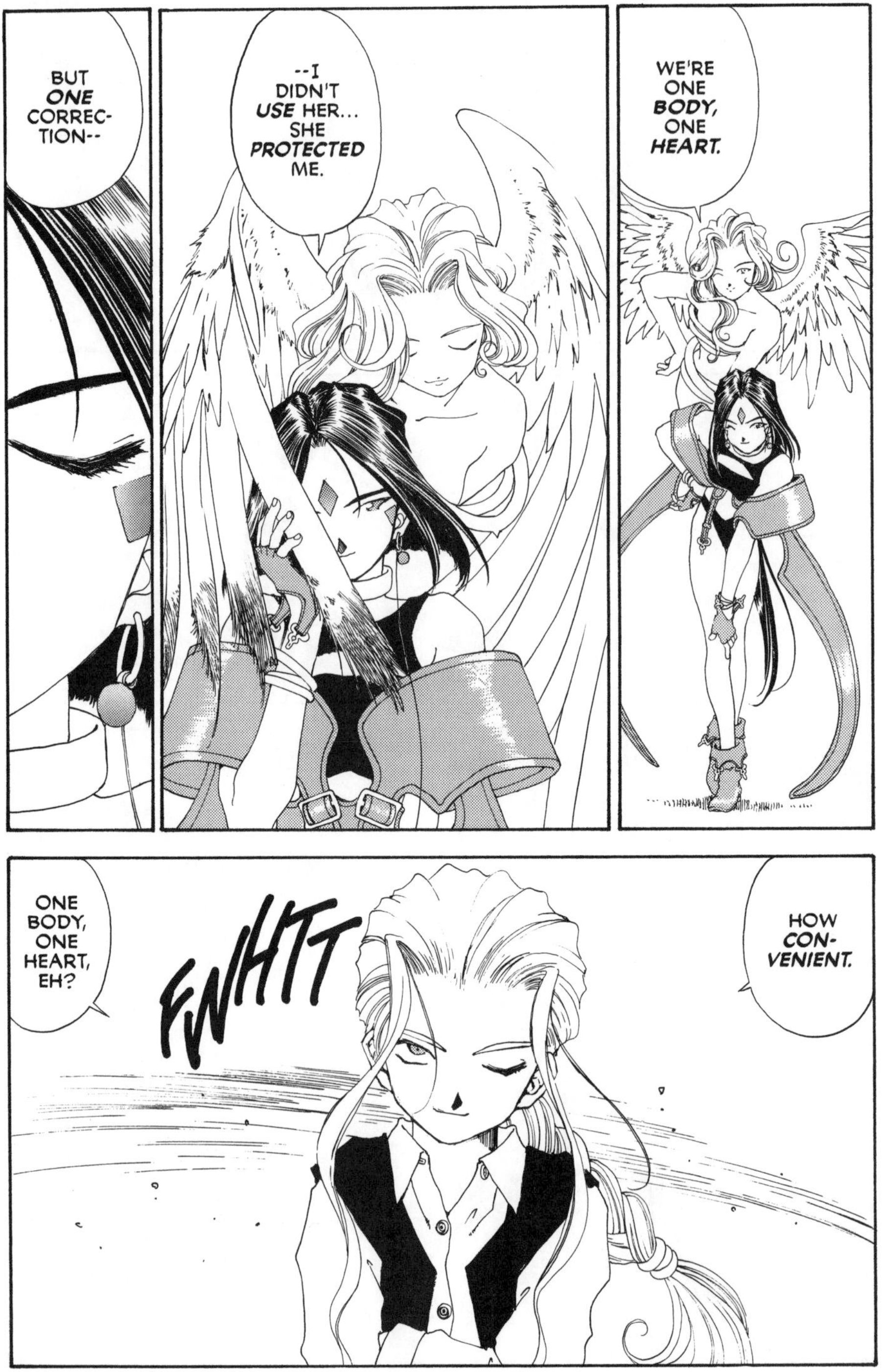
BUT *ONE* CORRECTION--
--I DIDN'T *USE* HER... SHE *PROTECTED* ME.
WE'RE ONE *BODY,* ONE *HEART.*
ONE BODY, ONE HEART, EH?
FWHTT
HOW *CONVENIENT.*

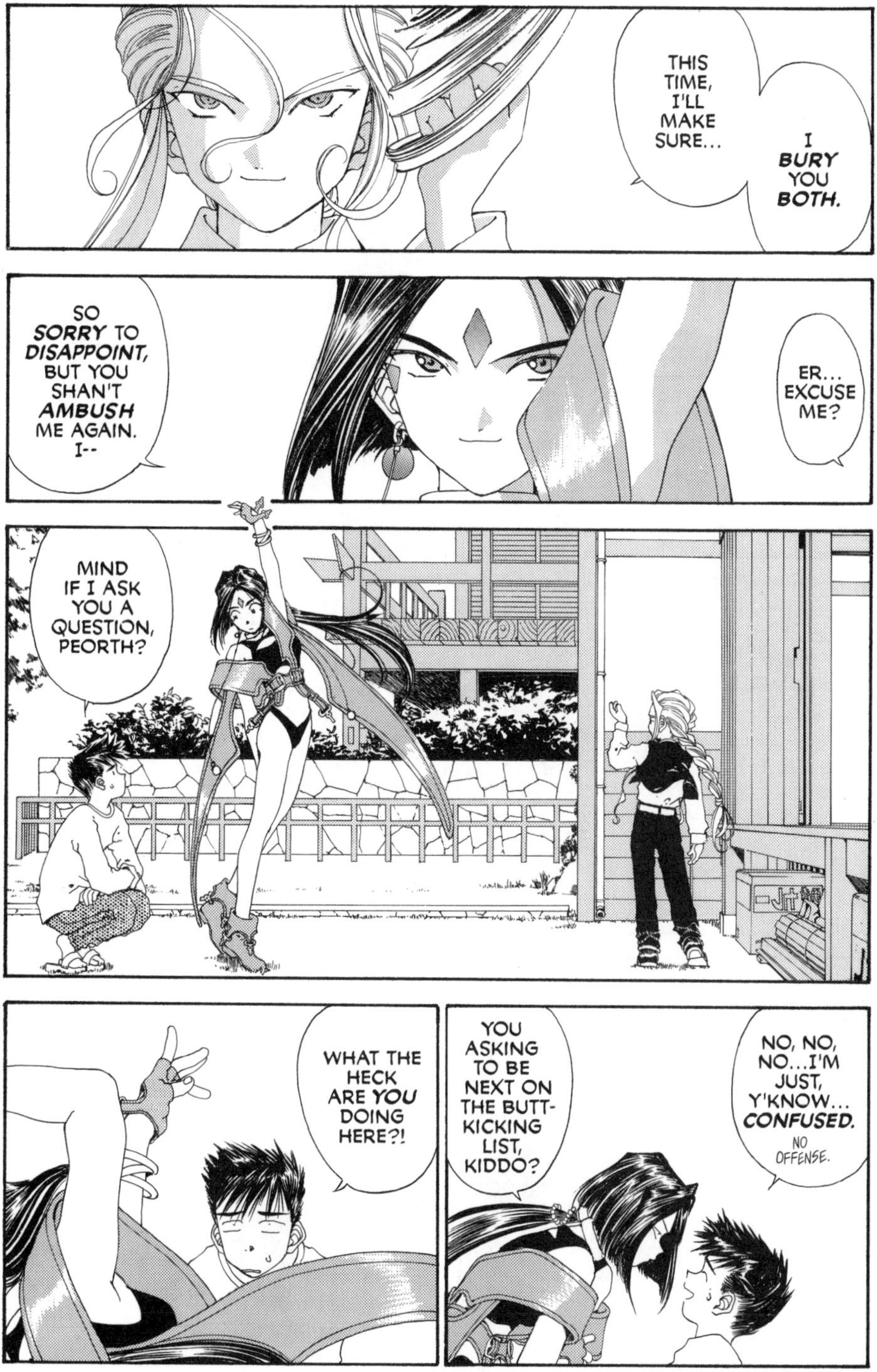
THIS TIME, I'LL MAKE SURE...
I BURY YOU BOTH.
SO SORRY TO DISAPPOINT, BUT YOU SHAN'T AMBUSH ME AGAIN. I--
ER... EXCUSE ME?
MIND IF I ASK YOU A QUESTION, PEORTH?
WHAT THE HECK ARE YOU DOING HERE?!
YOU ASKING TO BE NEXT ON THE BUTT-KICKING LIST, KIDDO?
NO, NO, NO...I'M JUST, Y'KNOW... CONFUSED.
NO OFFENSE.

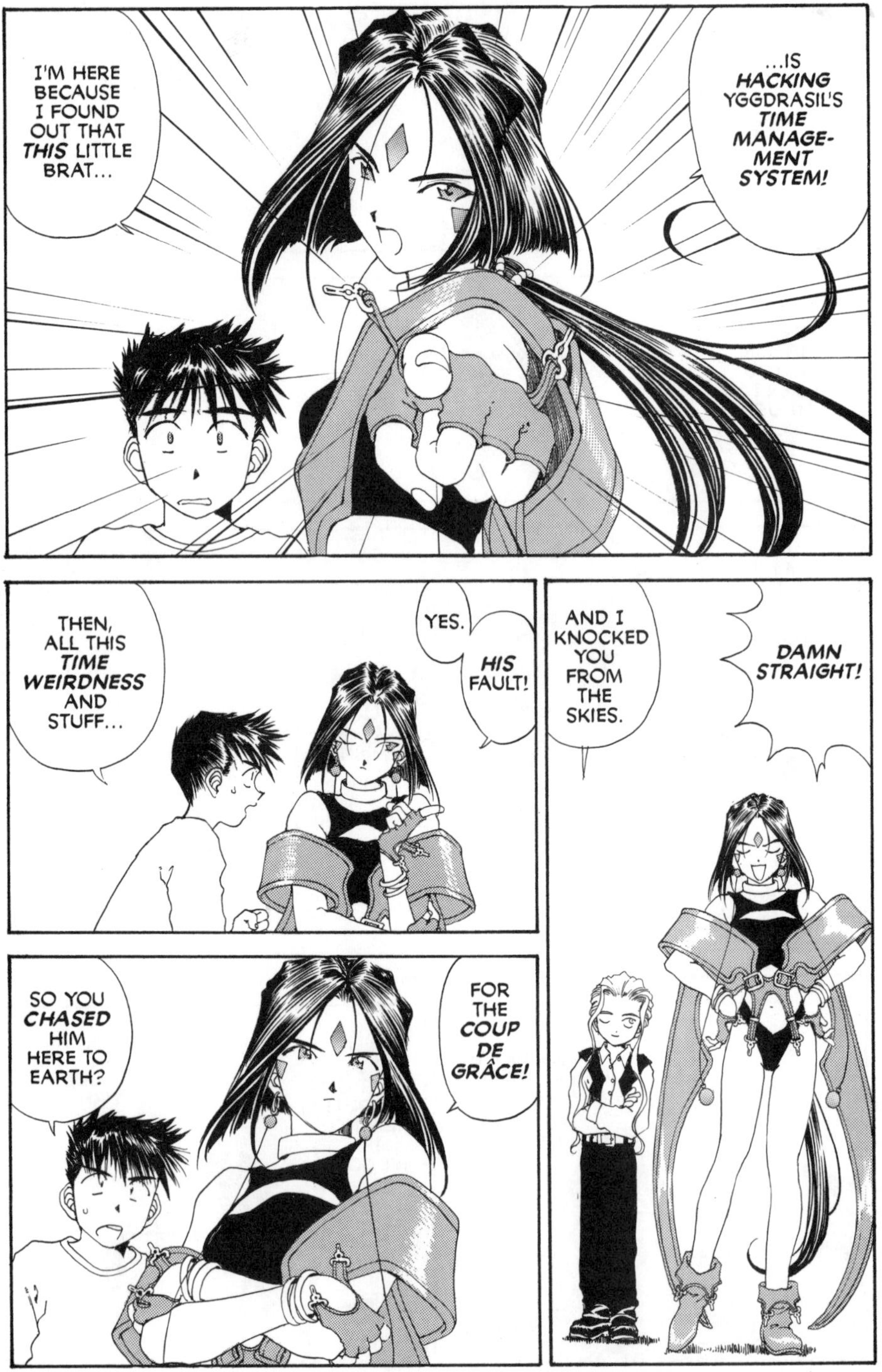
I'M HERE BECAUSE I FOUND OUT THAT THIS LITTLE BRAT...
...IS HACKING YGGDRASIL'S TIME MANAGEMENT SYSTEM!
THEN, ALL THIS TIME WEIRDNESS AND STUFF...
YES.
HIS FAULT!
SO YOU CHASED HIM HERE TO EARTH?
FOR THE COUP DE GRÂCE!
AND I KNOCKED YOU FROM THE SKIES.
DAMN STRAIGHT!

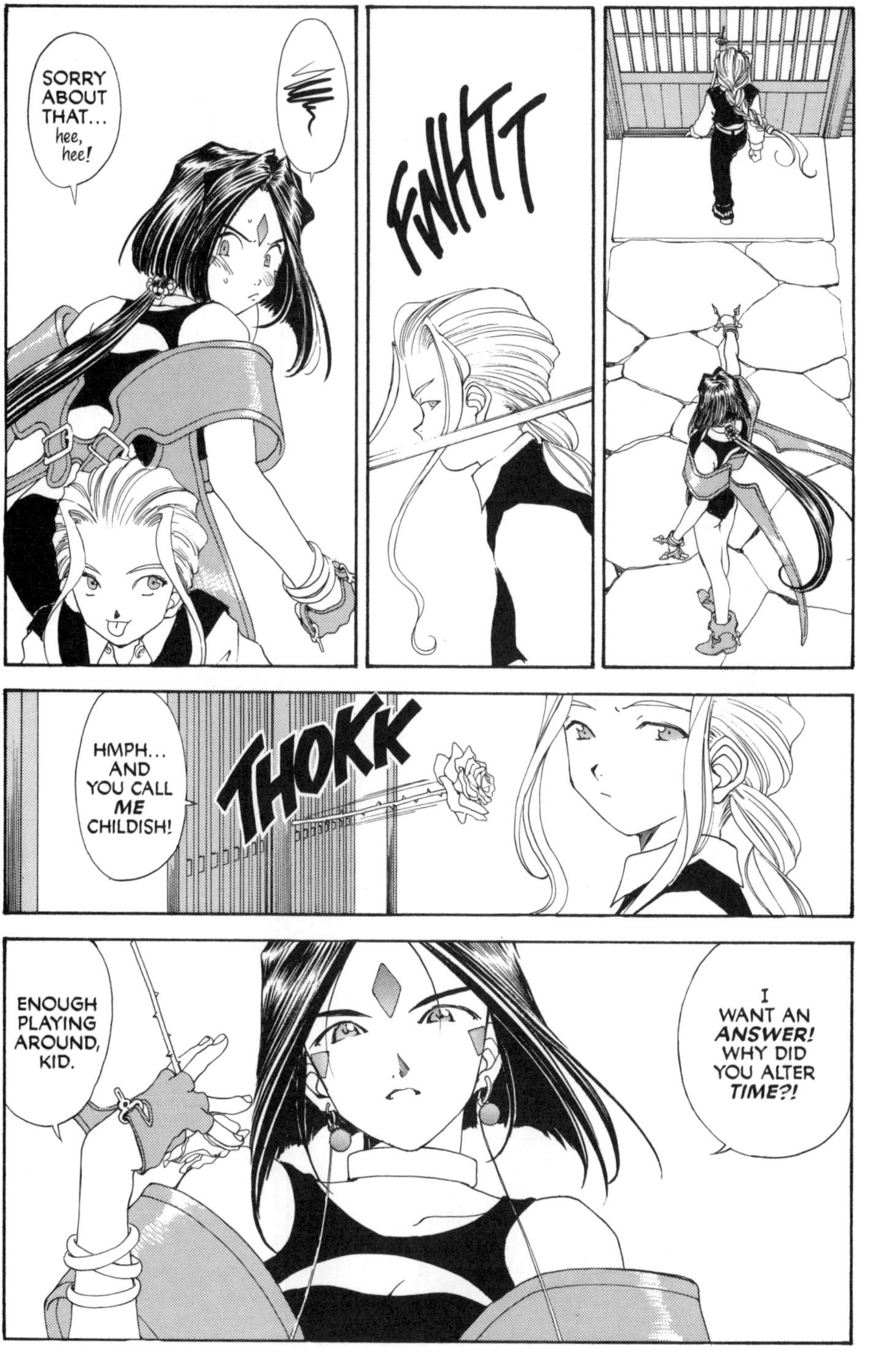
SORRY ABOUT THAT... hee, hee!
FWHTT
HMPH... AND YOU CALL *ME* CHILDISH!
THOKK
ENOUGH PLAYING AROUND, KID.
I WANT AN *ANSWER!* WHY DID YOU ALTER *TIME?!*

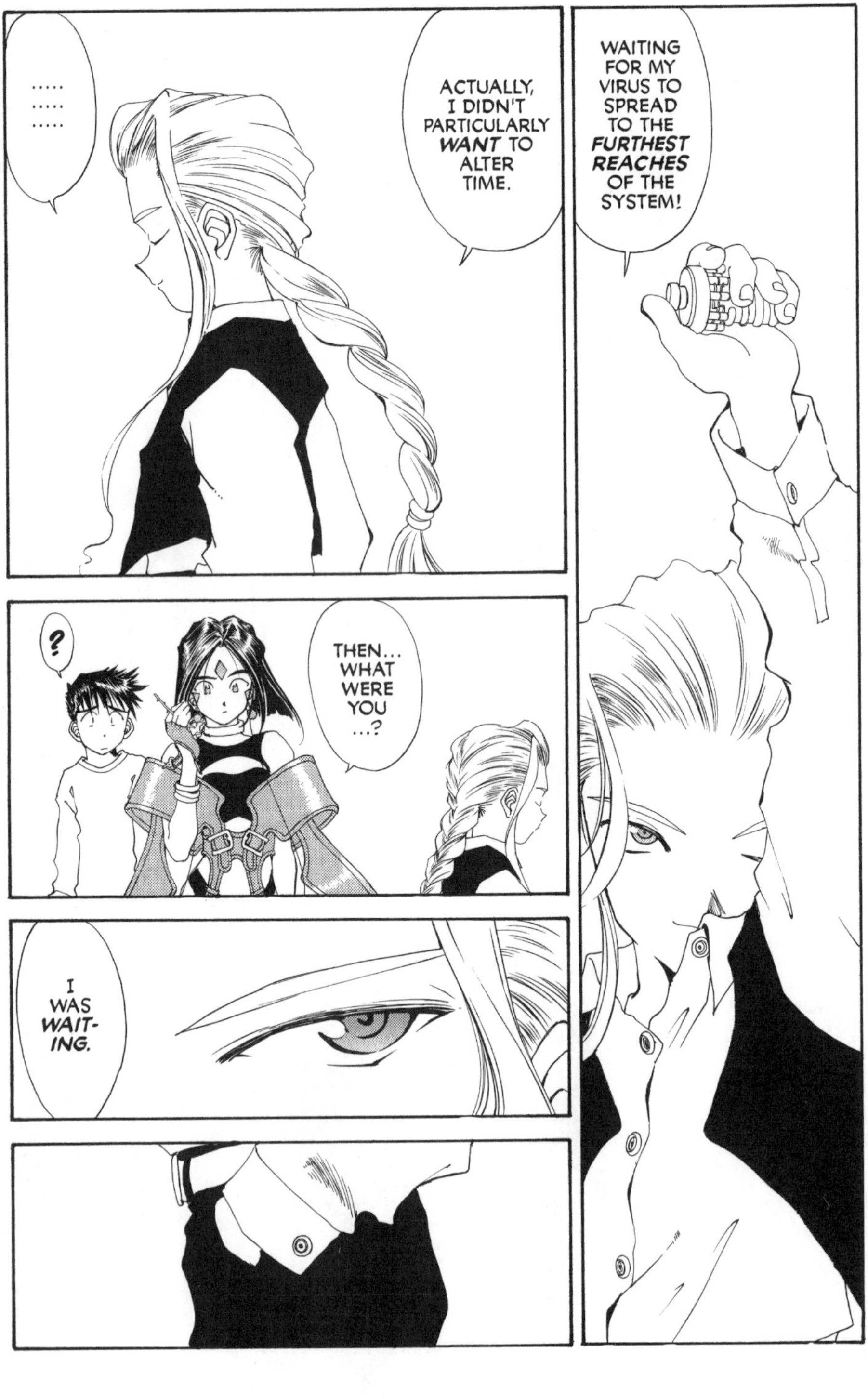

.....
.....
.....
ACTUALLY, I DIDN'T PARTICULARLY *WANT* TO ALTER TIME.
?
THEN... WHAT WERE YOU ...?
I WAS *WAIT-ING.*
WAITING FOR MY VIRUS TO SPREAD TO THE *FURTHEST REACHES* OF THE SYSTEM!

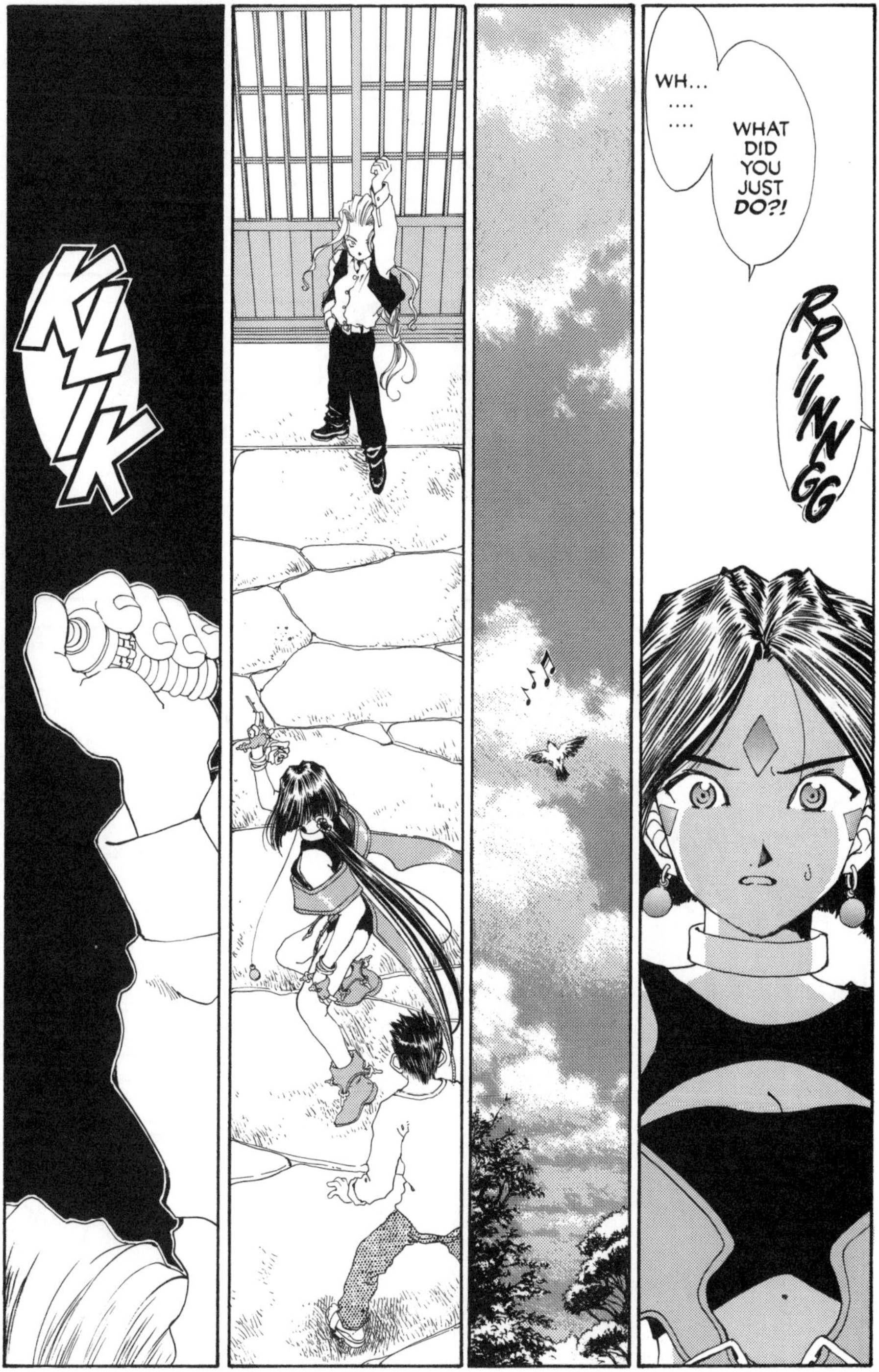
KLIK
WH... ....
WHAT DID YOU JUST DO?!
RRIINNGG

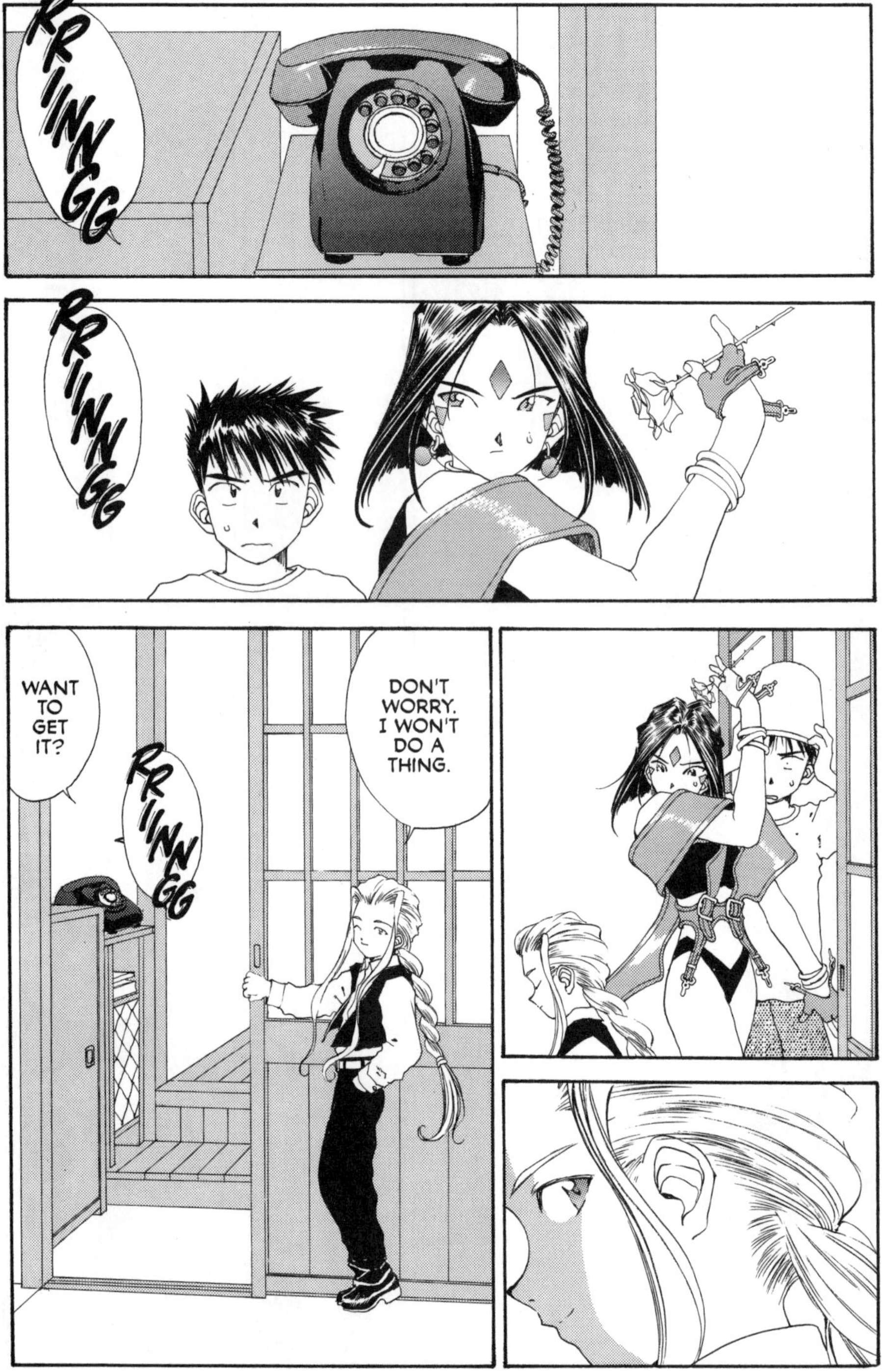
RRIINNGG
RRIINNGG
WANT TO GET IT?
RRIINNGG
DON'T WORRY. I WON'T DO A THING.

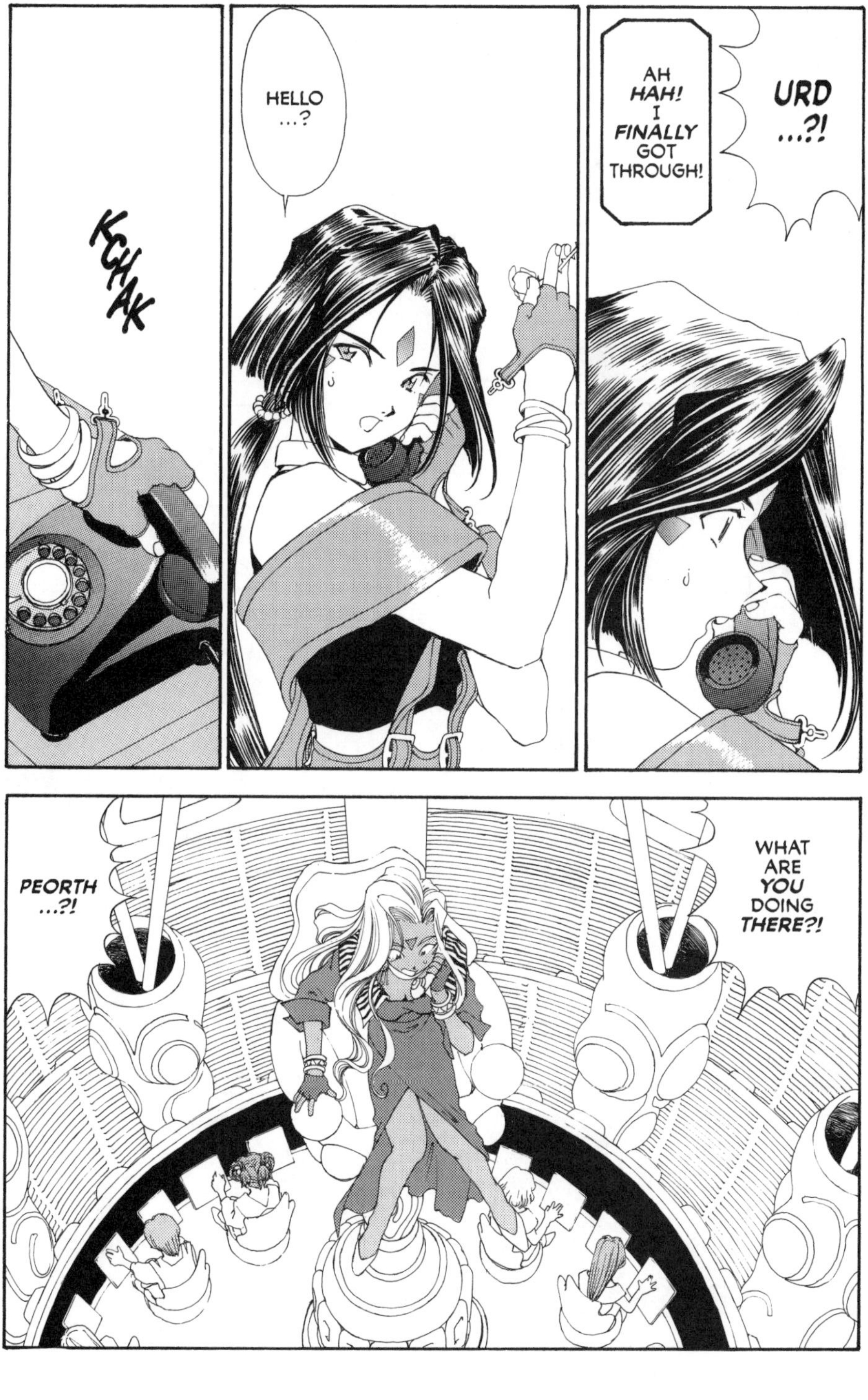
KCHAK
HELLO ...?
AH HAH! I FINALLY GOT THROUGH!
URD ...?!
PEORTH ...?!
WHAT ARE YOU DOING THERE?!

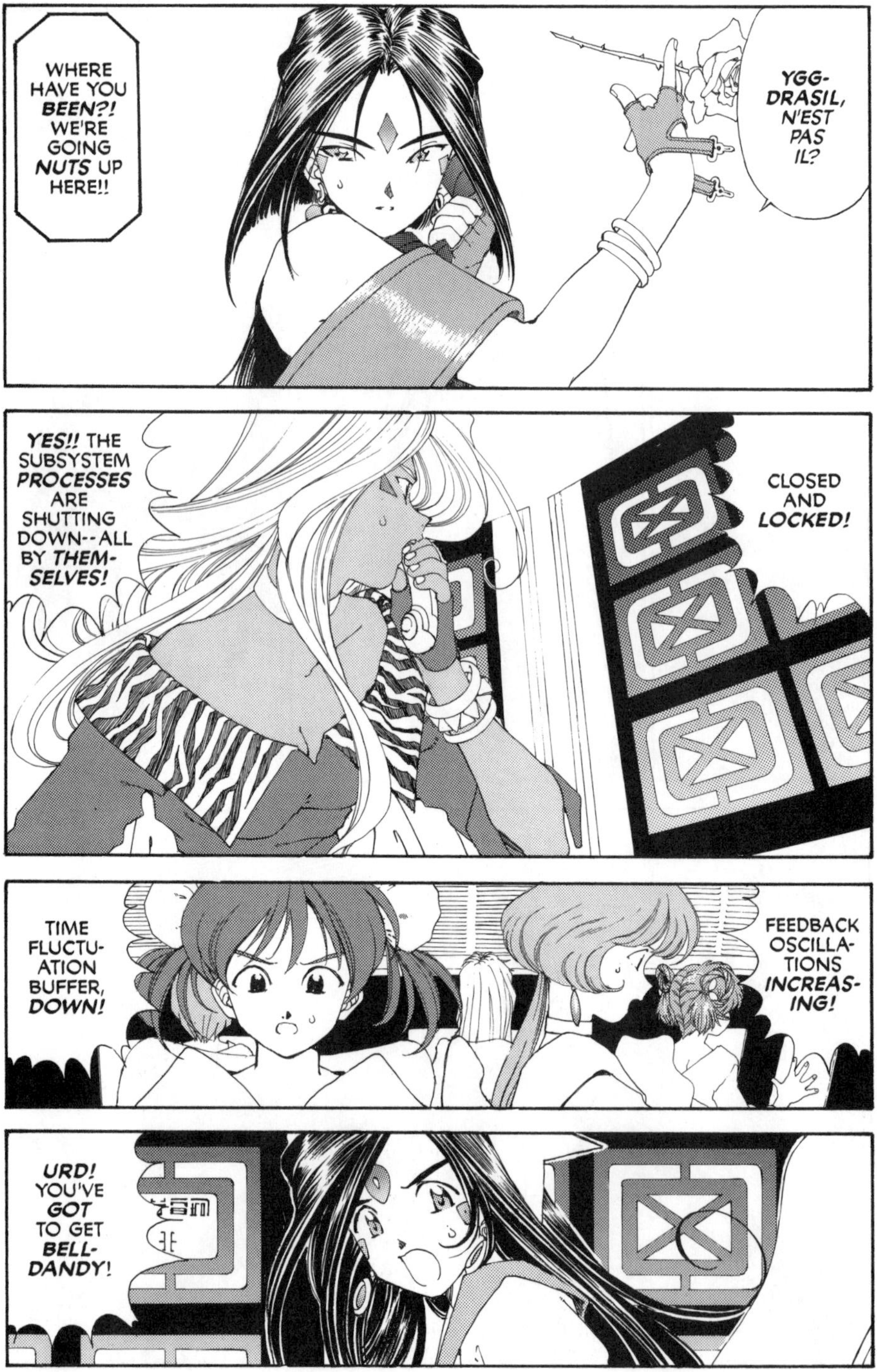
WHERE HAVE YOU BEEN?! WE'RE GOING NUTS UP HERE!!
YGG-DRASIL, N'EST PAS IL?
YES!! THE SUBSYSTEM PROCESSES ARE SHUTTING DOWN--ALL BY THEM-SELVES!
CLOSED AND LOCKED!
TIME FLUCTU-ATION BUFFER, DOWN!
FEEDBACK OSCILLA-TIONS INCREAS-ING!
URD! YOU'VE GOT TO GET BELL-DANDY!

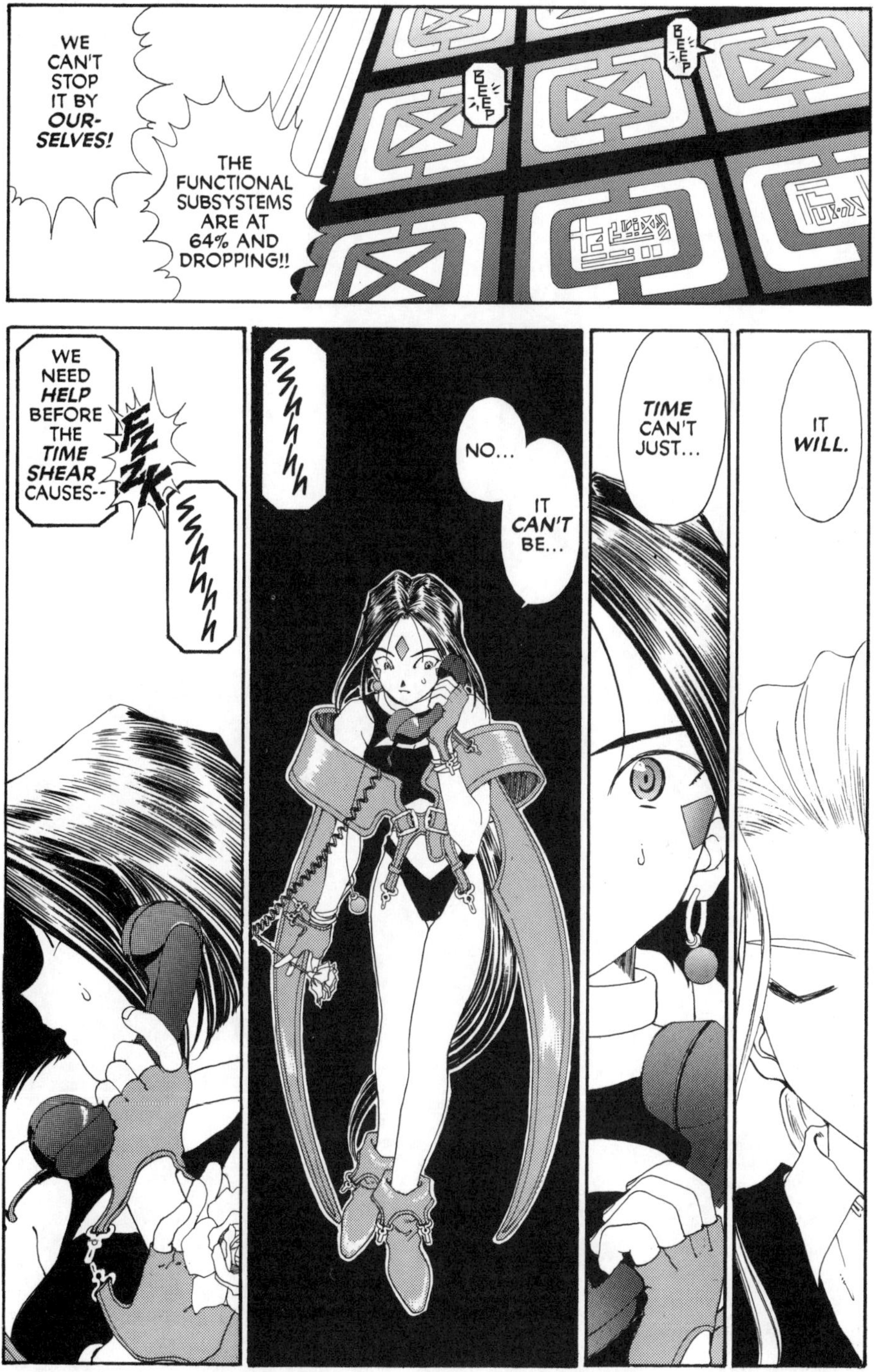
WE CAN'T STOP IT BY *OURSELVES!*
THE FUNCTIONAL SUBSYSTEMS ARE AT 64% AND DROPPING!!
BEEP
BEEP
WE NEED *HELP* BEFORE THE *TIME SHEAR* CAUSES--
FZZK
NO...
IT *CAN'T* BE...
TIME CAN'T JUST...
IT *WILL.*

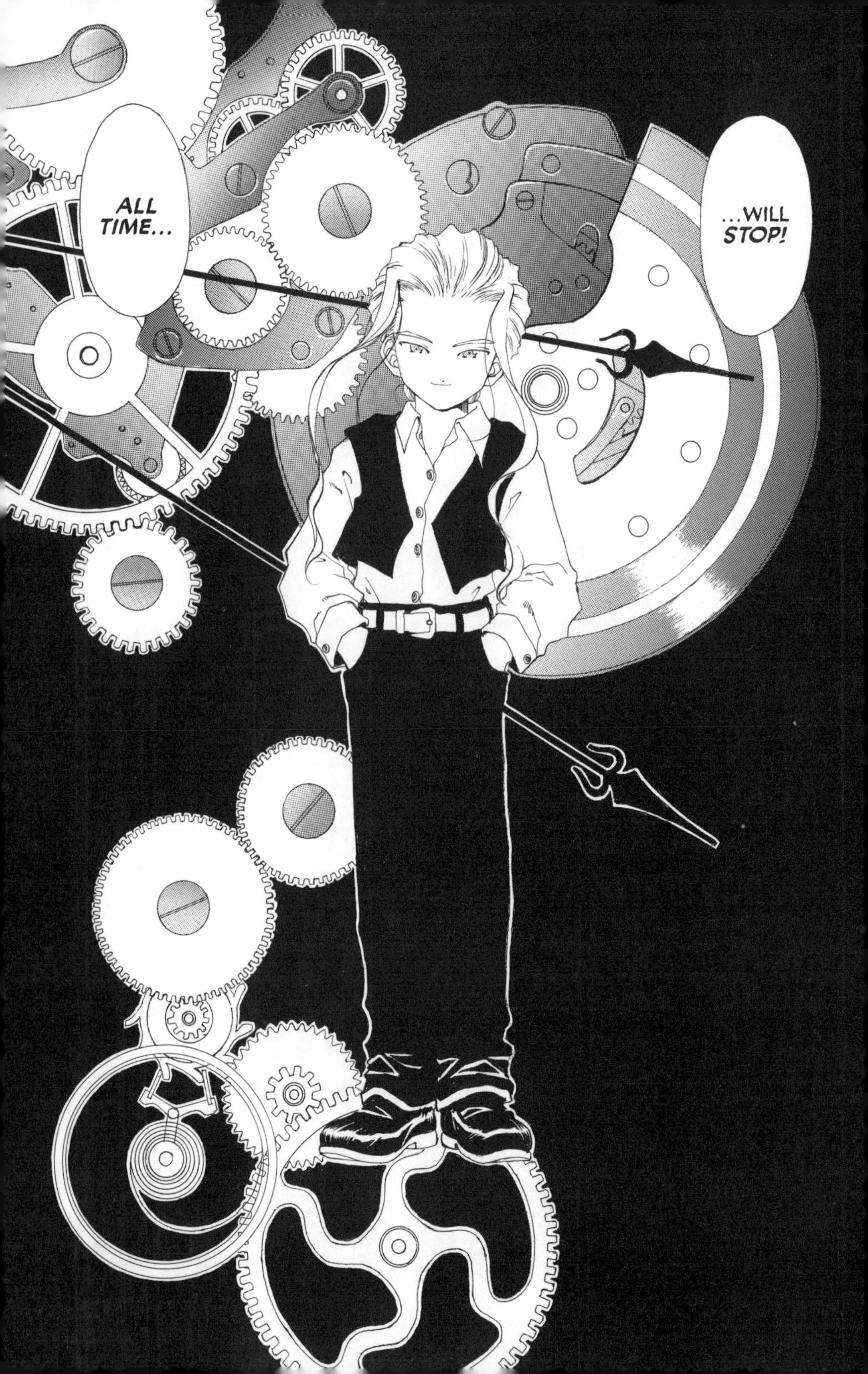
ALL TIME...
...WILL STOP!

Y-YOU CAN'T! *YOU CAN'T!!*
DON'T YOU *REALIZE* WHAT YOU'RE *DOING?!*
HEY... IT'S NO BIG DEAL.
IT'S NOT LIKE ANYONE *DIES.*
"NOT DYING" ...
...AND *"LIVING"*... ARE *NOT* THE SAME THING!!
YES, IT'S *TRUE* NO ONE WILL *SUFFER.*
FESTIMA WATCHES
2:00
PAROO 2
BIG PRESENT SALE

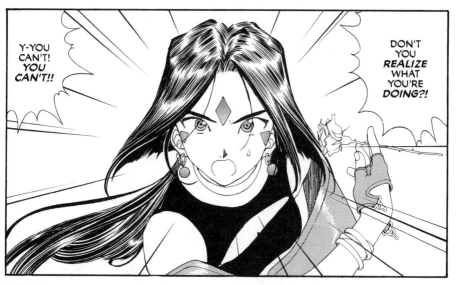

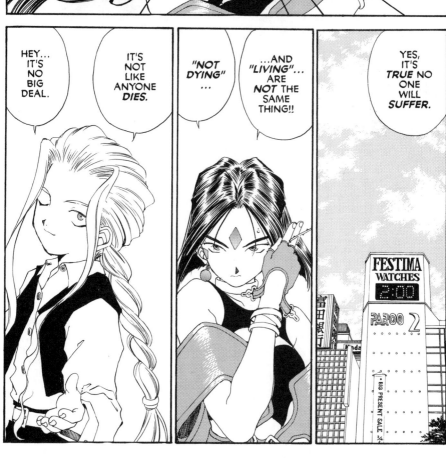

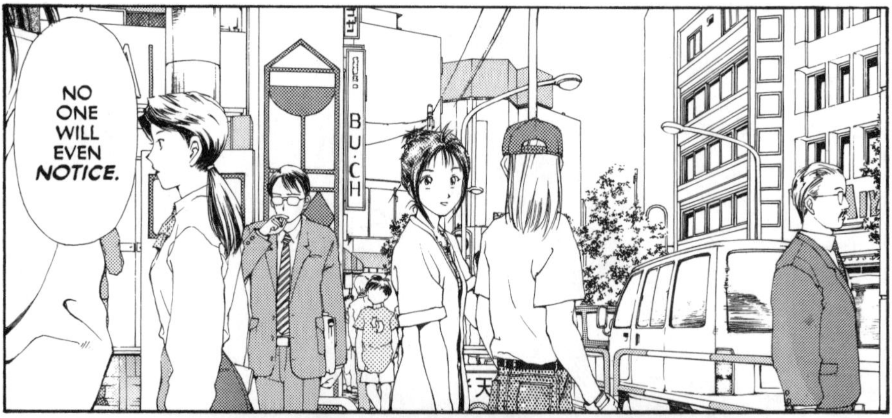
NO ONE WILL EVEN *NOTICE.*
BU·CH

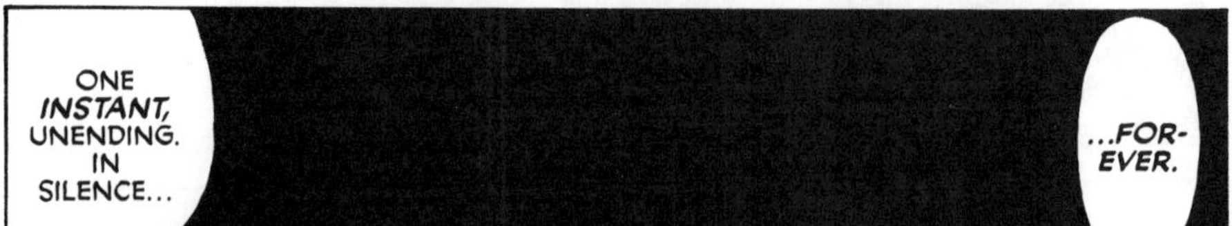
ONE *INSTANT,* UNENDING. IN SILENCE...
...*FOR-EVER.*
アトム
CABIN

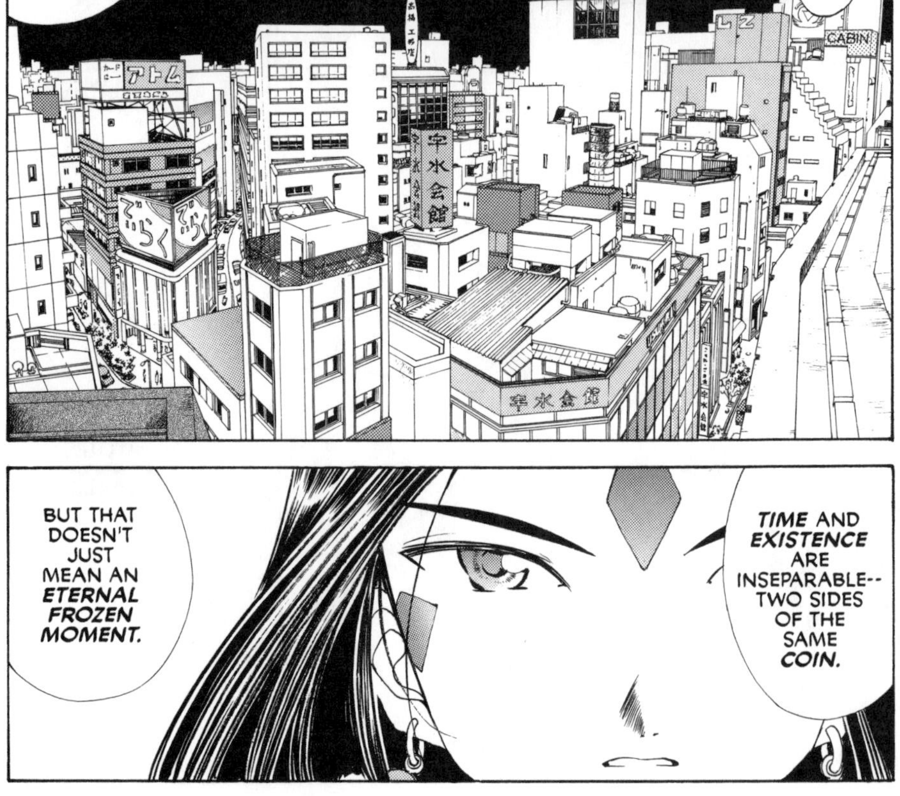
BUT THAT DOESN'T JUST MEAN AN ***ETERNAL FROZEN MOMENT.***
TIME AND ***EXISTENCE*** ARE INSEPARABLE-- TWO SIDES OF THE SAME ***COIN.***

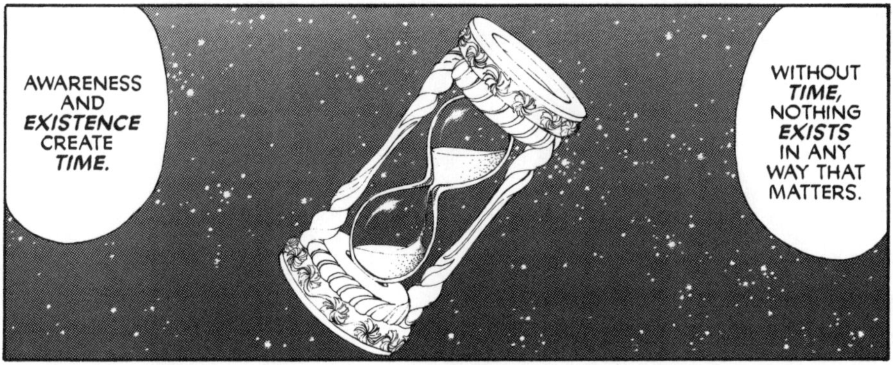
AWARENESS AND *EXISTENCE* CREATE *TIME.*
WITHOUT *TIME,* NOTHING *EXISTS* IN ANY WAY THAT MATTERS.

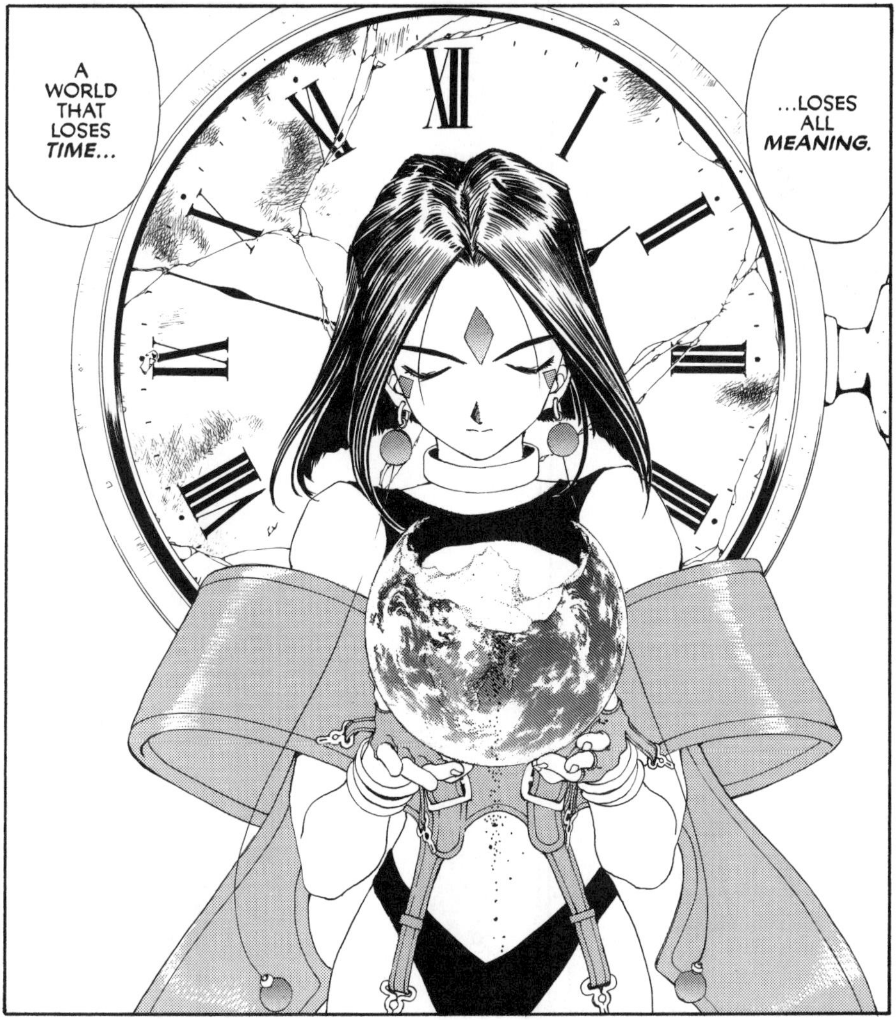
A WORLD THAT LOSES *TIME...*
...LOSES ALL *MEANING.*

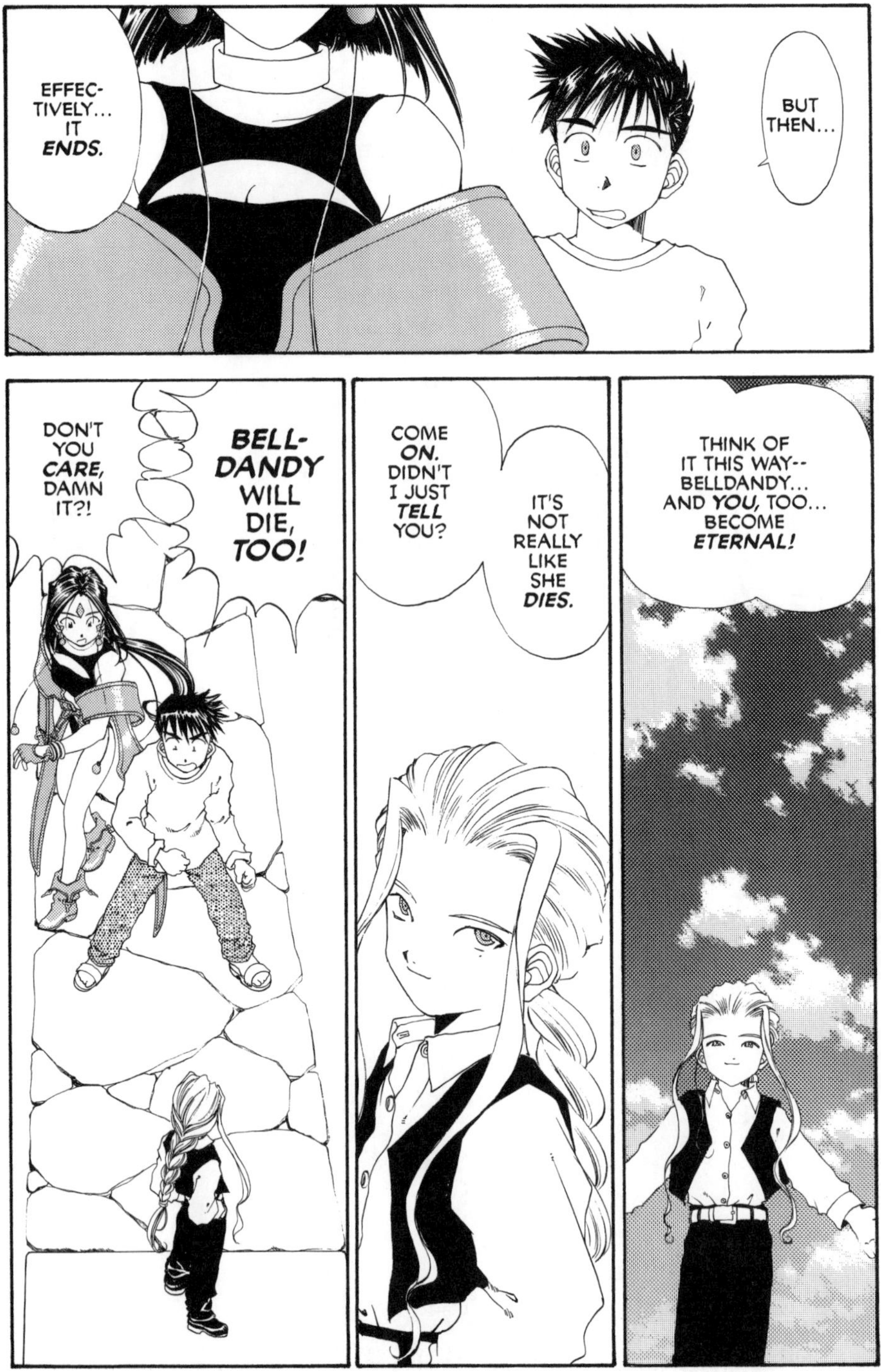
EFFECTIVELY... IT ENDS.
BUT THEN...
DON'T YOU CARE, DAMN IT?!
BELLDANDY WILL DIE, TOO!
COME ON. DIDN'T I JUST TELL YOU?
IT'S NOT REALLY LIKE SHE DIES.
THINK OF IT THIS WAY-- BELLDANDY... AND YOU, TOO... BECOME ETERNAL!

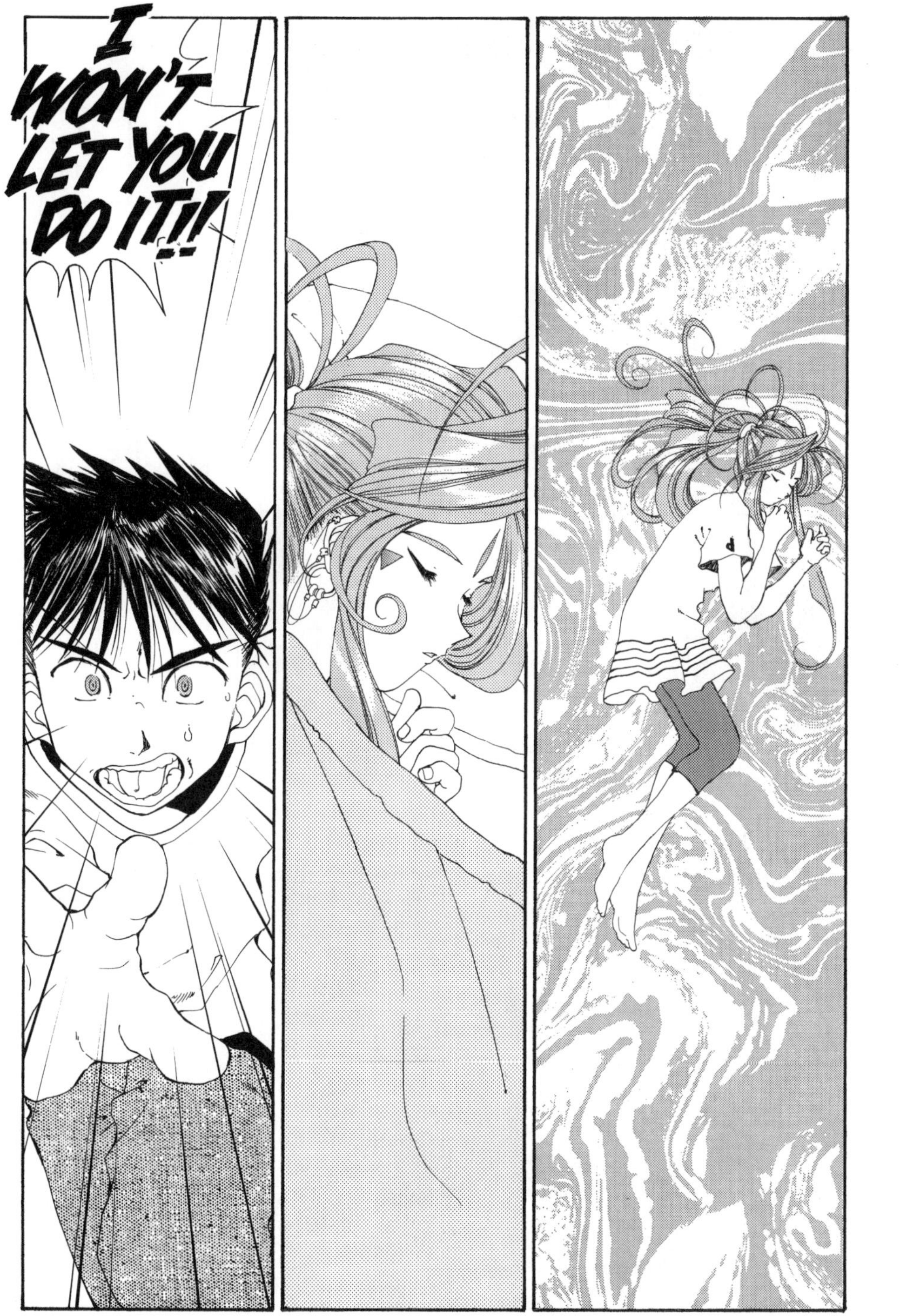
I WON'T LET YOU DO IT!!

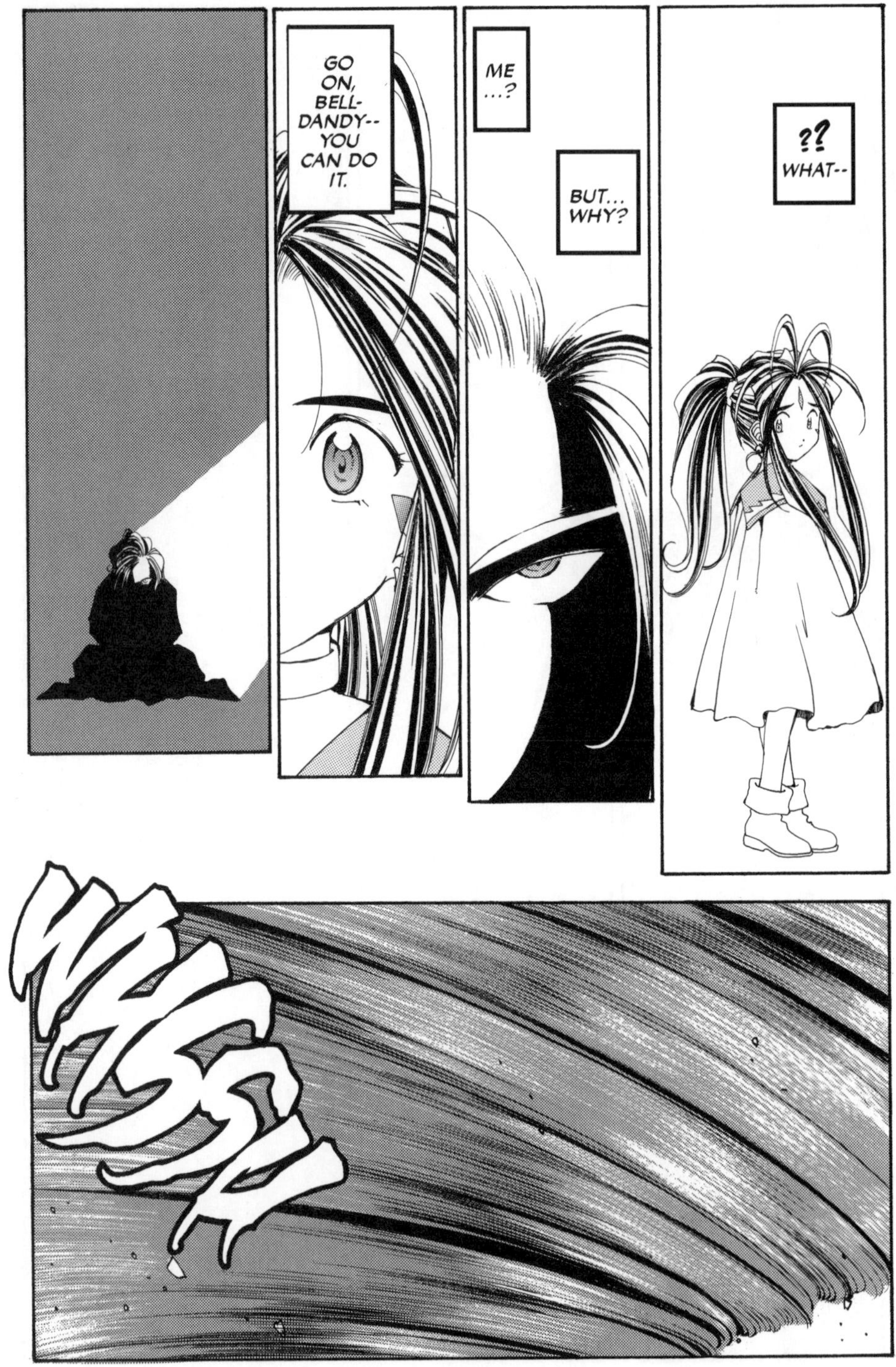
GO ON, BELL-DANDY-- YOU CAN DO IT.
ME ...?
BUT... WHY?
?? WHAT--
WHSSH

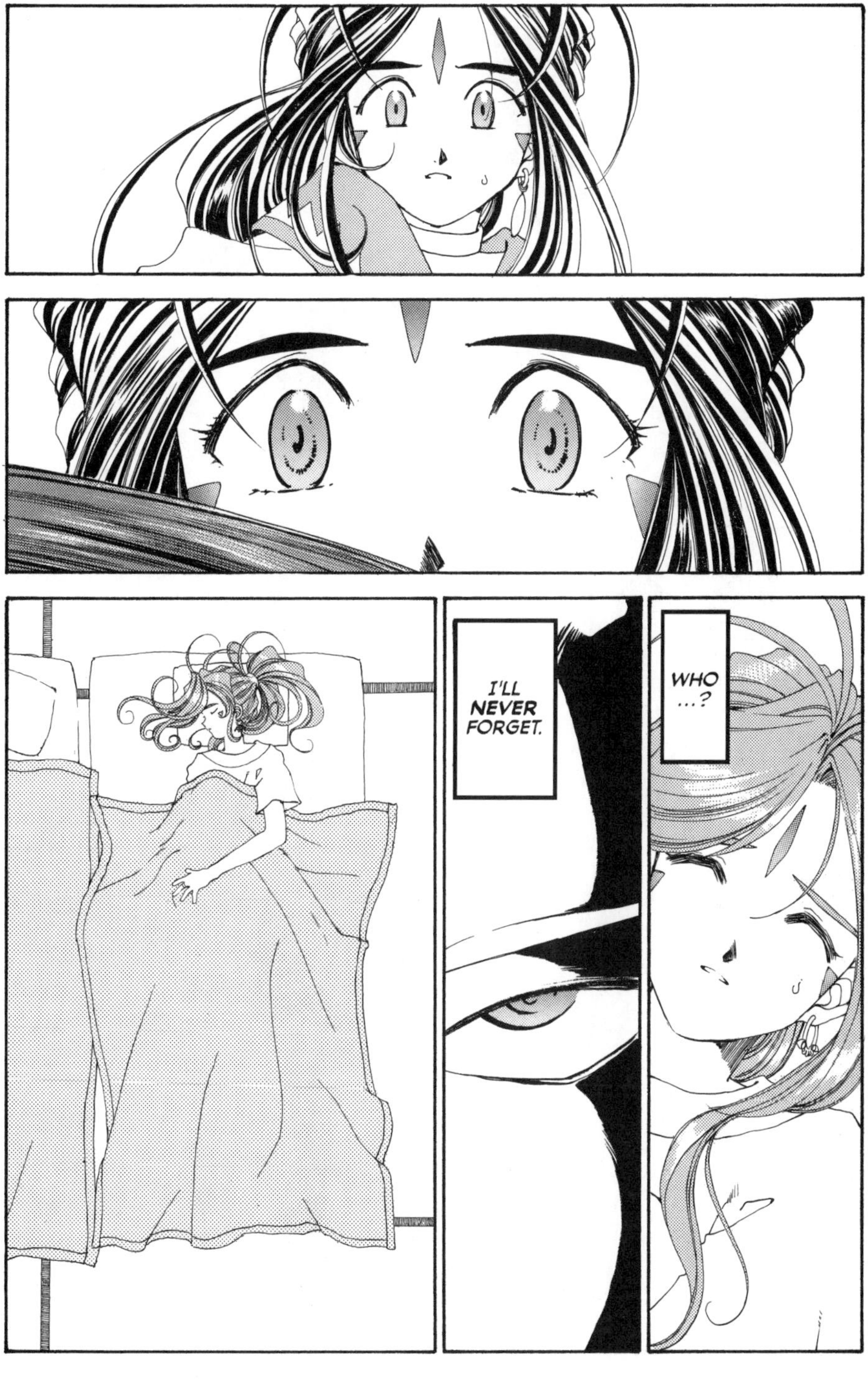
I'LL NEVER FORGET.
WHO ...?

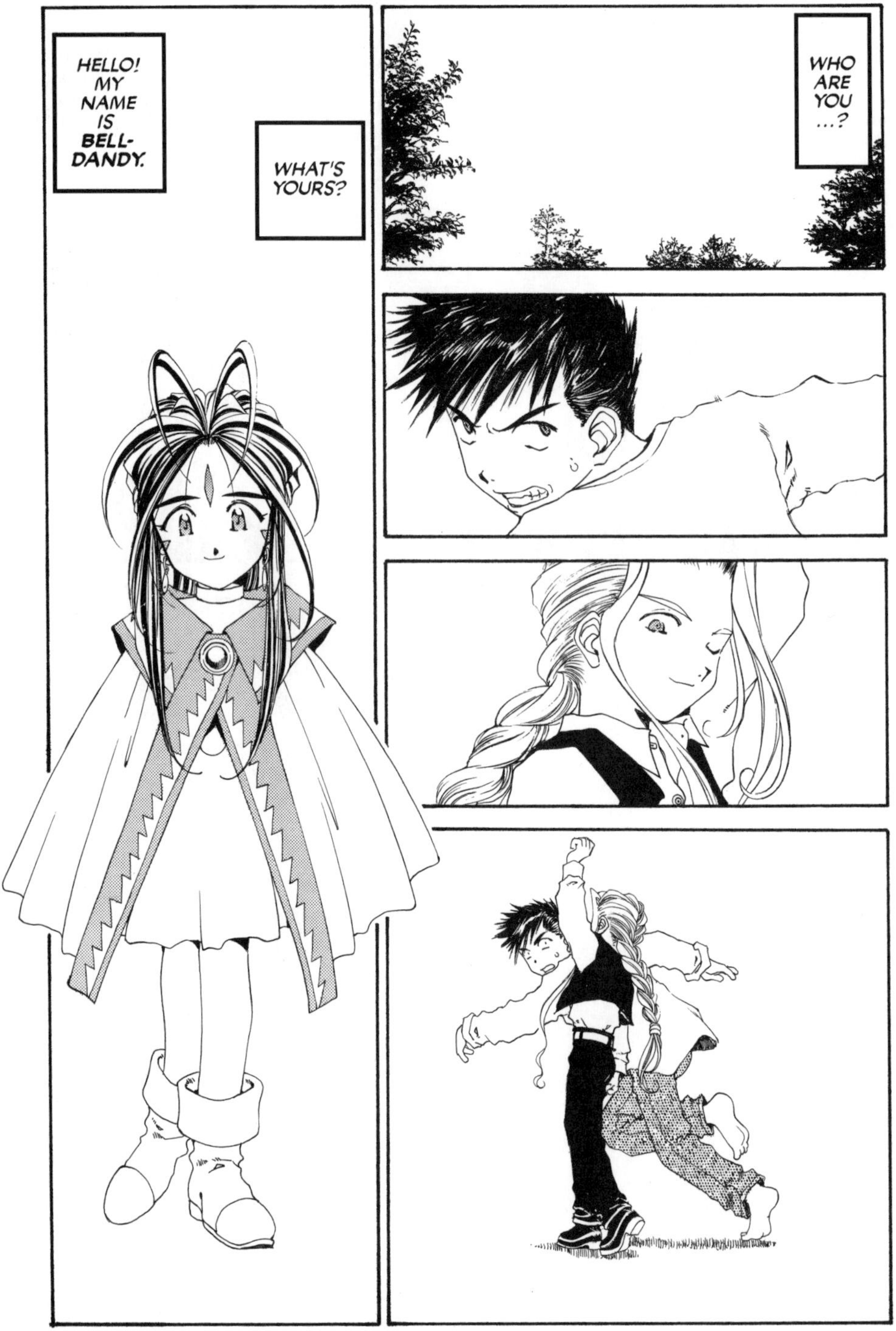
HELLO! MY NAME IS BELL-DANDY.
WHAT'S YOURS?
WHO ARE YOU ...?

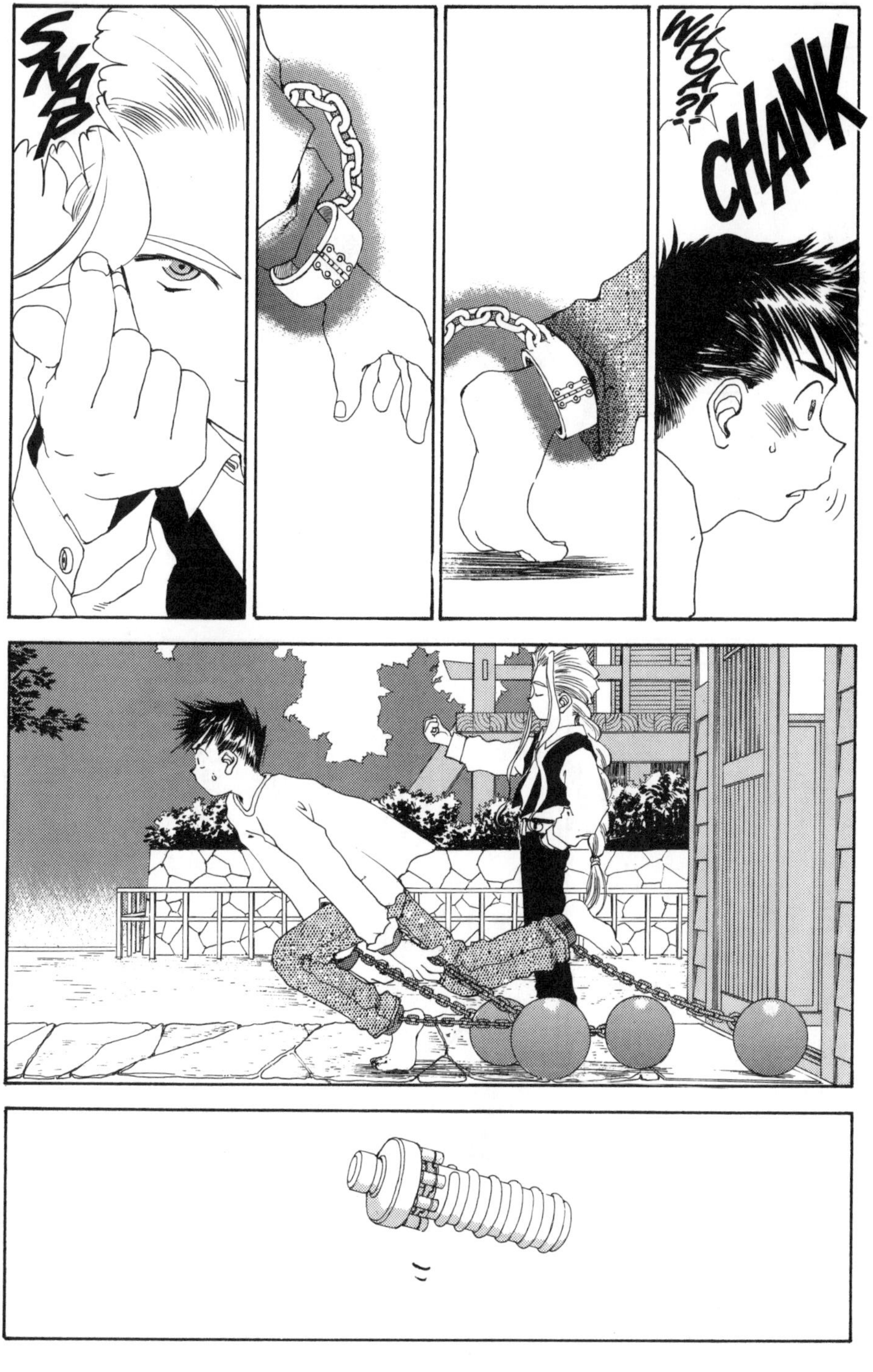
SNAP
WHOA?!
CHANK

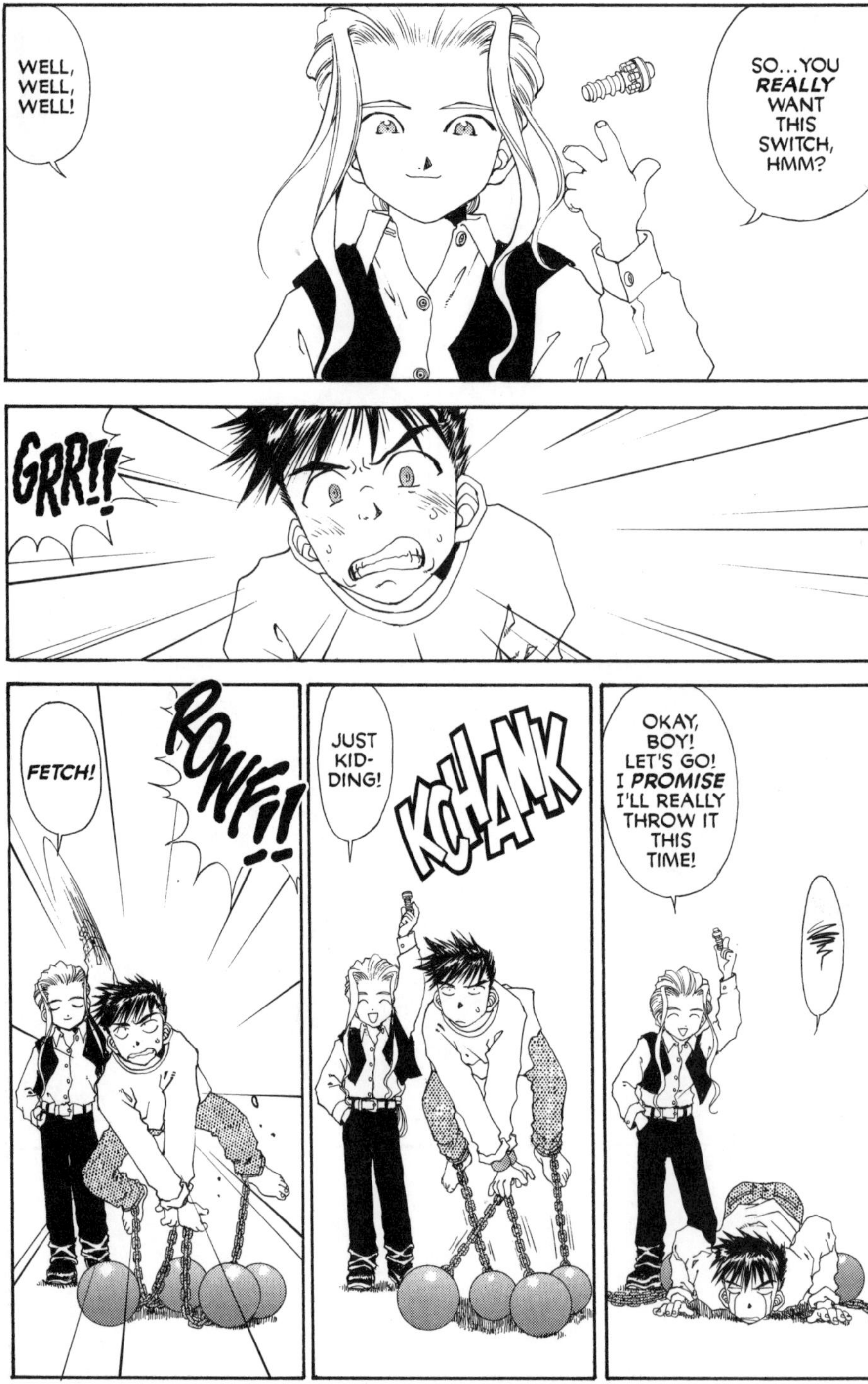
WELL, WELL, WELL!
SO...YOU *REALLY* WANT THIS SWITCH, HMM?
GRR!!
FETCH!
ROWF!!
JUST KID-DING!
KCHANK
OKAY, BOY! LET'S GO! I *PROMISE* I'LL REALLY THROW IT THIS TIME!

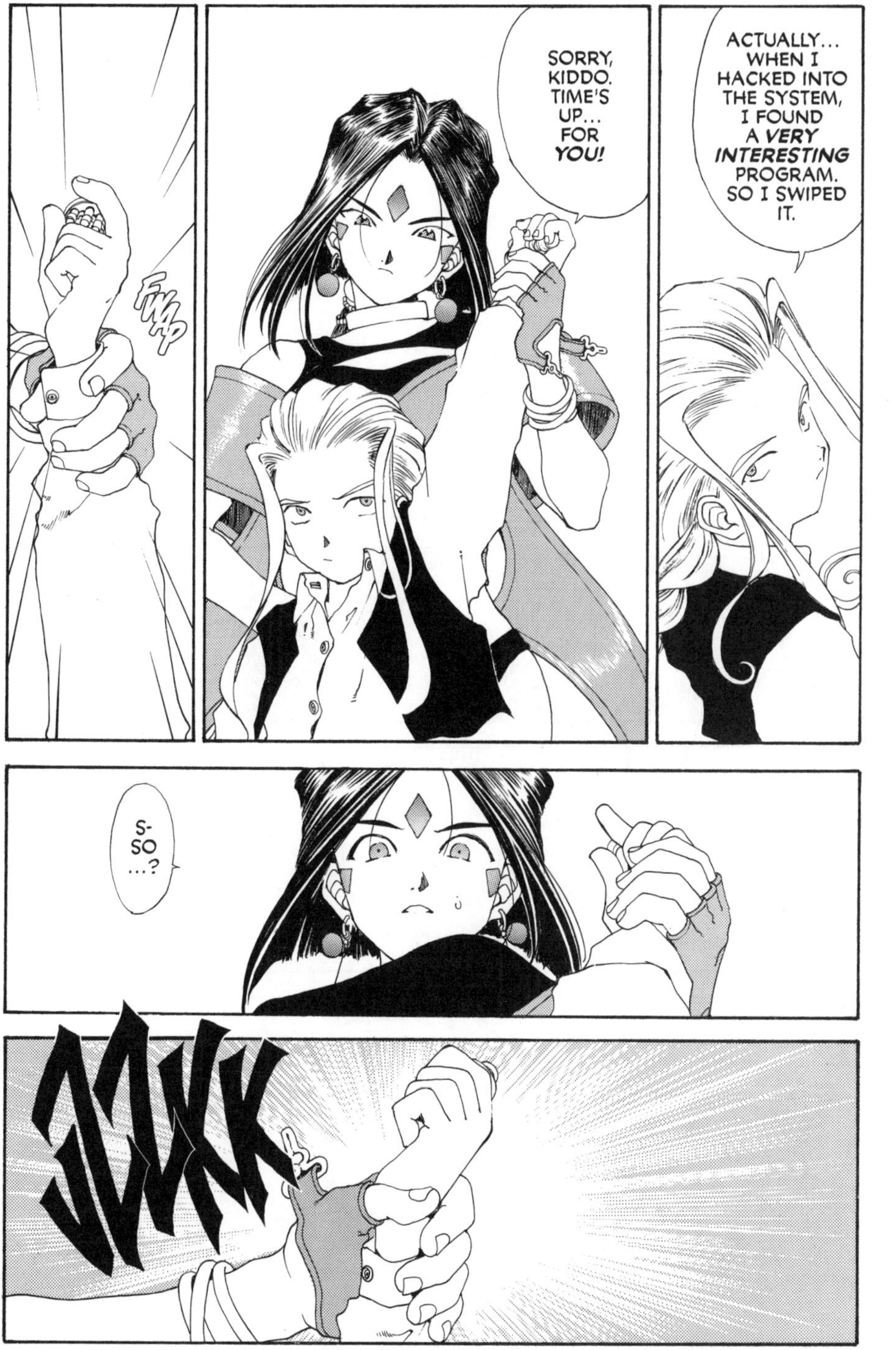
FWAP
SORRY, KIDDO. TIME'S UP... FOR *YOU!*
ACTUALLY... WHEN I HACKED INTO THE SYSTEM, I FOUND A ***VERY INTERESTING*** PROGRAM. SO I SWIPED IT.
S-SO ...?
JINK

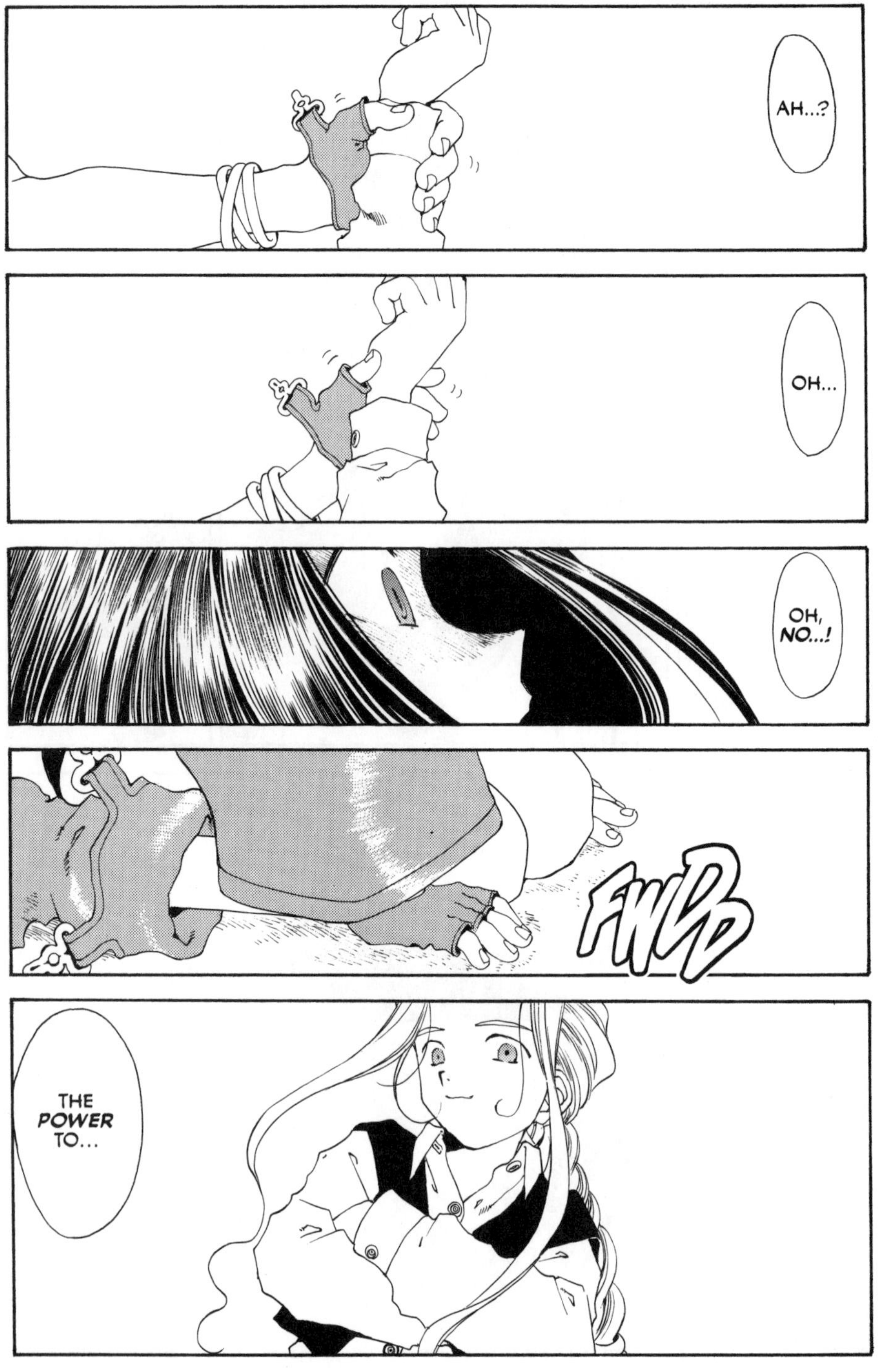
AH...?
OH...
OH, NO...!
FWUD
THE POWER TO...

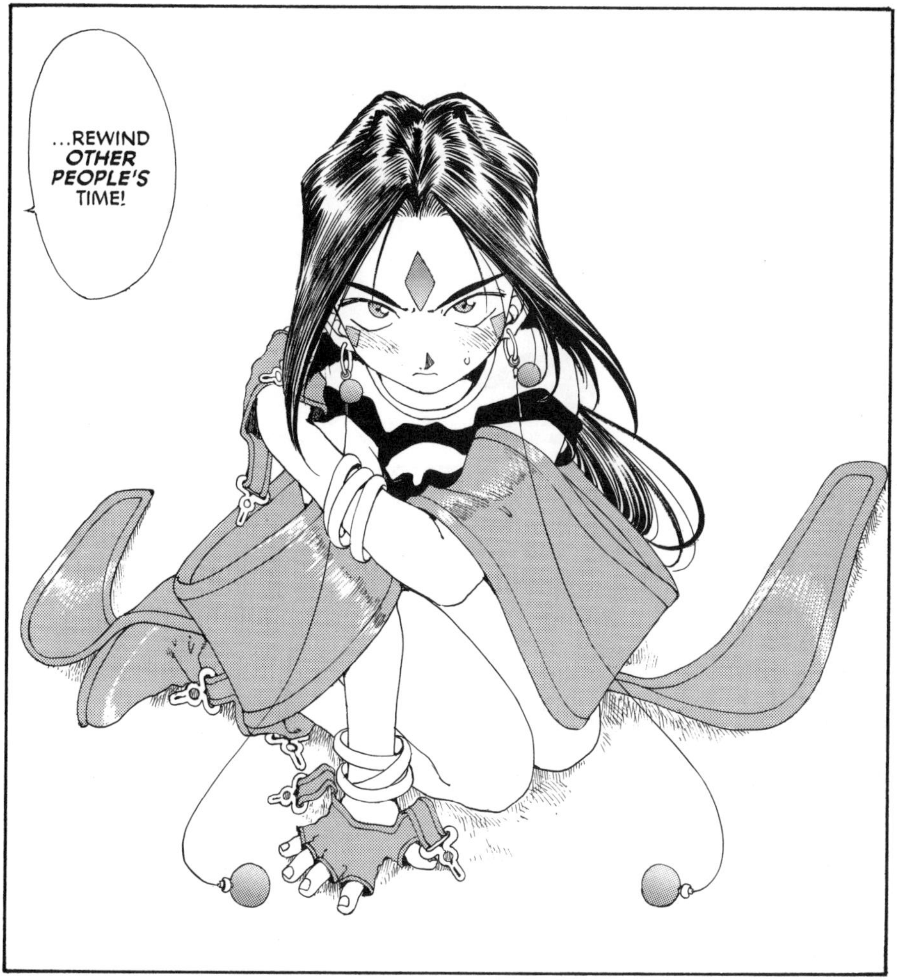
...REWIND OTHER PEOPLE'S TIME!

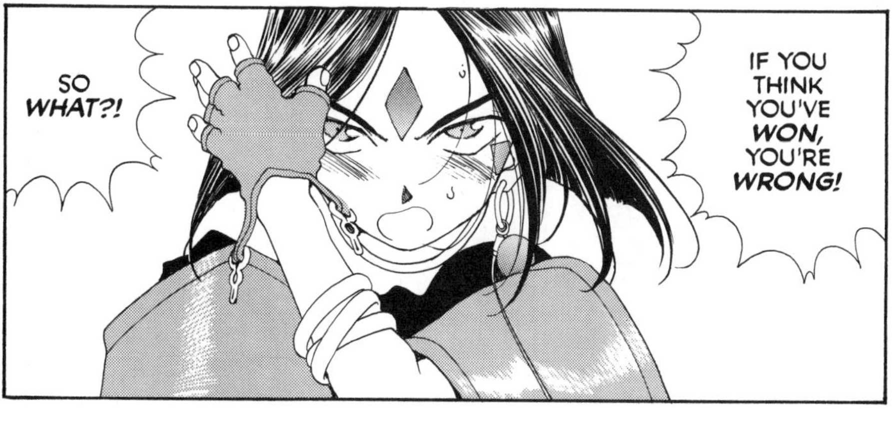
SO WHAT?!
IF YOU THINK YOU'VE WON, YOU'RE WRONG!

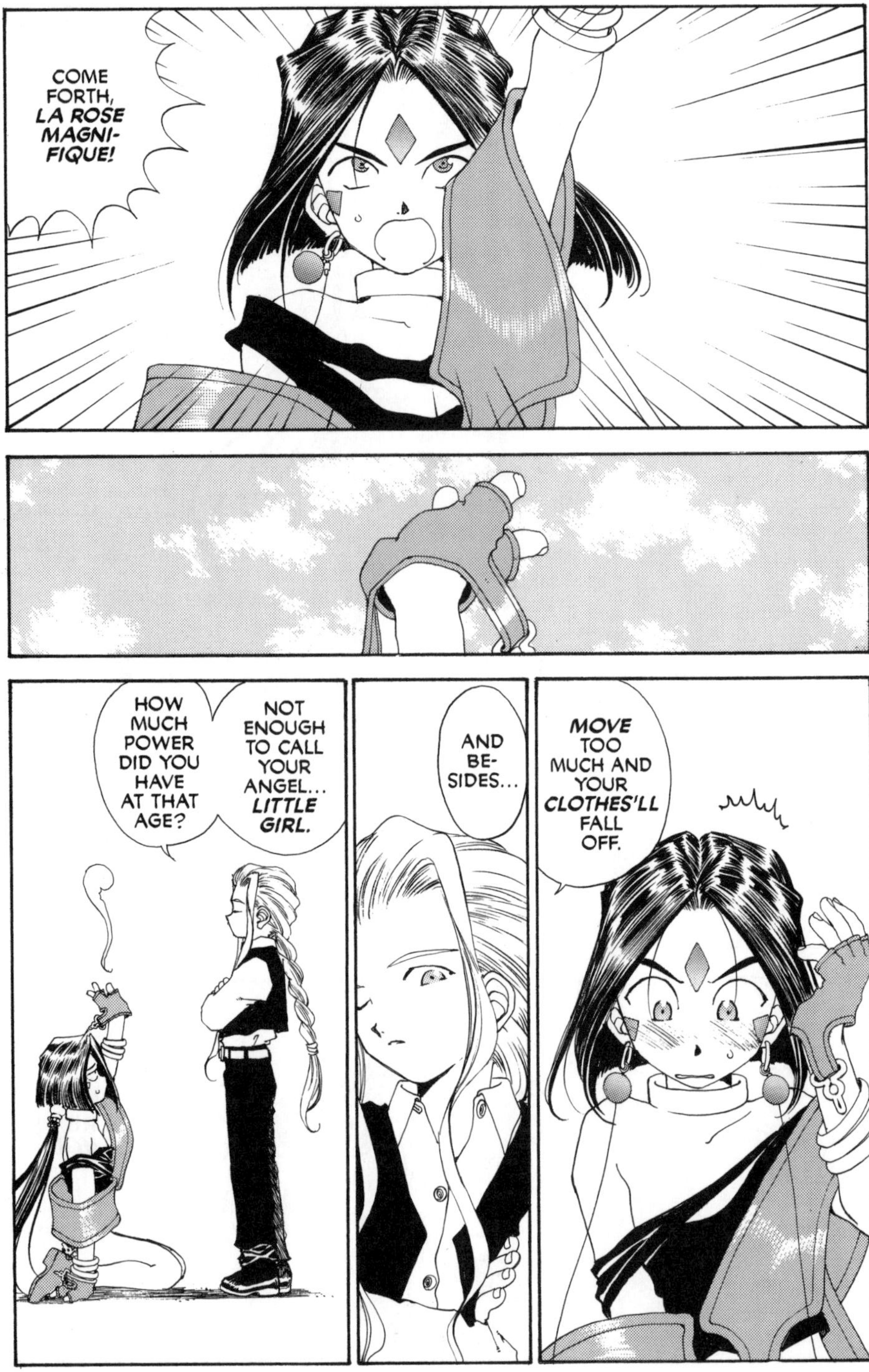
COME FORTH, LA ROSE MAGNI- FIQUE!
HOW MUCH POWER DID YOU HAVE AT THAT AGE?
NOT ENOUGH TO CALL YOUR ANGEL... LITTLE GIRL.
AND BE- SIDES...
MOVE TOO MUCH AND YOUR CLOTHES'LL FALL OFF.

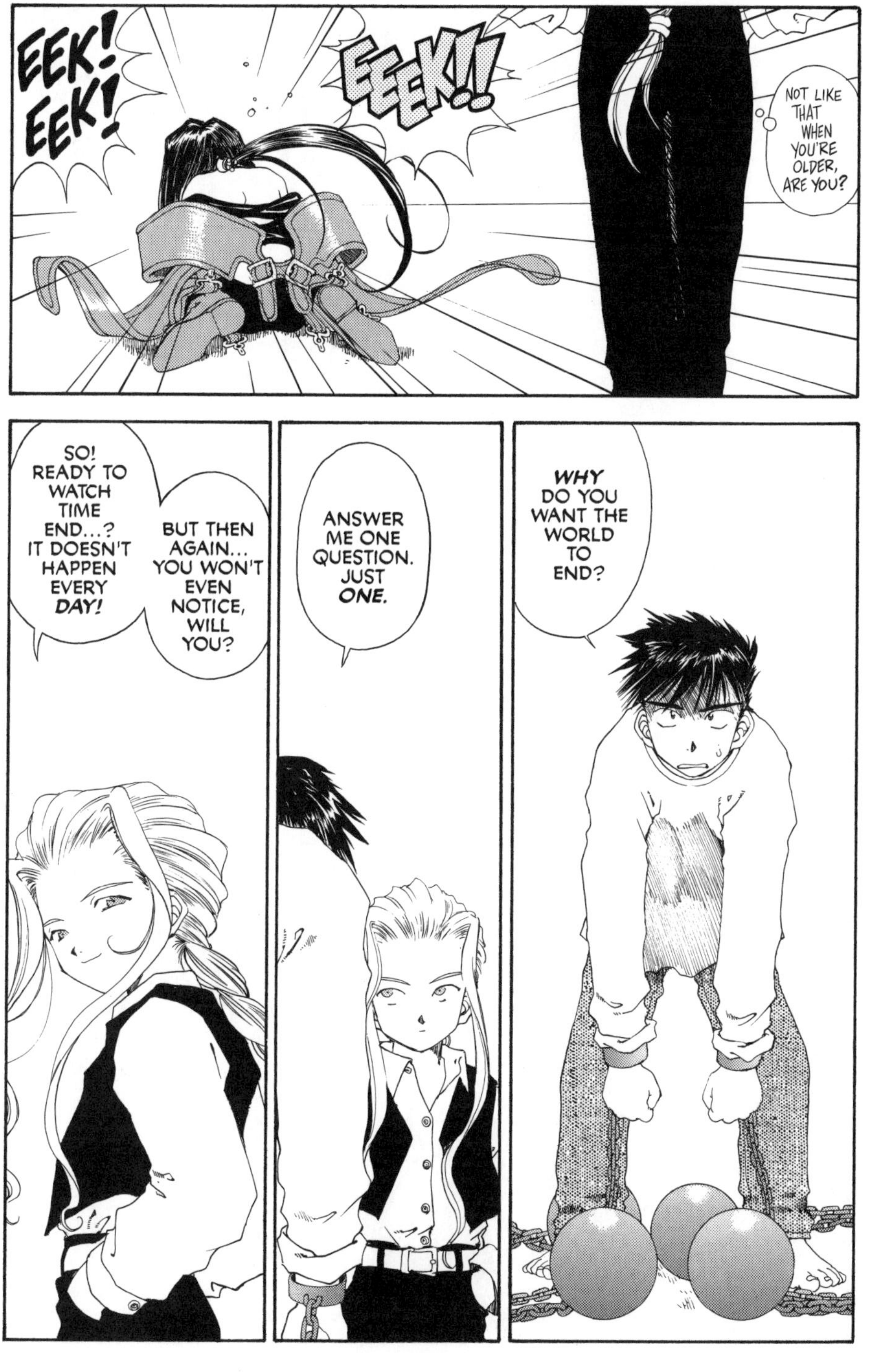
EEK! EEK!
EEEK!!
NOT LIKE THAT WHEN YOU'RE OLDER, ARE YOU?
SO! READY TO WATCH TIME END...? IT DOESN'T HAPPEN EVERY *DAY!*
BUT THEN AGAIN... YOU WON'T EVEN NOTICE, WILL YOU?
ANSWER ME ONE QUESTION. JUST *ONE.*
WHY DO YOU WANT THE WORLD TO END?

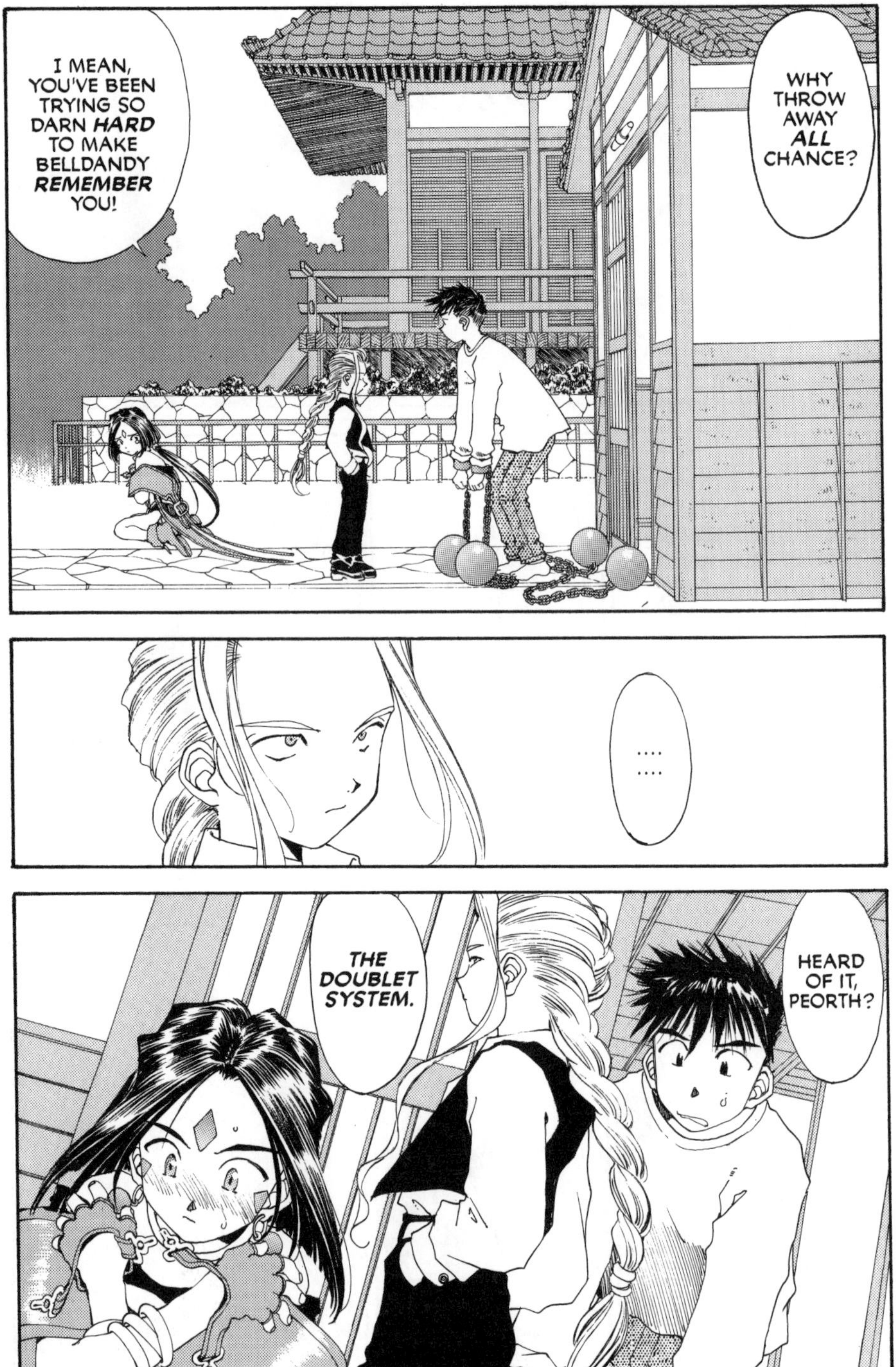
I MEAN, YOU'VE BEEN TRYING SO DARN HARD TO MAKE BELLDANDY REMEMBER YOU!
WHY THROW AWAY ALL CHANCE?
....
....
THE DOUBLET SYSTEM.
HEARD OF IT, PEORTH?

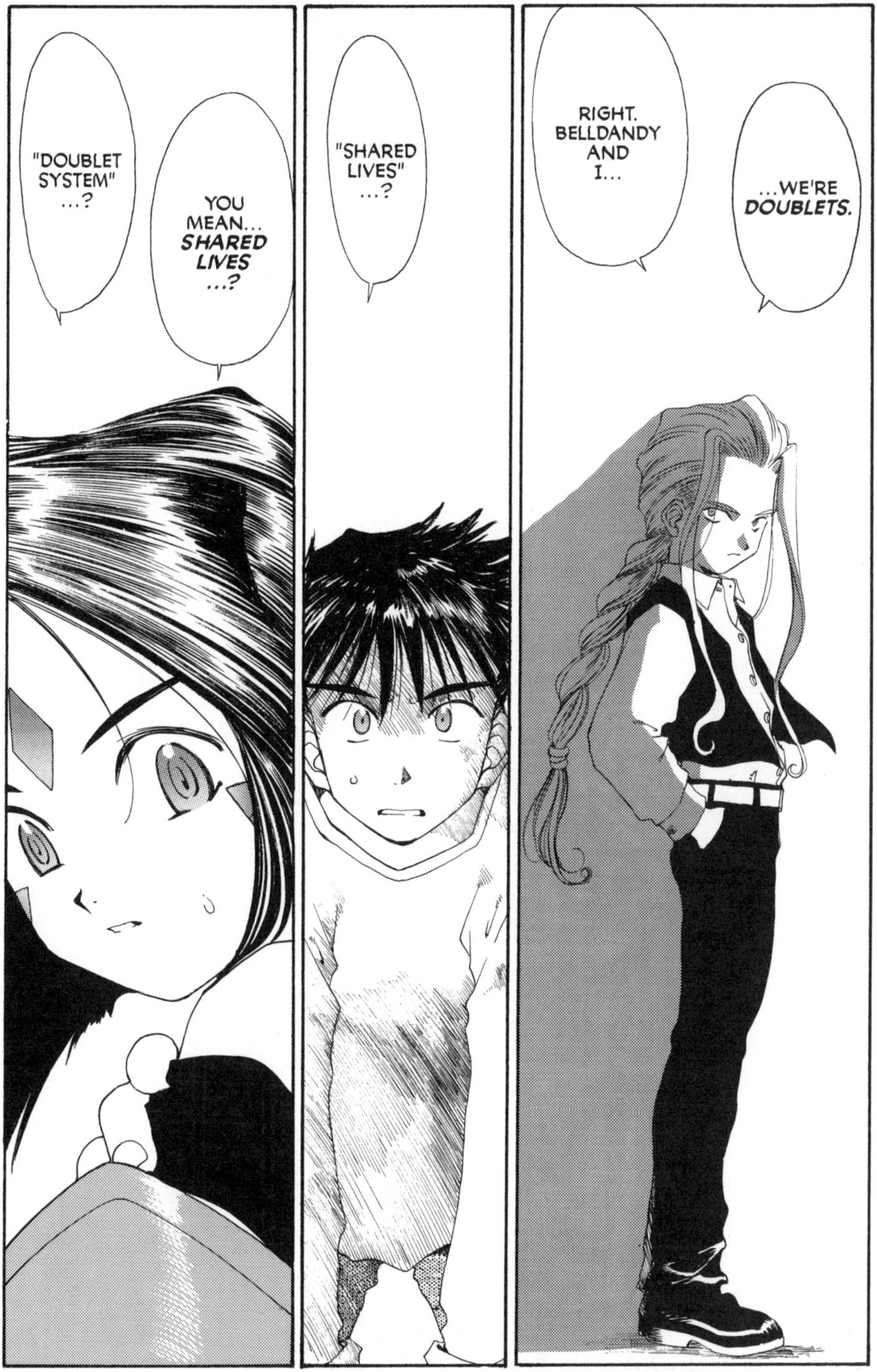
"DOUBLET SYSTEM" ...?
YOU MEAN... *SHARED LIVES* ...?
"SHARED LIVES" ...?
RIGHT. BELLDANDY AND I...
...WE'RE *DOUBLETS.*

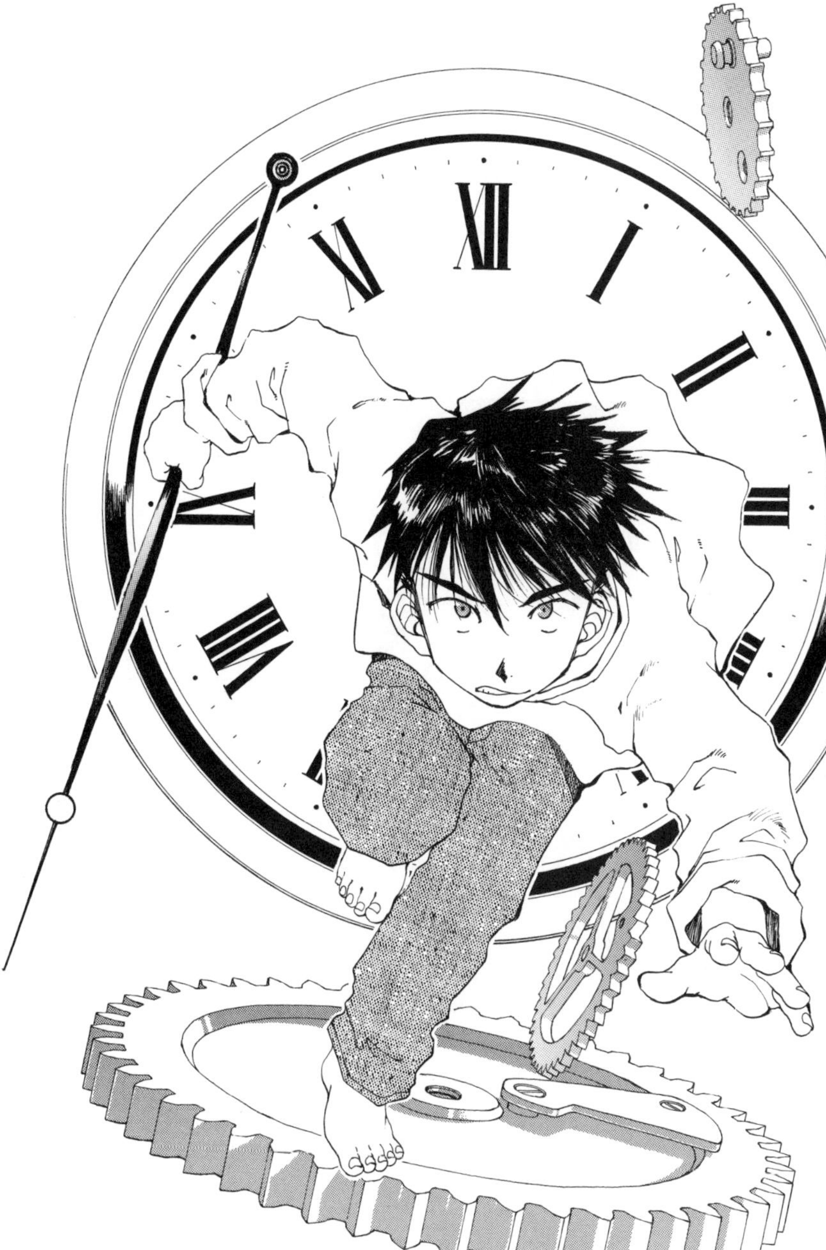

THE TROUBLE WITH DOUBLETS

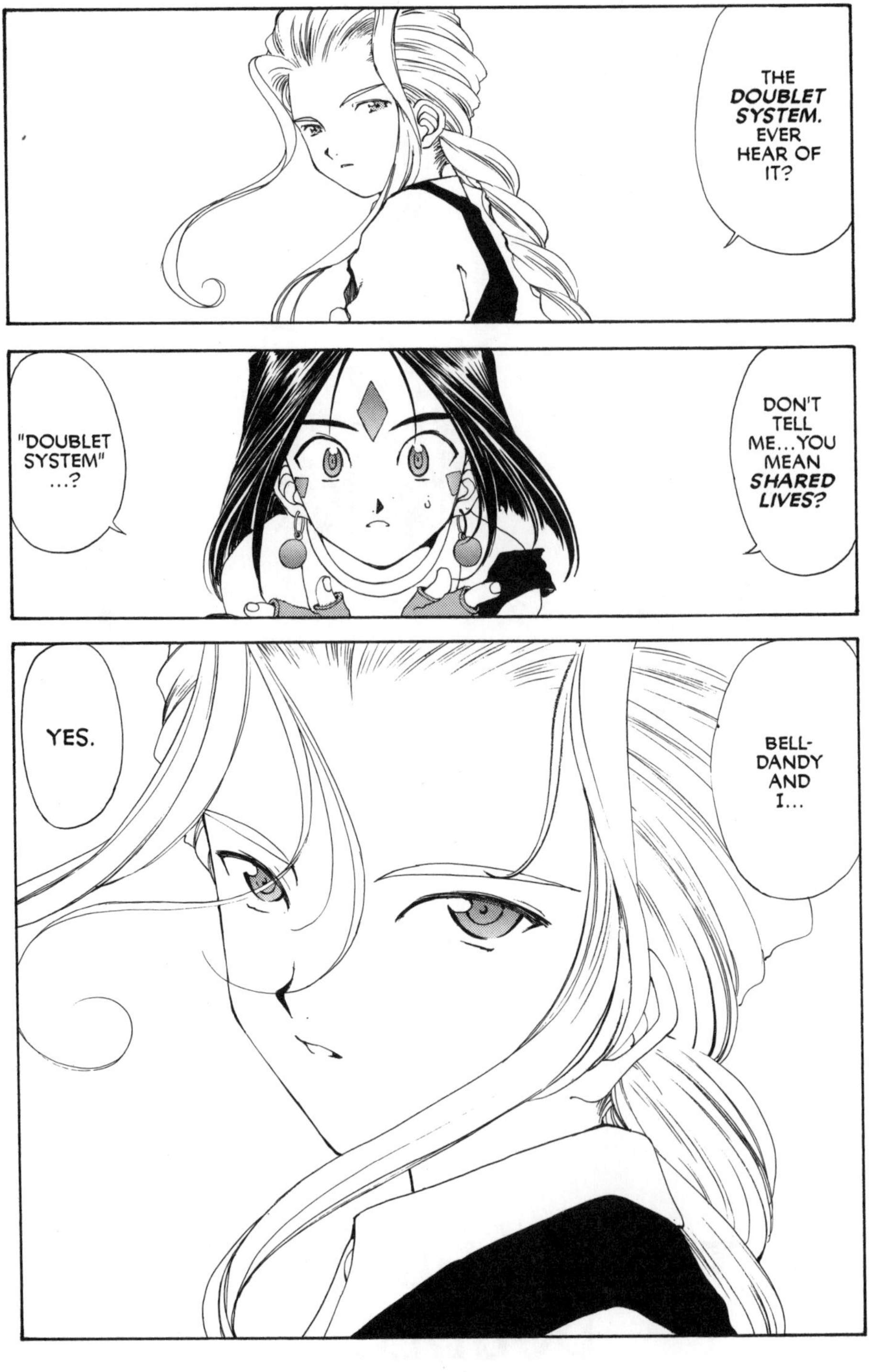
THE DOUBLET SYSTEM. EVER HEAR OF IT?
"DOUBLET SYSTEM" ...?
DON'T TELL ME...YOU MEAN SHARED LIVES?
YES.
BELL-DANDY AND I...

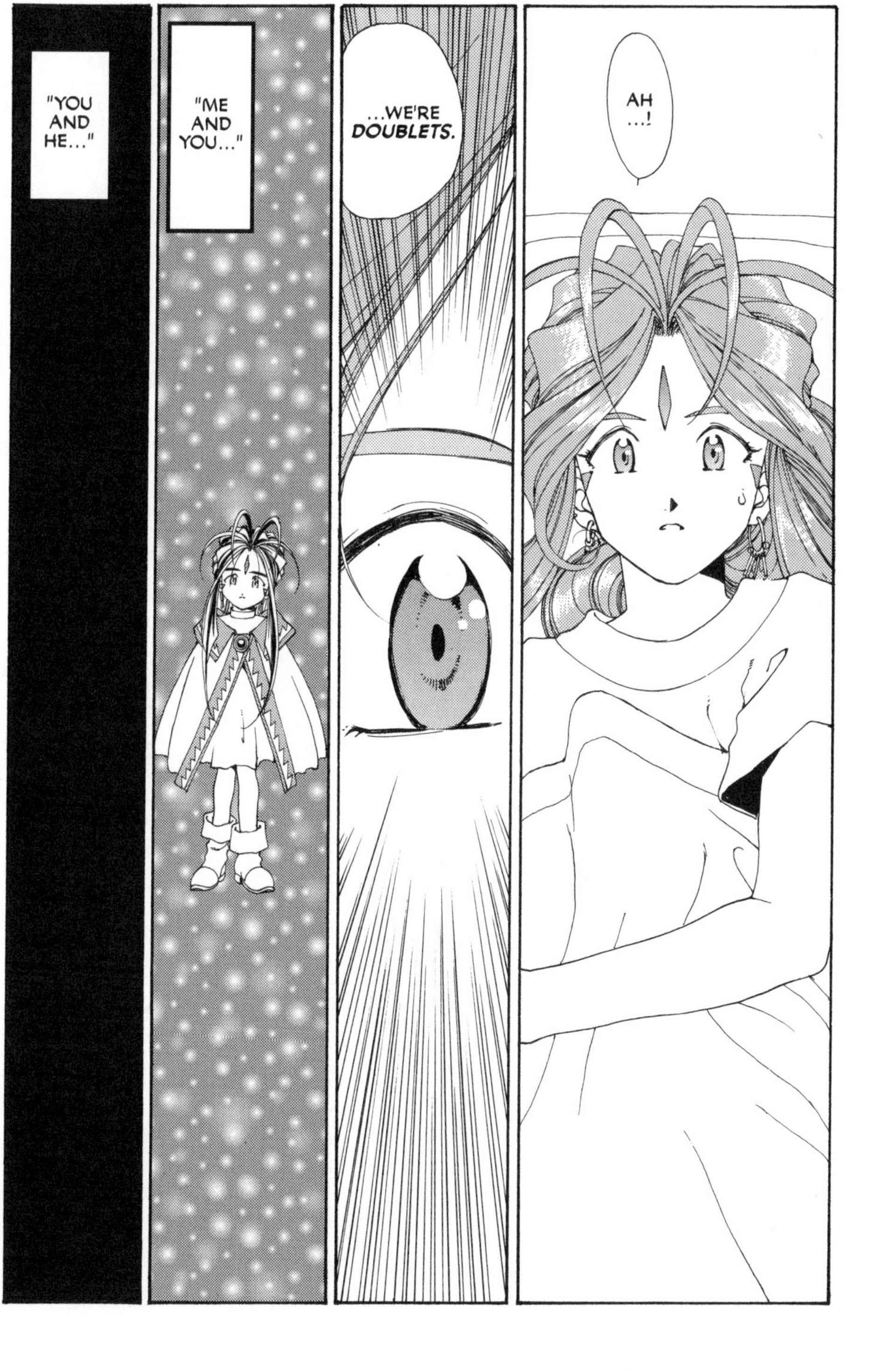
"YOU AND HE..."
"ME AND YOU..."
...WE'RE *DOUBLETS.*
AH ...!

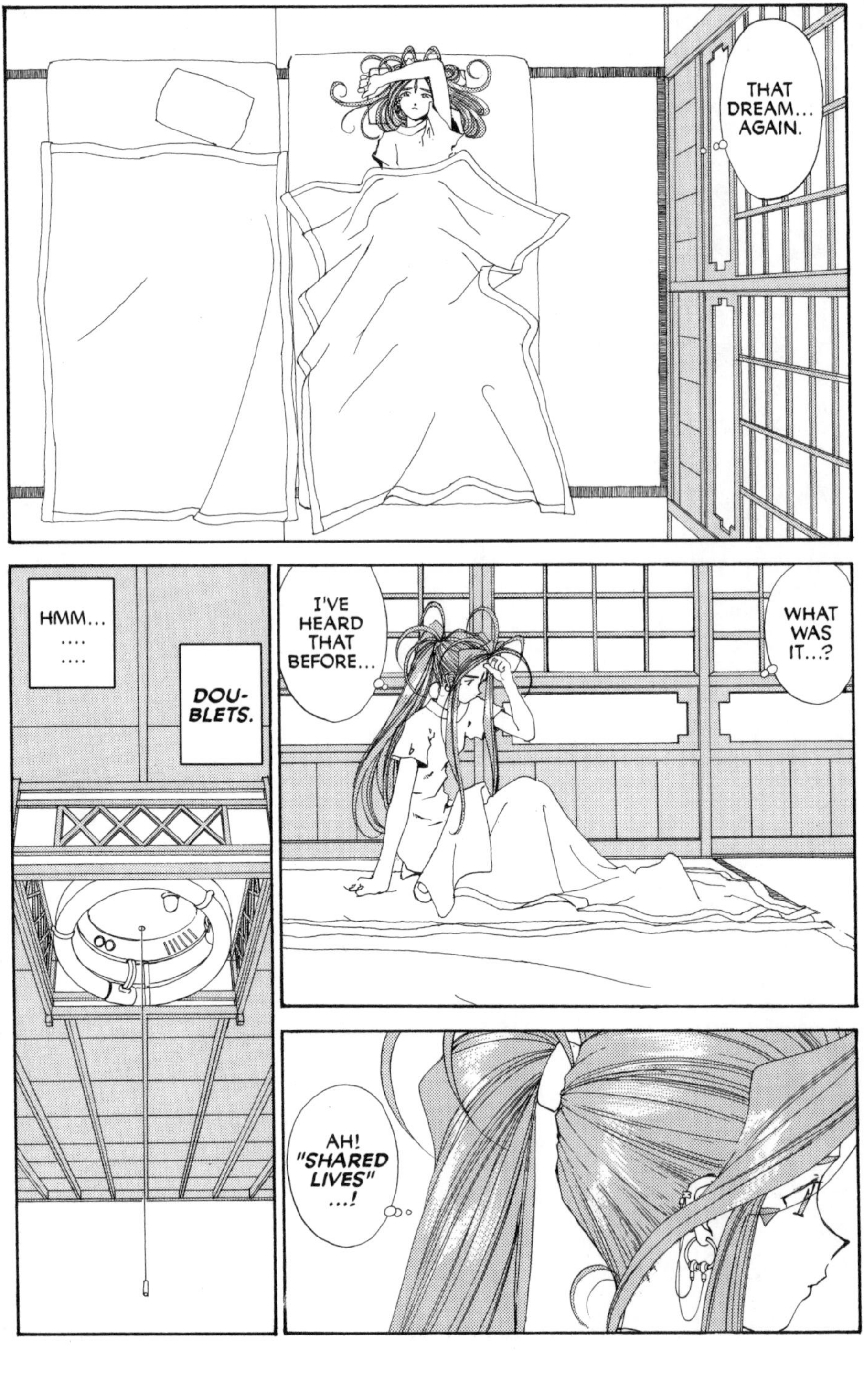
THAT DREAM... AGAIN.
HMM... ....
DOU-BLETS.
I'VE HEARD THAT BEFORE...
WHAT WAS IT...?
AH! "SHARED LIVES" ...!

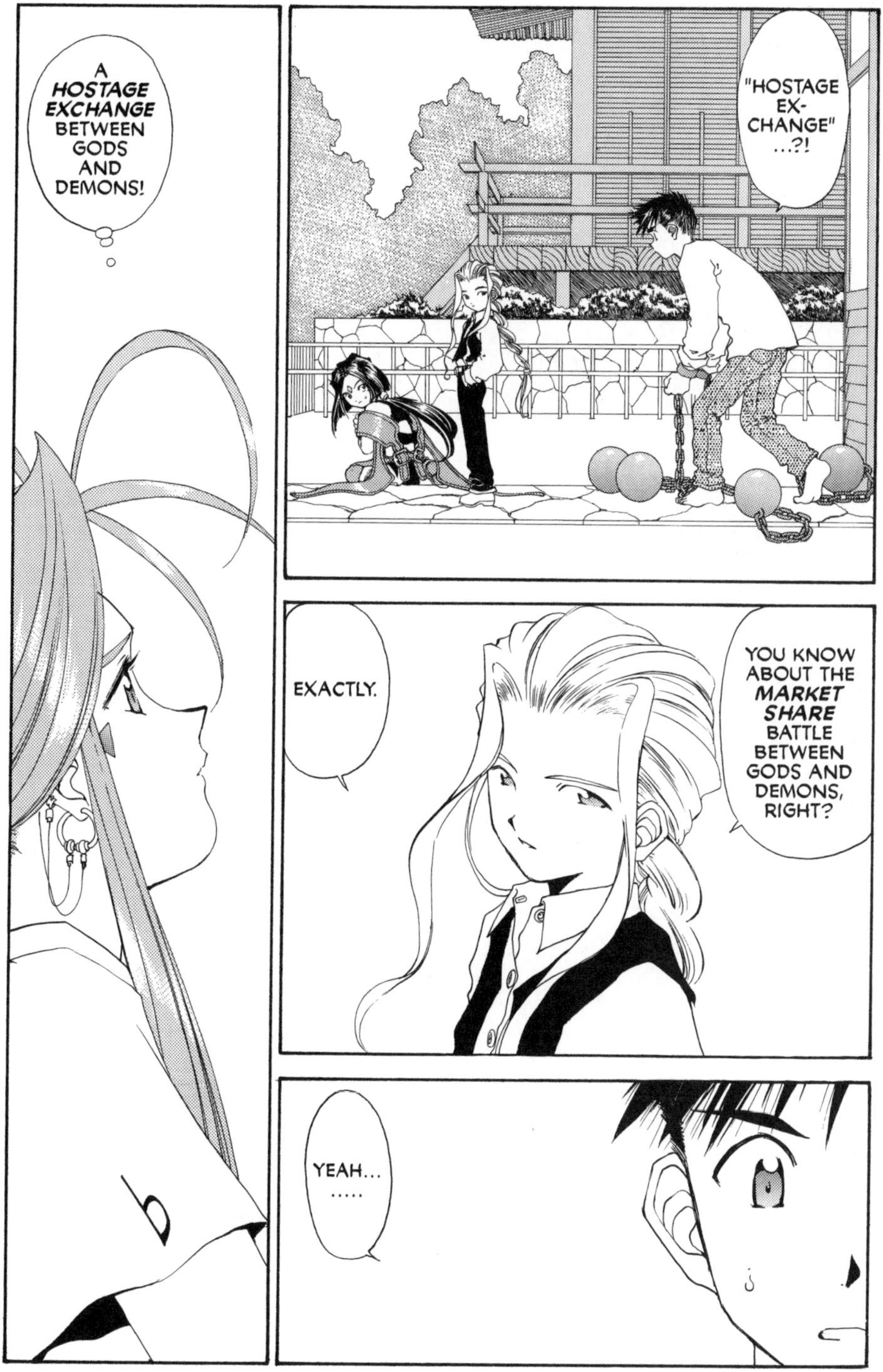
A *HOSTAGE EXCHANGE* BETWEEN GODS AND DEMONS!
"HOSTAGE EX-CHANGE" ...?!
EXACTLY.
YOU KNOW ABOUT THE *MARKET SHARE* BATTLE BETWEEN GODS AND DEMONS, RIGHT?
YEAH... .....

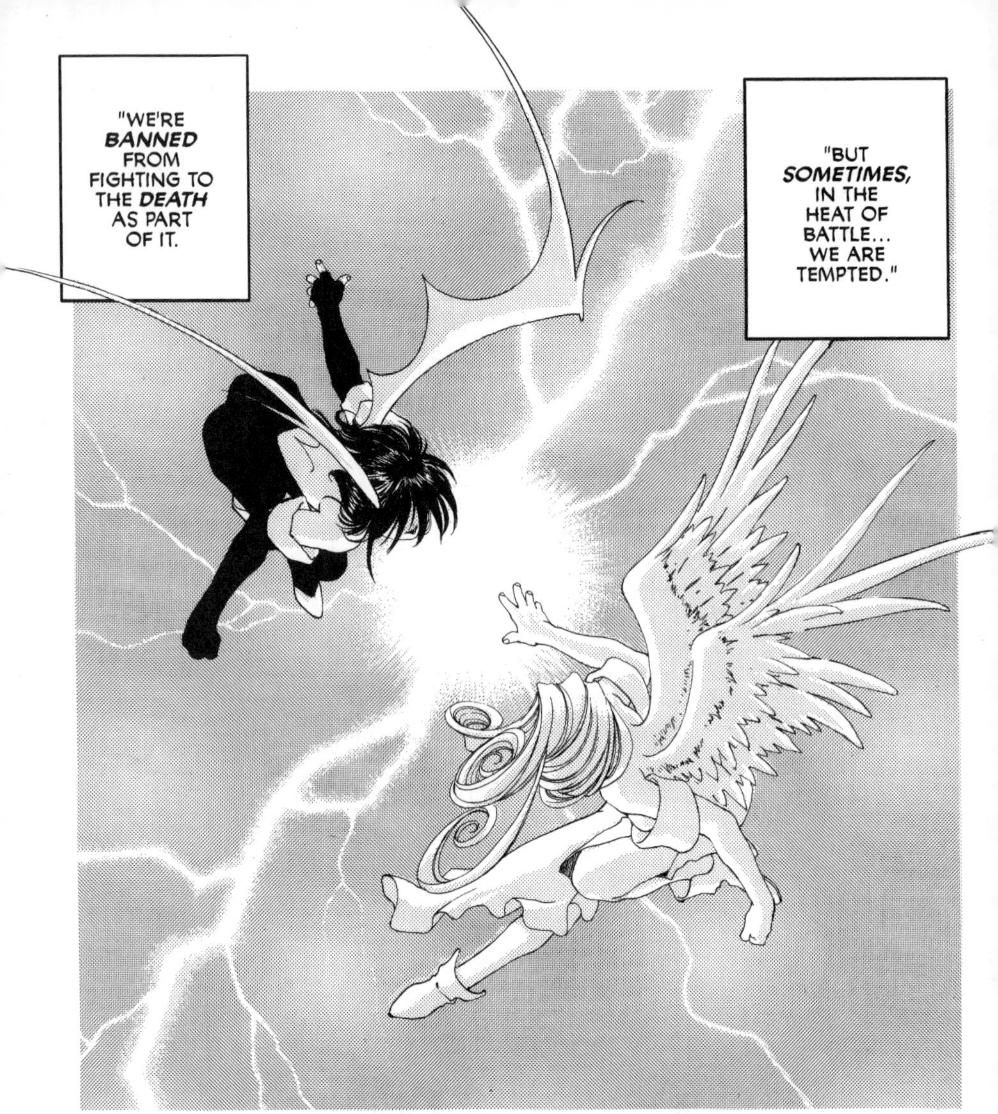
"WE'RE *BANNED* FROM FIGHTING TO THE *DEATH* AS PART OF IT.
"BUT *SOMETIMES,* IN THE HEAT OF BATTLE... WE ARE TEMPTED."
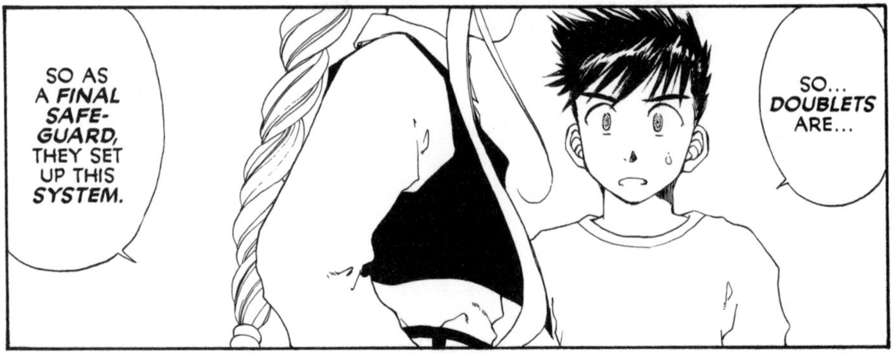
SO AS A *FINAL SAFE-GUARD,* THEY SET UP THIS *SYSTEM.*
SO... *DOUBLETS* ARE...

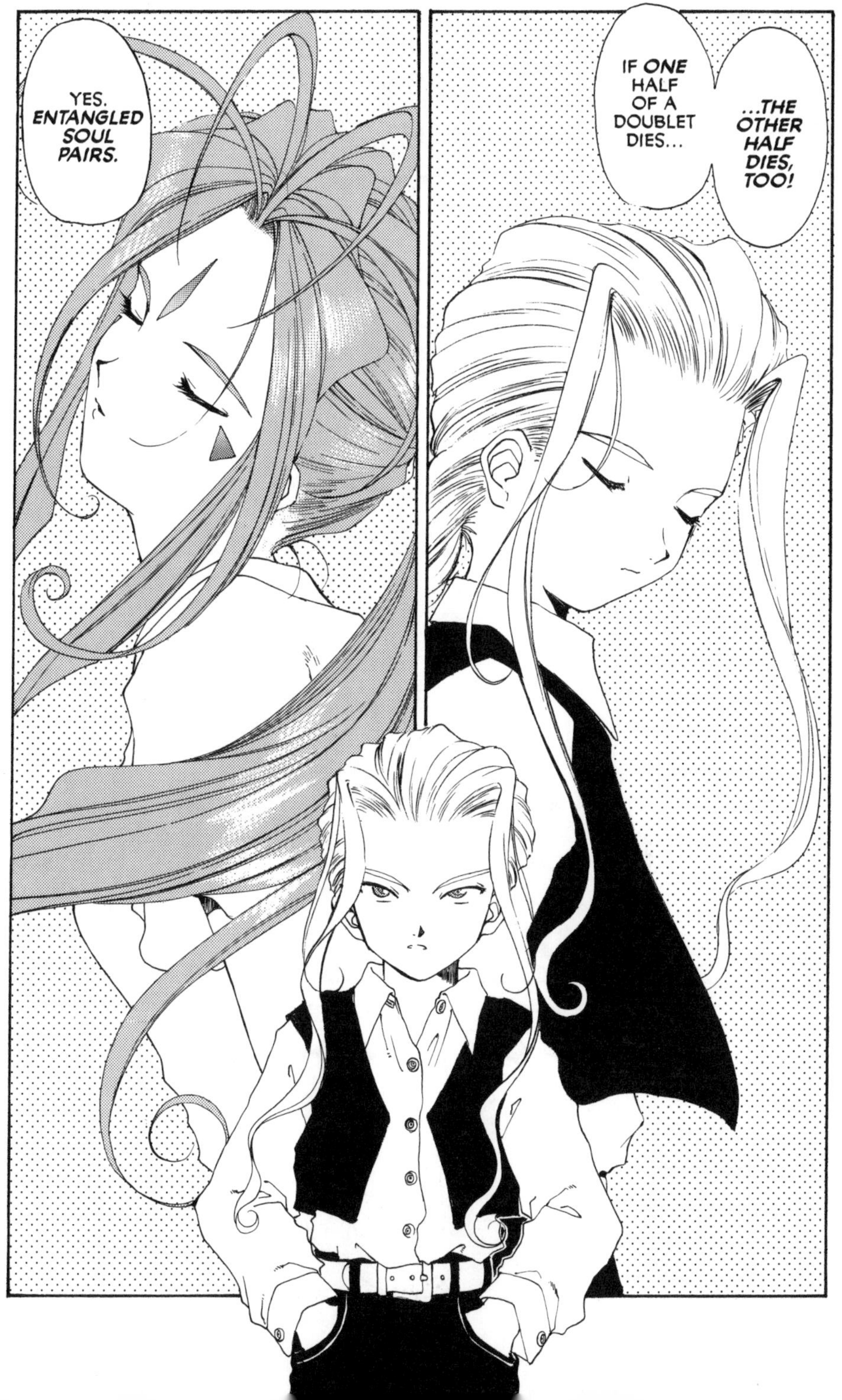
YES. ENTANGLED SOUL PAIRS.
IF ONE HALF OF A DOUBLET DIES...
...THE OTHER HALF DIES, TOO!

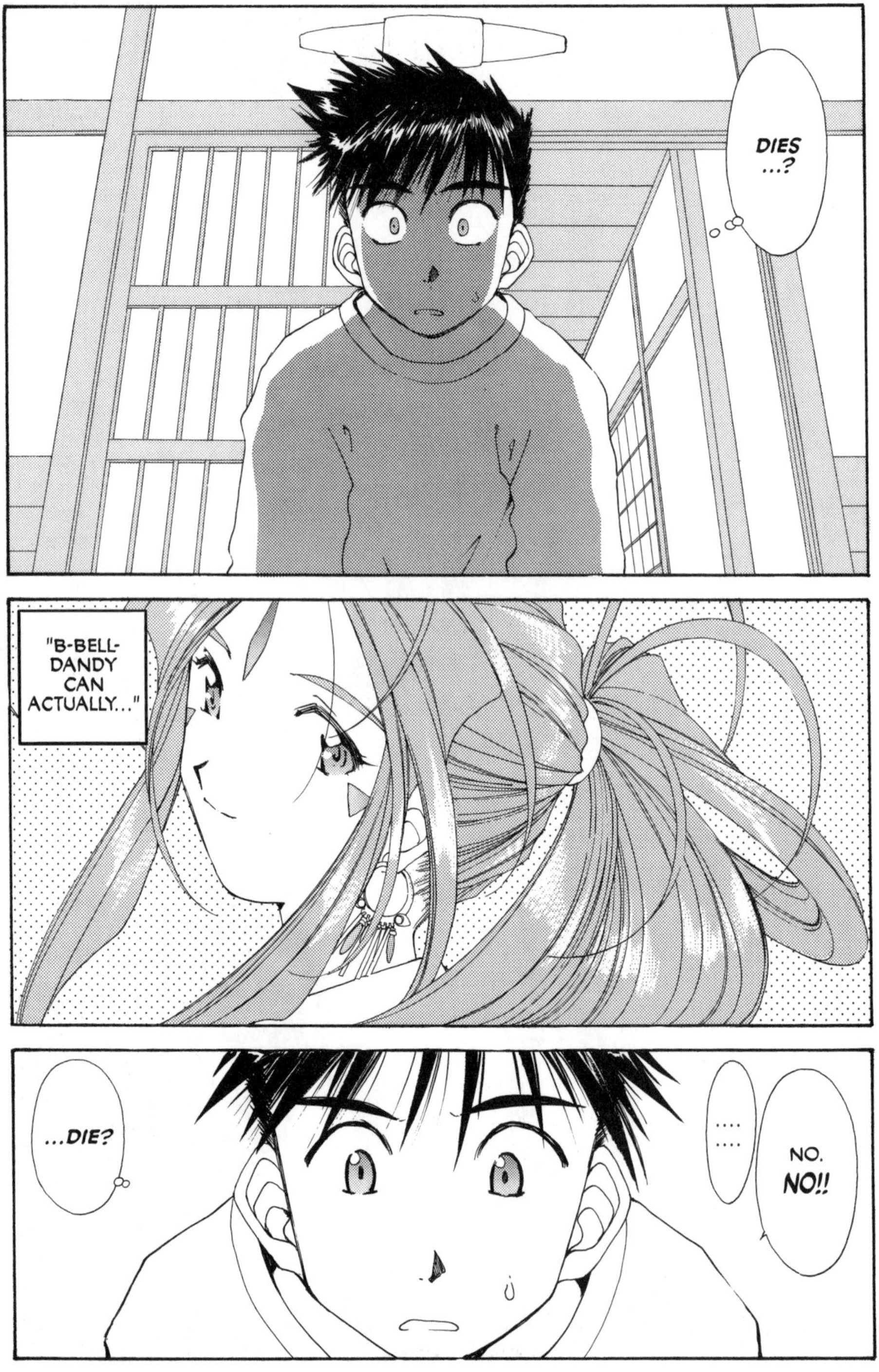
DIES ...?
"B-BELL-DANDY CAN ACTUALLY..."
...DIE?
....
NO. NO!!

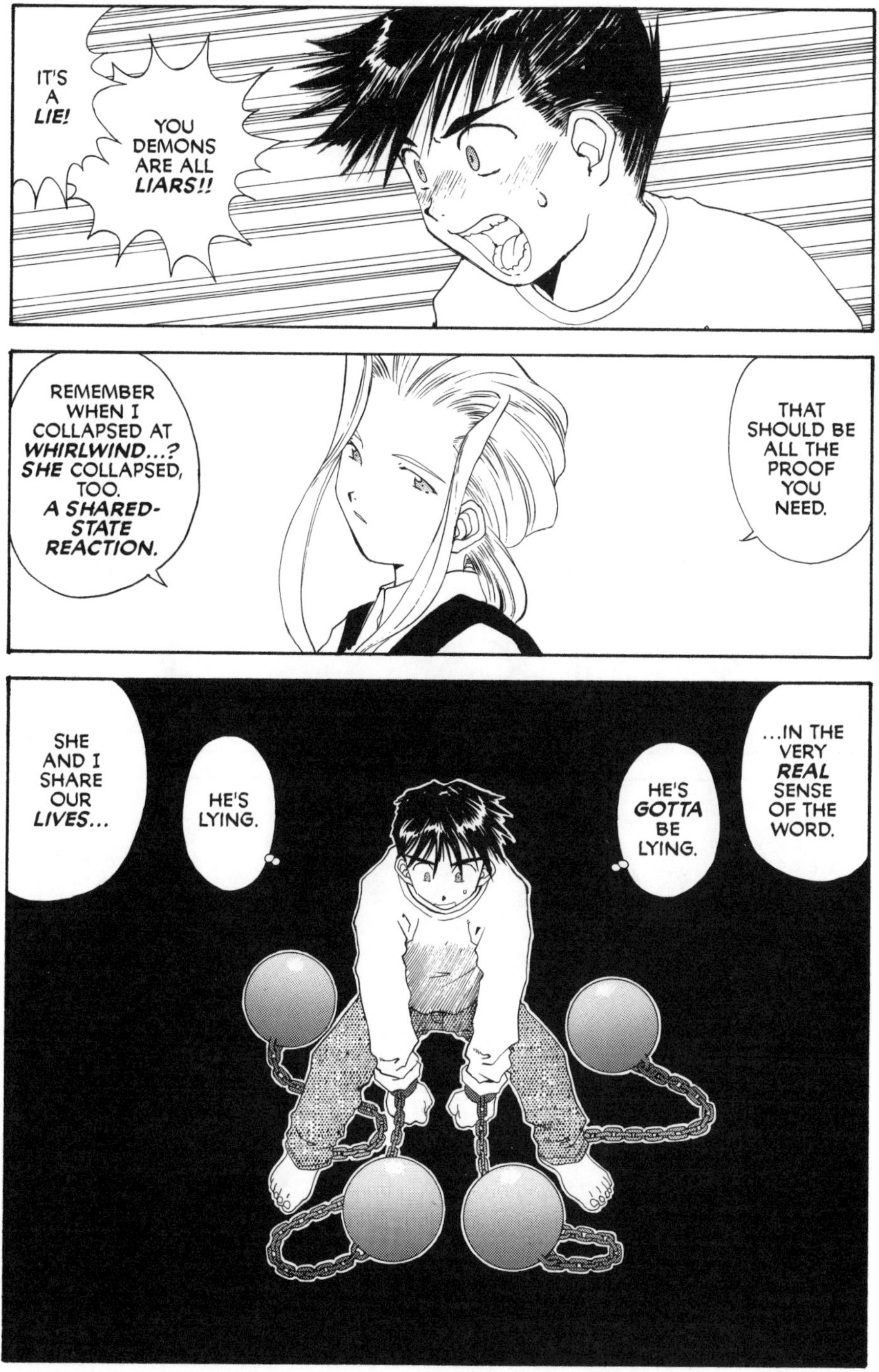
IT'S A LIE!
YOU DEMONS ARE ALL LIARS!!
REMEMBER WHEN I COLLAPSED AT WHIRLWIND...? SHE COLLAPSED, TOO. A SHARED-STATE REACTION.
THAT SHOULD BE ALL THE PROOF YOU NEED.
SHE AND I SHARE OUR LIVES...
HE'S LYING.
HE'S GOTTA BE LYING.
...IN THE VERY REAL SENSE OF THE WORD.

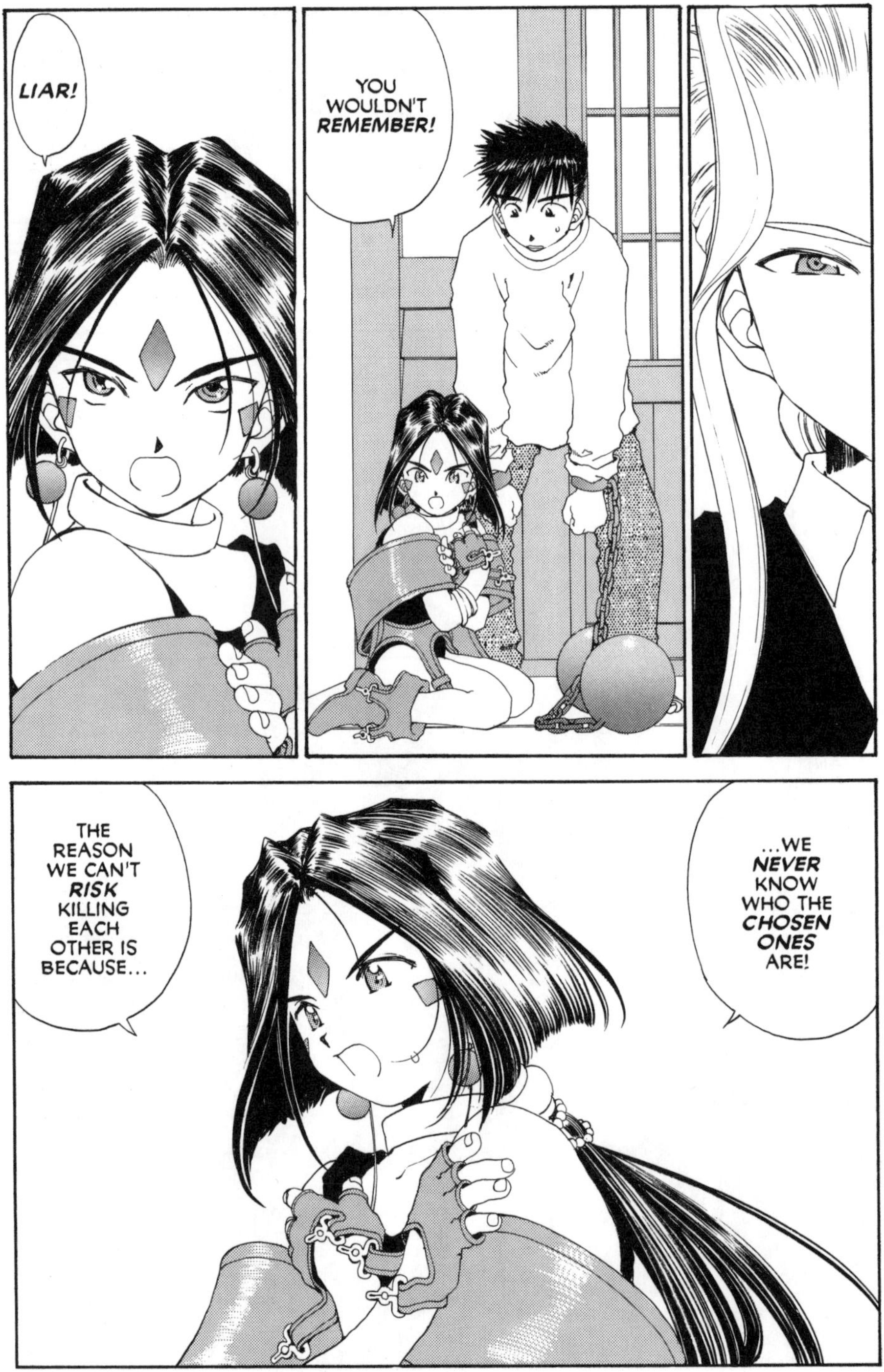
LIAR!
YOU WOULDN'T REMEMBER!
THE REASON WE CAN'T RISK KILLING EACH OTHER IS BECAUSE...
...WE NEVER KNOW WHO THE CHOSEN ONES ARE!

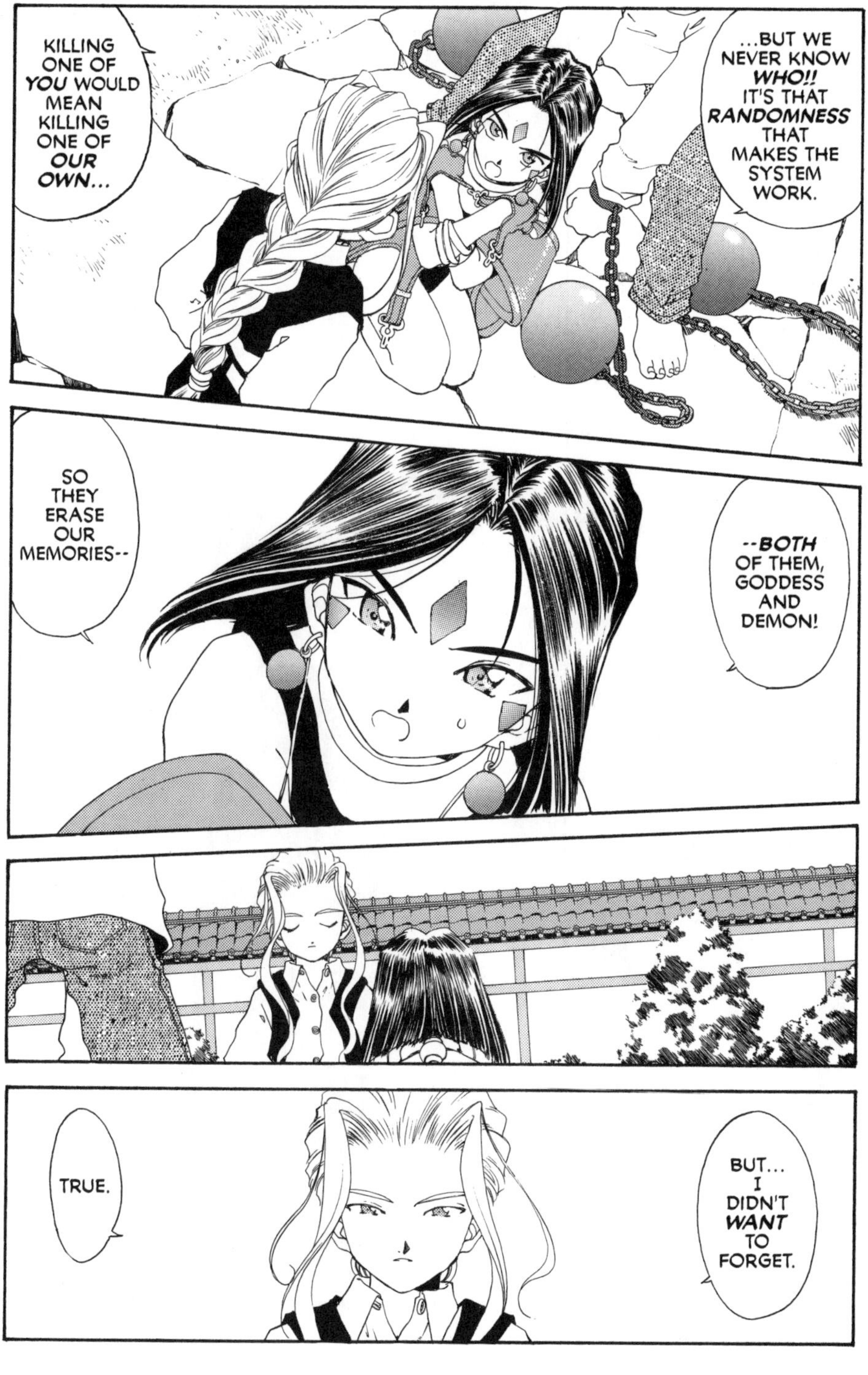
KILLING ONE OF *YOU* WOULD MEAN KILLING ONE OF *OUR OWN*...
...BUT WE NEVER KNOW *WHO!!* IT'S THAT *RANDOMNESS* THAT MAKES THE SYSTEM WORK.
SO THEY ERASE OUR MEMORIES--
--*BOTH* OF THEM, GODDESS AND DEMON!
TRUE.
BUT... I DIDN'T *WANT* TO FORGET.

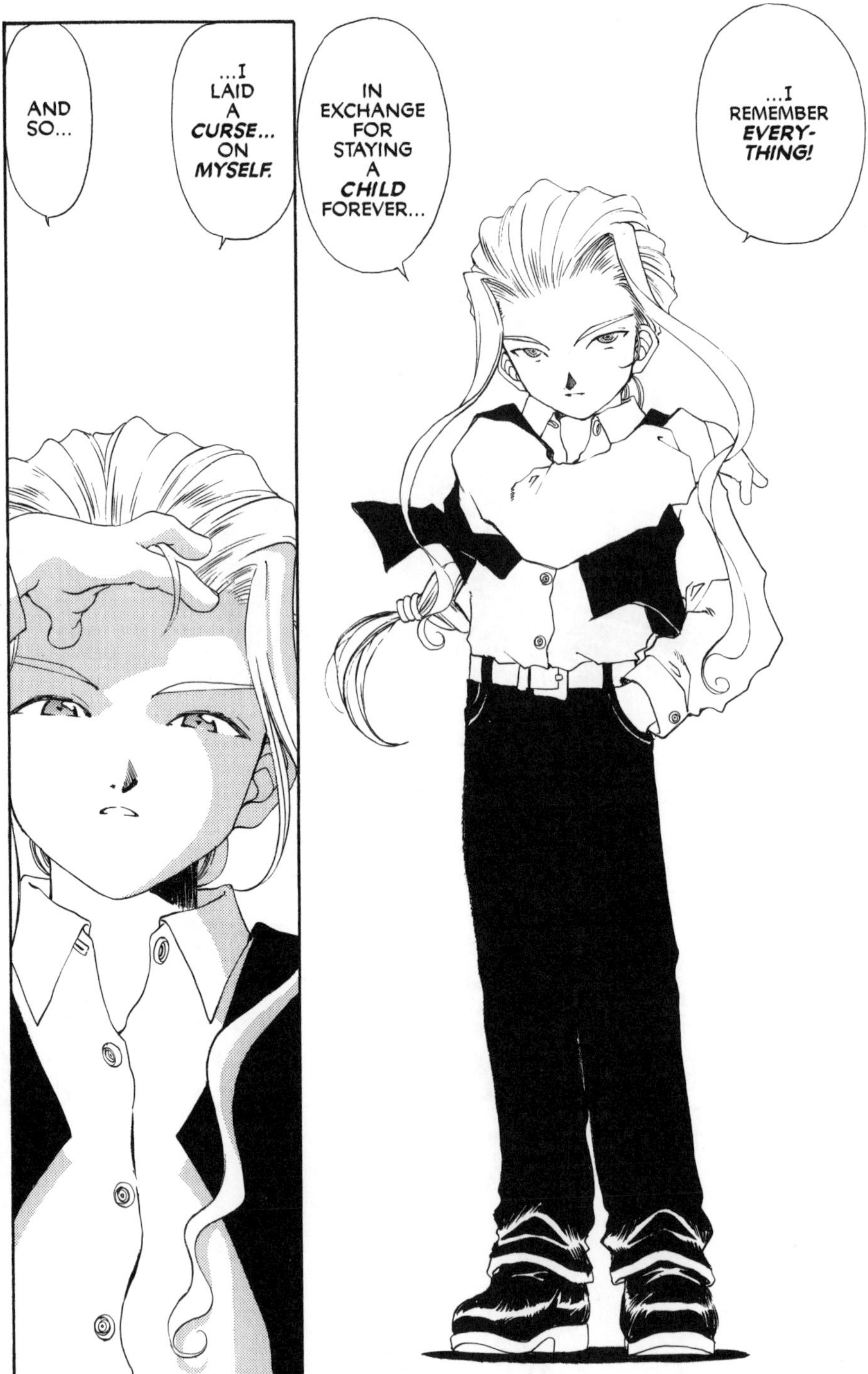
AND SO...
...I LAID A CURSE... ON MYSELF.
IN EXCHANGE FOR STAYING A CHILD FOREVER...
...I REMEMBER EVERYTHING!

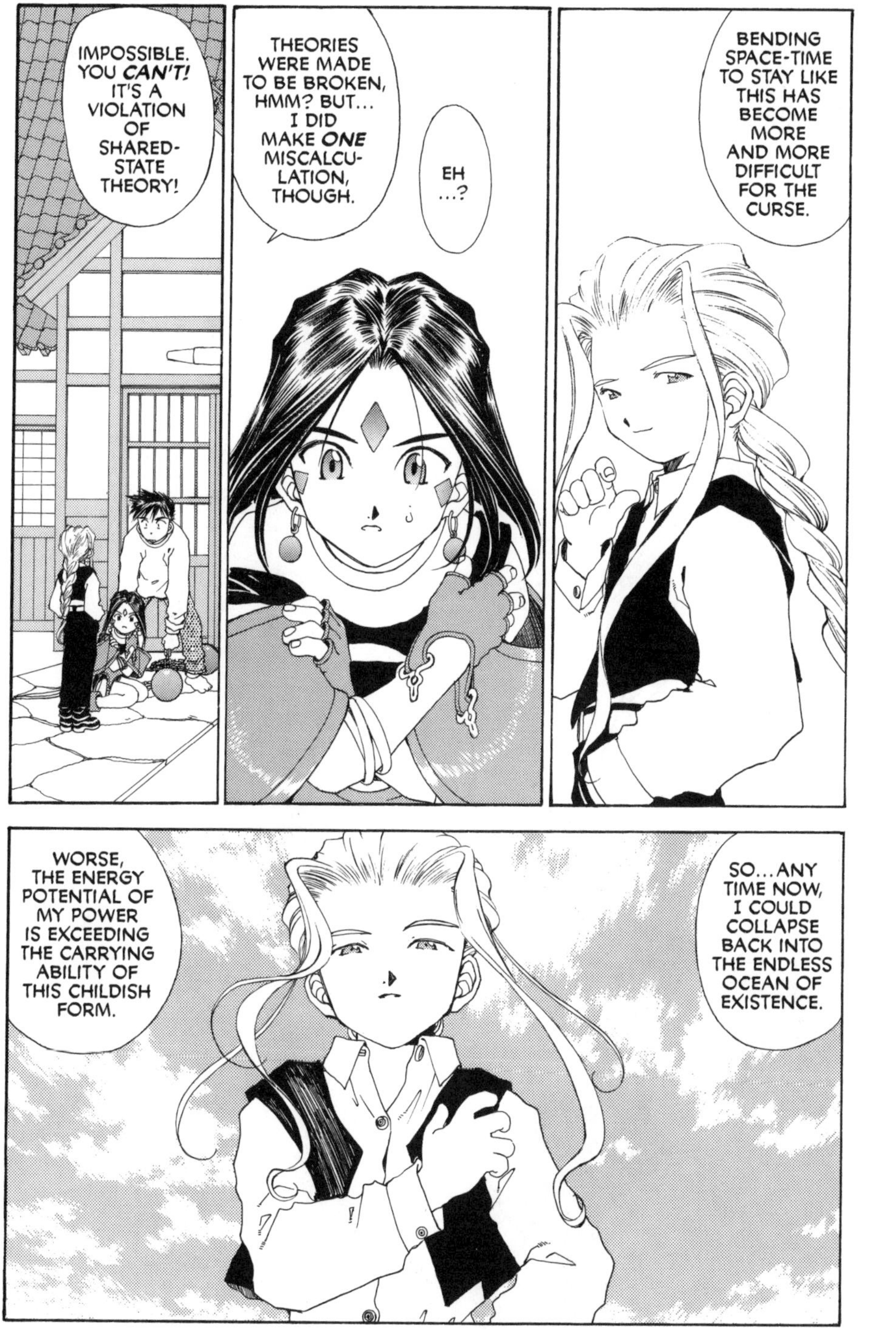
IMPOSSIBLE. YOU **CAN'T!** IT'S A VIOLATION OF SHARED-STATE THEORY!
THEORIES WERE MADE TO BE BROKEN, HMM? BUT... I DID MAKE **ONE** MISCALCULATION, THOUGH.
EH ...?
BENDING SPACE-TIME TO STAY LIKE THIS HAS BECOME MORE AND MORE DIFFICULT FOR THE CURSE.
WORSE, THE ENERGY POTENTIAL OF MY POWER IS EXCEEDING THE CARRYING ABILITY OF THIS CHILDISH FORM.
SO... ANY TIME NOW, I COULD COLLAPSE BACK INTO THE ENDLESS OCEAN OF EXISTENCE.

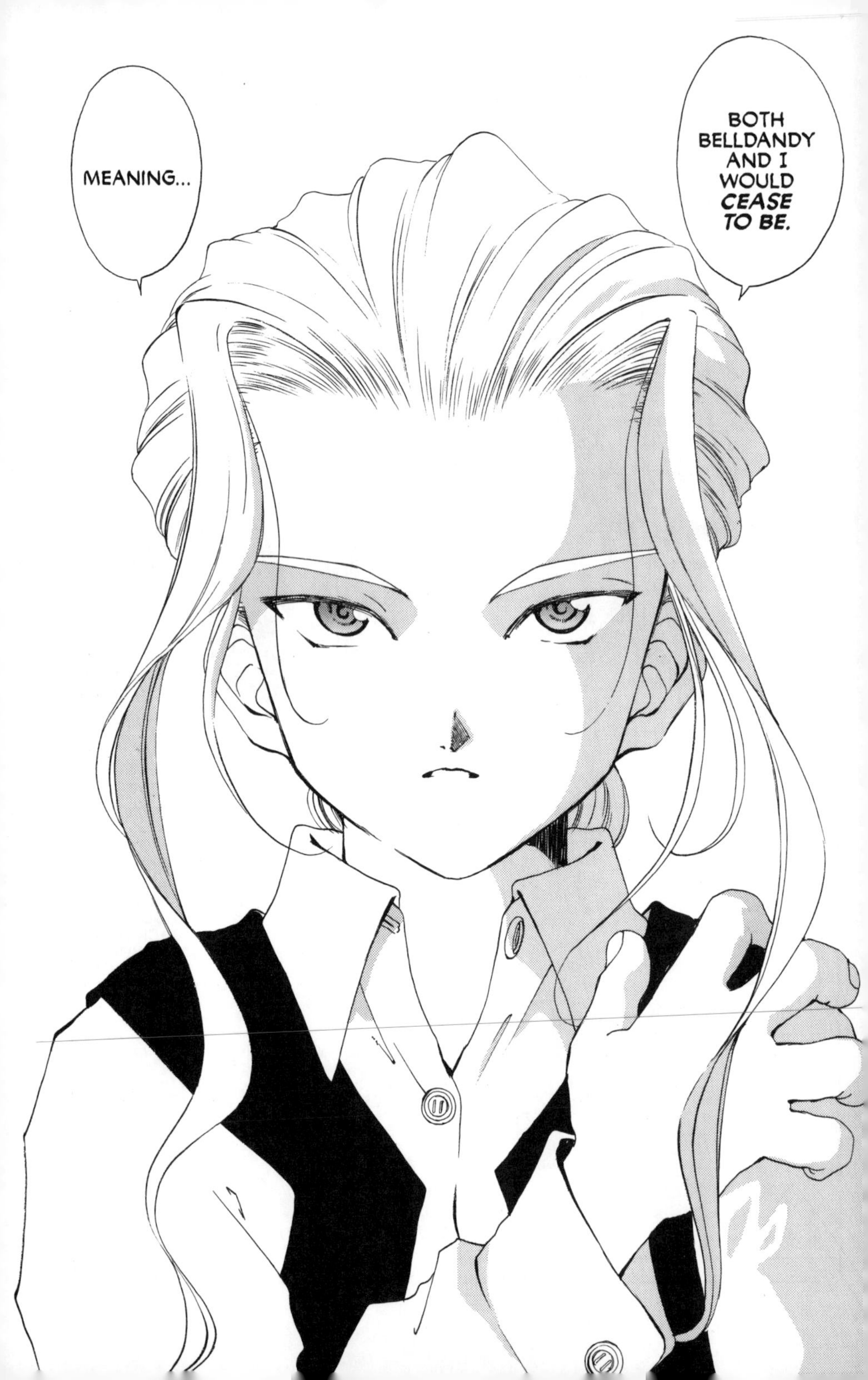
MEANING...
BOTH BELLDANDY AND I WOULD *CEASE TO BE.*

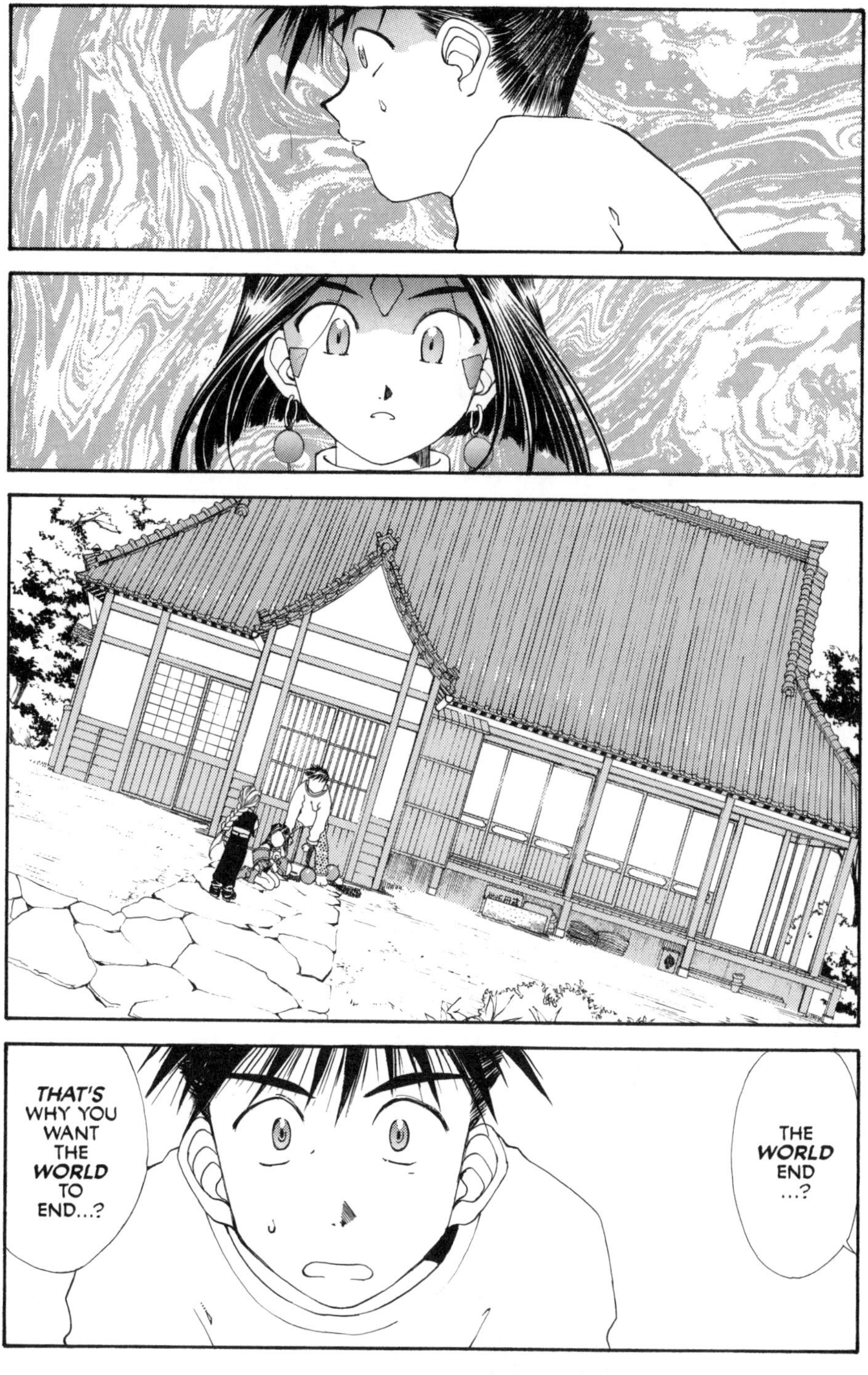
THAT'S WHY YOU WANT THE WORLD TO END...?
THE WORLD END ...?

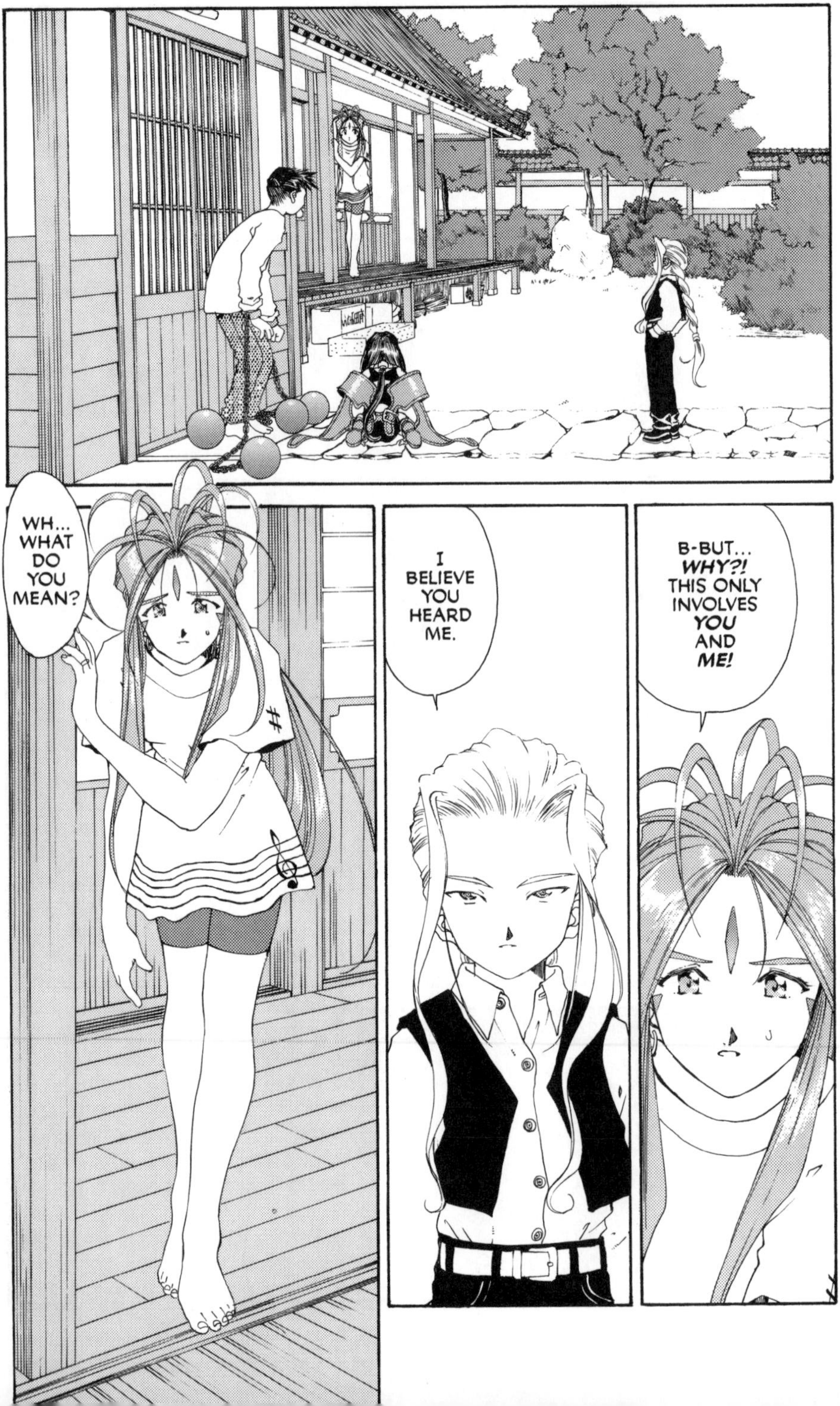
WH... WHAT DO YOU MEAN?
I BELIEVE YOU HEARD ME.
B-BUT... *WHY?!* THIS ONLY INVOLVES *YOU* AND *ME!*

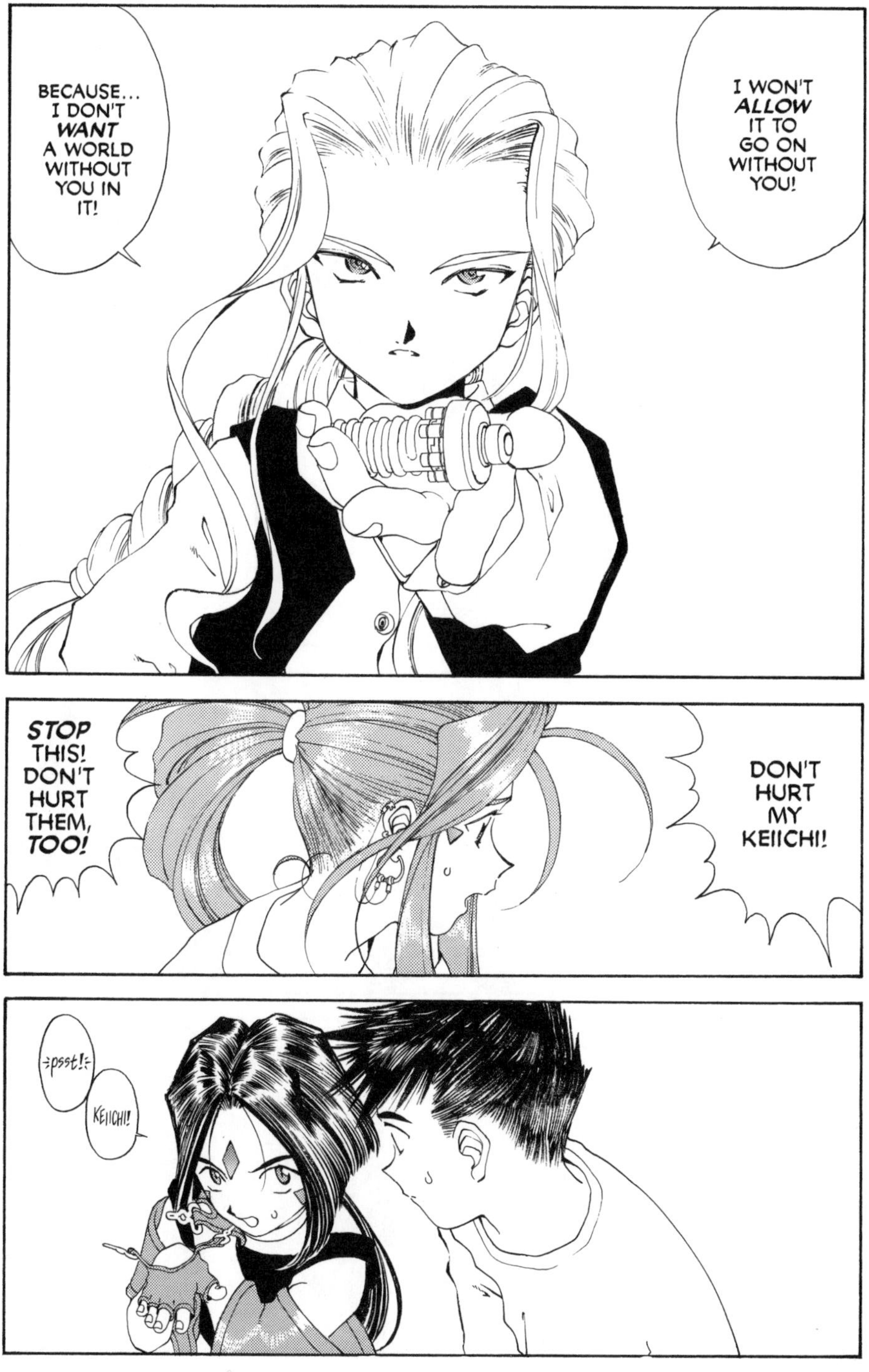
BECAUSE... I DON'T WANT A WORLD WITHOUT YOU IN IT!
I WON'T ALLOW IT TO GO ON WITHOUT YOU!
STOP THIS! DON'T HURT THEM, TOO!
DON'T HURT MY KEIICHI!
psst!
KEIICHI!

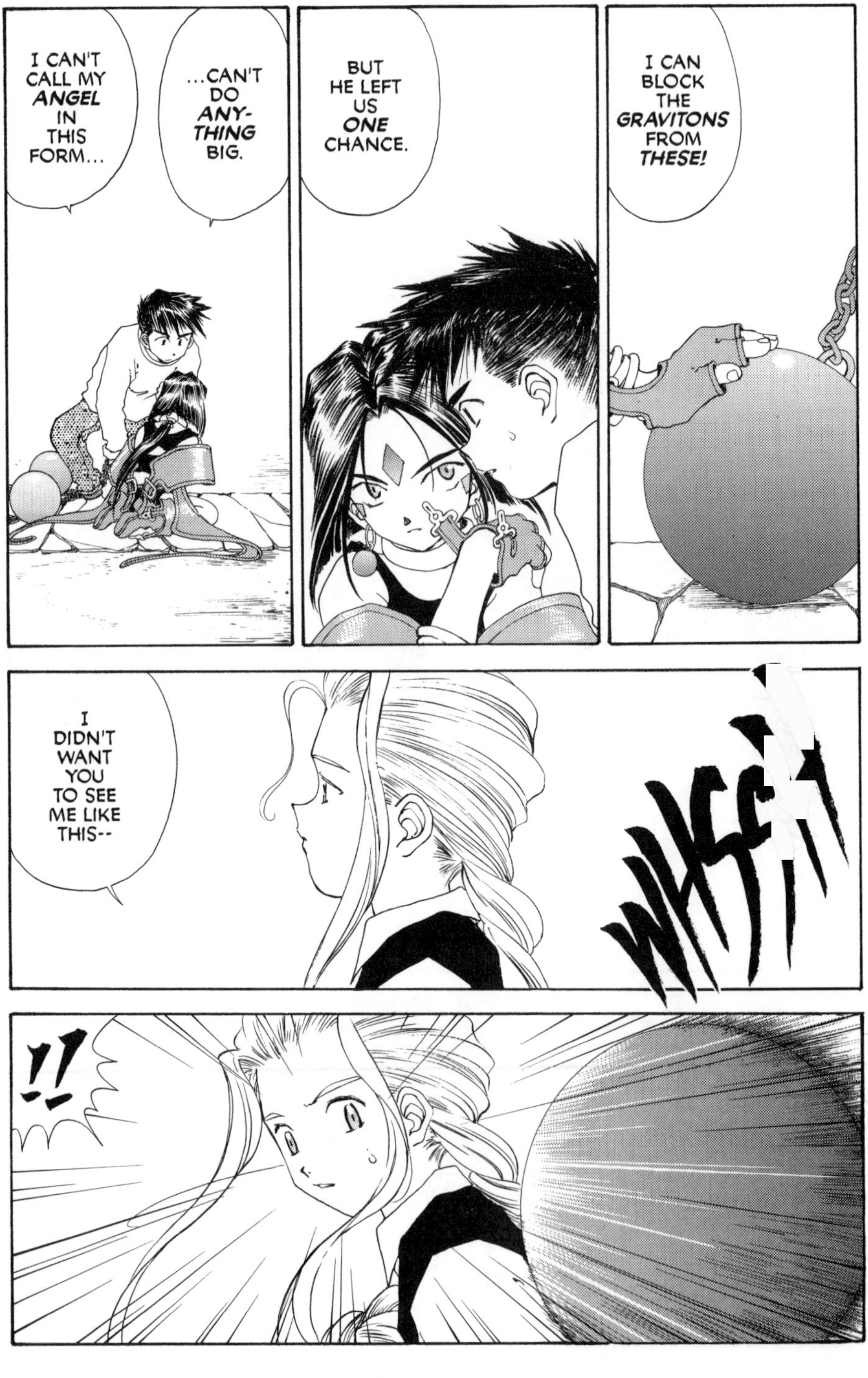
I CAN'T CALL MY ANGEL IN THIS FORM...
...CAN'T DO ANYTHING BIG.
BUT HE LEFT US ONE CHANCE.
I CAN BLOCK THE GRAVITONS FROM THESE!
I DIDN'T WANT YOU TO SEE ME LIKE THIS--
!!

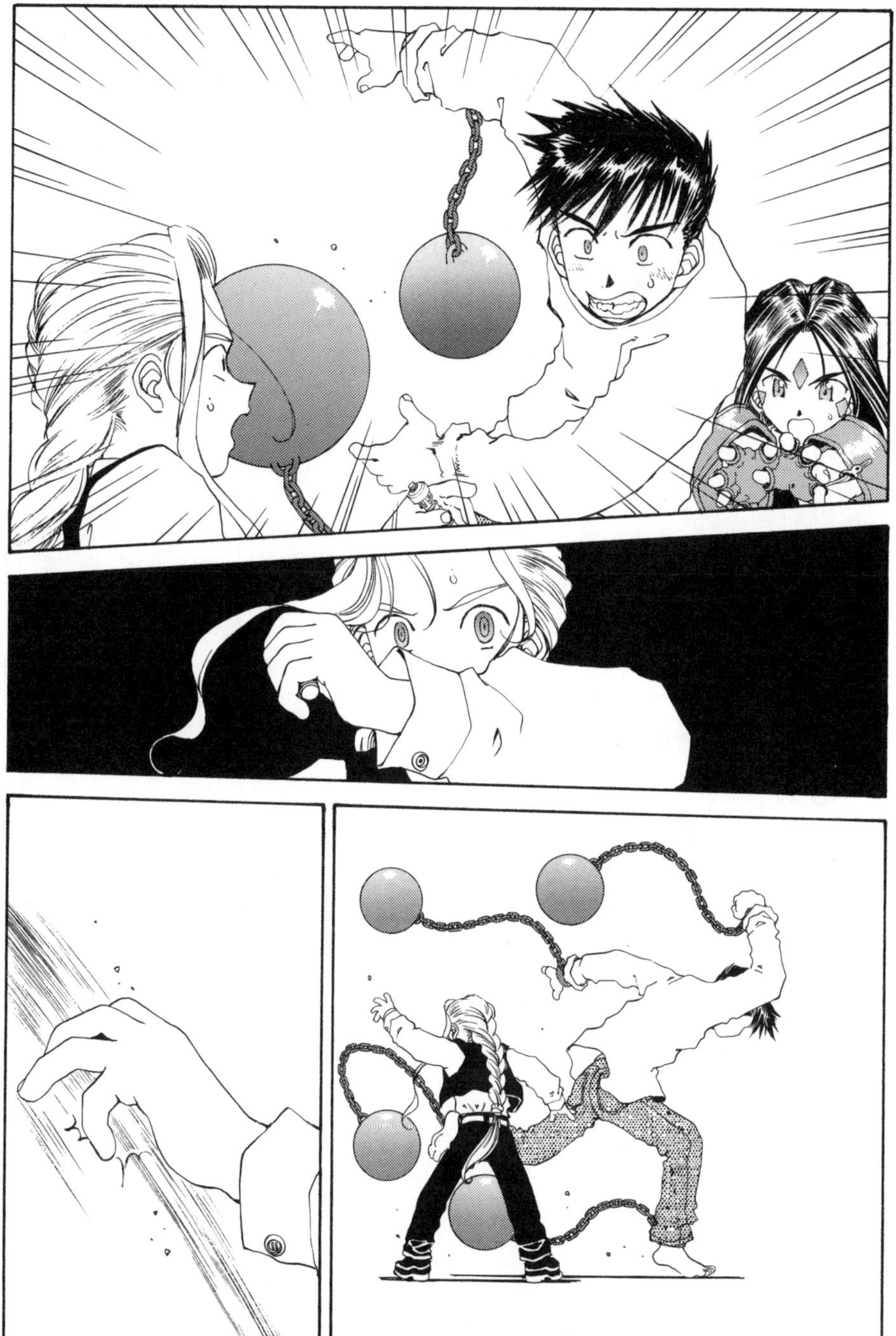

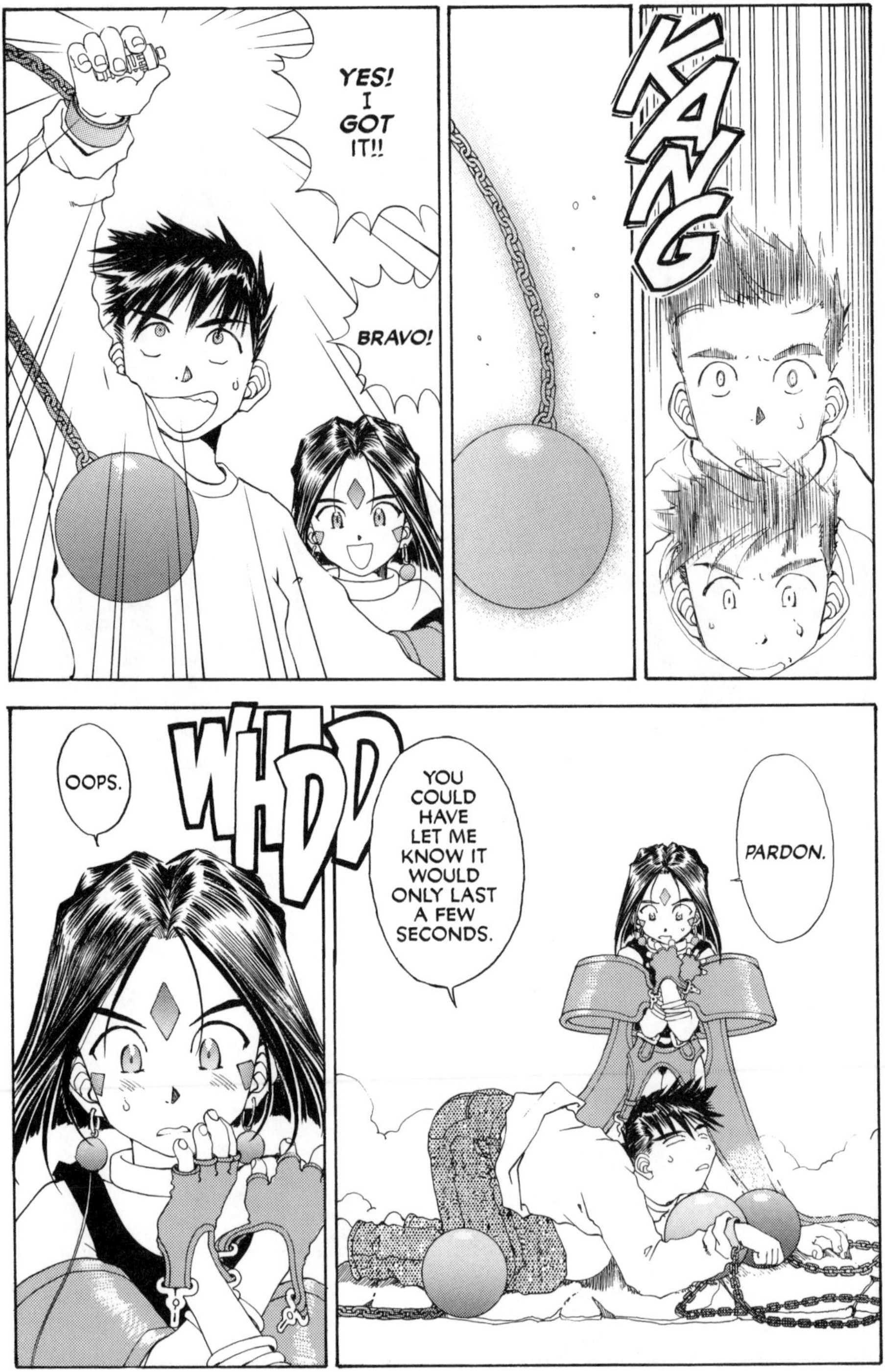
YES! I GOT IT!!
BRAVO!
KANG
OOPS.
WHDD
YOU COULD HAVE LET ME KNOW IT WOULD ONLY LAST A FEW SECONDS.
PARDON.

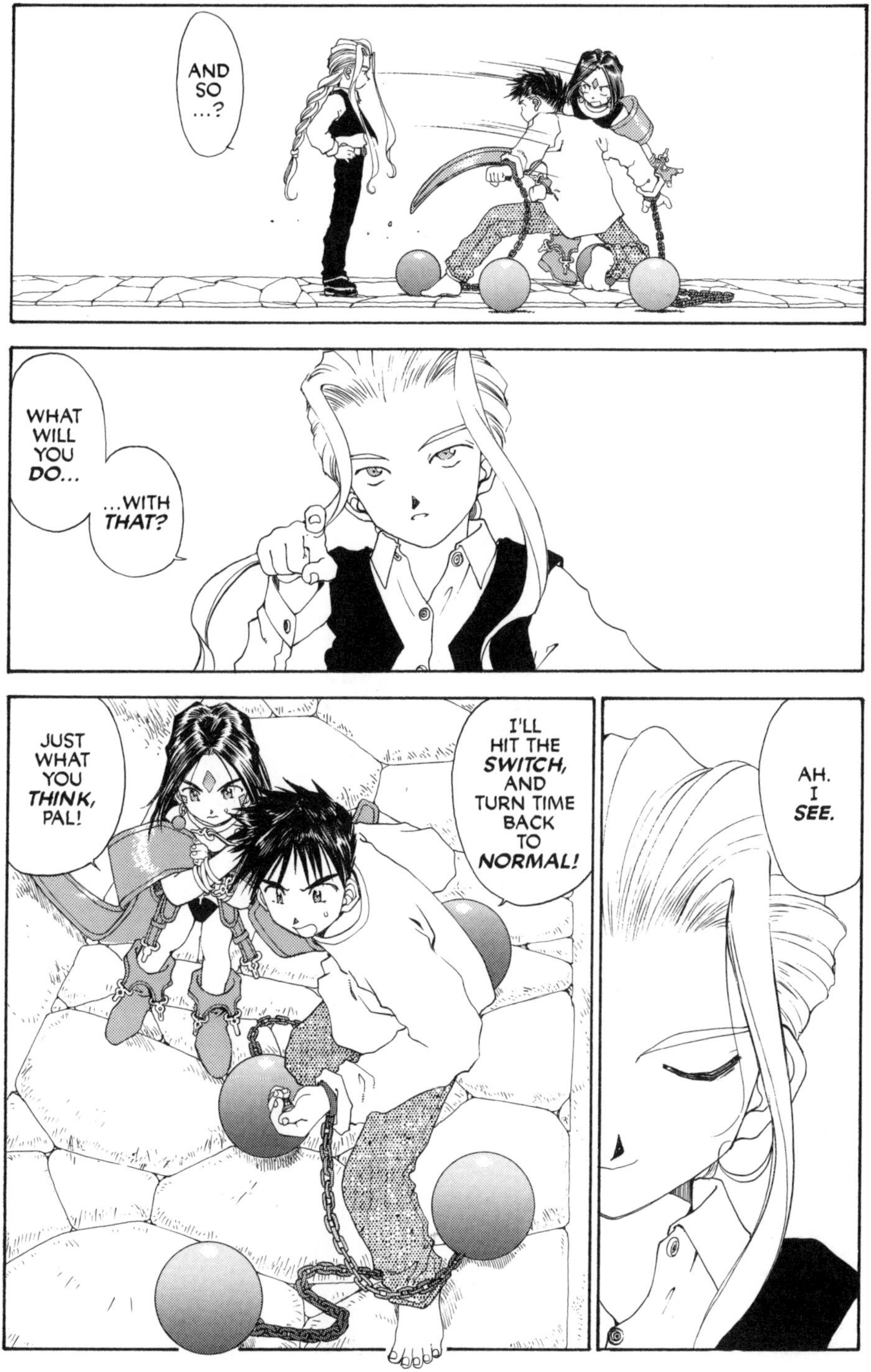
AND SO ...?
WHAT WILL YOU *DO...*
...WITH *THAT?*
JUST WHAT YOU *THINK,* PAL!
I'LL HIT THE *SWITCH,* AND TURN TIME BACK TO *NORMAL!*
AH. I *SEE.*

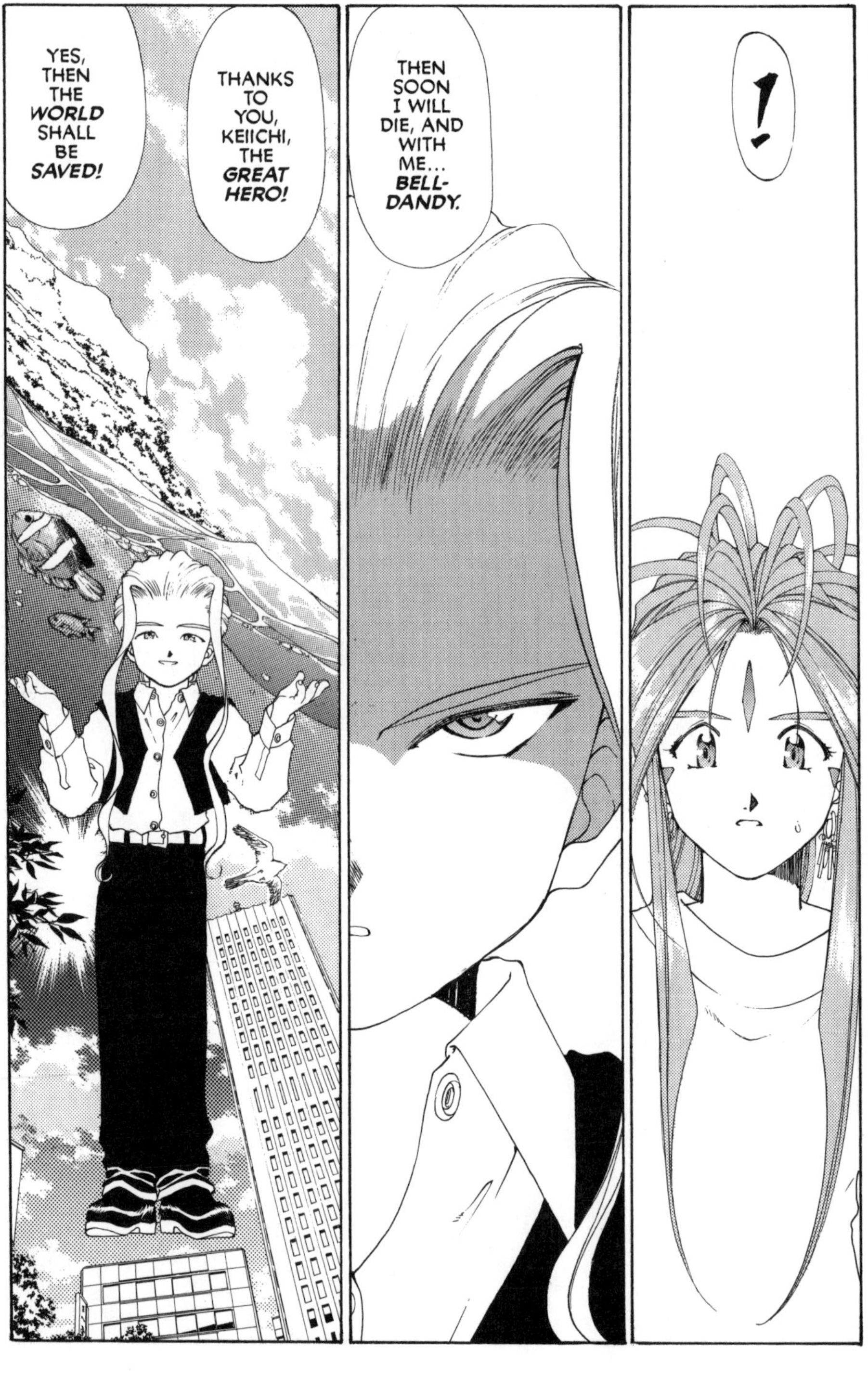
YES, THEN THE WORLD SHALL BE SAVED!
THANKS TO YOU, KEIICHI, THE GREAT HERO!
THEN SOON I WILL DIE, AND WITH ME... BELL-DANDY.
!

SO WHAT WILL YOU *DO*, KEIICHI?

PUSH THE BUTTON... AND *KILL* YOUR LADY LOVE...?

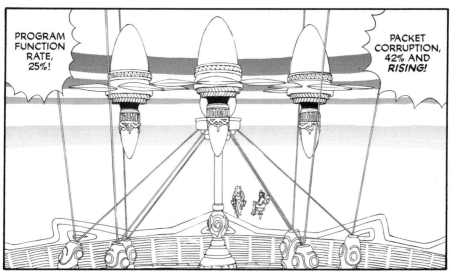

PROGRAM FUNCTION RATE, 25%!

PACKET CORRUPTION, 42% AND *RISING!*

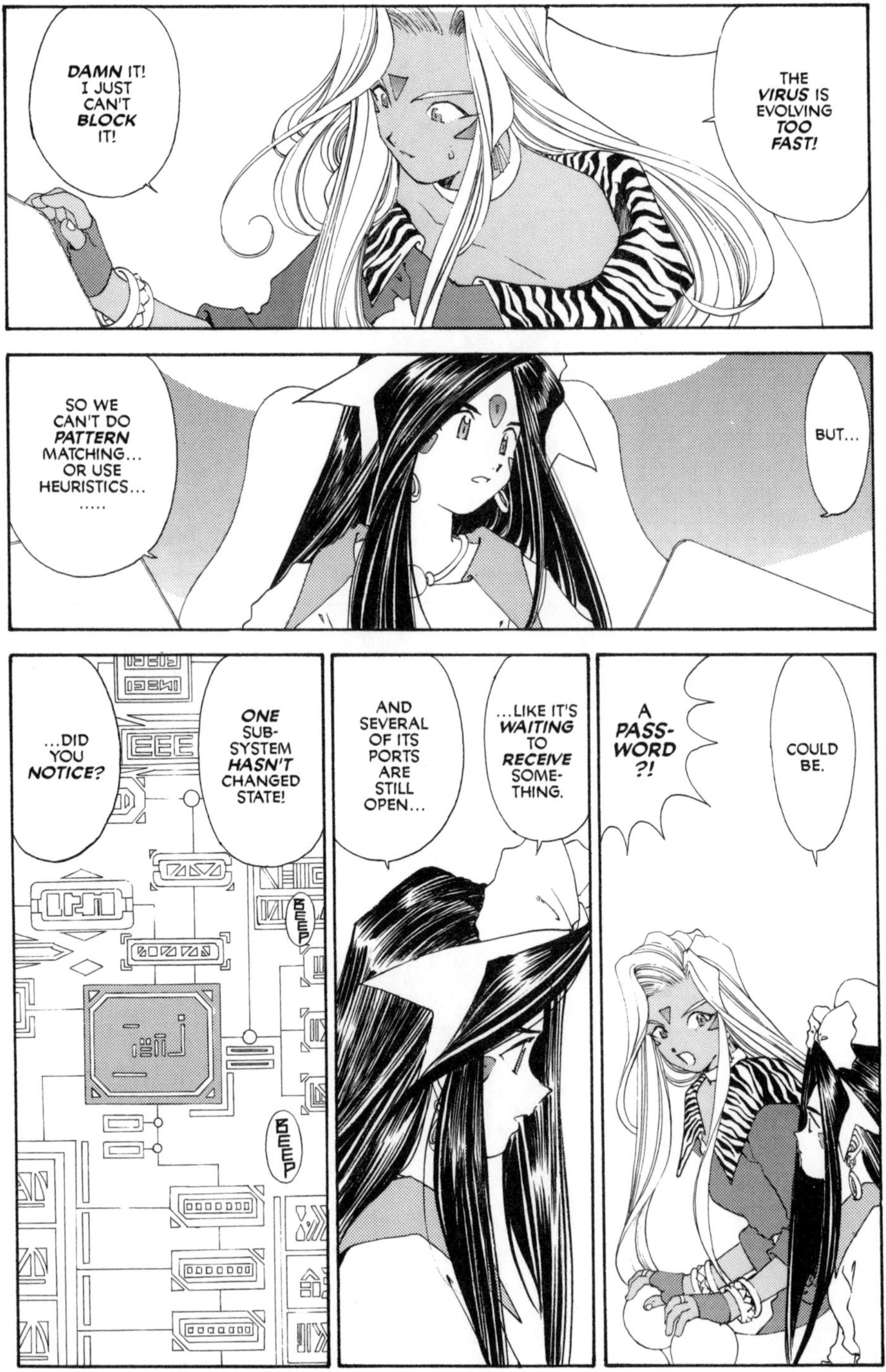
DAMN IT! I JUST CAN'T BLOCK IT!
THE VIRUS IS EVOLVING TOO FAST!
SO WE CAN'T DO PATTERN MATCHING... OR USE HEURISTICS... .....
BUT...
...DID YOU NOTICE?
ONE SUB-SYSTEM HASN'T CHANGED STATE!
BEEP
BEEP
AND SEVERAL OF ITS PORTS ARE STILL OPEN...
...LIKE IT'S WAITING TO RECEIVE SOME-THING.
A PASS-WORD?!
COULD BE.

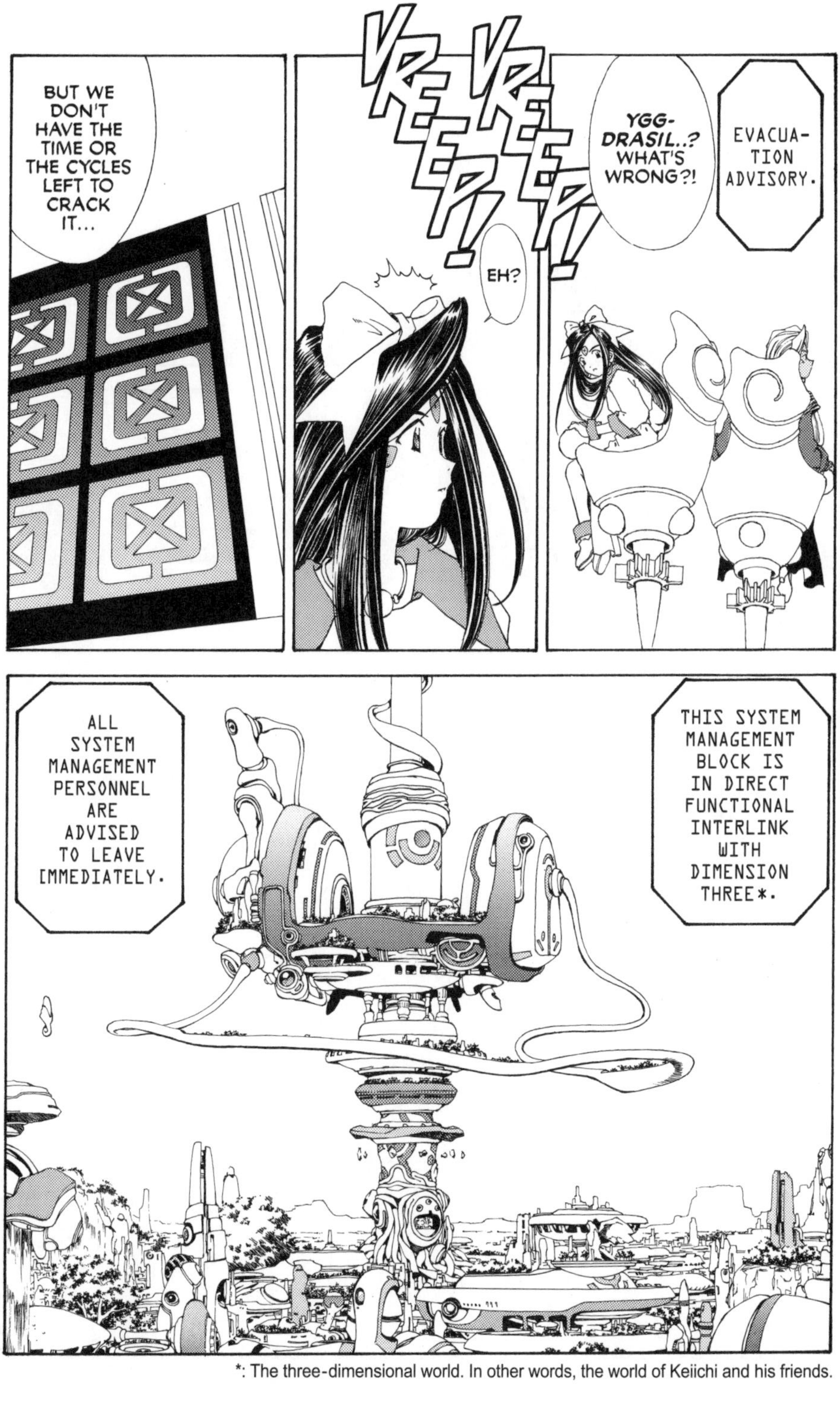
BUT WE DON'T HAVE THE TIME OR THE CYCLES LEFT TO CRACK IT...
VREEP! VREEP!
EH?
YGG-DRASIL..? WHAT'S WRONG?!
EVACUATION ADVISORY.
ALL SYSTEM MANAGEMENT PERSONNEL ARE ADVISED TO LEAVE IMMEDIATELY.
THIS SYSTEM MANAGEMENT BLOCK IS IN DIRECT FUNCTIONAL INTERLINK WITH DIMENSION THREE*.

*: The three-dimensional world. In other words, the world of Keiichi and his friends.

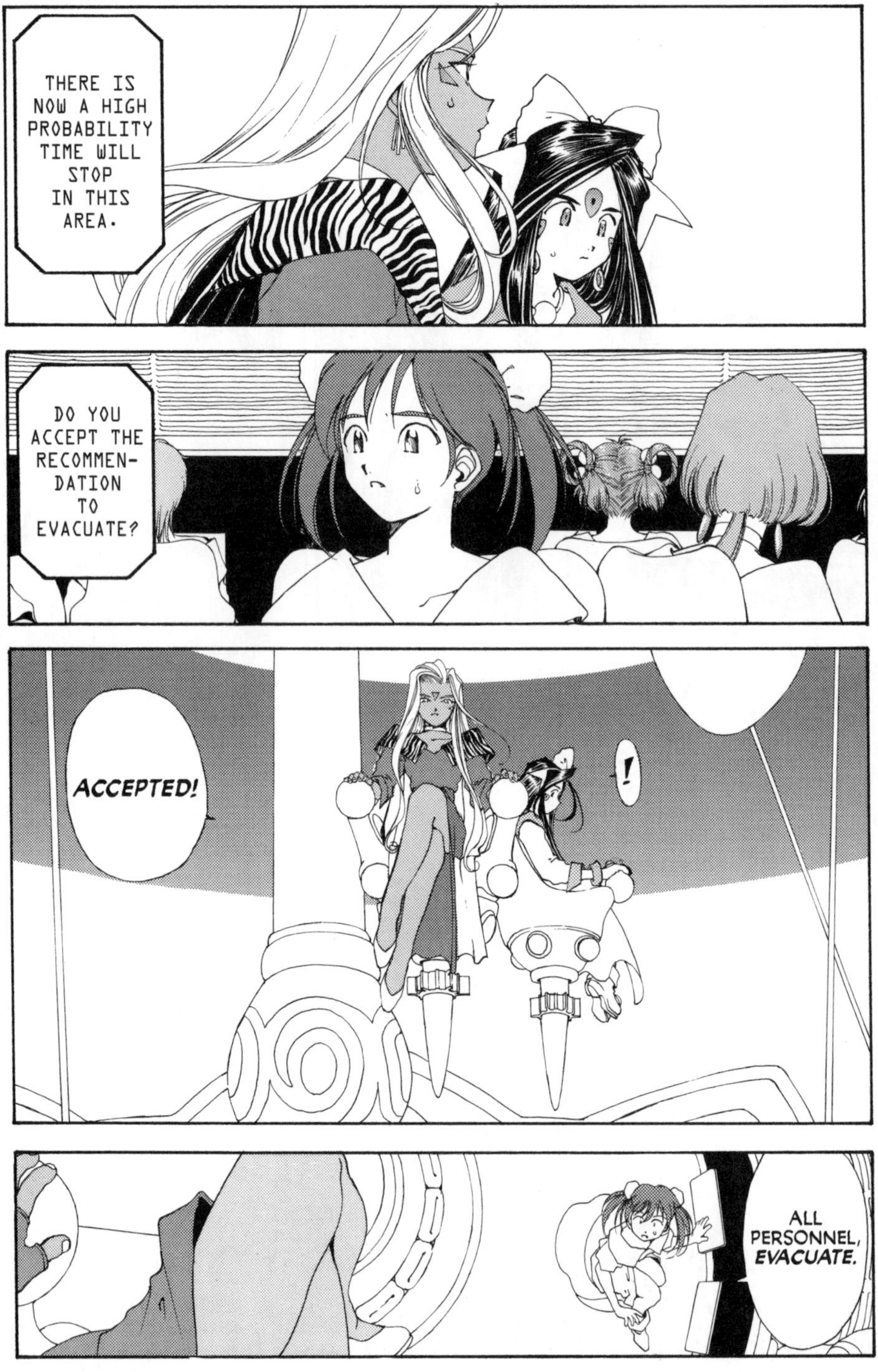
THERE IS NOW A HIGH PROBABILITY TIME WILL STOP IN THIS AREA.
DO YOU ACCEPT THE RECOMMENDATION TO EVACUATE?
ACCEPTED!
!
ALL PERSONNEL, EVACUATE.

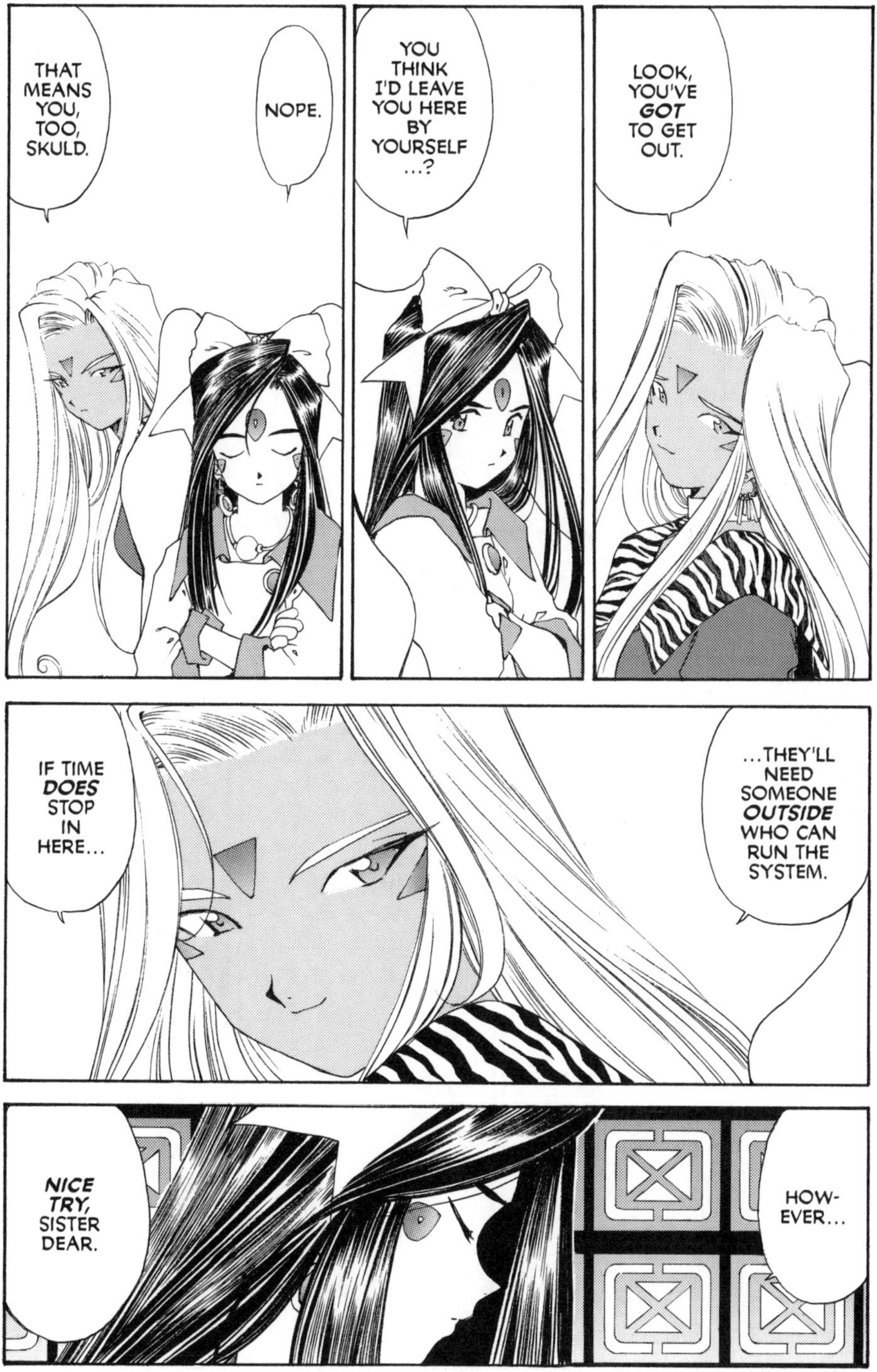
THAT MEANS YOU, TOO, SKULD.
NOPE.
YOU THINK I'D LEAVE YOU HERE BY YOURSELF ...?
LOOK, YOU'VE ***GOT*** TO GET OUT.
IF TIME ***DOES*** STOP IN HERE...
...THEY'LL NEED SOMEONE ***OUTSIDE*** WHO CAN RUN THE SYSTEM.
NICE TRY, SISTER DEAR.
HOW-EVER...

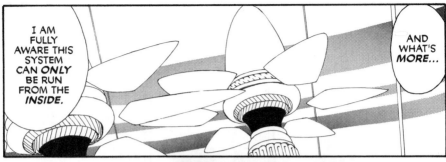

I AM FULLY AWARE THIS SYSTEM CAN *ONLY* BE RUN FROM THE *INSIDE.*

AND WHAT'S *MORE...*

...YOU CAN'T *RE-ENTER* A SPACE WHERE TIME HAS STOPPED.

I'M NOT LETTING YOU BE THE BIG *HERO!* NO *WAY!*

RATS!

SAW RIGHT THROUGH ME.

ALL RIGHT... YOU CAN STAY. JUST DON'T GET IN MY *WAY!*

HAH! SAME TO *YOU,* URD!

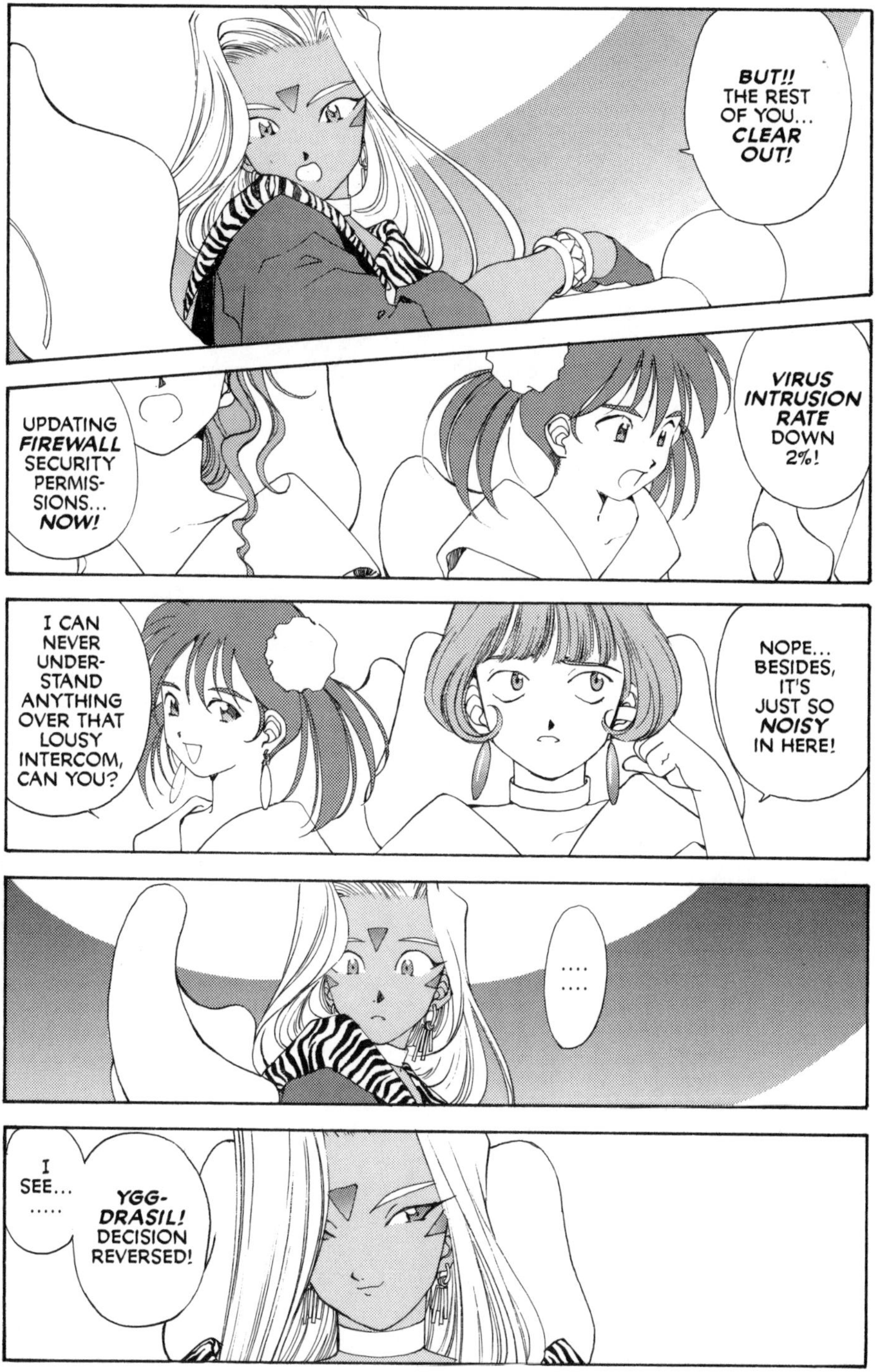
BUT!! THE REST OF YOU... CLEAR OUT!
UPDATING FIREWALL SECURITY PERMIS-SIONS... NOW!
VIRUS INTRUSION RATE DOWN 2%!
I CAN NEVER UNDER-STAND ANYTHING OVER THAT LOUSY INTERCOM, CAN YOU?
NOPE... BESIDES, IT'S JUST SO NOISY IN HERE!
....
I SEE... .....
YGG-DRASIL! DECISION REVERSED!

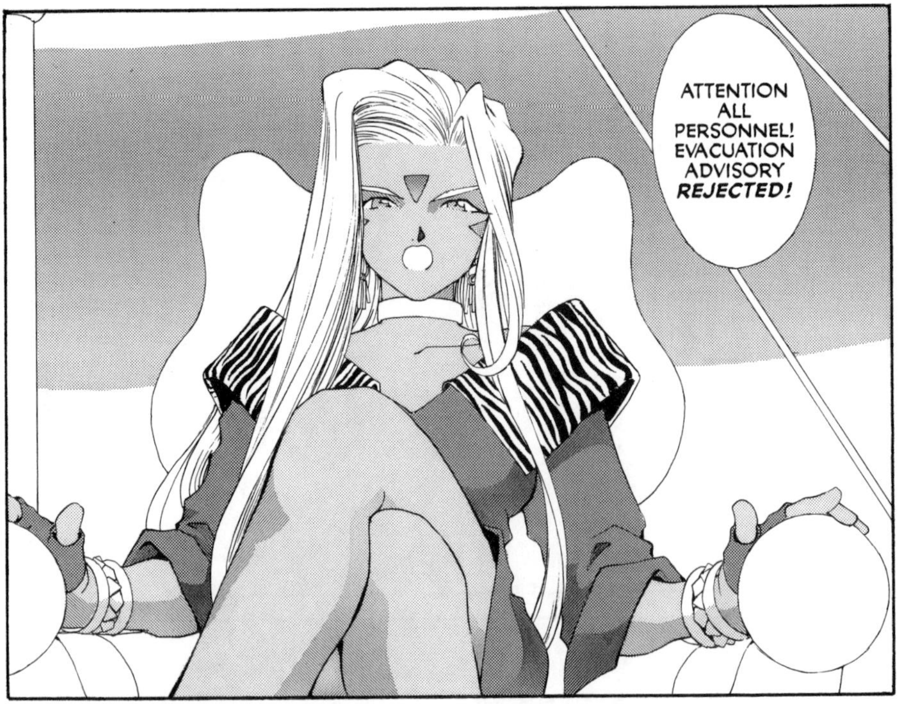
ATTENTION ALL PERSONNEL! EVACUATION ADVISORY *REJECTED!*

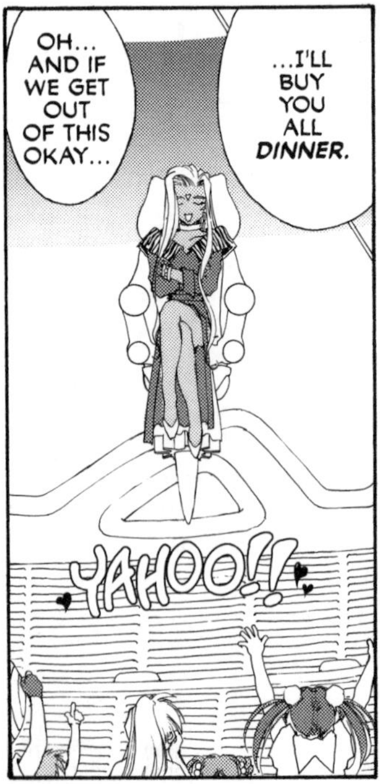
OH... AND IF WE GET OUT OF THIS OKAY...
...I'LL BUY YOU ALL *DINNER.*
YAHOO!!

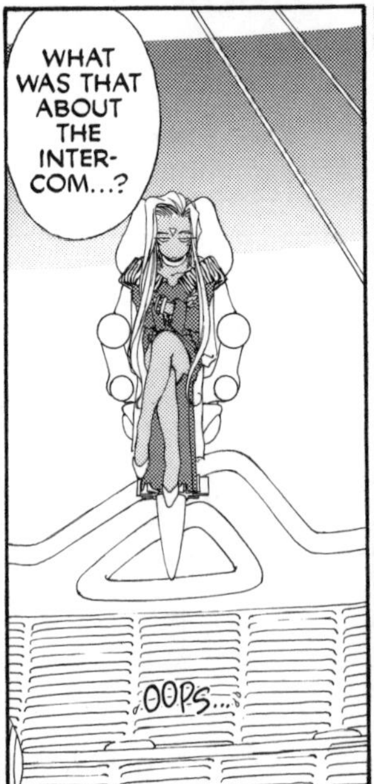
WHAT WAS THAT ABOUT THE INTER-COM...?
OOPS...

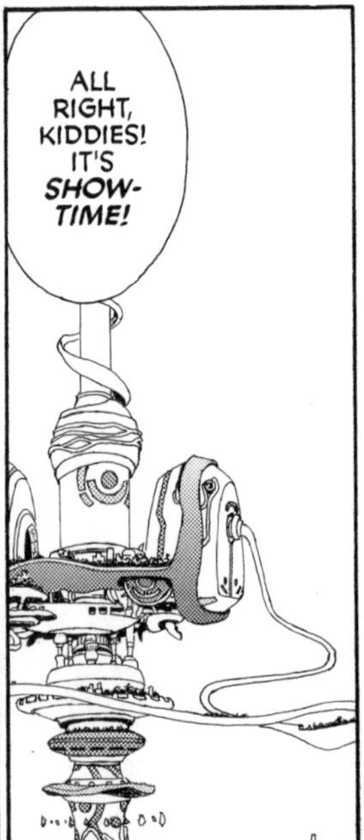
ALL RIGHT, KIDDIES! IT'S *SHOW-TIME!*

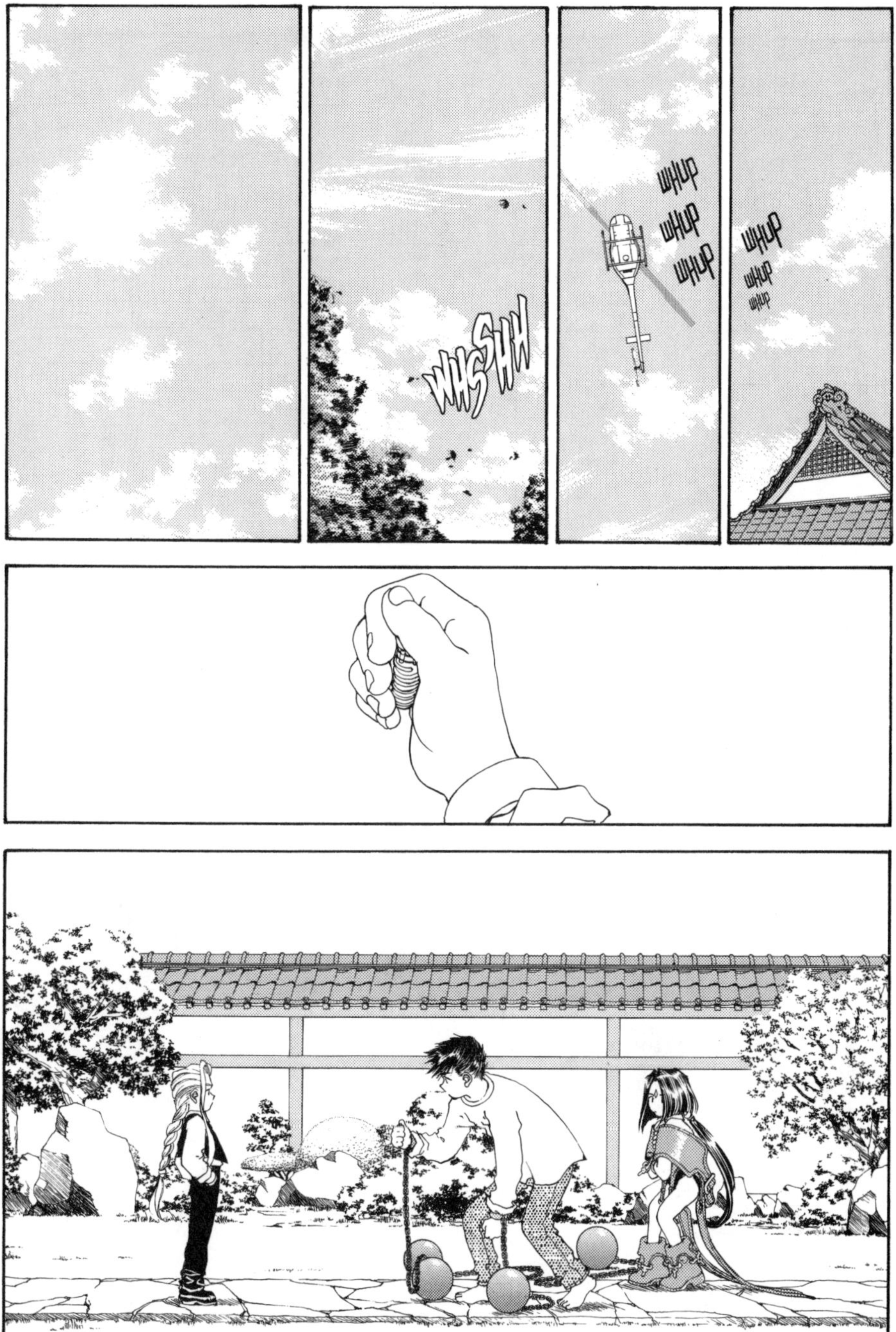
WHSHH
WHUP
WHUP
WHUP
WHUP
WHUP
WHUP

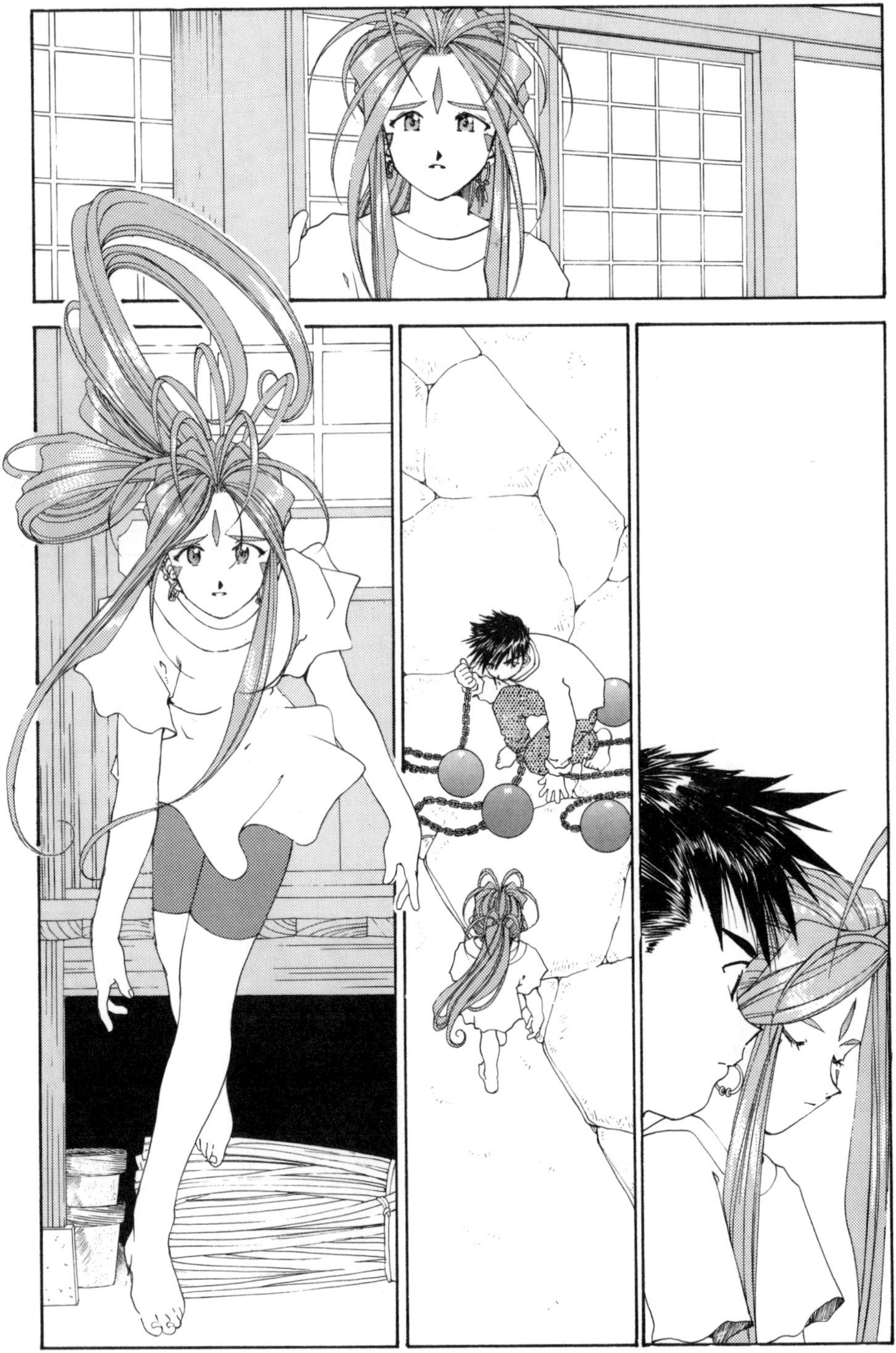

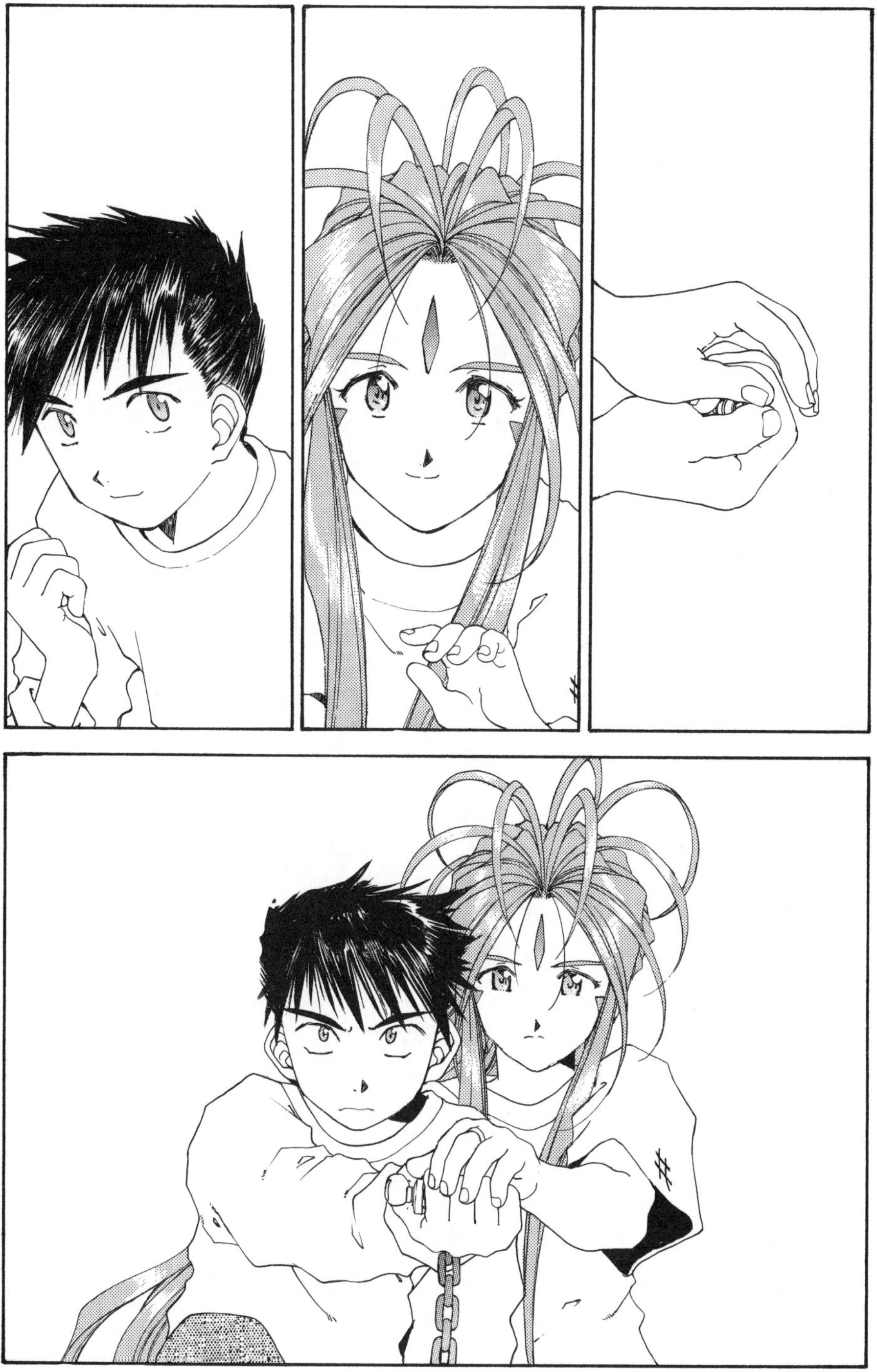

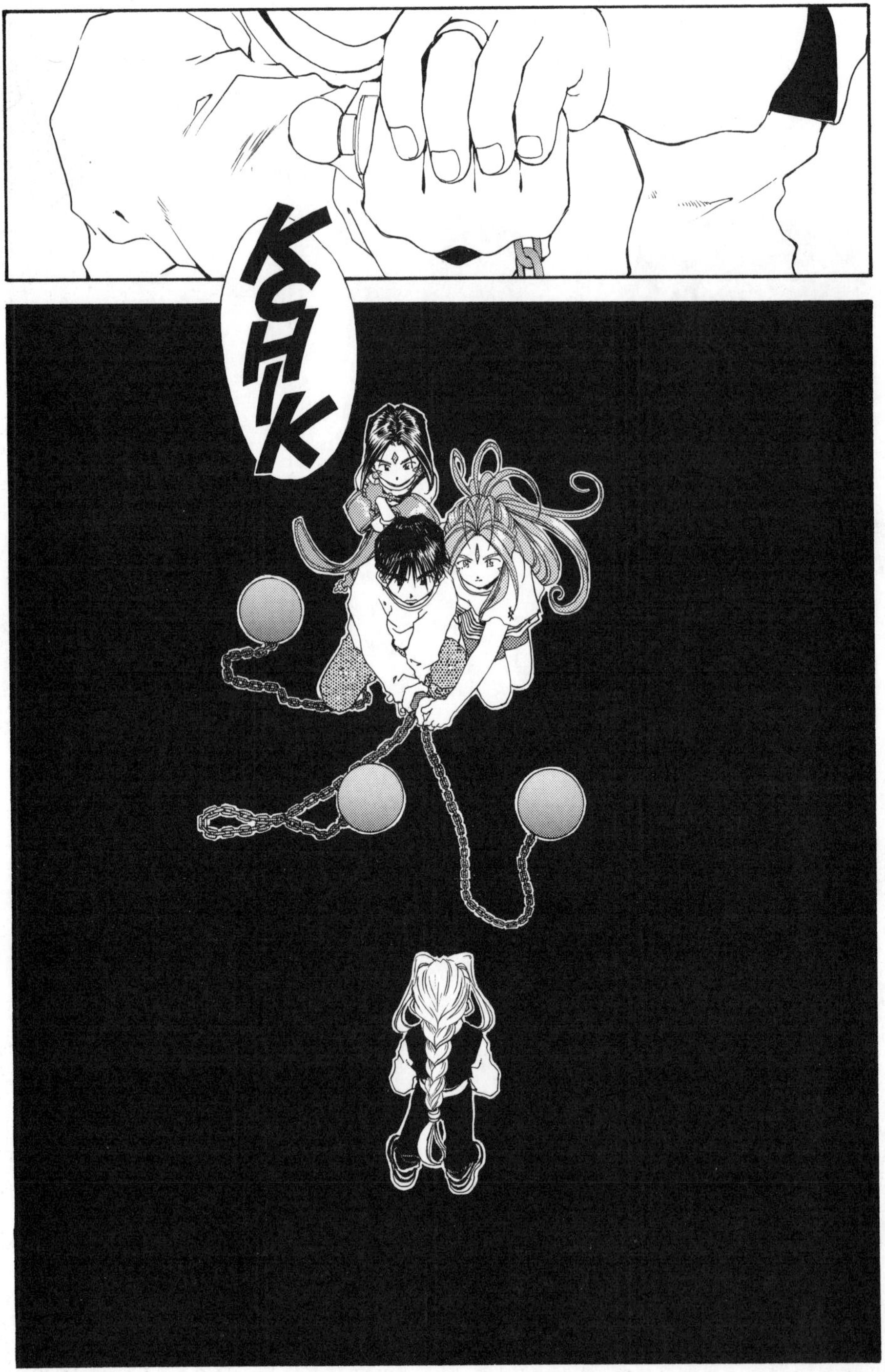
KCHIK

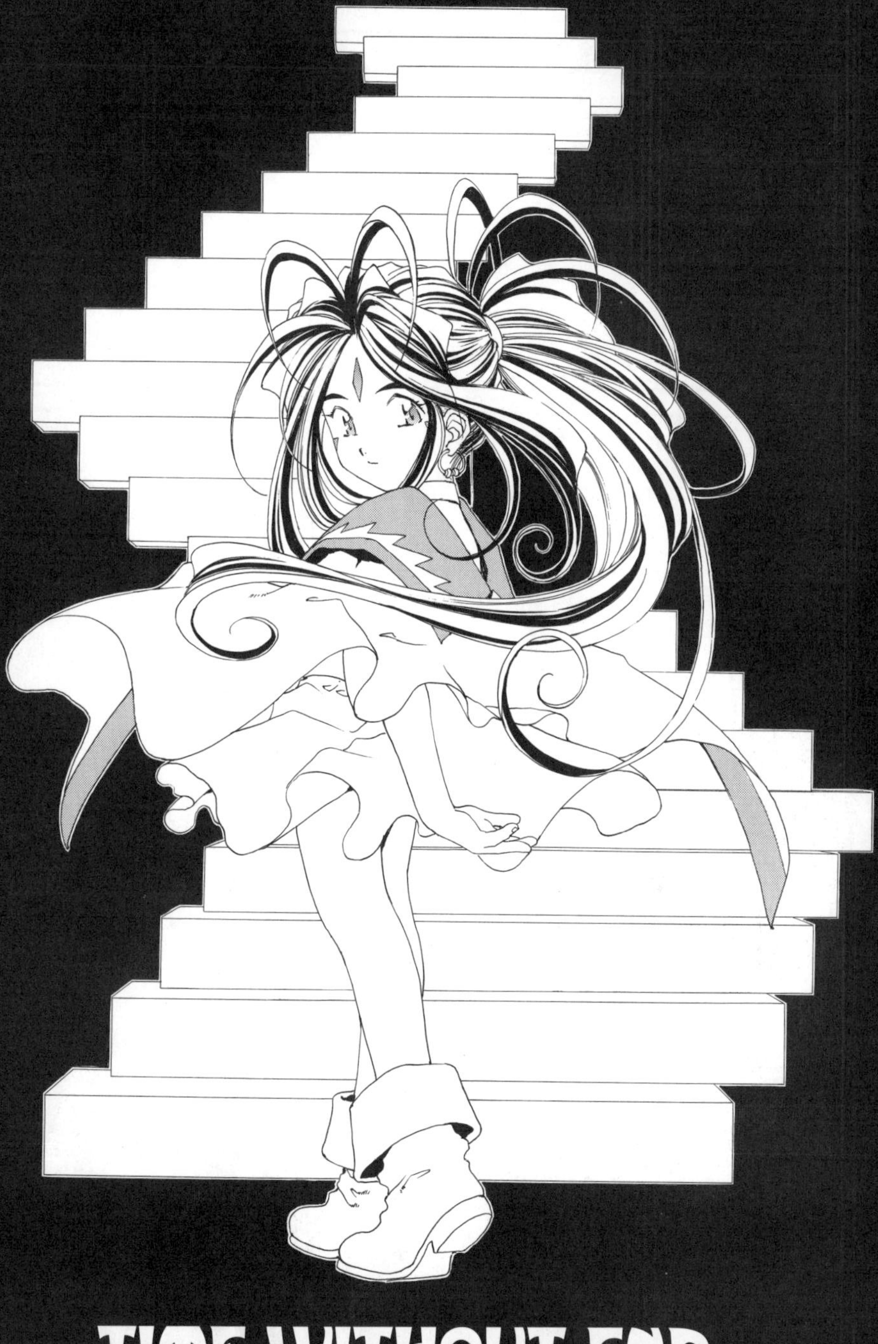

TIME WITHOUT END, HOPE WITHOUT END

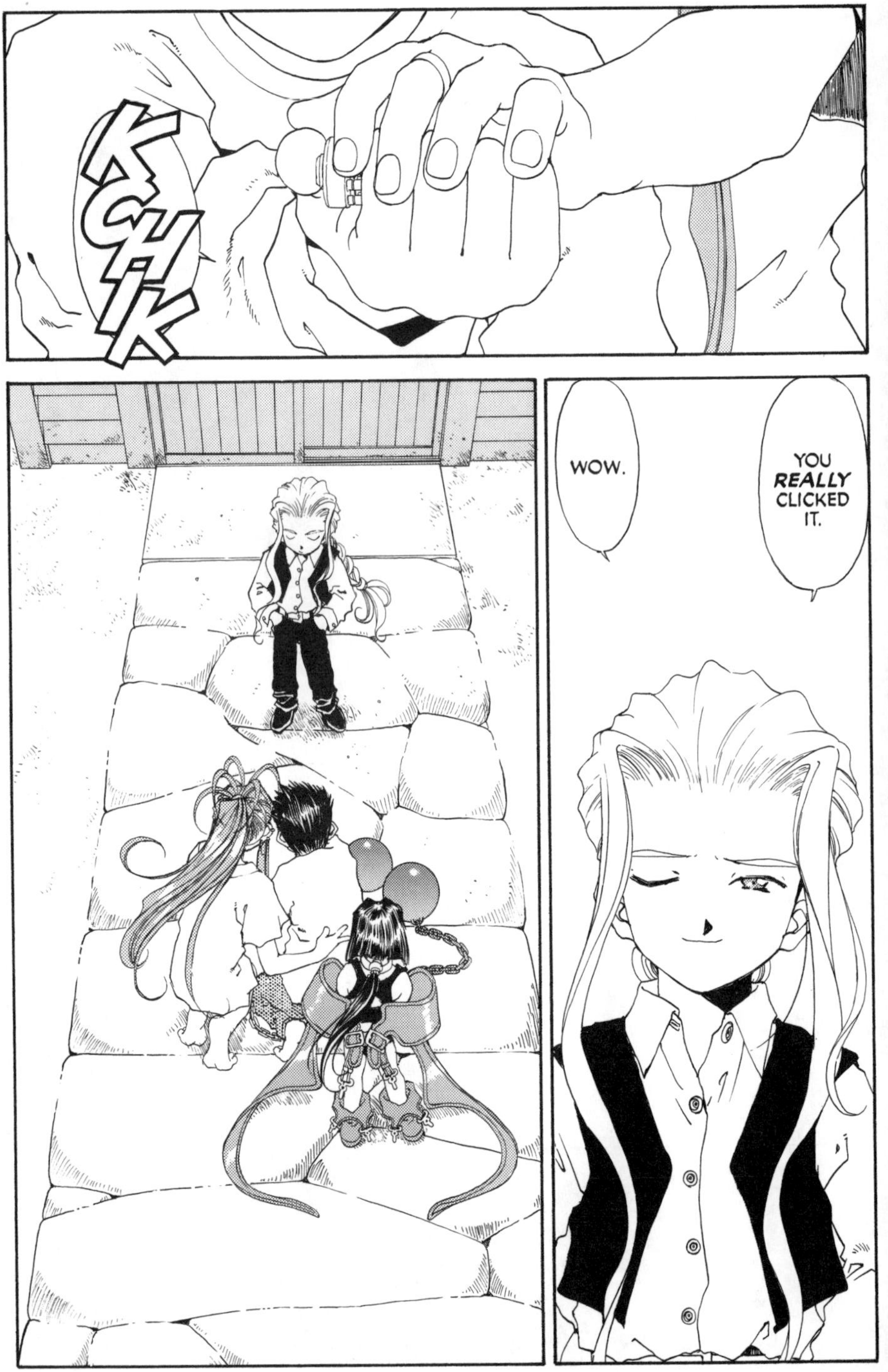
KCHIK
WOW.
YOU *REALLY* CLICKED IT.

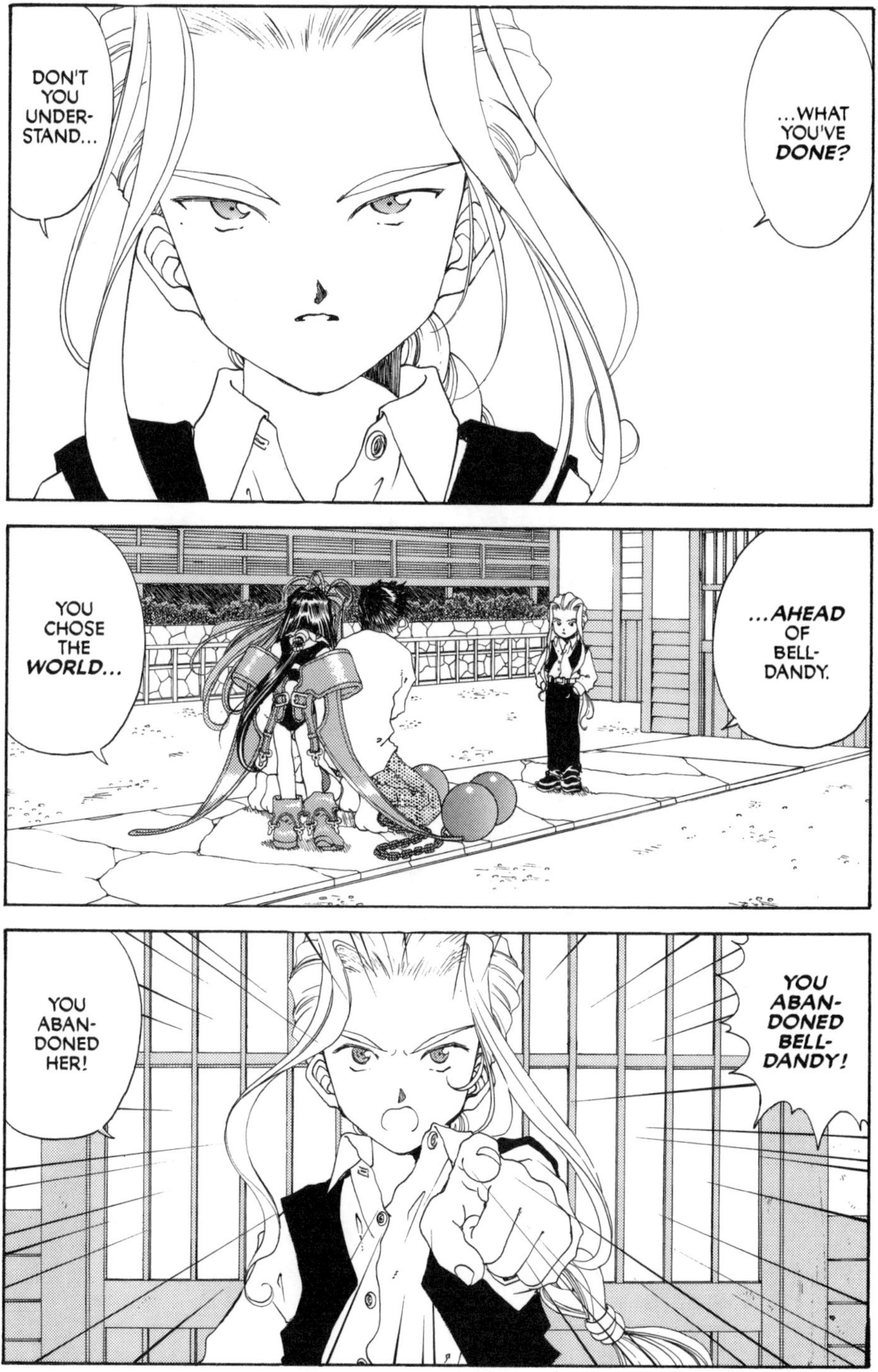
DON'T YOU UNDER-STAND...
...WHAT YOU'VE *DONE?*
YOU CHOSE THE *WORLD...*
...AHEAD OF BELL-DANDY.
YOU ABAN-DONED HER!
YOU ABAN-DONED BELL-DANDY!

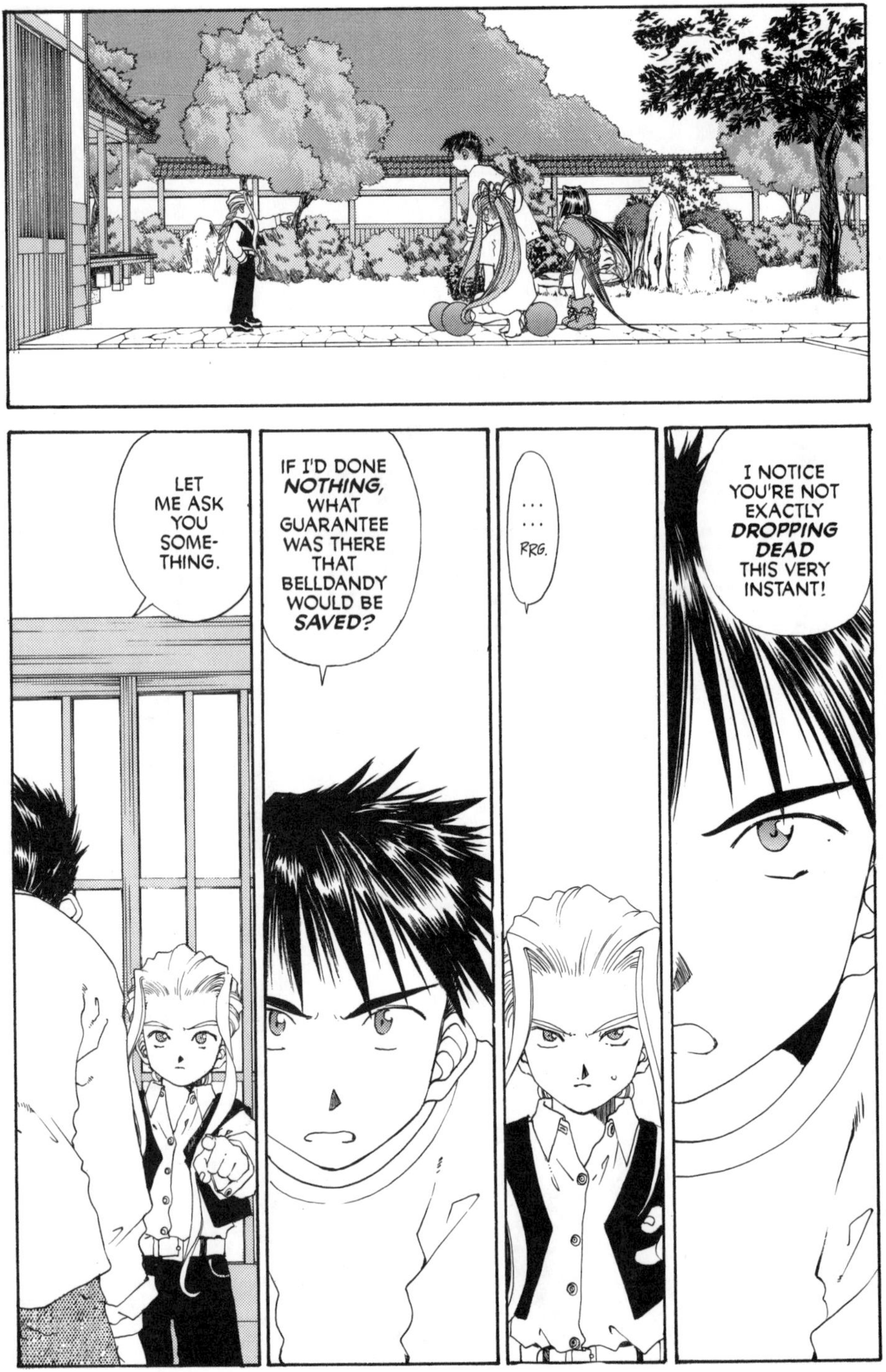

LET ME ASK YOU SOME-THING.
IF I'D DONE **NOTHING,** WHAT GUARANTEE WAS THERE THAT BELLDANDY WOULD BE **SAVED?**
... ... RRG.
I NOTICE YOU'RE NOT EXACTLY **DROPPING DEAD** THIS VERY INSTANT!

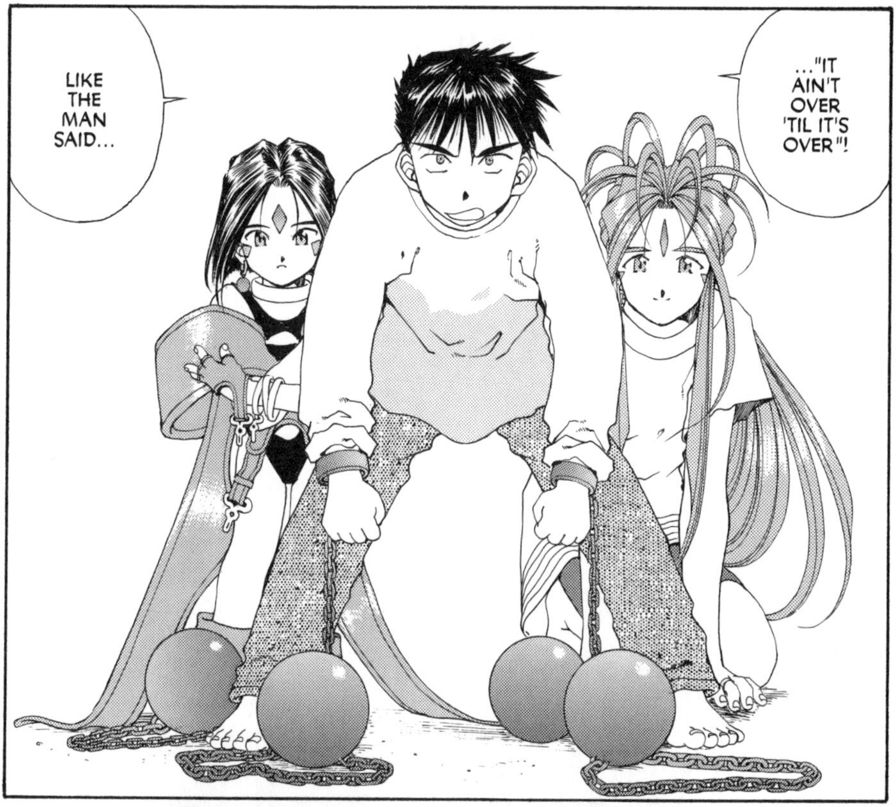
LIKE THE MAN SAID...
..."IT AIN'T OVER 'TIL IT'S OVER"!
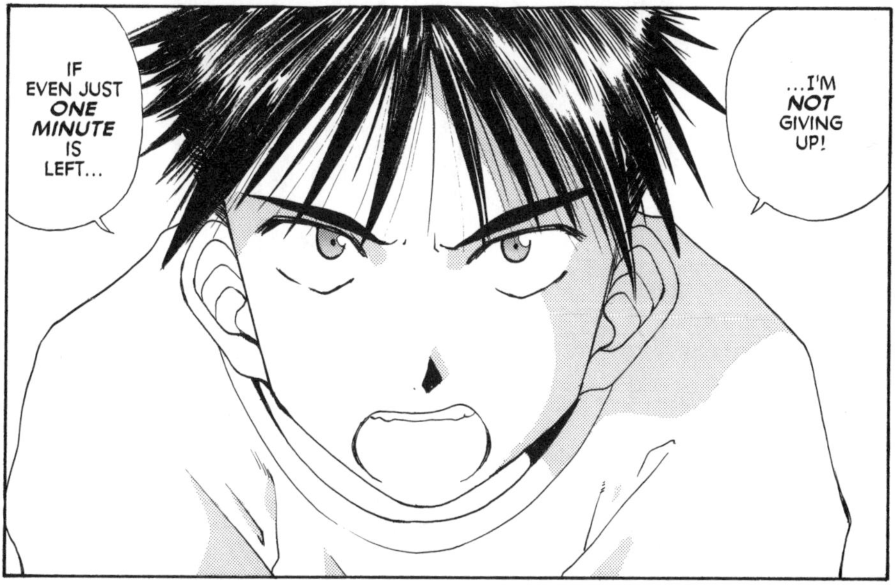
IF EVEN JUST ***ONE MINUTE*** IS LEFT...
...I'M ***NOT*** GIVING UP!

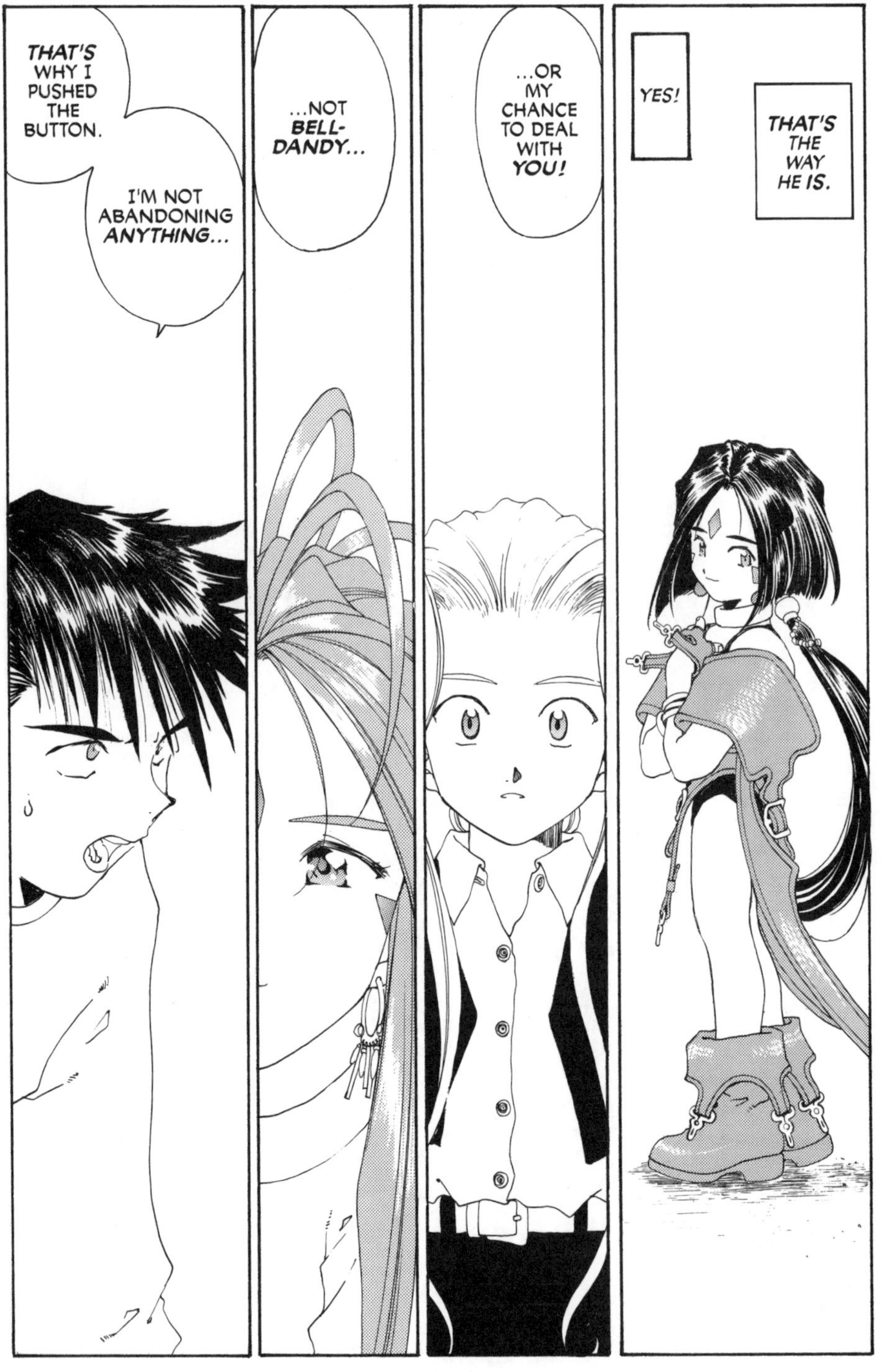
THAT'S WHY I PUSHED THE BUTTON.
I'M NOT ABANDONING ANYTHING...
...NOT BELL-DANDY...
...OR MY CHANCE TO DEAL WITH YOU!
YES!
THAT'S THE WAY HE IS.

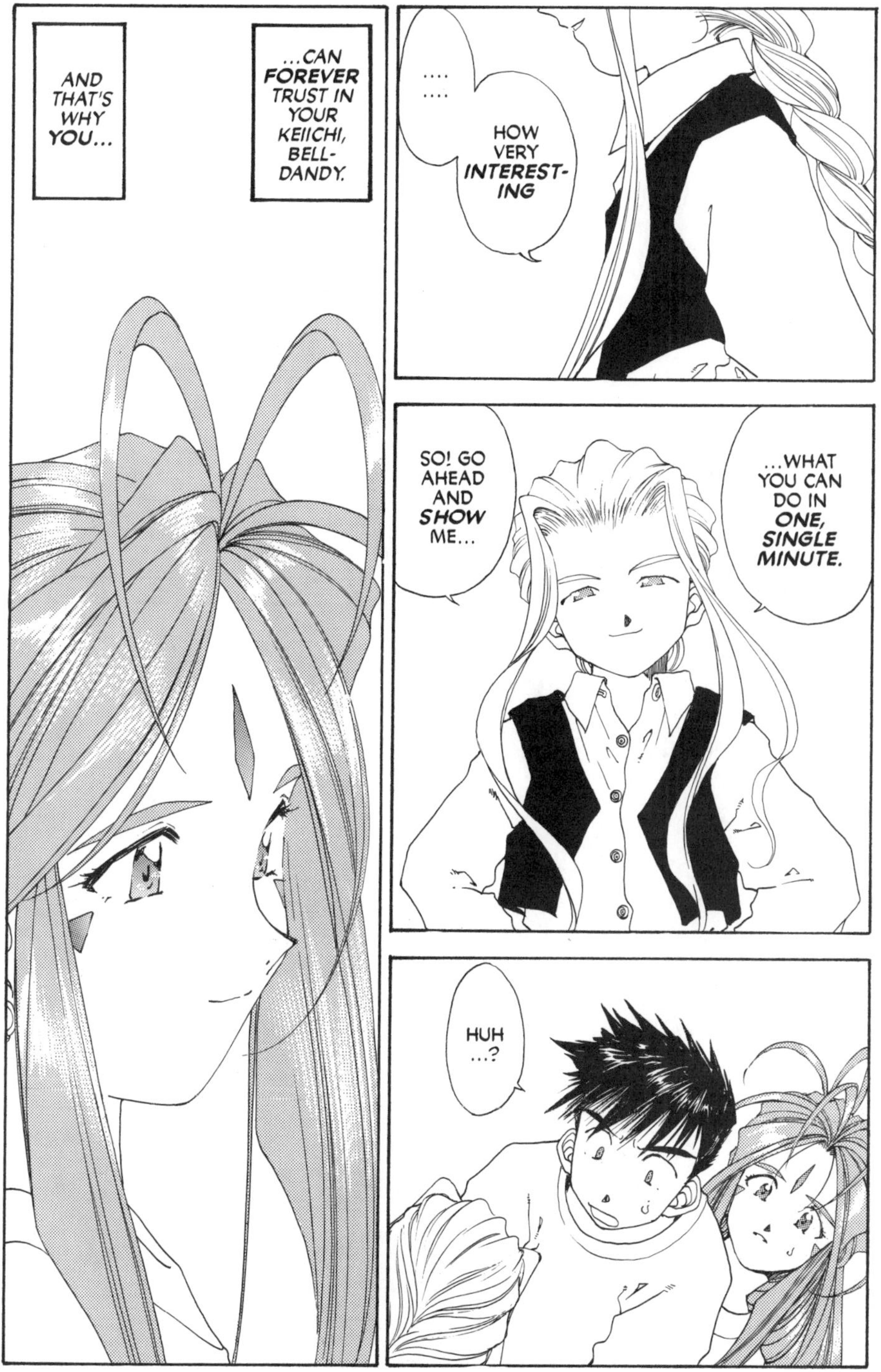
AND THAT'S WHY YOU...
...CAN FOREVER TRUST IN YOUR KEIICHI, BELL-DANDY.
....
....
HOW VERY INTEREST-ING
SO! GO AHEAD AND SHOW ME...
...WHAT YOU CAN DO IN ONE, SINGLE MINUTE.
HUH ...?

BECAUSE, IN FACT, THAT'S **ALL** YOU'VE GOT-- **BEFORE TIME STOPS!**

WHA --?!

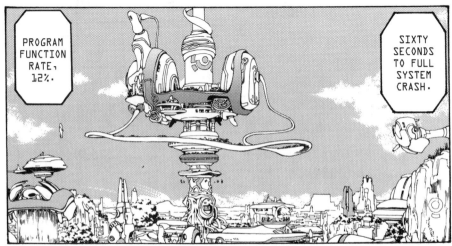

PROGRAM FUNCTION RATE, 12%.

SIXTY SECONDS TO FULL SYSTEM CRASH.

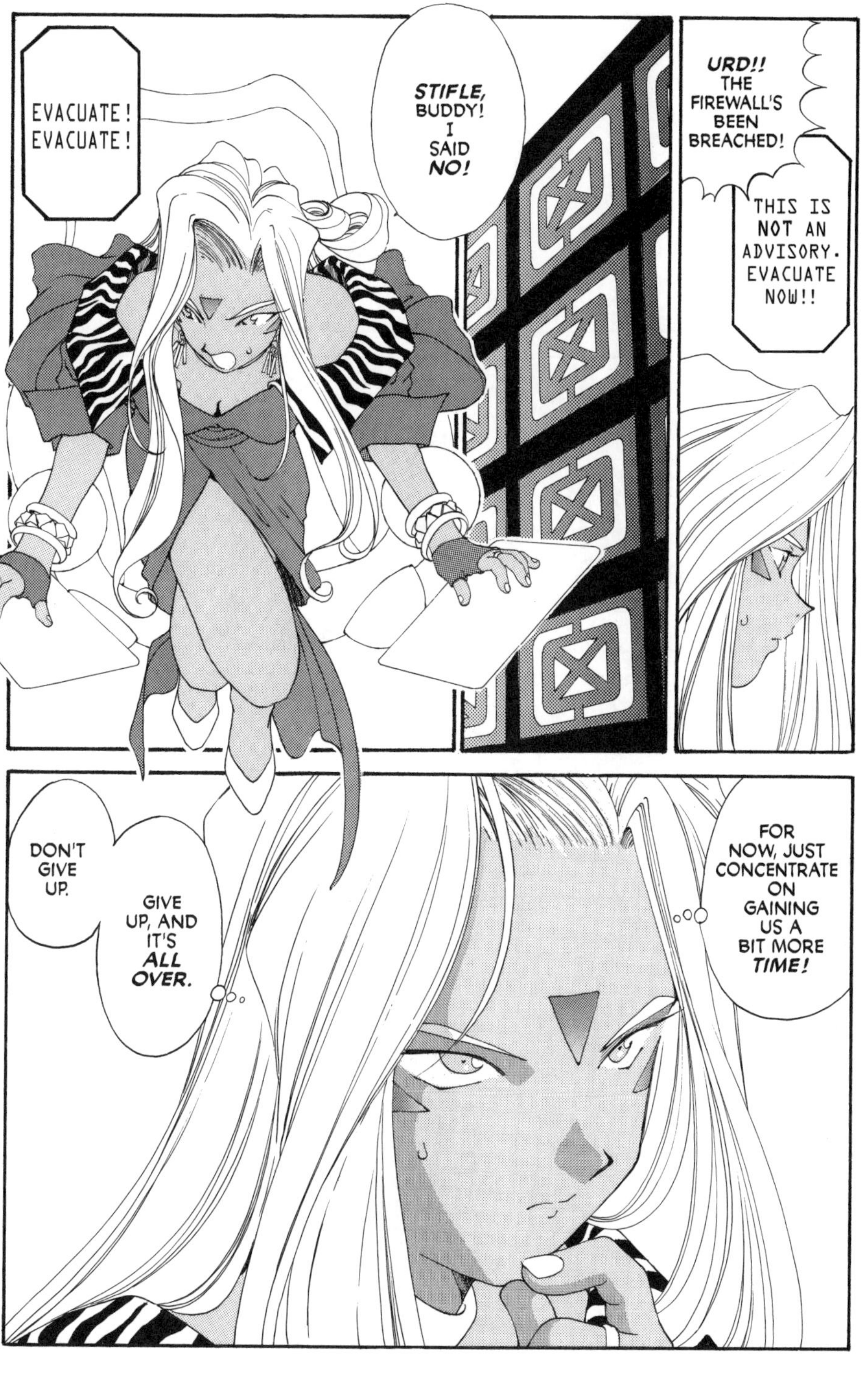
EVACUATE! EVACUATE!
STIFLE, BUDDY! I SAID NO!
URD!! THE FIREWALL'S BEEN BREACHED!
THIS IS NOT AN ADVISORY. EVACUATE NOW!!
DON'T GIVE UP.
GIVE UP, AND IT'S ALL OVER.
FOR NOW, JUST CONCENTRATE ON GAINING US A BIT MORE TIME!

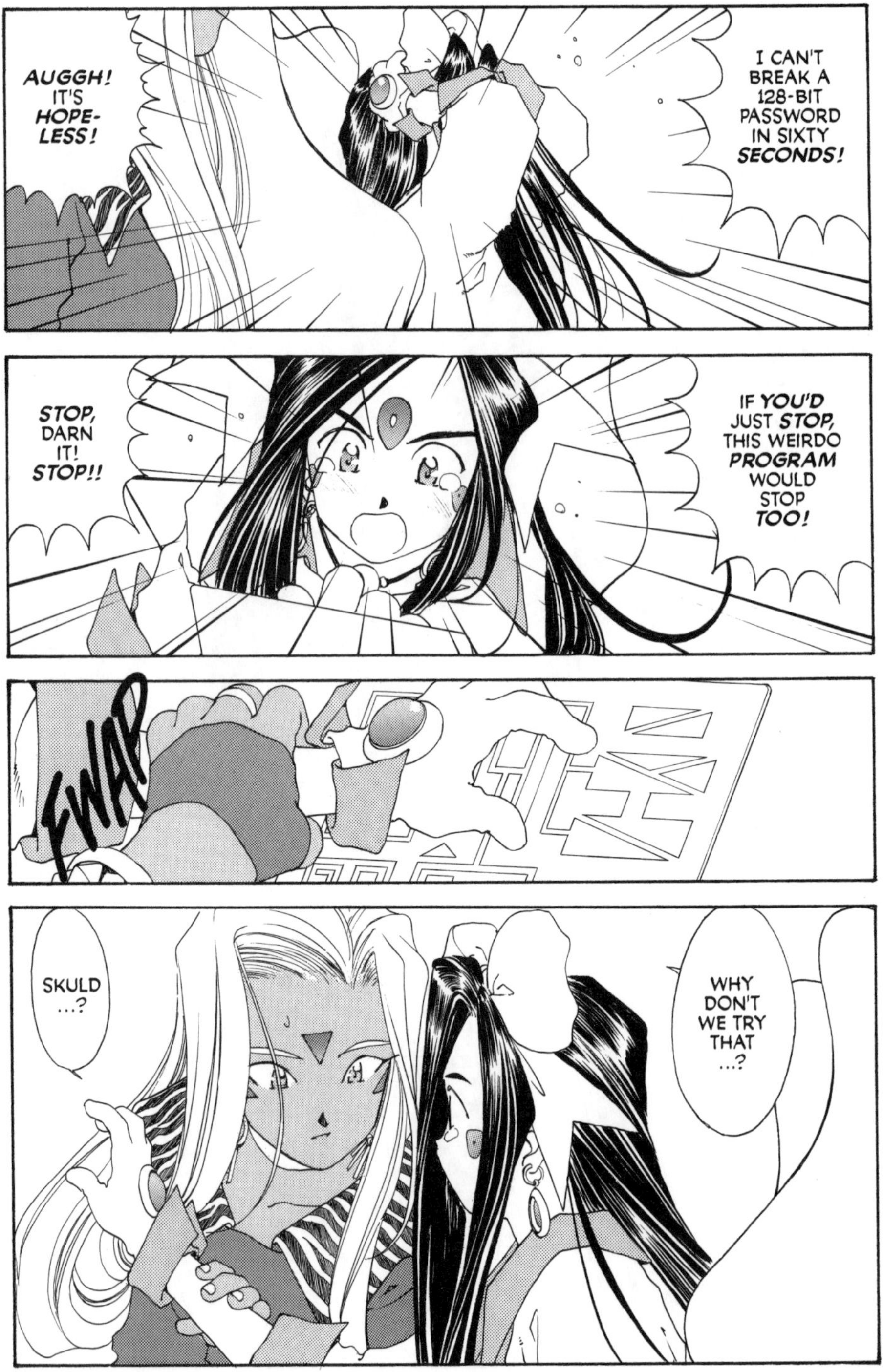
AUGGH! IT'S HOPE-LESS!
I CAN'T BREAK A 128-BIT PASSWORD IN SIXTY SECONDS!
STOP, DARN IT! STOP!!
IF YOU'D JUST STOP, THIS WEIRDO PROGRAM WOULD STOP TOO!
FWAP
SKULD ...?
WHY DON'T WE TRY THAT ...?

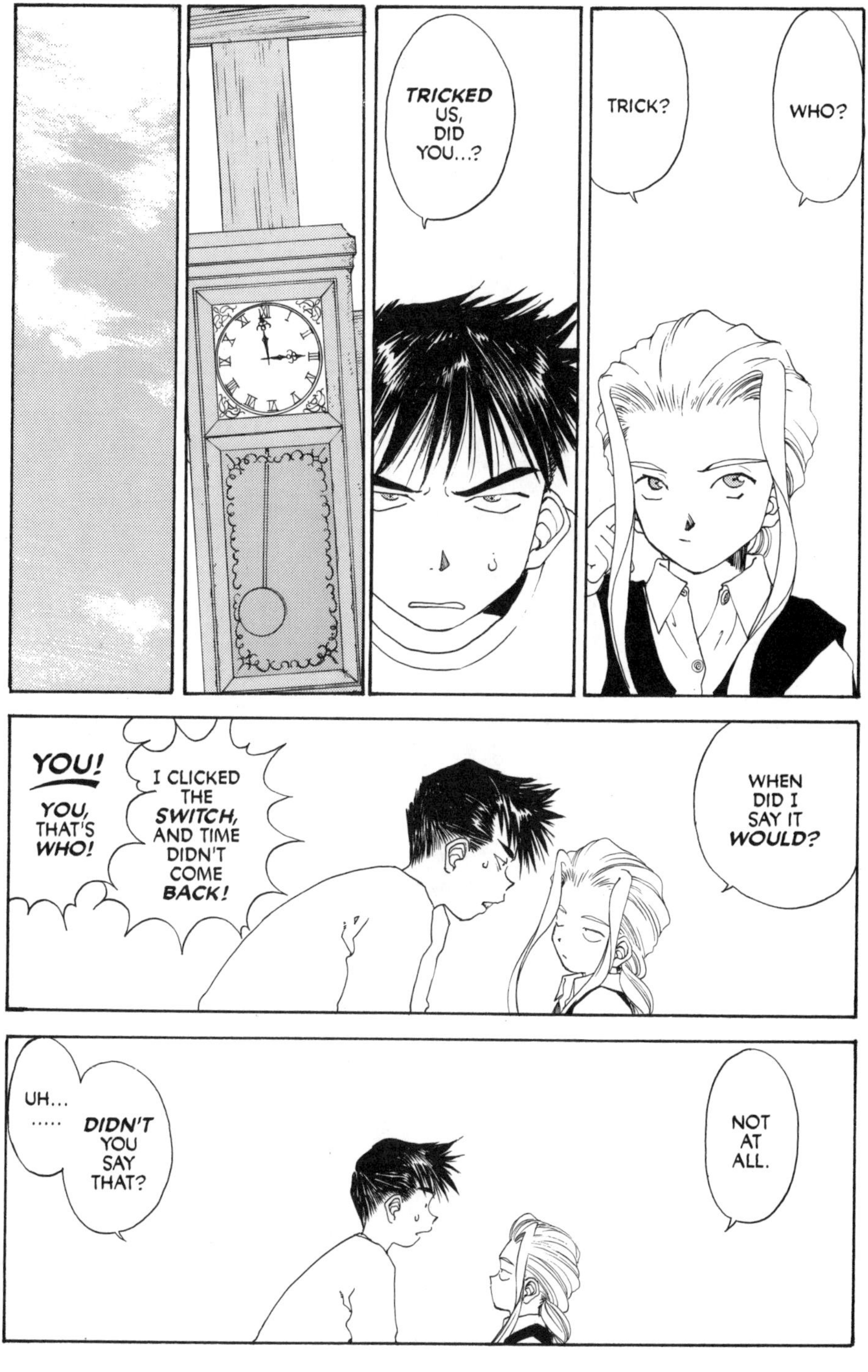
TRICKED US, DID YOU...?
TRICK?
WHO?
YOU! YOU, THAT'S WHO!
I CLICKED THE SWITCH, AND TIME DIDN'T COME BACK!
WHEN DID I SAY IT WOULD?
UH... ..... DIDN'T YOU SAY THAT?
NOT AT ALL.

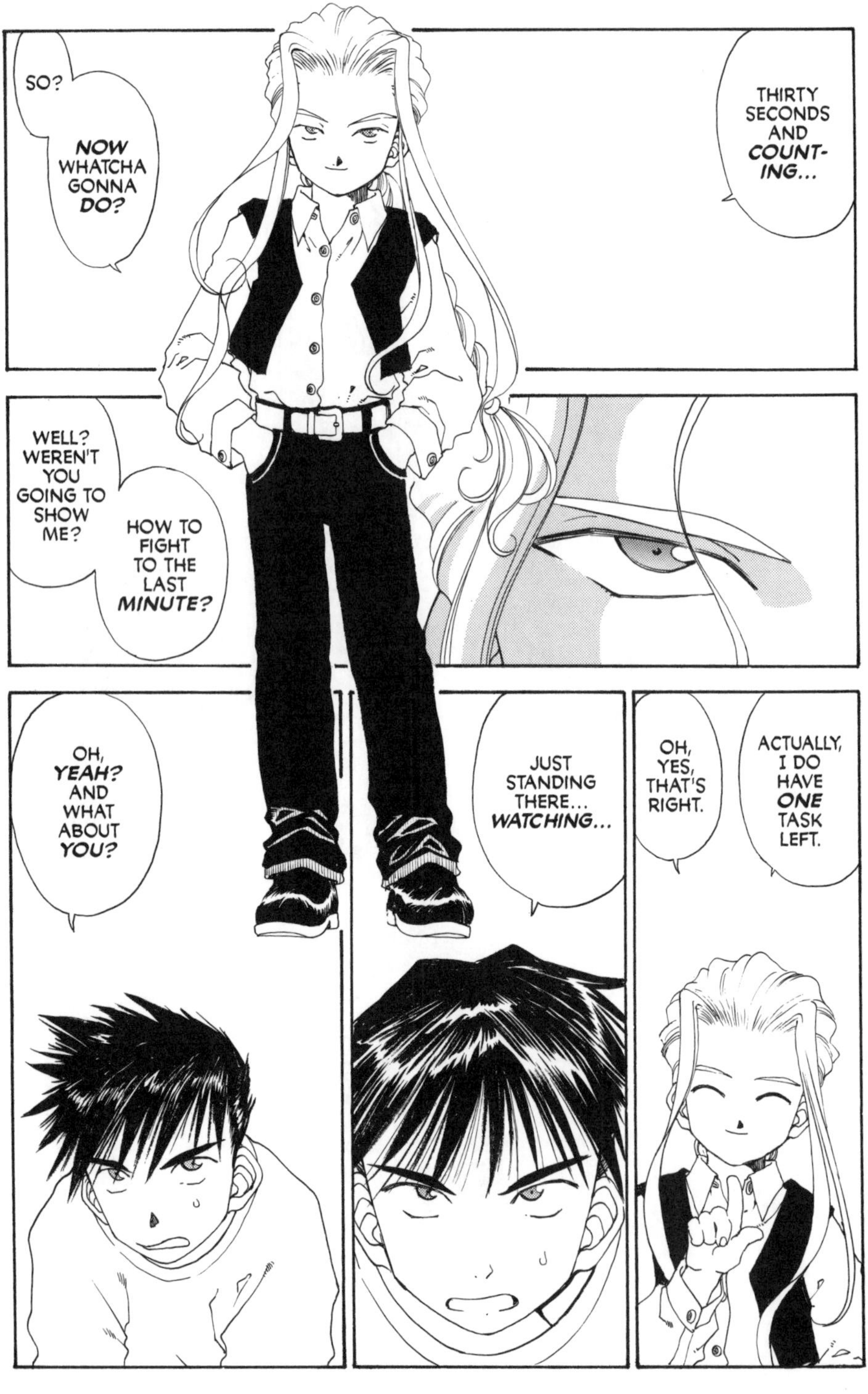
SO?
NOW WHATCHA GONNA DO?
THIRTY SECONDS AND COUNTING...
WELL? WEREN'T YOU GOING TO SHOW ME?
HOW TO FIGHT TO THE LAST MINUTE?
OH, YEAH? AND WHAT ABOUT YOU?
JUST STANDING THERE... WATCHING...
OH, YES, THAT'S RIGHT.
ACTUALLY, I DO HAVE ONE TASK LEFT.

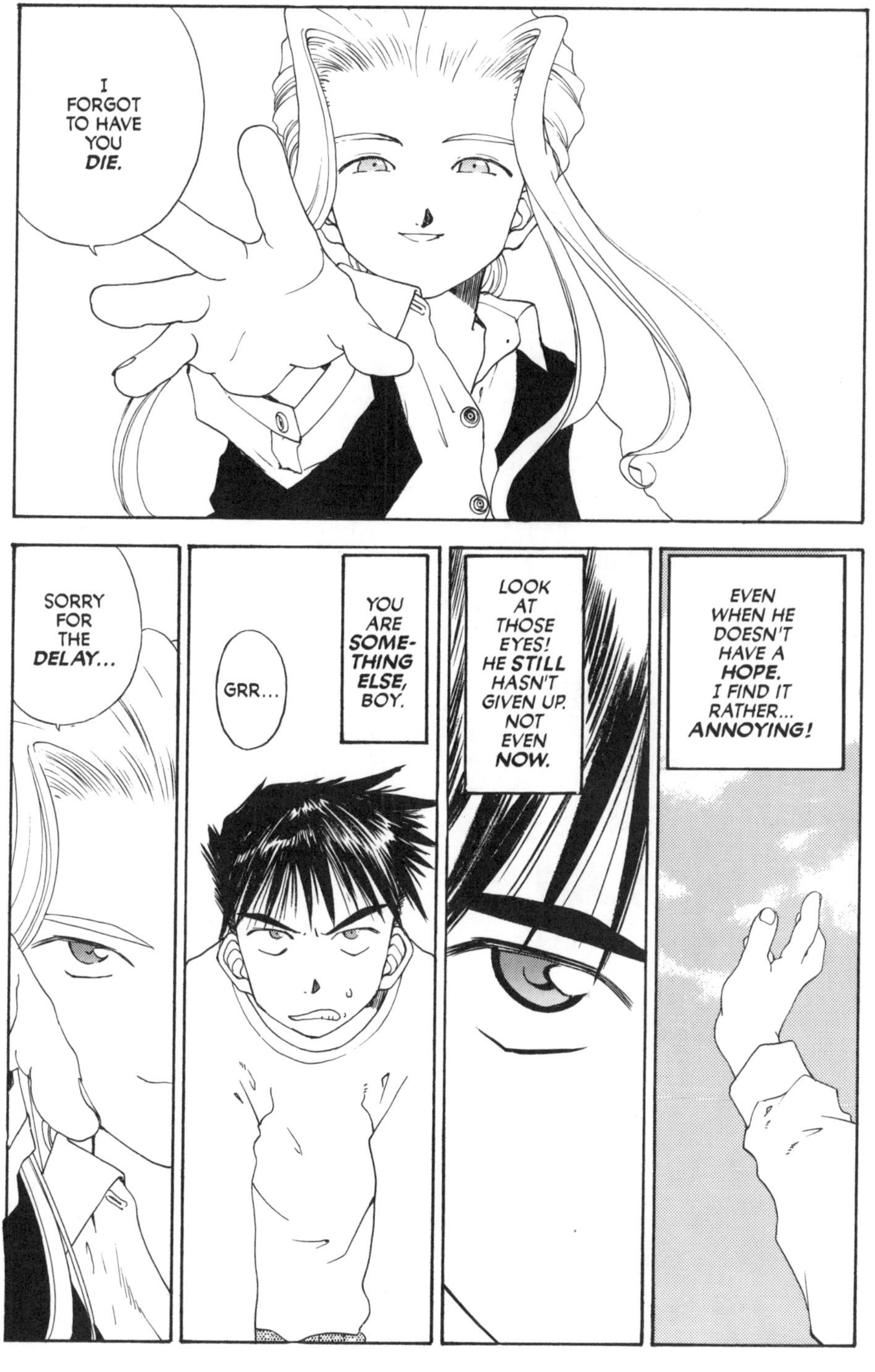
I FORGOT TO HAVE YOU *DIE.*
SORRY FOR THE *DELAY...*
GRR...
YOU ARE ***SOME-THING ELSE,*** *BOY.*
LOOK AT THOSE EYES! HE **STILL** *HASN'T GIVEN UP. NOT EVEN* **NOW.**
EVEN WHEN HE DOESN'T HAVE A ***HOPE.*** *I FIND IT RATHER...* ***ANNOYING!***

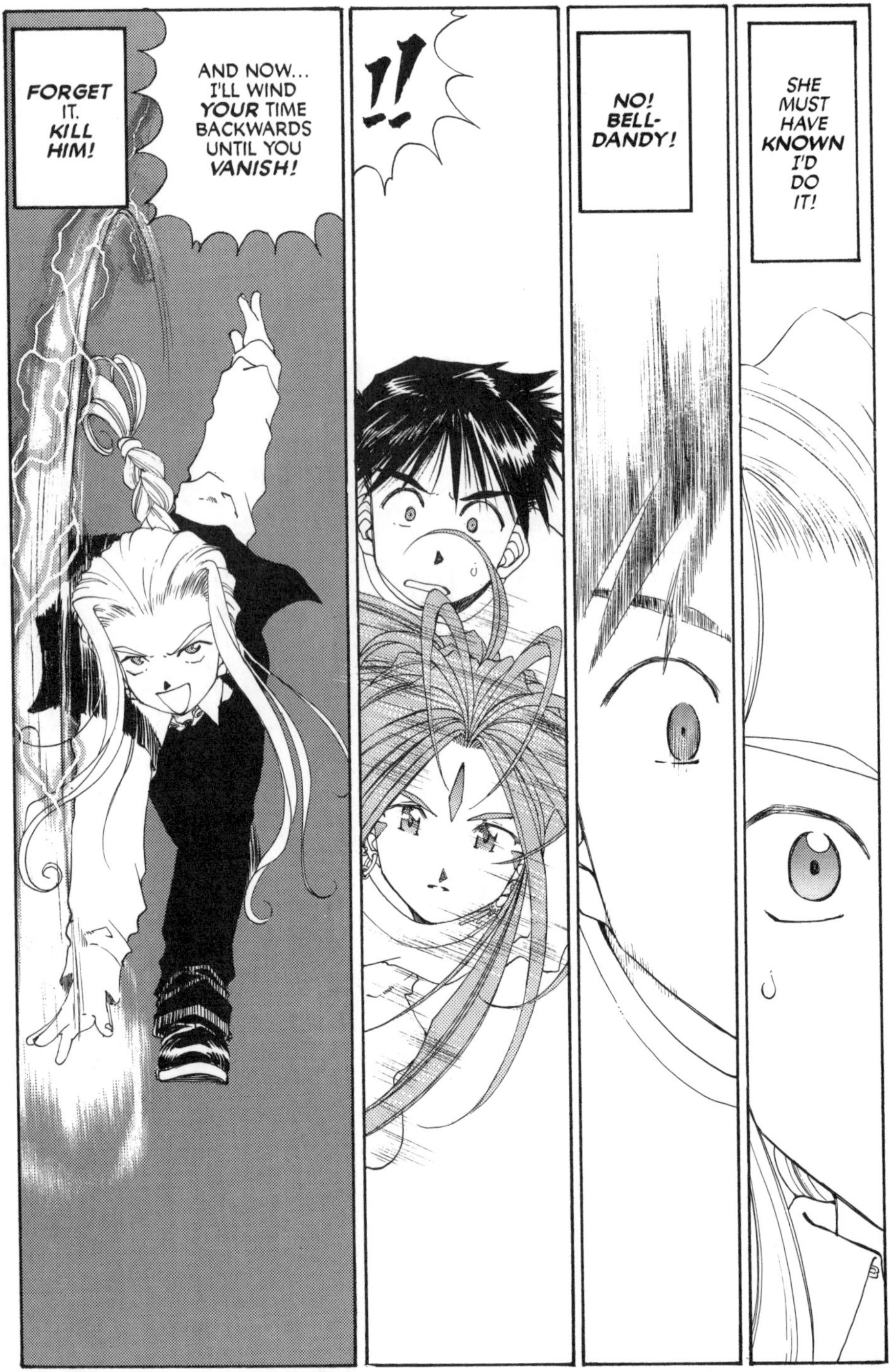

FORGET IT. KILL HIM!
AND NOW... I'LL WIND YOUR TIME BACKWARDS UNTIL YOU VANISH!
!!
NO! BELL-DANDY!
SHE MUST HAVE KNOWN I'D DO IT!

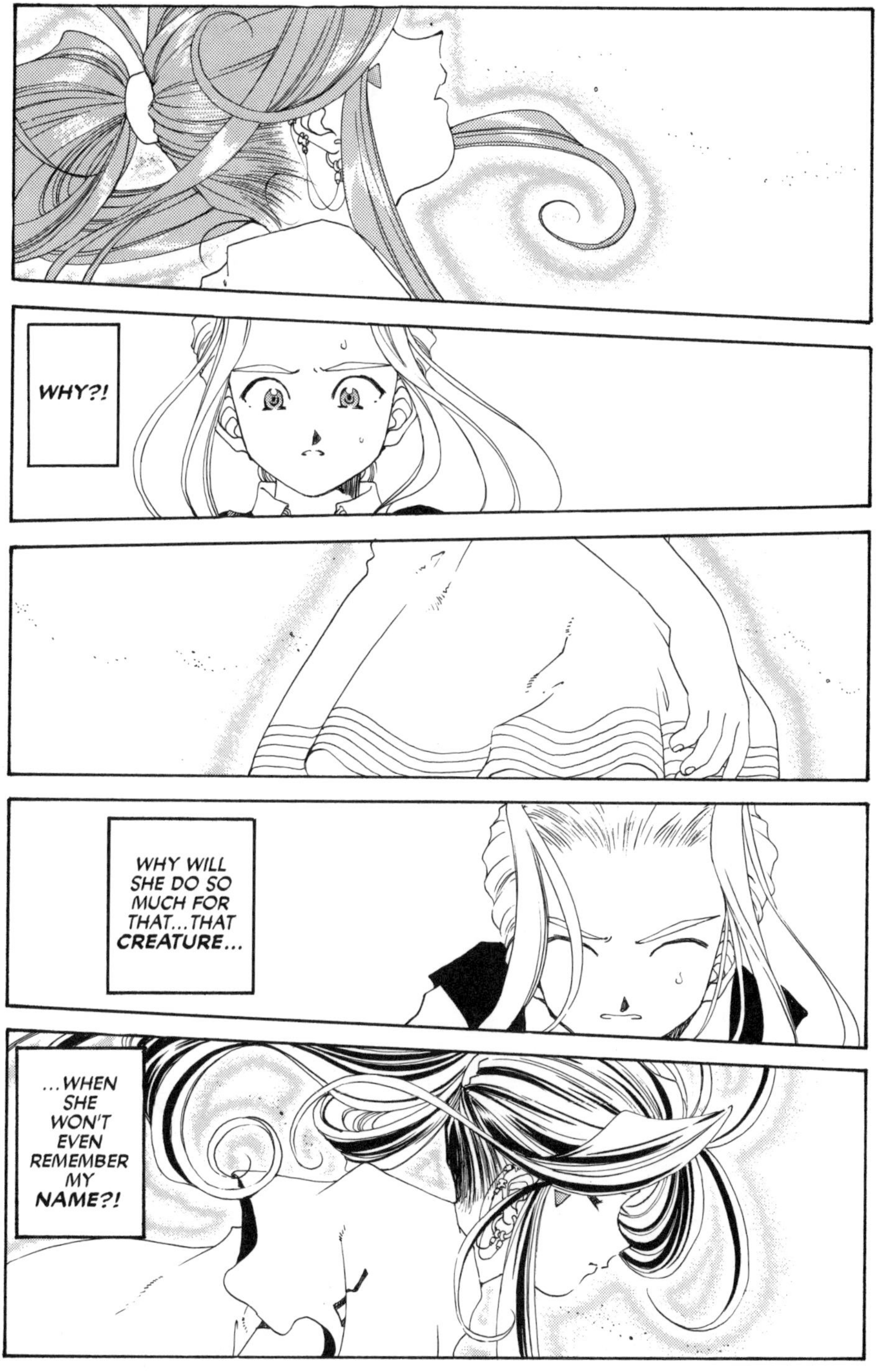
WHY?!
WHY WILL SHE DO SO MUCH FOR THAT...THAT **CREATURE...**
...WHEN SHE WON'T EVEN REMEMBER MY **NAME?!**

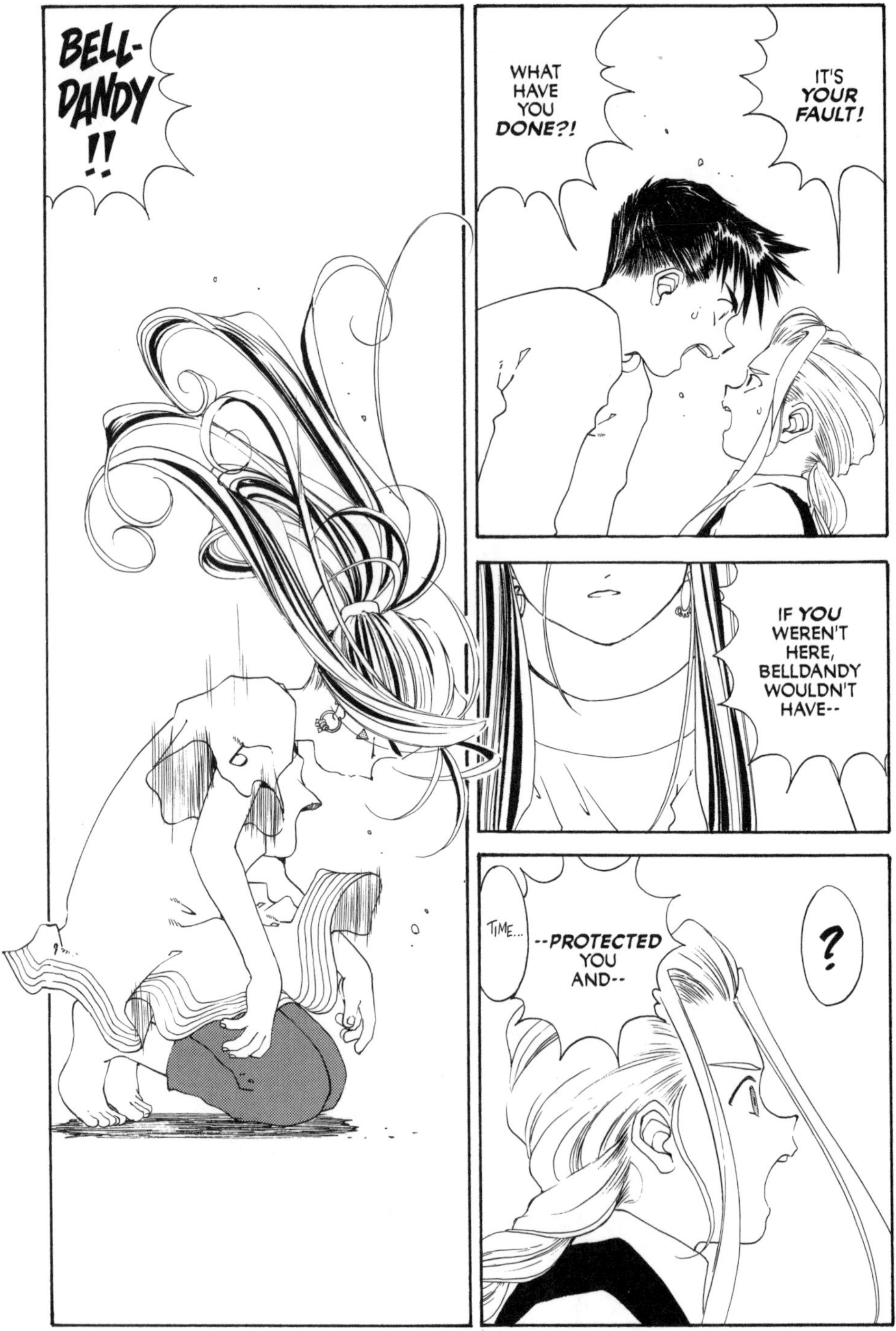
BELL-DANDY!!
WHAT HAVE YOU DONE?!
IT'S YOUR FAULT!
IF YOU WEREN'T HERE, BELLDANDY WOULDN'T HAVE--
TIME...
--PROTECTED YOU AND--
?

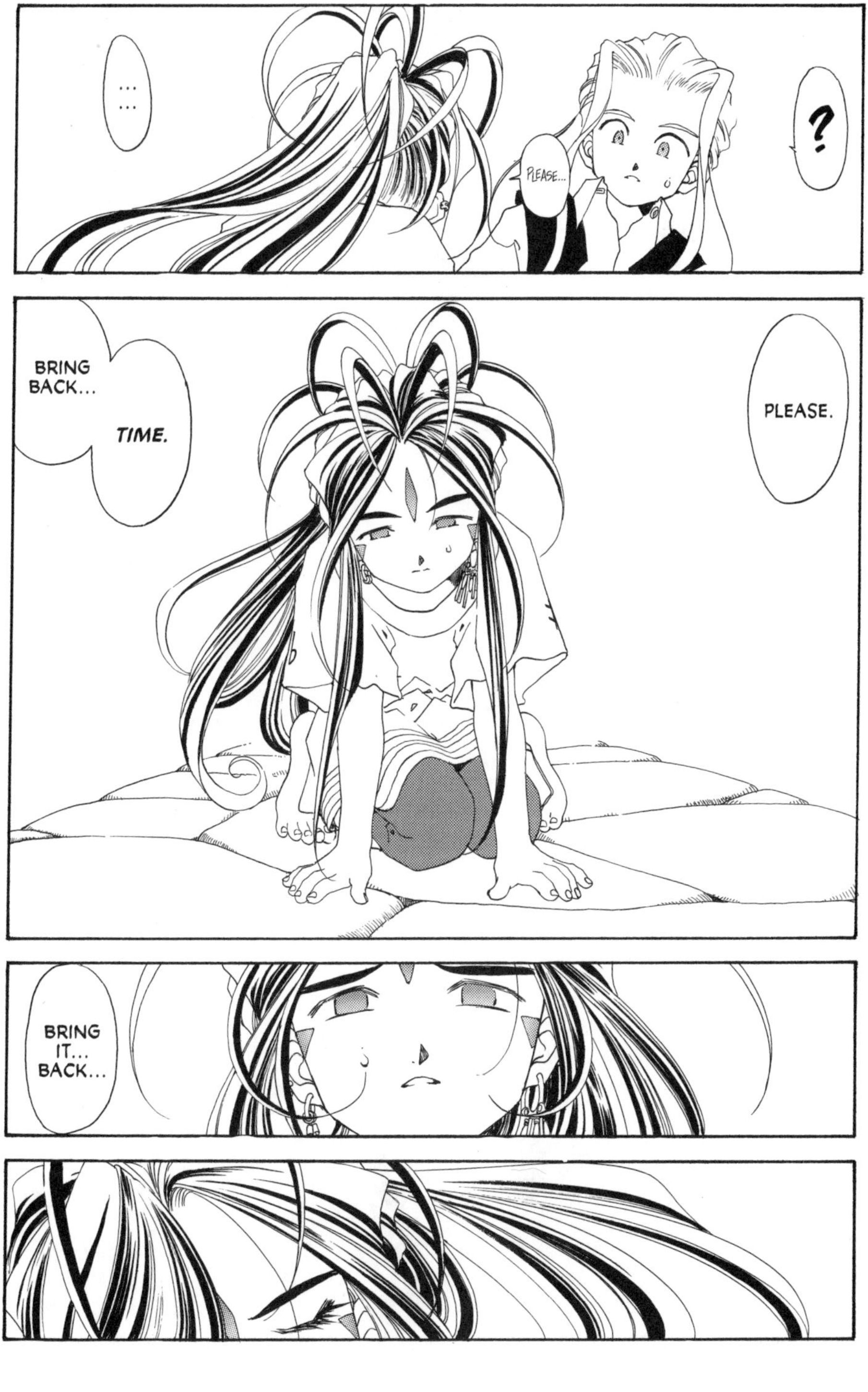
……
PLEASE…
?
BRING BACK… TIME.
PLEASE.
BRING IT… BACK…

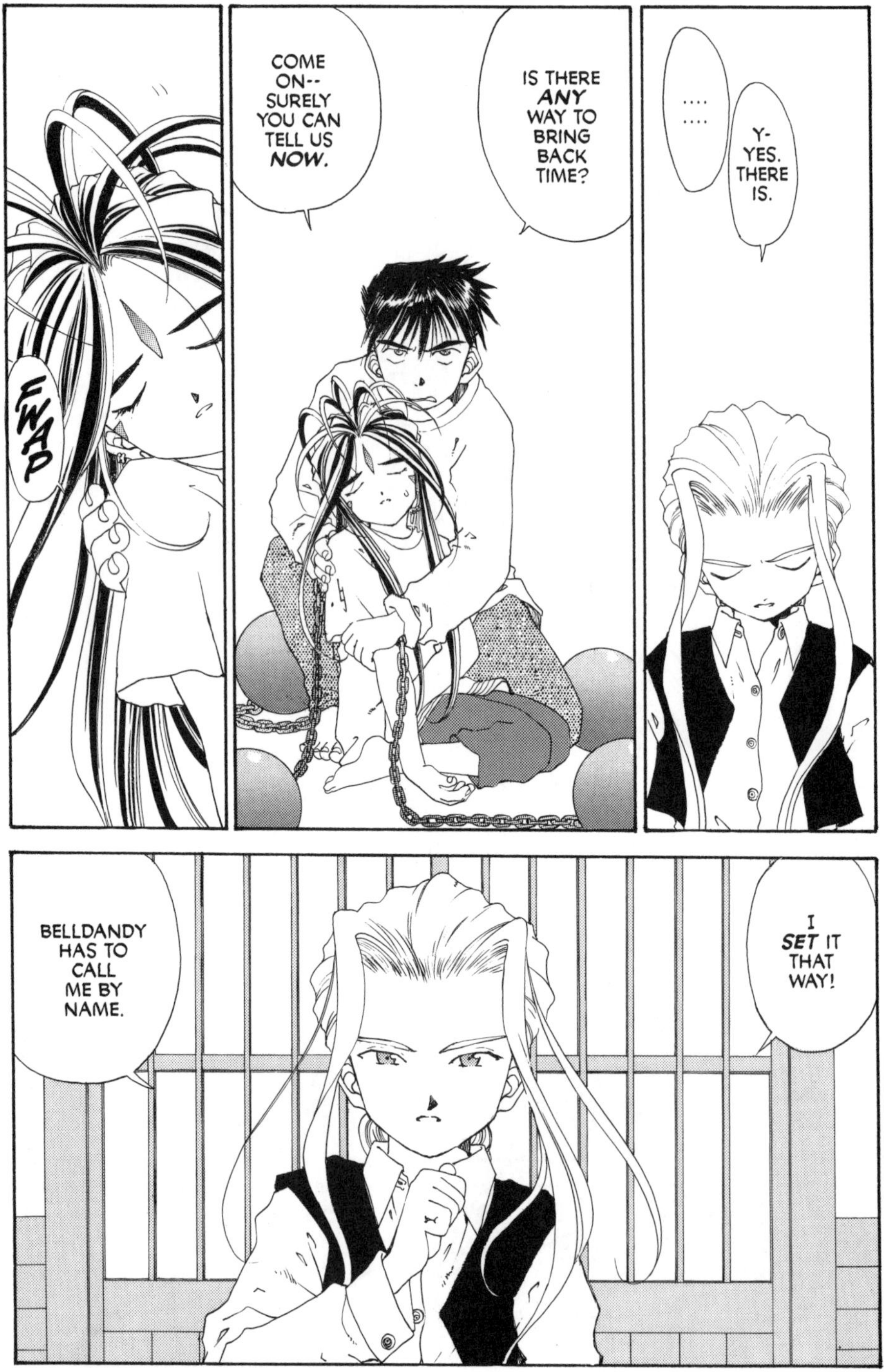
FWAP
COME ON-- SURELY YOU CAN TELL US NOW.
IS THERE ANY WAY TO BRING BACK TIME?
....
Y- YES. THERE IS.
BELLDANDY HAS TO CALL ME BY NAME.
I SET IT THAT WAY!

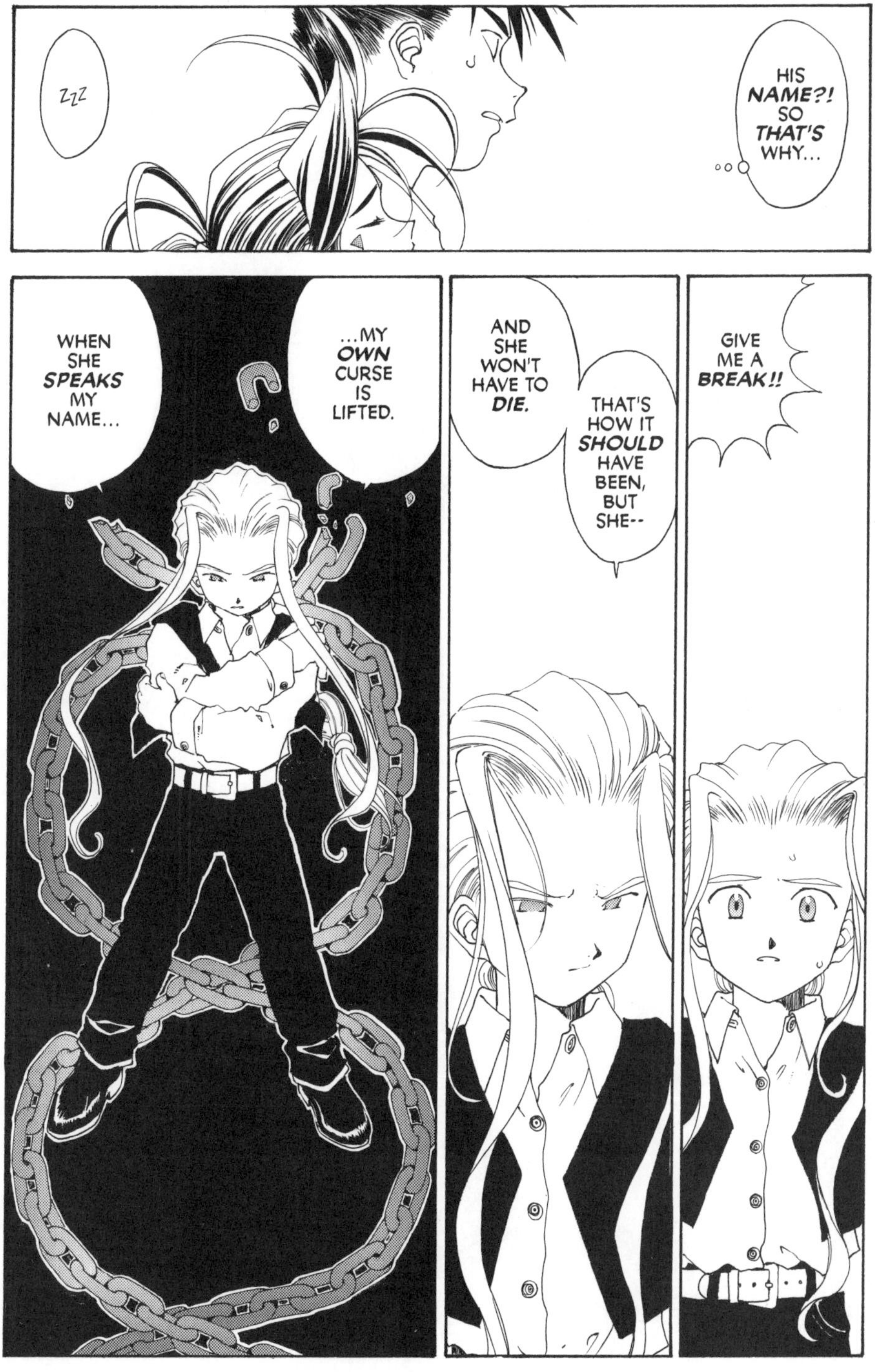
ZZZ
HIS NAME?! SO THAT'S WHY...
WHEN SHE SPEAKS MY NAME...
...MY OWN CURSE IS LIFTED.
AND SHE WON'T HAVE TO DIE.
THAT'S HOW IT SHOULD HAVE BEEN, BUT SHE--
GIVE ME A BREAK!!

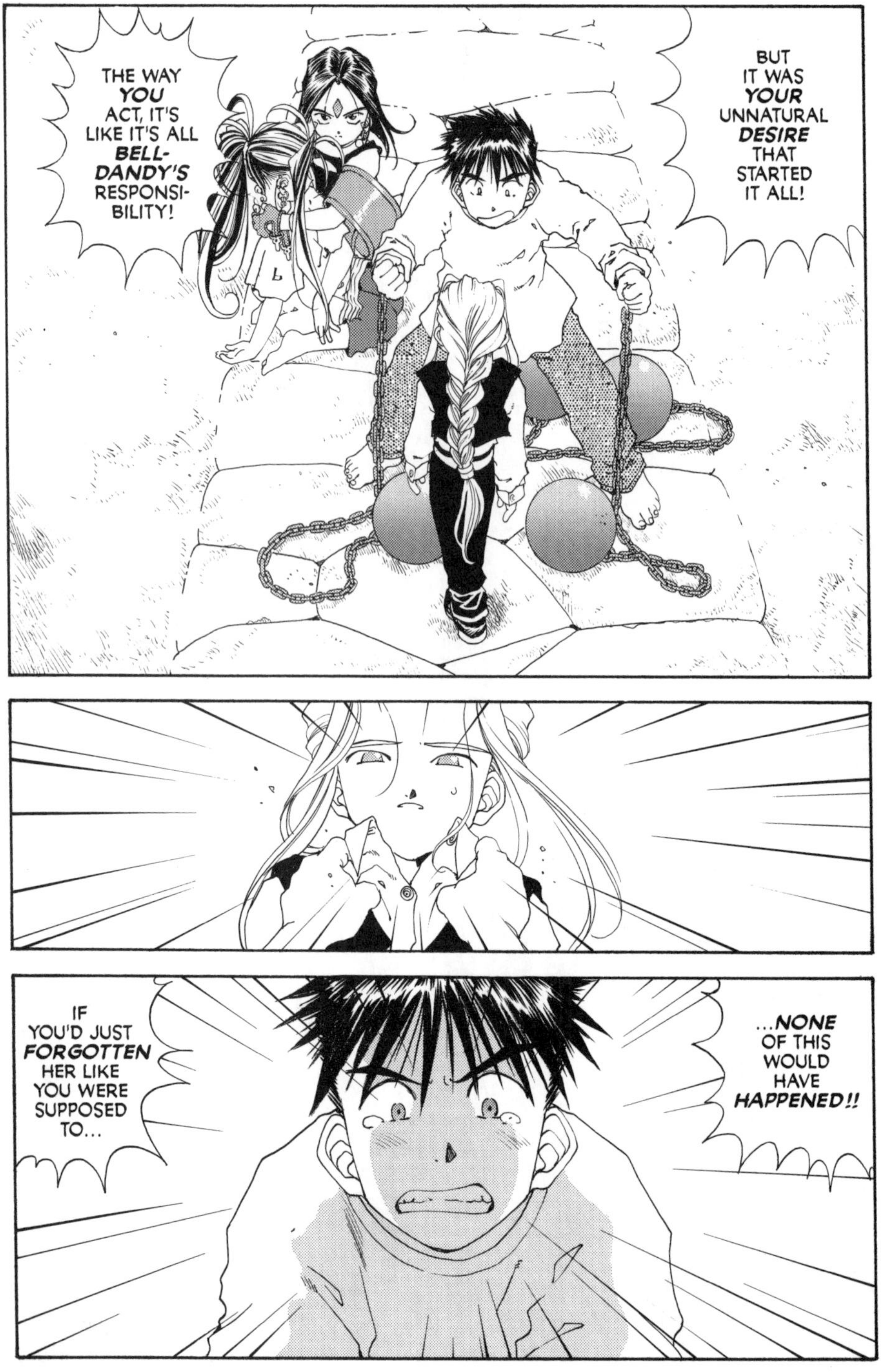
THE WAY *YOU* ACT, IT'S LIKE IT'S ALL *BELL-DANDY'S* RESPONSI-BILITY!
BUT IT WAS *YOUR* UNNATURAL *DESIRE* THAT STARTED IT ALL!
IF YOU'D JUST *FORGOTTEN* HER LIKE YOU WERE SUPPOSED TO...
...*NONE* OF THIS WOULD HAVE *HAPPENED!!*

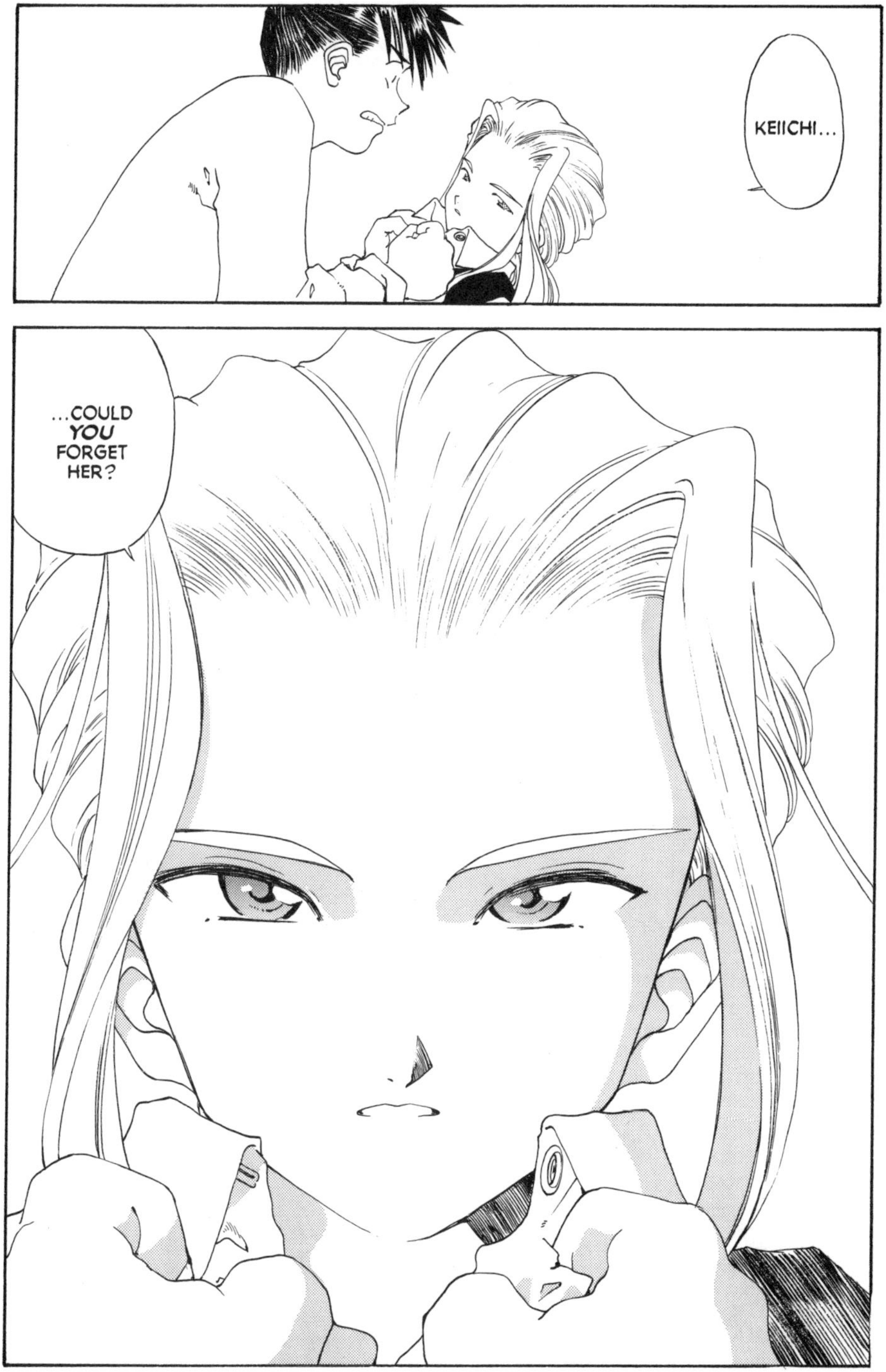
KEIICHI...
...COULD *YOU* FORGET HER?

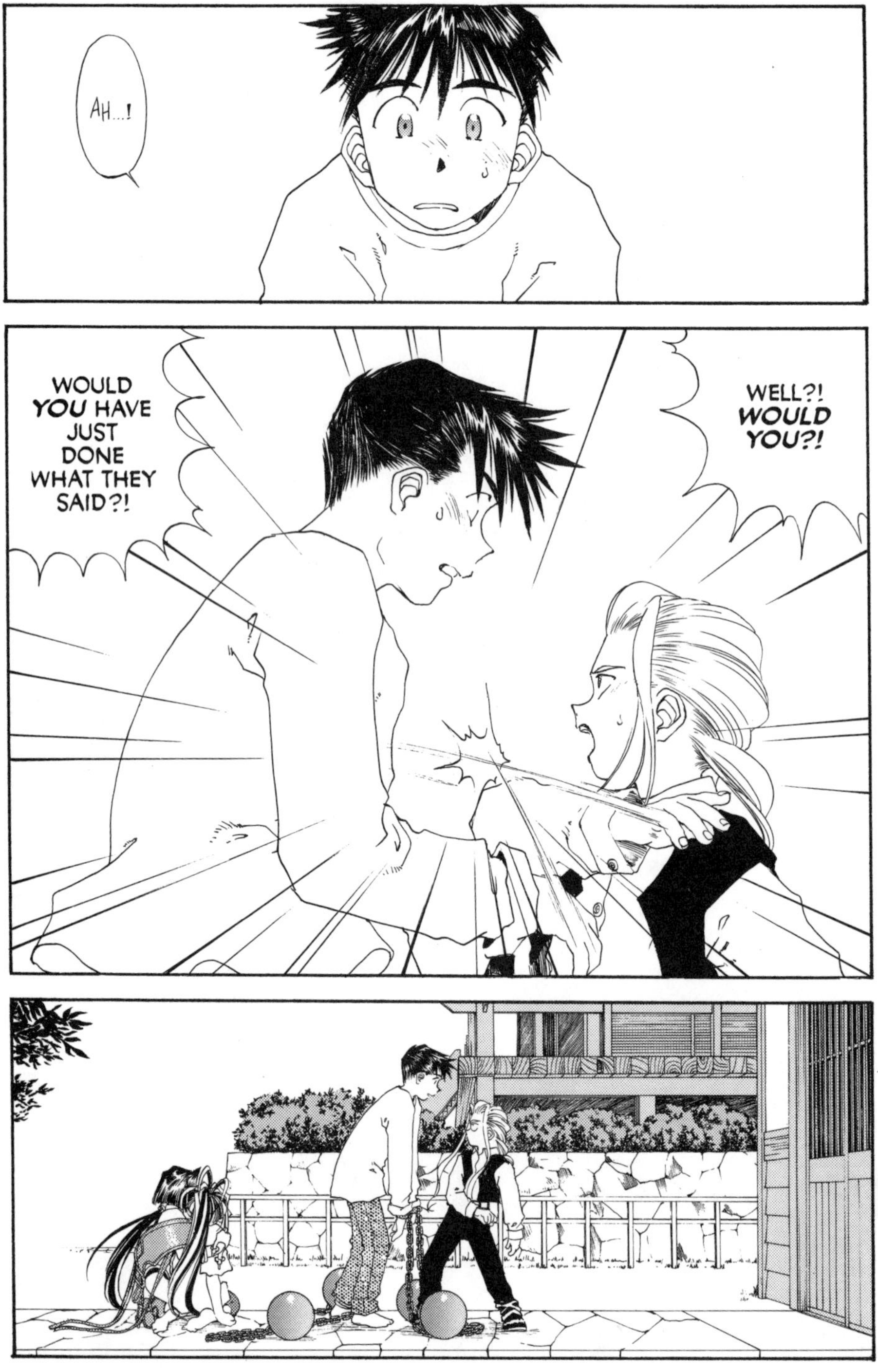
AH...!
WOULD YOU HAVE JUST DONE WHAT THEY SAID?!
WELL?! WOULD YOU?!

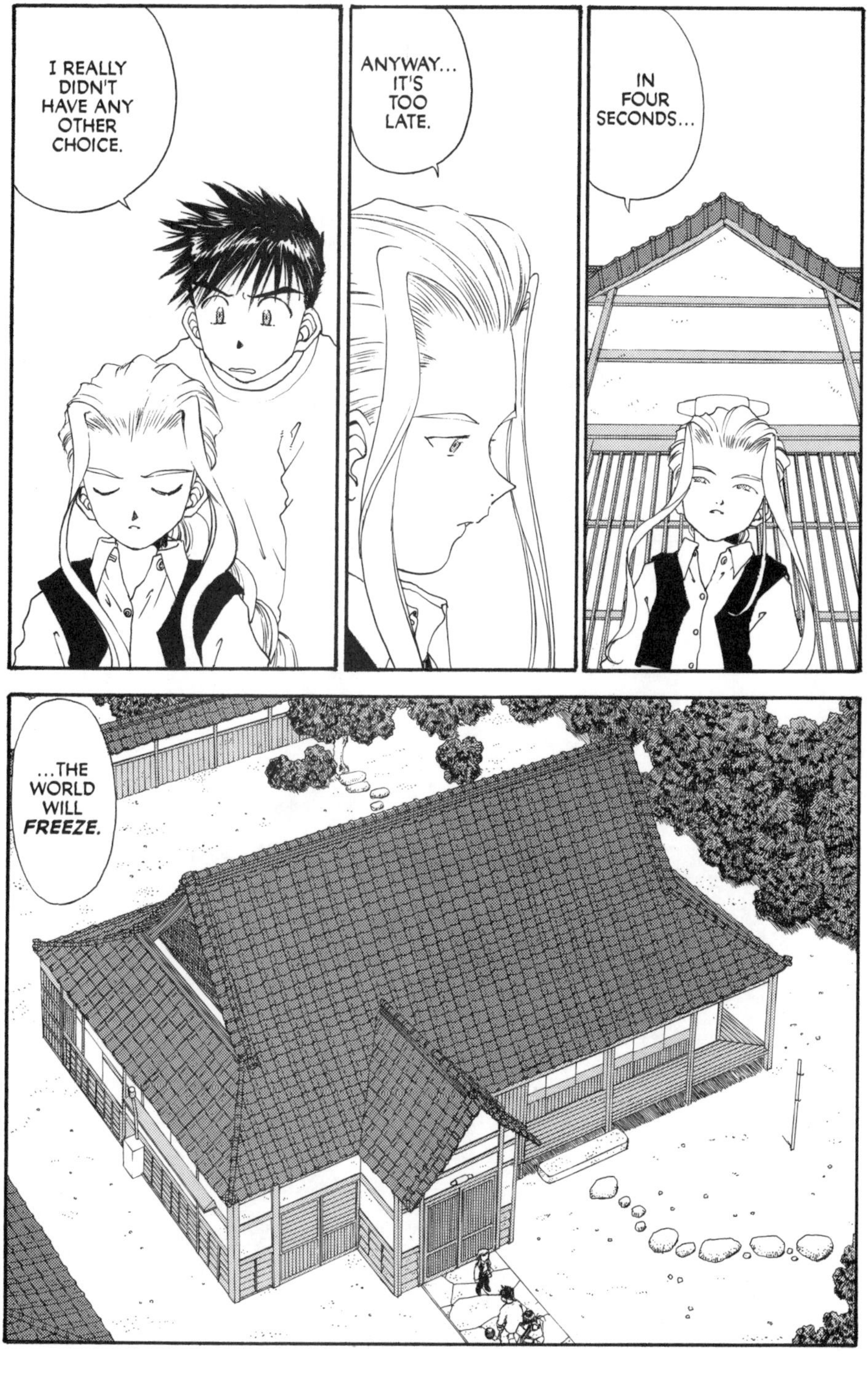
I REALLY DIDN'T HAVE ANY OTHER CHOICE.
ANYWAY... IT'S TOO LATE.
IN FOUR SECONDS...
...THE WORLD WILL *FREEZE.*

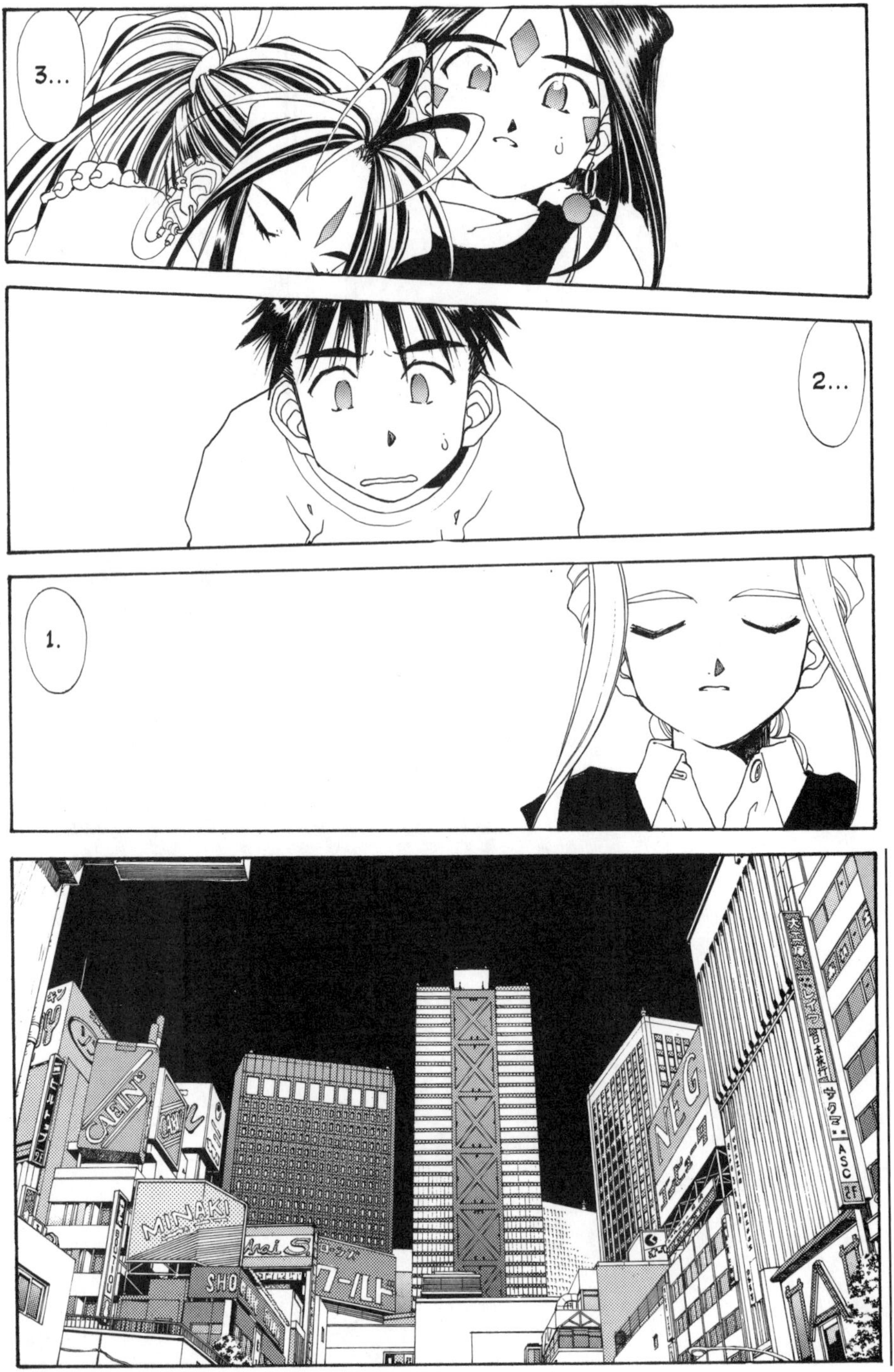
3...
2...
1.

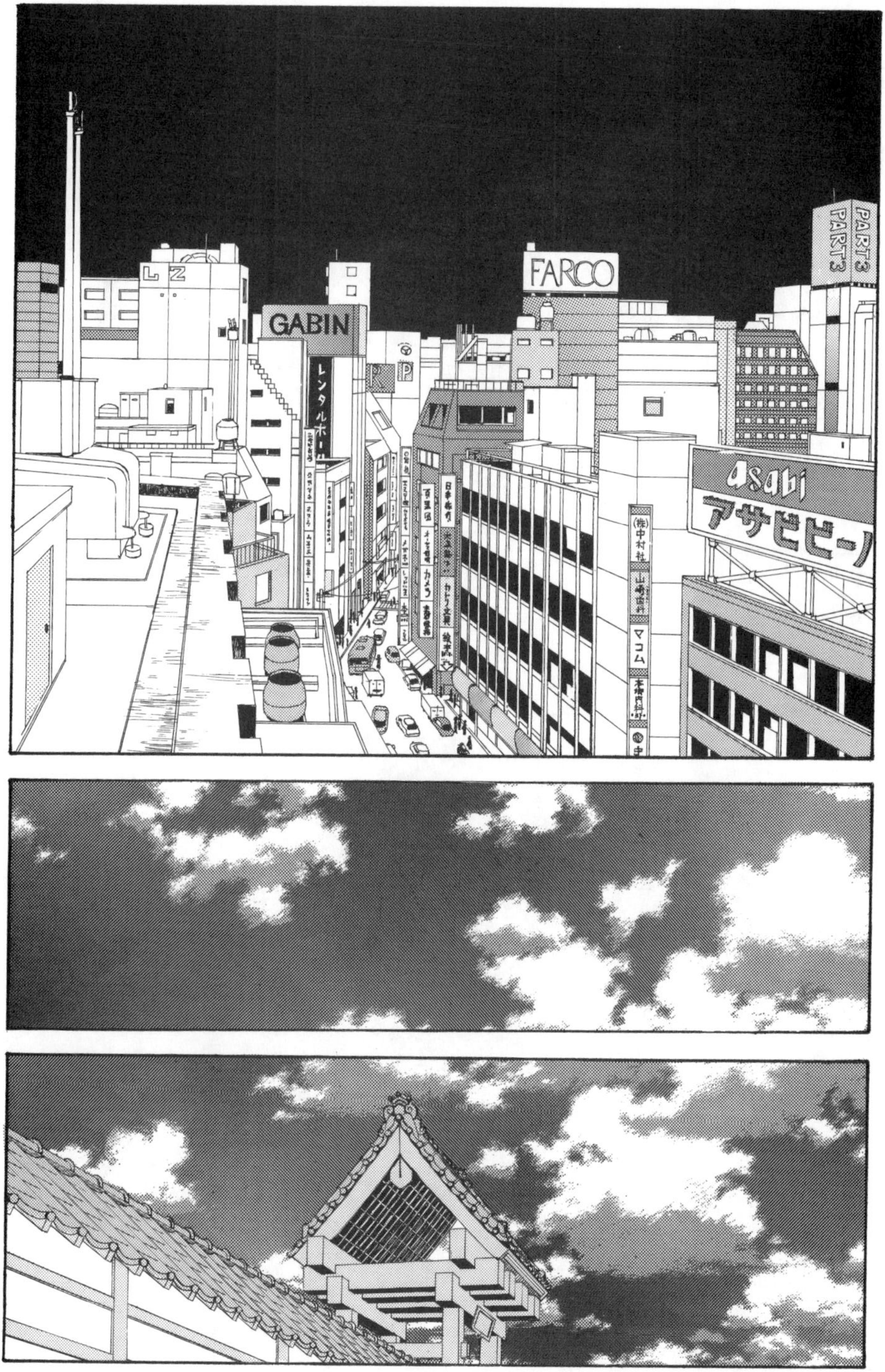
GABIN
FARCO
PART3
PART3
asabi

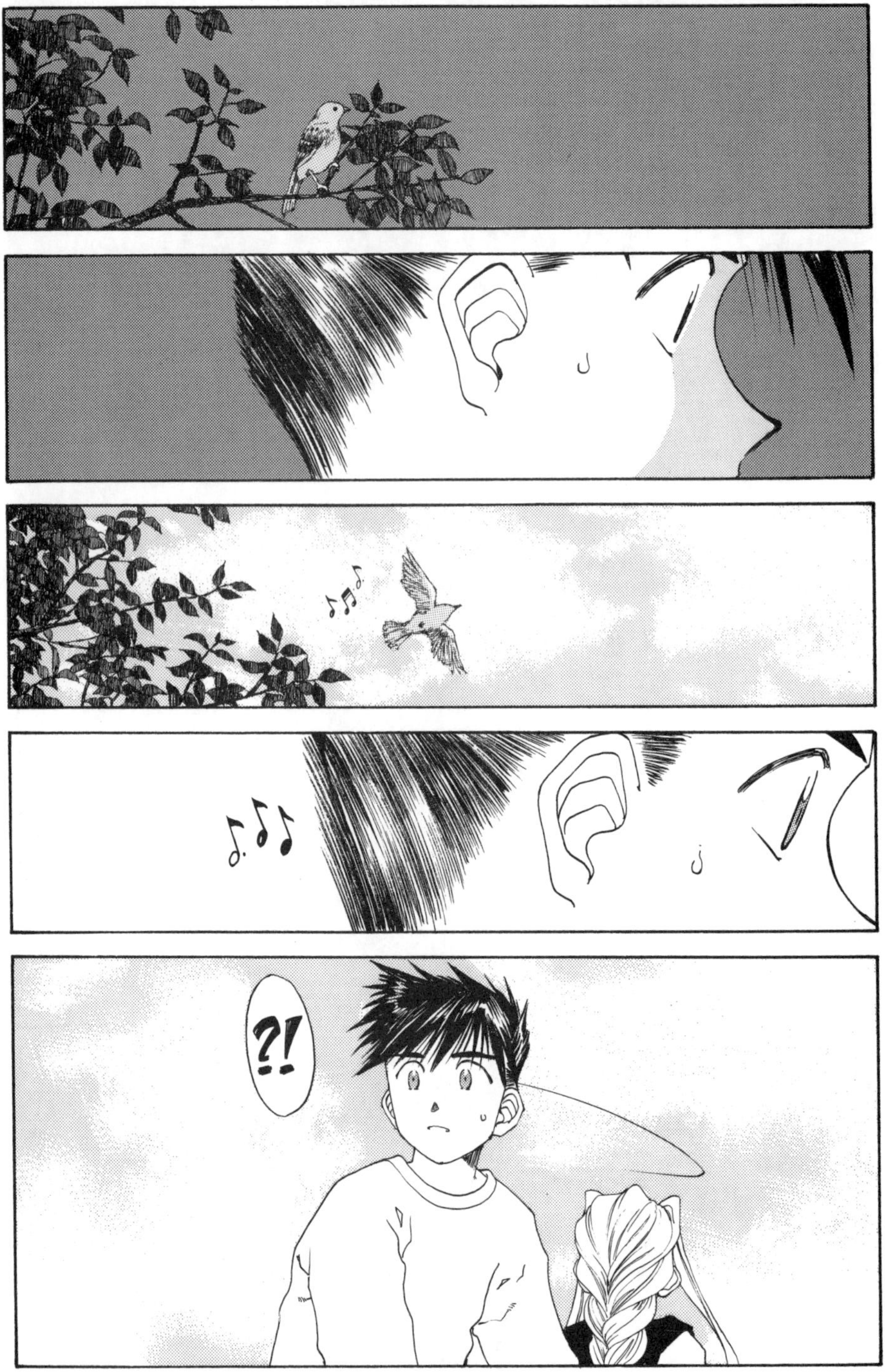
?!

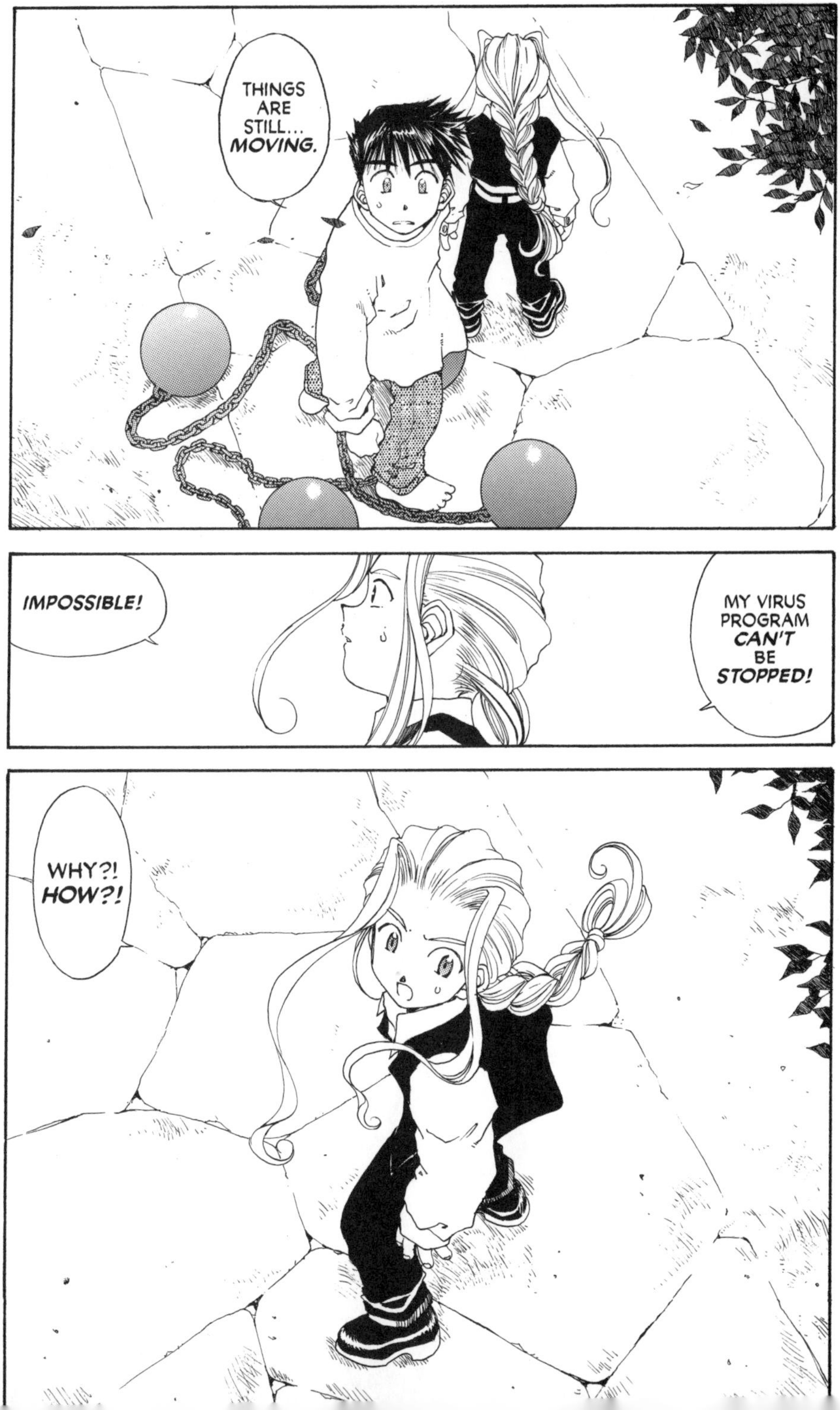
THINGS ARE STILL... MOVING.
IMPOSSIBLE!
MY VIRUS PROGRAM CAN'T BE STOPPED!
WHY?! HOW?!

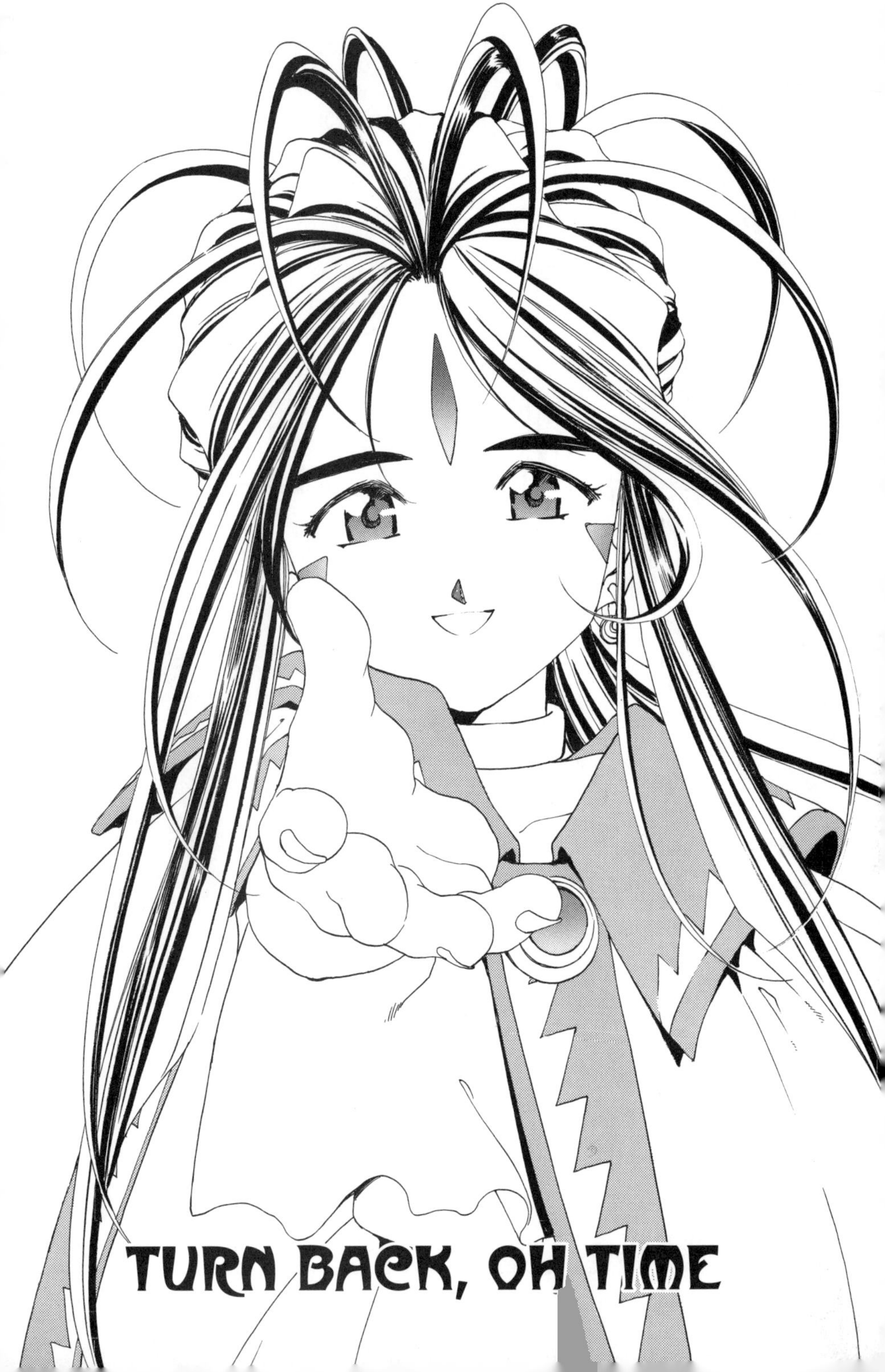
TURN BACK, OH TIME

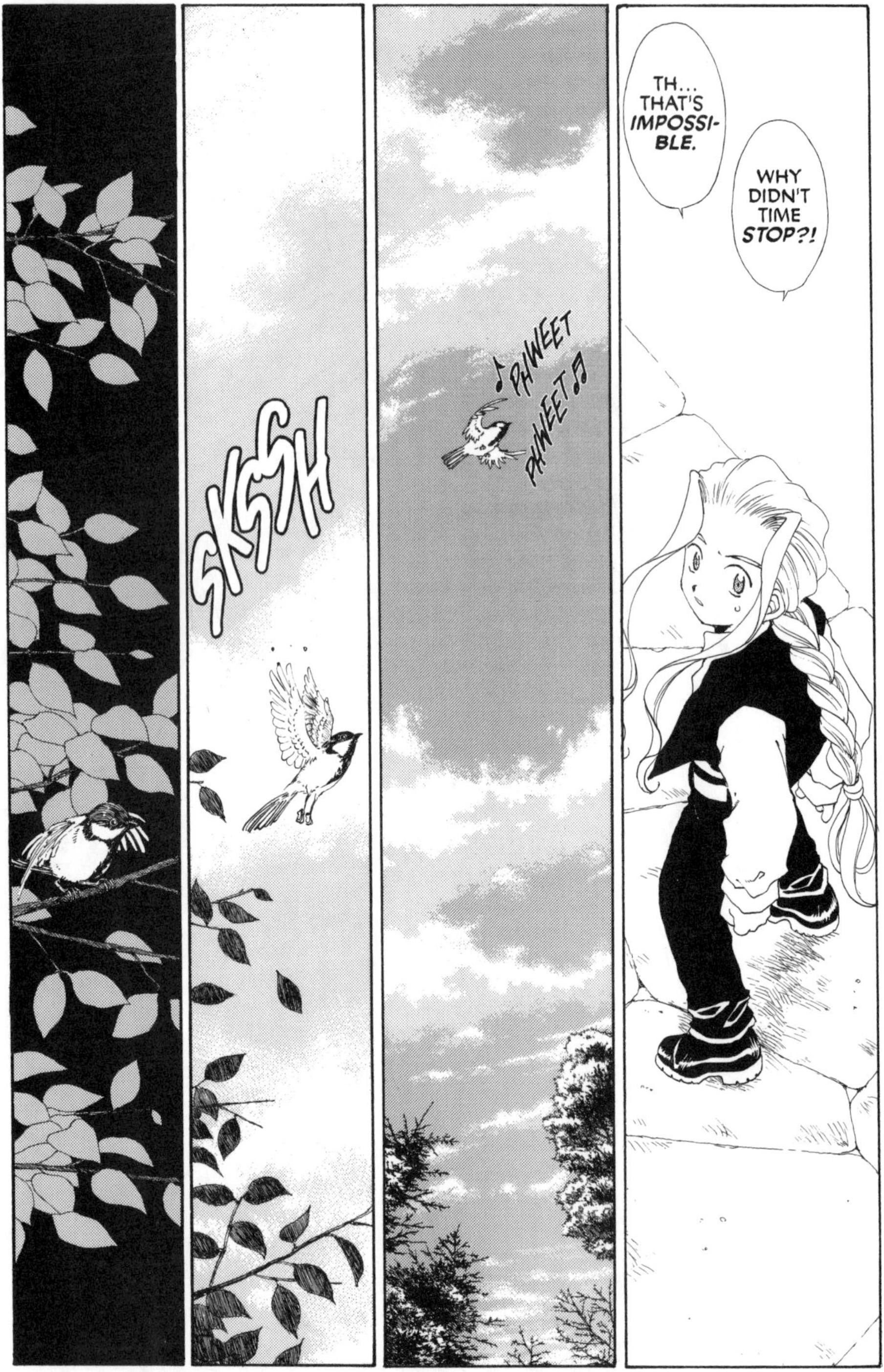

SKSSH
♪ PHWEET PHWEET ♫
TH... THAT'S *IMPOSSI-BLE.*
WHY DIDN'T TIME *STOP?!*

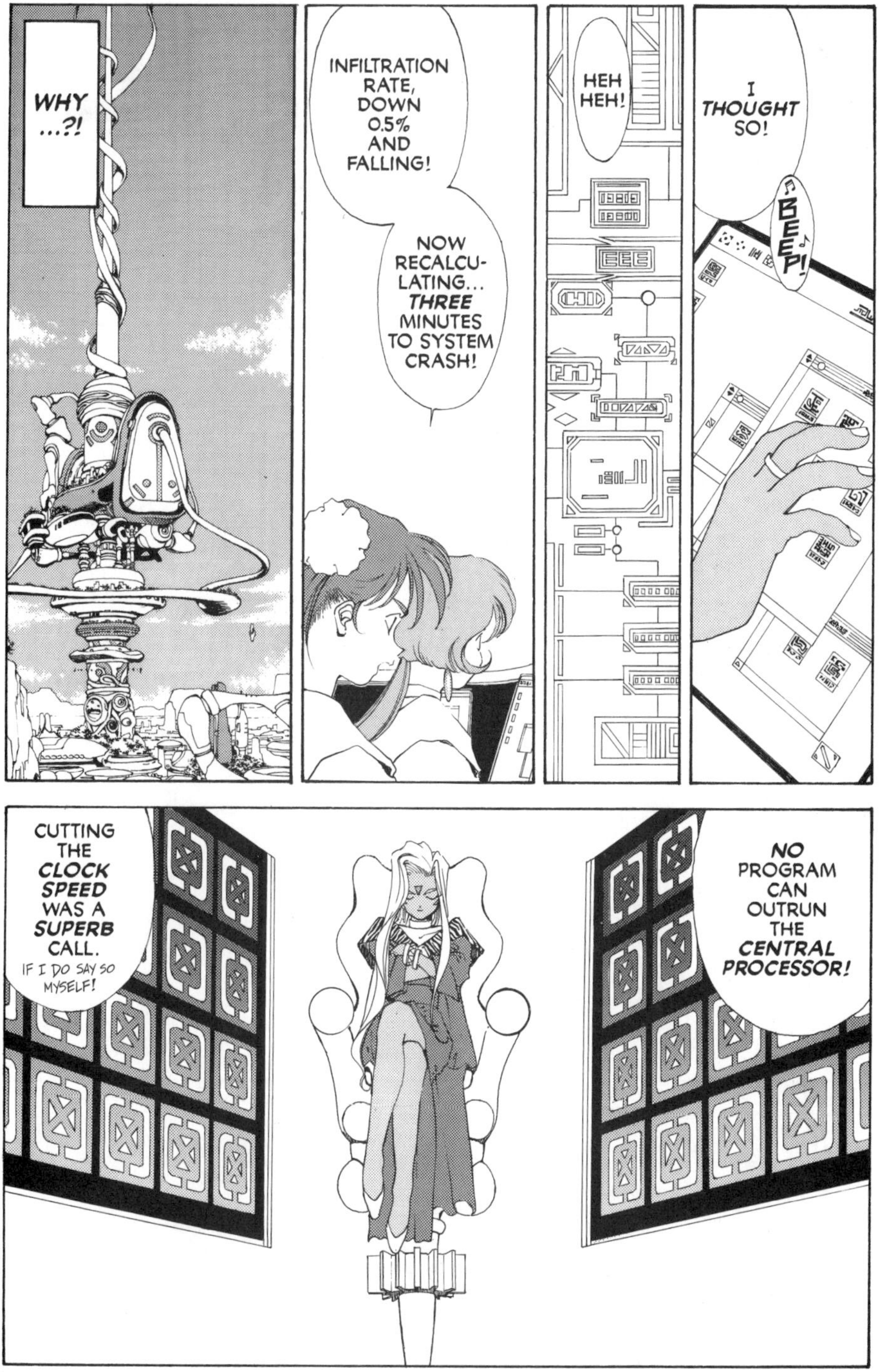
WHY ...?!
INFILTRATION RATE, DOWN 0.5% AND FALLING!
NOW RECALCU-LATING... THREE MINUTES TO SYSTEM CRASH!
HEH HEH!
I THOUGHT SO!
BEEP!
CUTTING THE CLOCK SPEED WAS A SUPERB CALL.
IF I DO SAY SO MYSELF!
NO PROGRAM CAN OUTRUN THE CENTRAL PROCESSOR!

BUT IT'S NOT LIKE WE CAN JUST SIT ON OUR HANDS, URD.

AT *THIS* SPEED, THE TIME DISTORTION WILL GO OFF THE SCALE IN *DIMENSION THREE.*

TRUE.

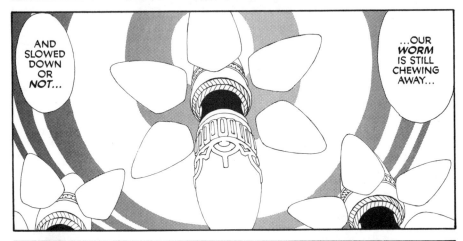

AND SLOWED DOWN OR *NOT...*

...OUR *WORM* IS STILL CHEWING AWAY...

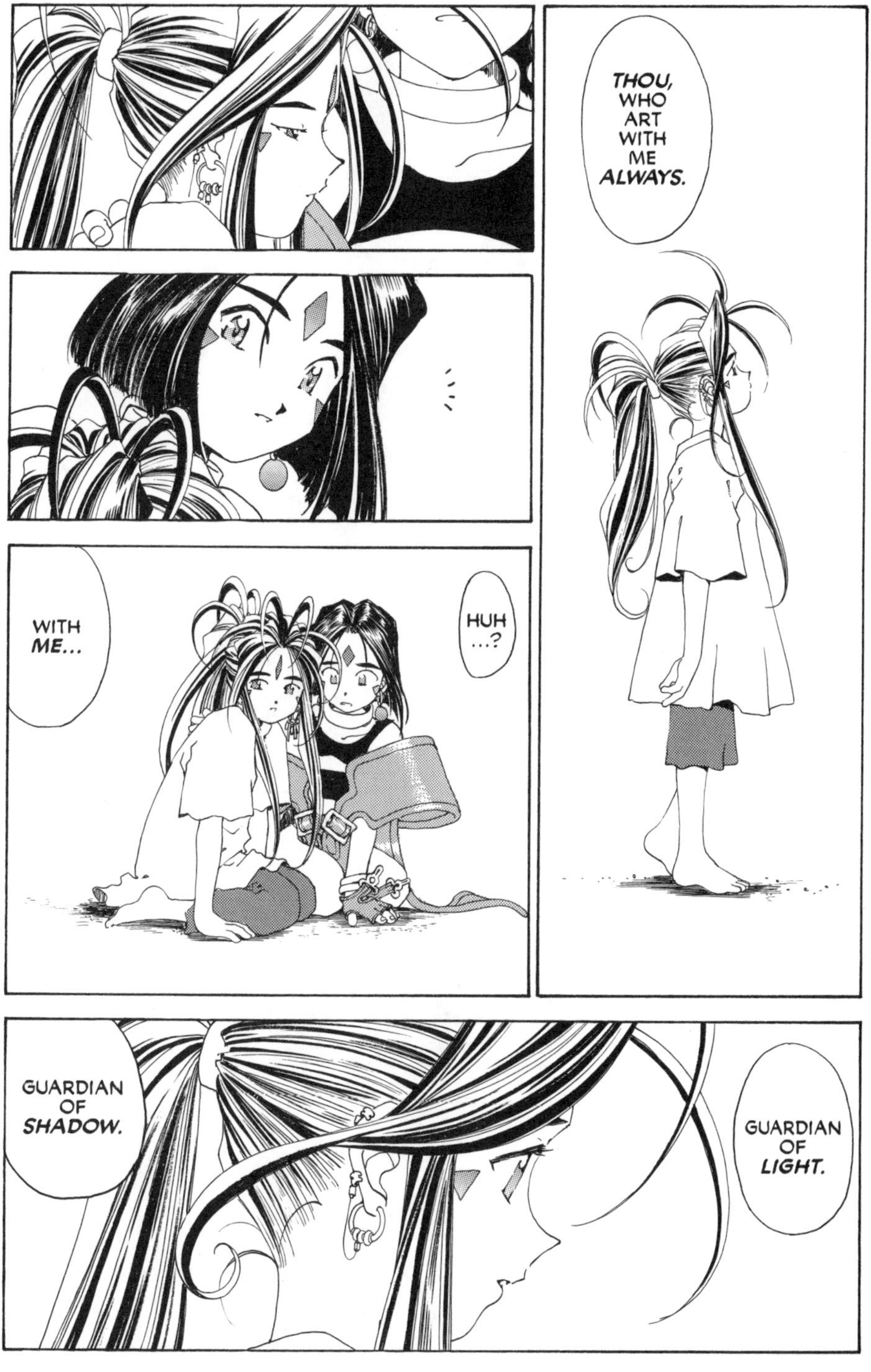
WITH ME...
HUH ...?
THOU, WHO ART WITH ME ALWAYS.
GUARDIAN OF SHADOW.
GUARDIAN OF LIGHT.

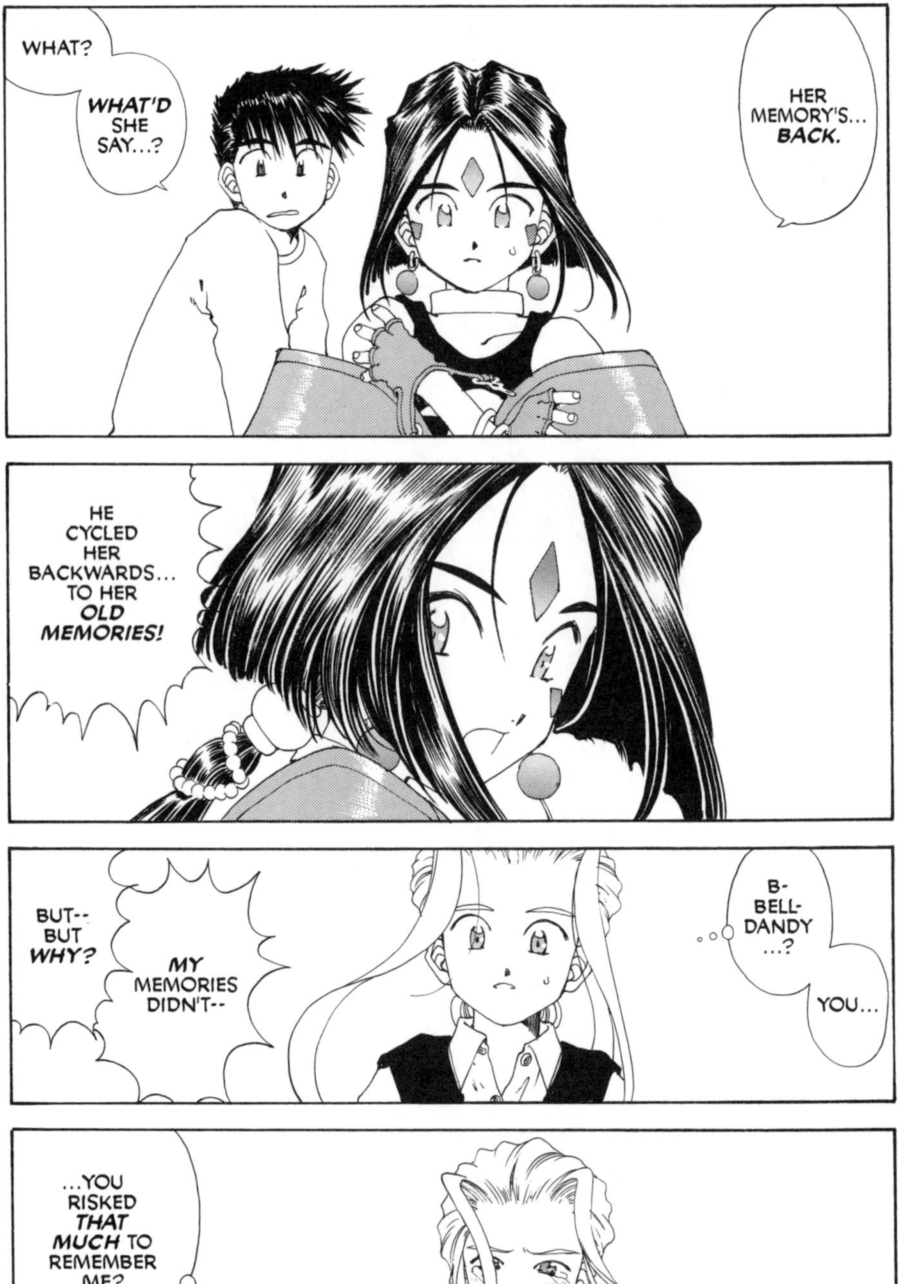
WHAT? WHAT'D SHE SAY...?
HER MEMORY'S... BACK.
HE CYCLED HER BACKWARDS... TO HER OLD MEMORIES!
BUT-- BUT WHY?
MY MEMORIES DIDN'T--
B- BELL-DANDY ...?
YOU...
...YOU RISKED THAT MUCH TO REMEMBER ME?

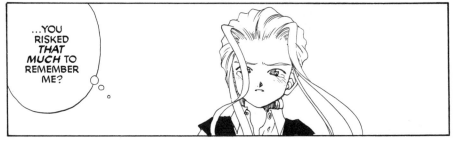

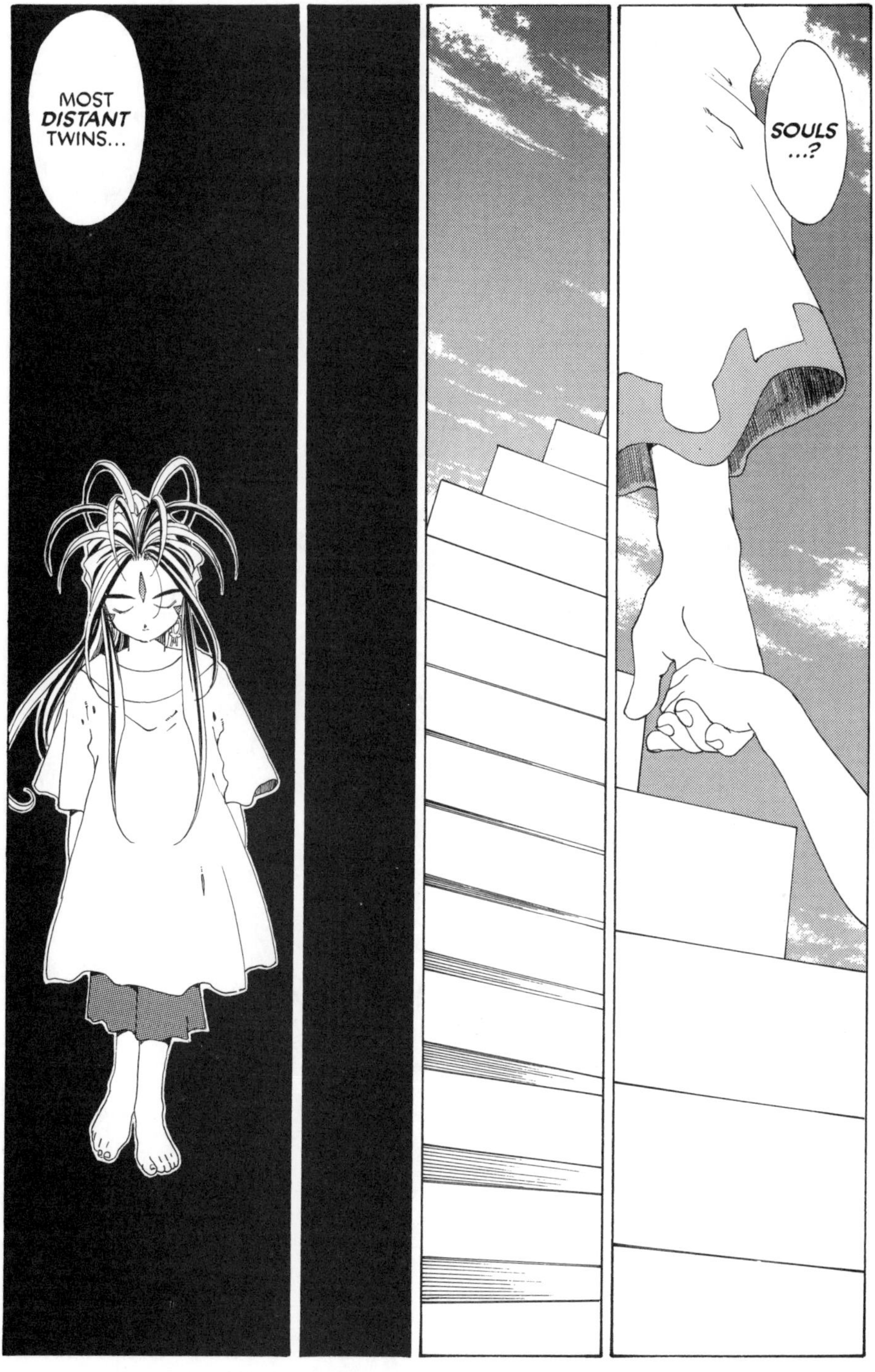
MOST *DISTANT* TWINS...
SOULS ...?

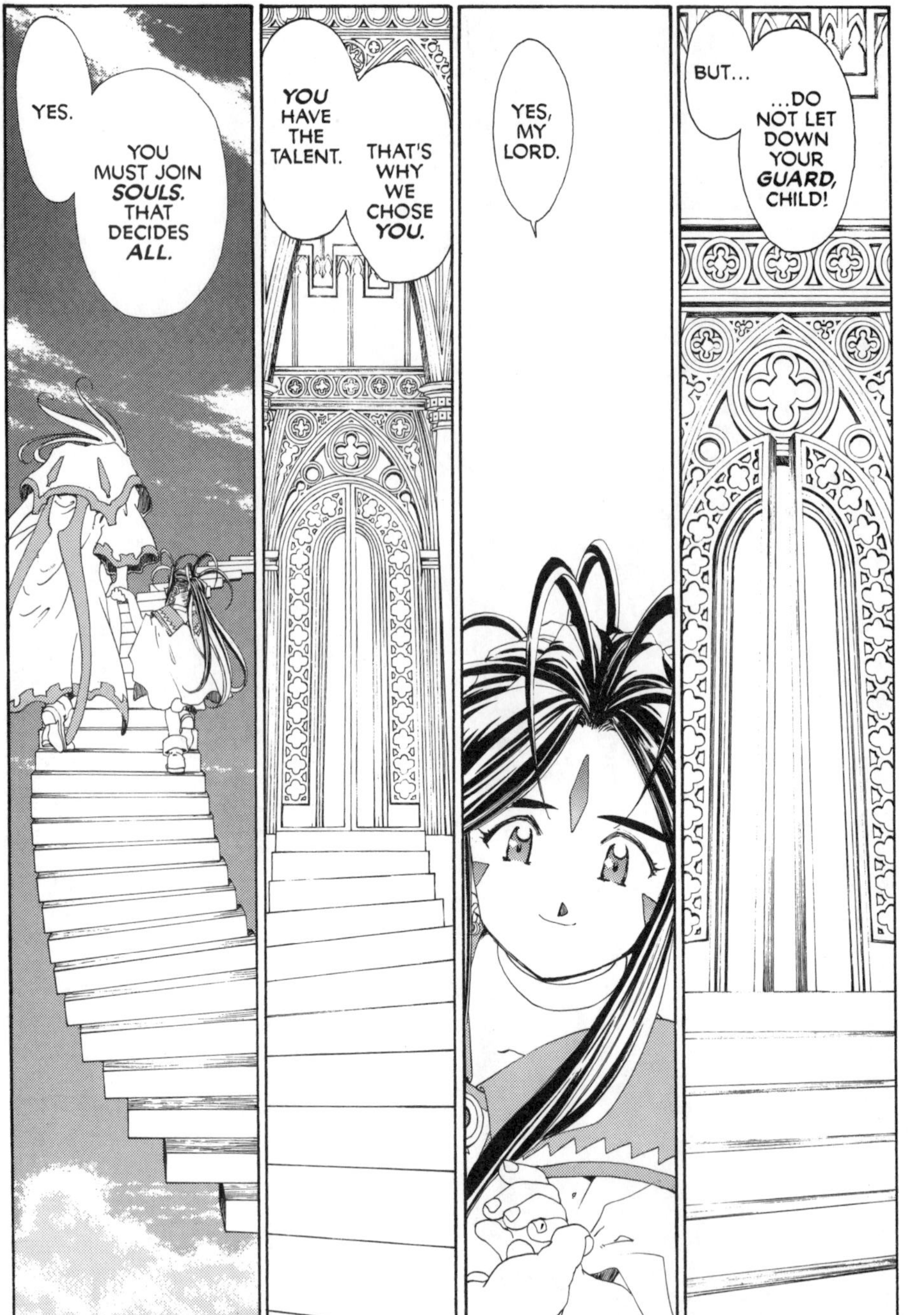
YES.
YOU MUST JOIN *SOULS.* THAT DECIDES *ALL.*
YOU HAVE THE TALENT.
THAT'S WHY WE CHOSE *YOU.*
YES, MY LORD.
BUT...
...DO NOT LET DOWN YOUR *GUARD,* CHILD!

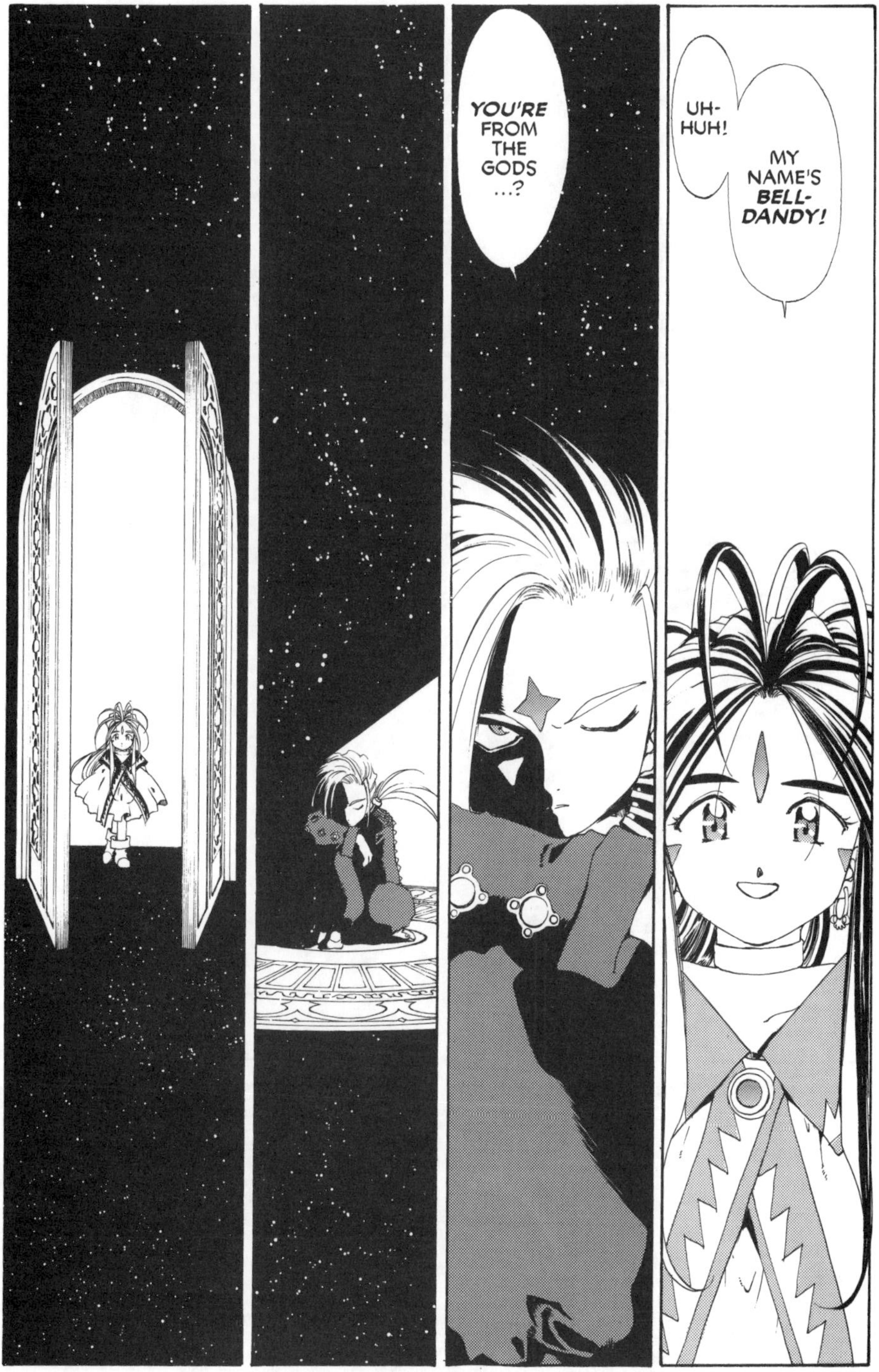
YOU'RE FROM THE GODS ...?
UH-HUH!
MY NAME'S BELL-DANDY!

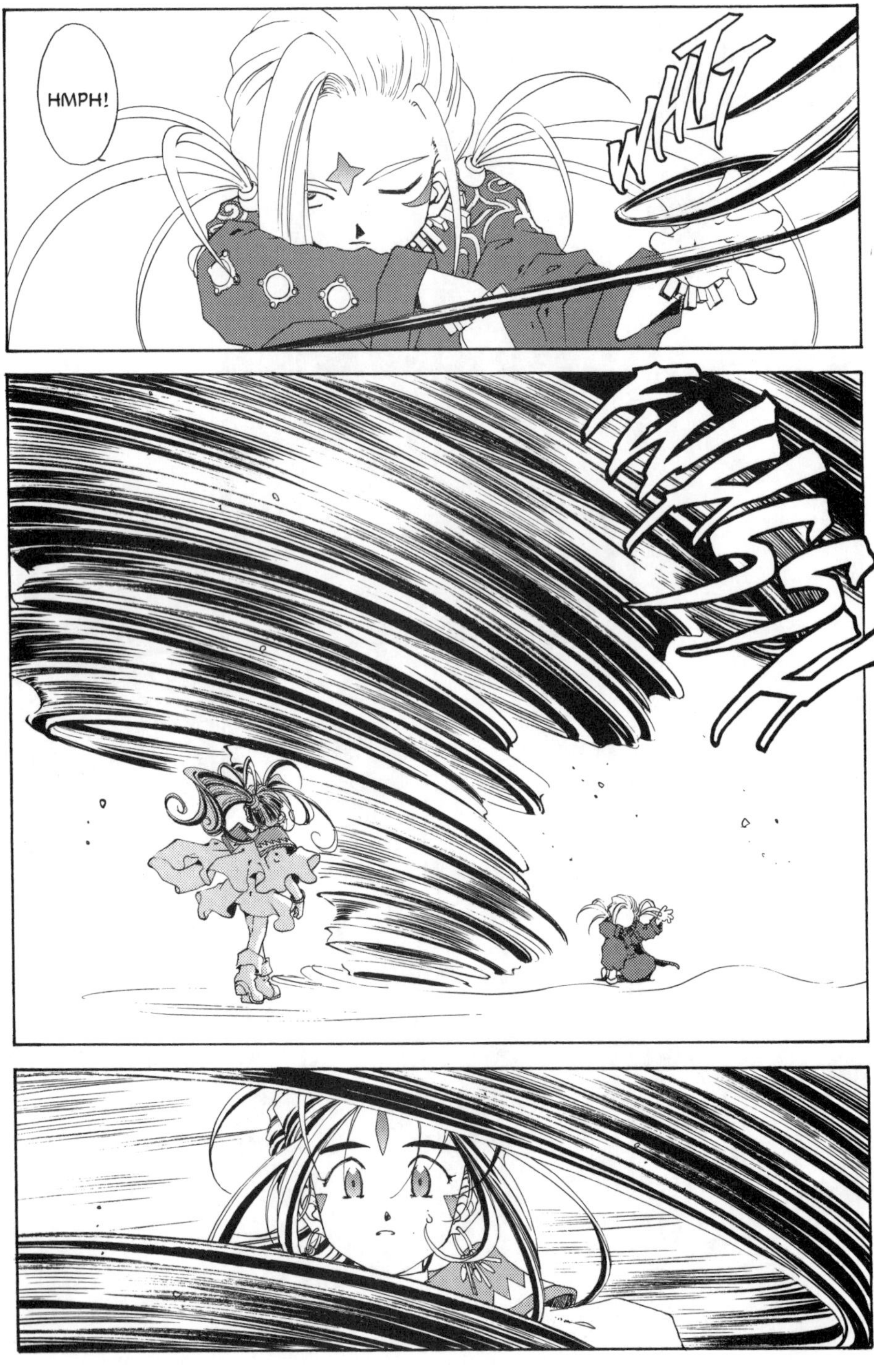
HMPH!
WHTT
FWHSSH

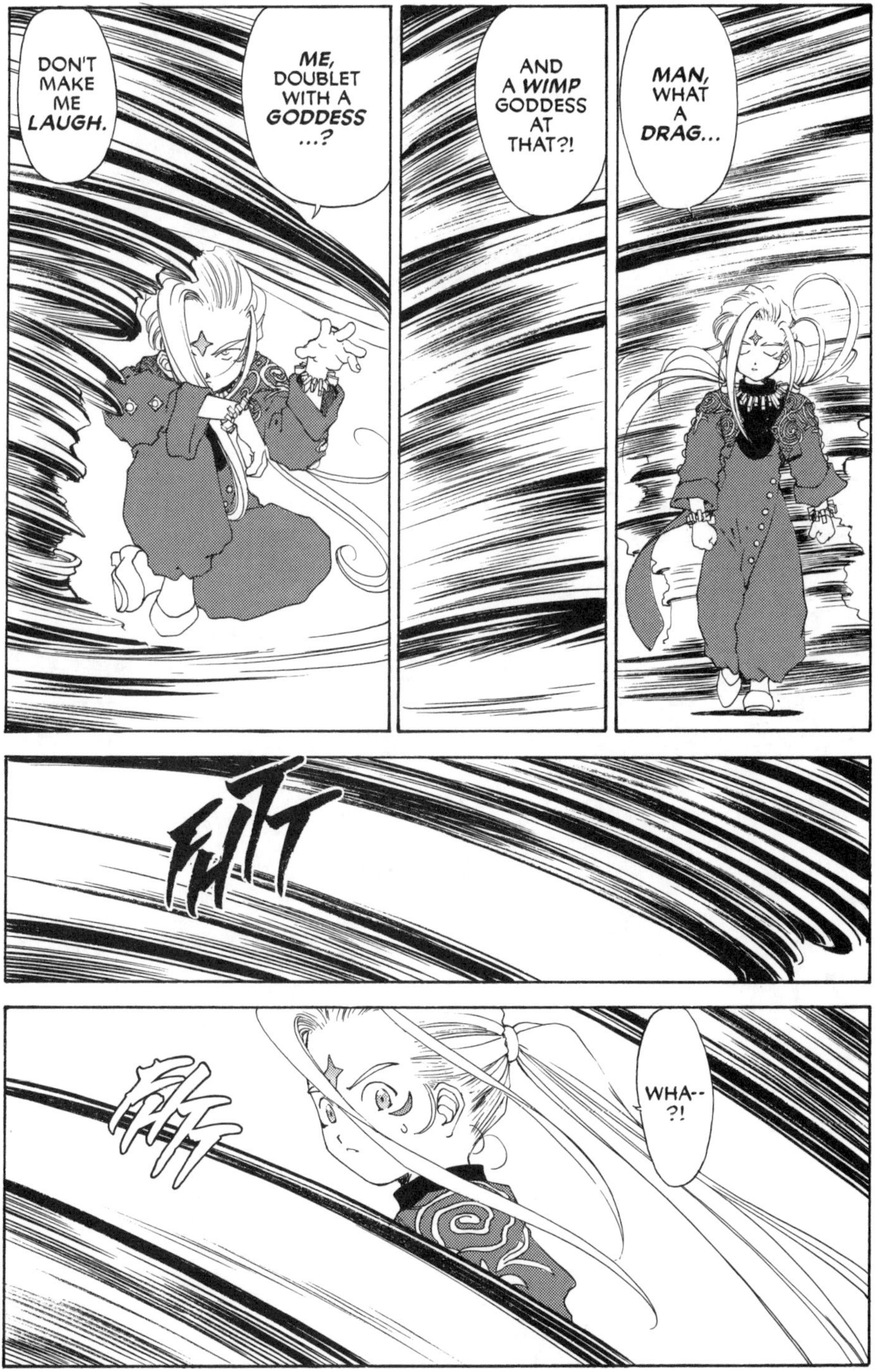
DON'T MAKE ME LAUGH.
ME, DOUBLET WITH A GODDESS ...?
AND A WIMP GODDESS AT THAT?!
MAN, WHAT A DRAG...
WHA-- ?!

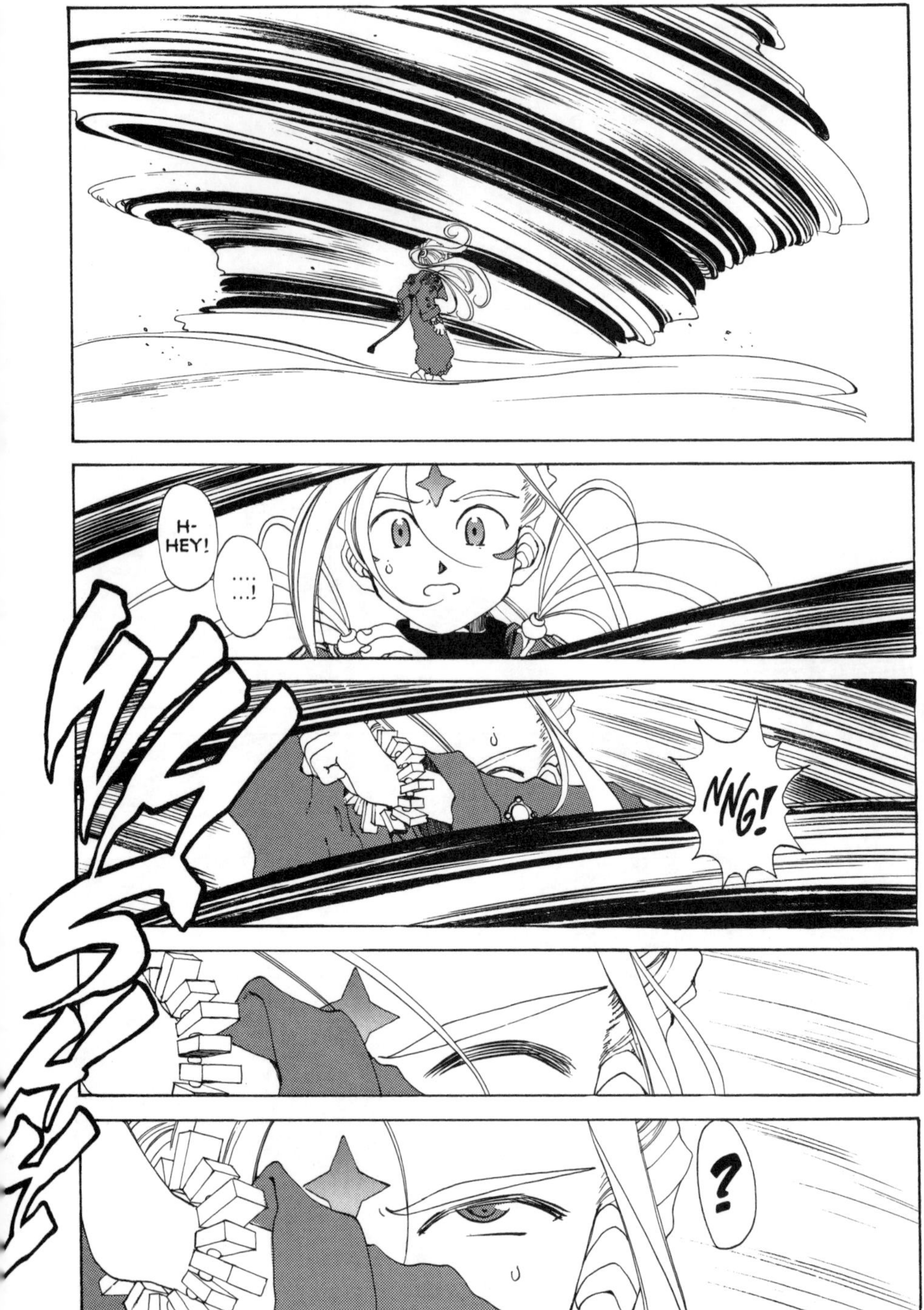
H- HEY!
......!
NNG!
?

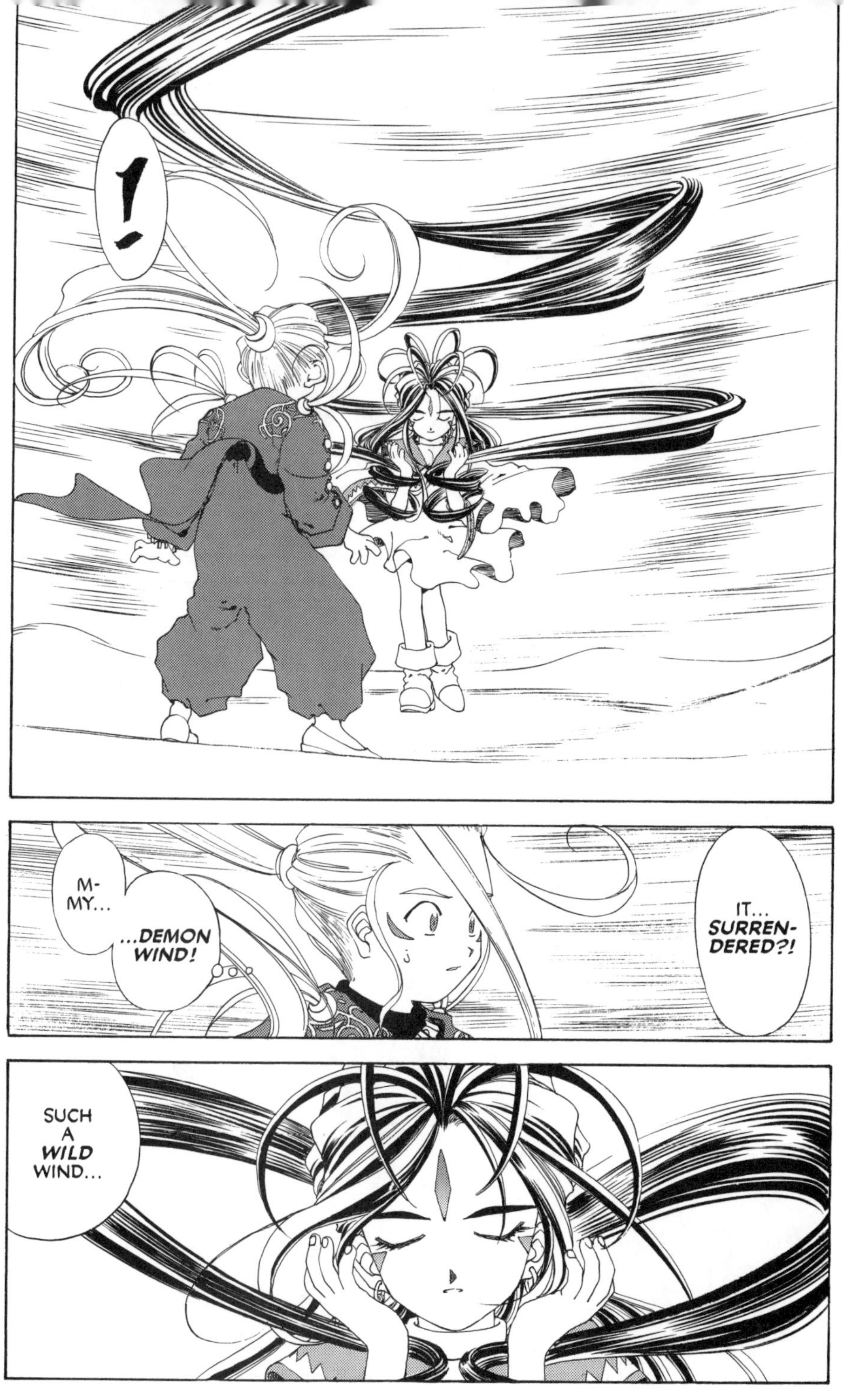
!
M-MY... ...DEMON WIND!
IT... SURREN-DERED?!
SUCH A WILD WIND...

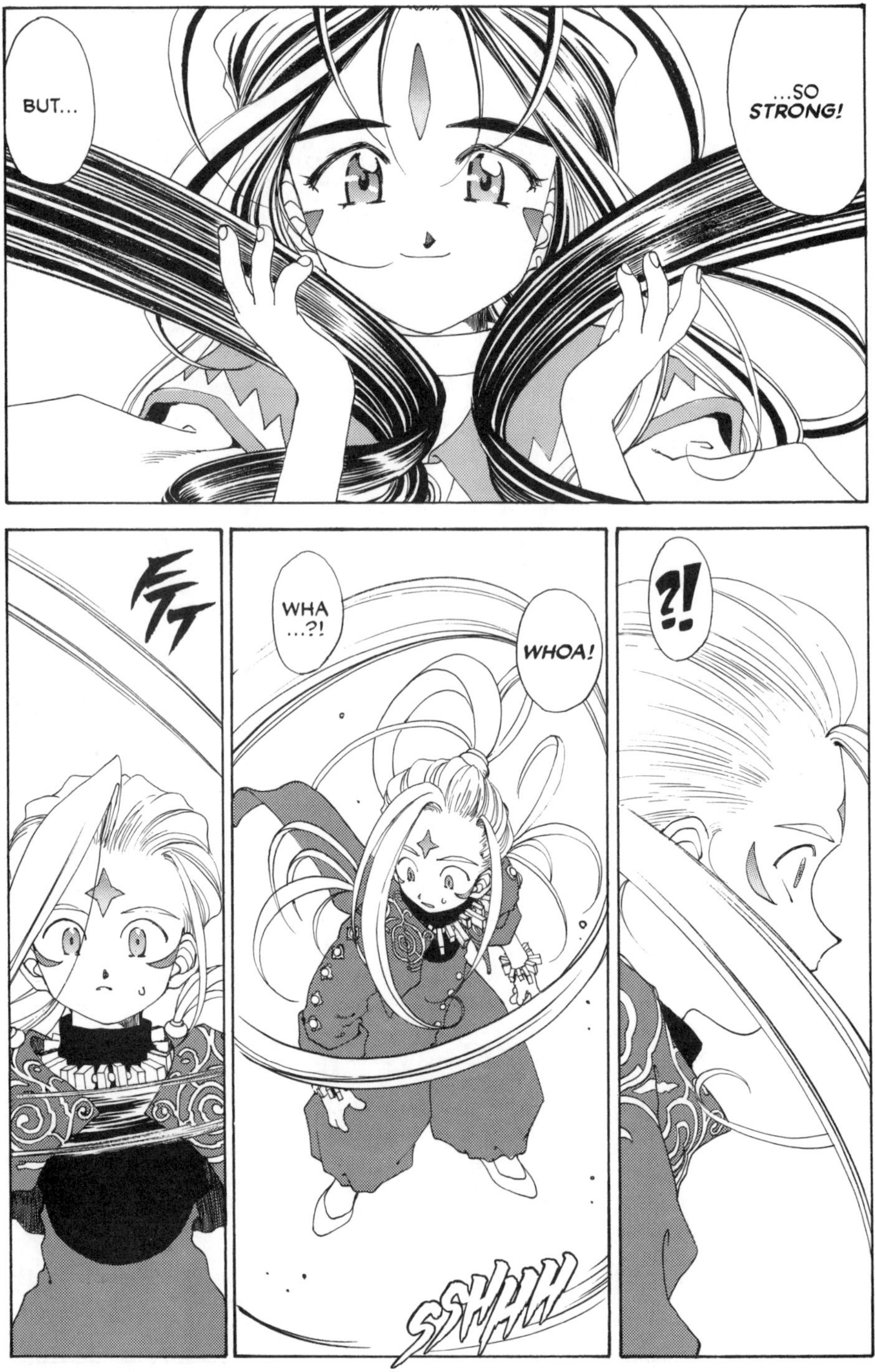
BUT...
...SO STRONG!
WHA ...?!
WHOA!
SSHHH
?!

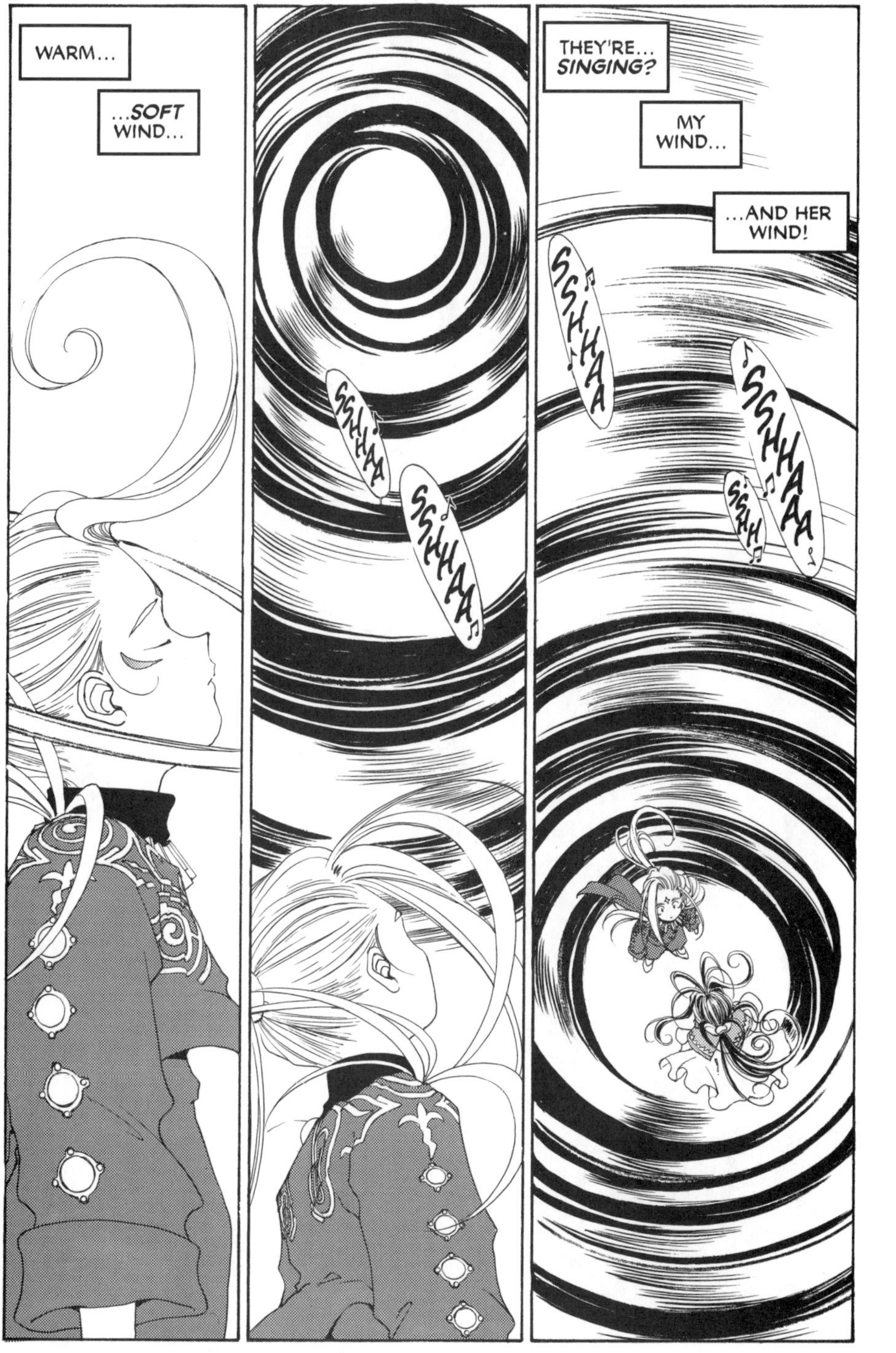
WARM...
...SOFT WIND...
SSHHAA
SSHHAAA
THEY'RE... SINGING?
MY WIND...
...AND HER WIND!
SSHHAA
SSHHAAA
SSHH

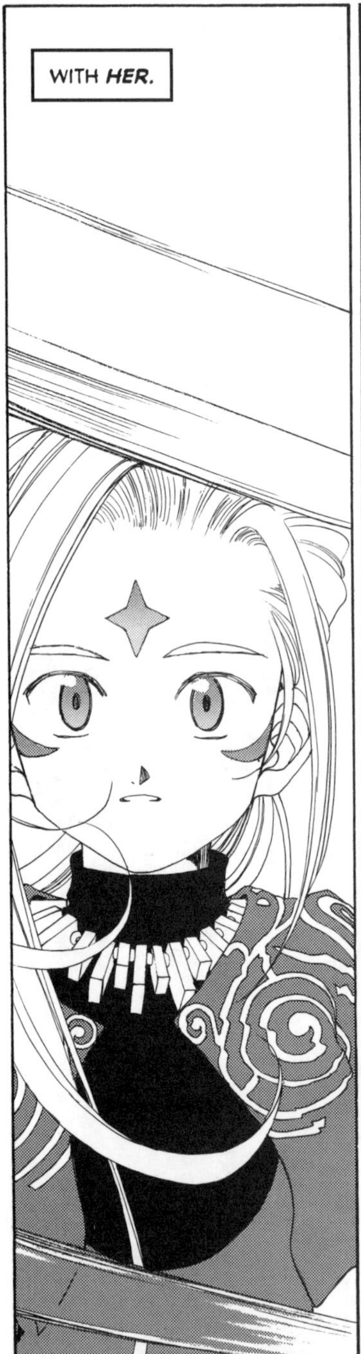
WITH **HER.**

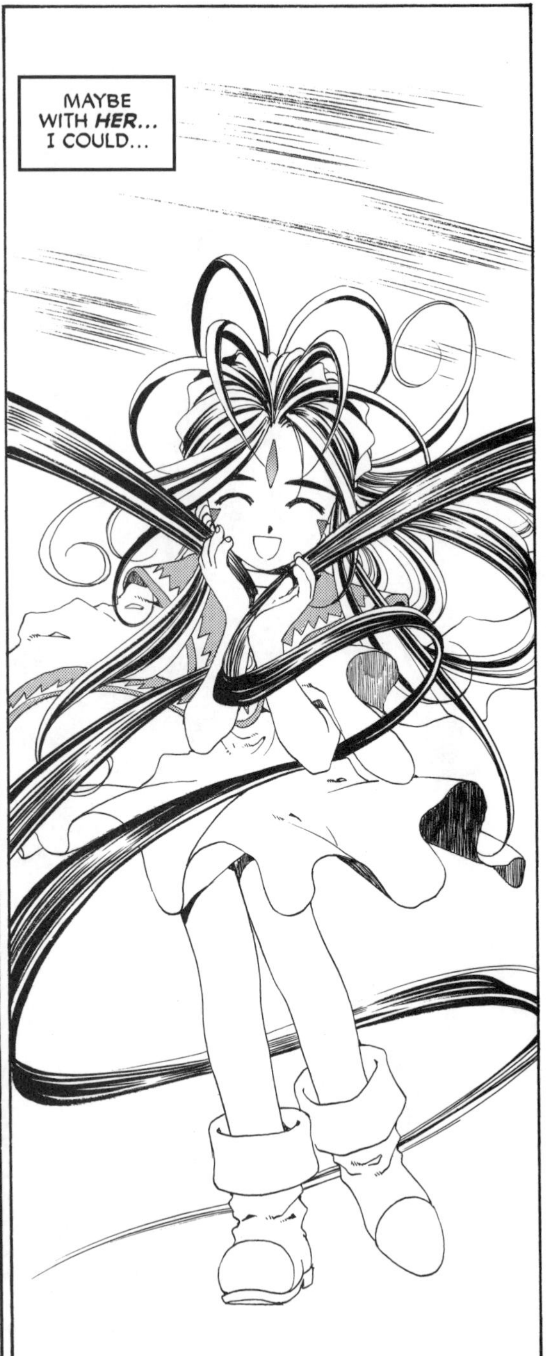
MAYBE WITH **HER...** I COULD...

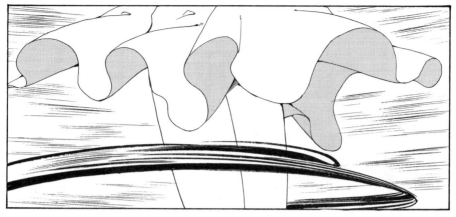

OOH, GOOD ONE.

DEMON WIND OF MINE...

THOU, WHO ART WITH ME ALWAYS...

EH ...?

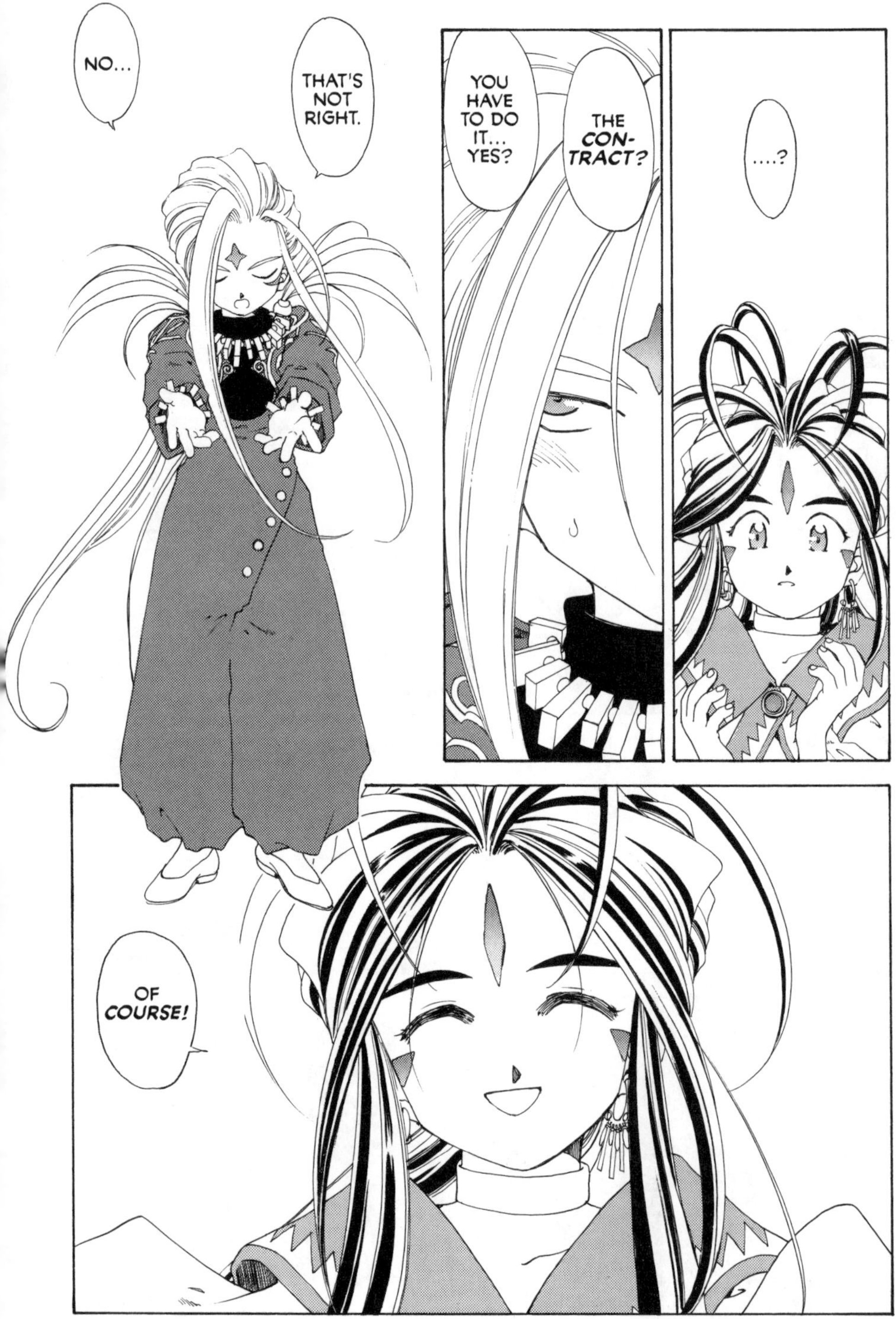
NO...
THAT'S NOT RIGHT.
YOU HAVE TO DO IT... YES?
THE CONTRACT?
....?
OF COURSE!

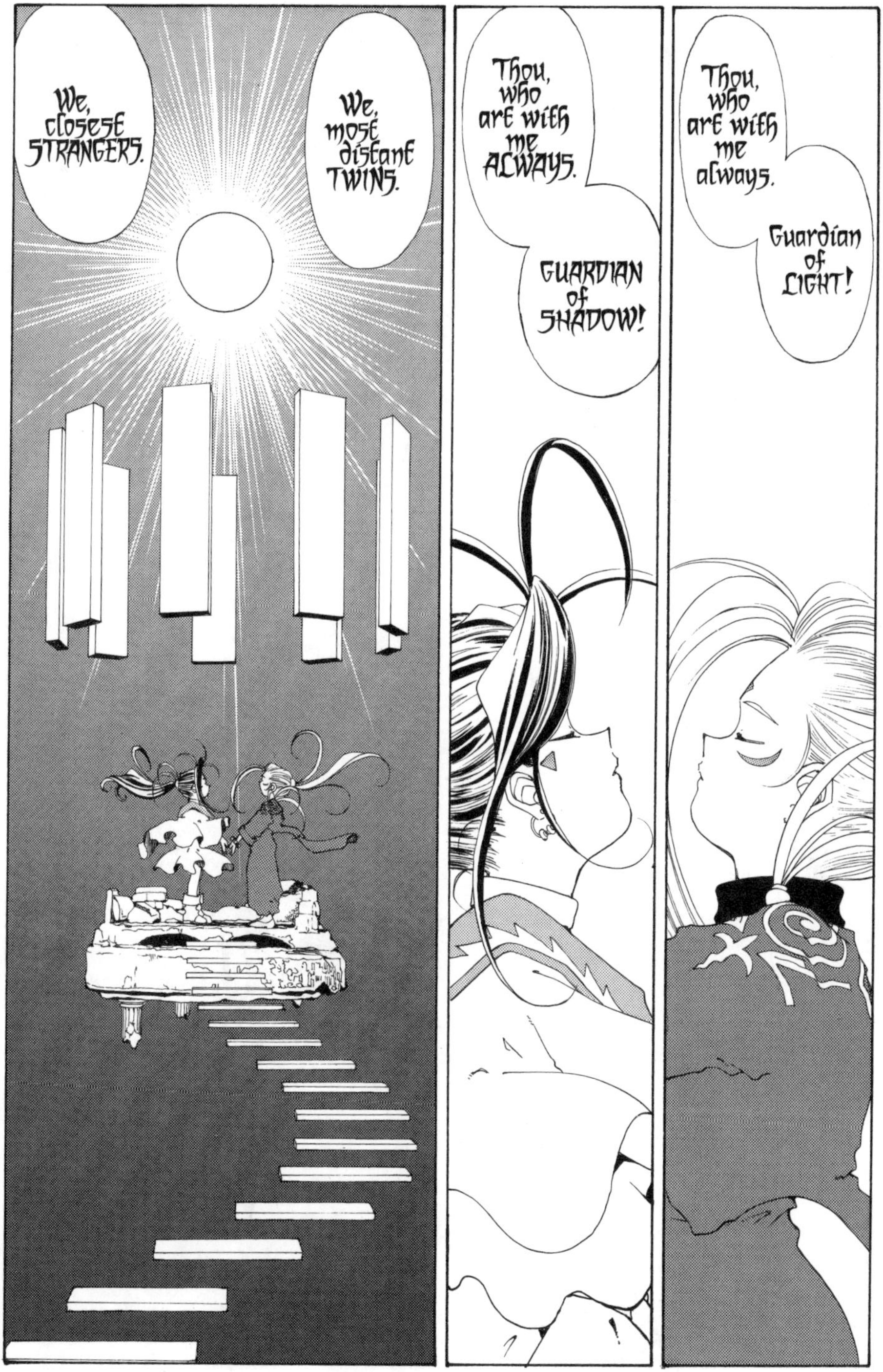
We, closest STRANGERS.
We, most distant TWINS.
Thou, who are with me ALWAYS.
GUARDIAN of SHADOW!
Thou, who are with me always.
Guardian of LIGHT!

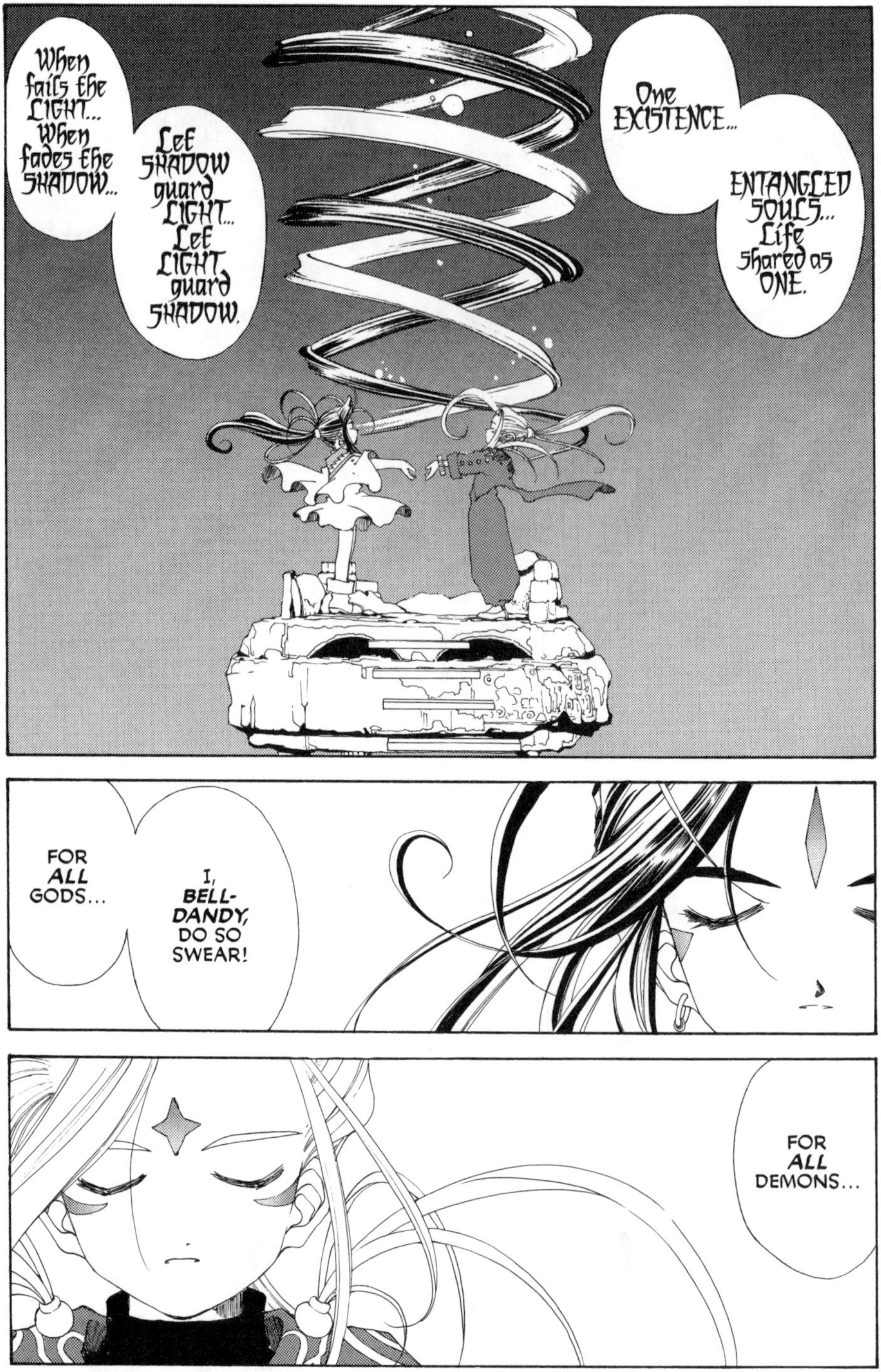
When fails the LIGHT... When fades the SHADOW...
Let SHADOW guard LIGHT... Let LIGHT guard SHADOW.
One EXISTENCE...
ENTANGLED SOULS... Life shared as ONE.
FOR *ALL* GODS...
I, *BELL-DANDY,* DO SO SWEAR!
FOR *ALL* DEMONS...

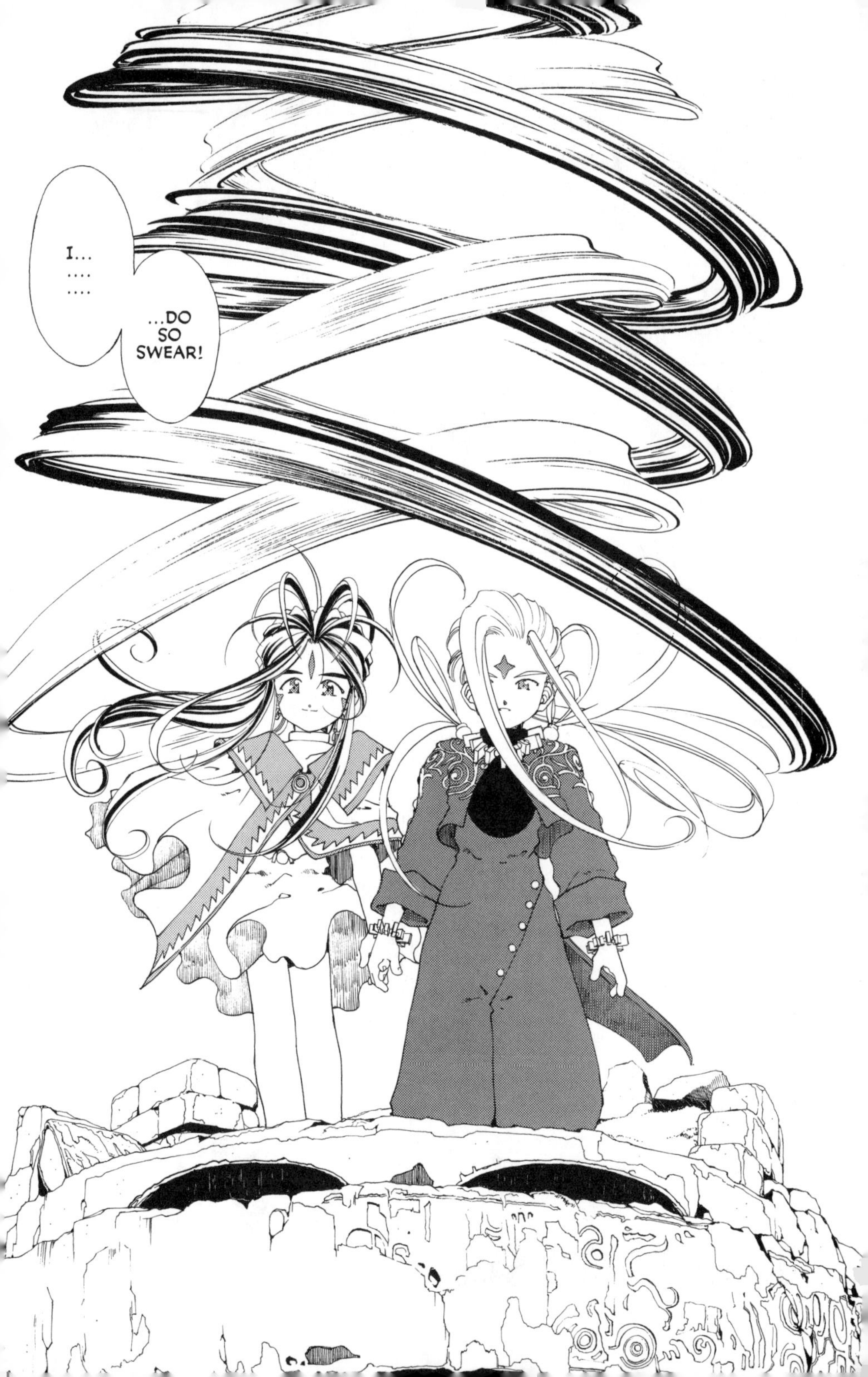

I...
....
....
...DO SO SWEAR!

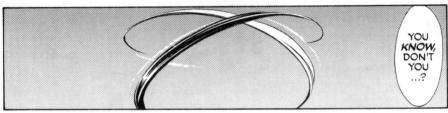

YOU *KNOW,* DON'T YOU ...?

WHEN WE LEAVE HERE, WE'LL *FORGET.*

ABOUT EACH OTHER. ABOUT EVERY-THING.

I KNOW.

I WON'T. I *WON'T* FORGET.

I... I'M SORRY...

...BUT THAT JUST ISN'T *POSSIBLE.*

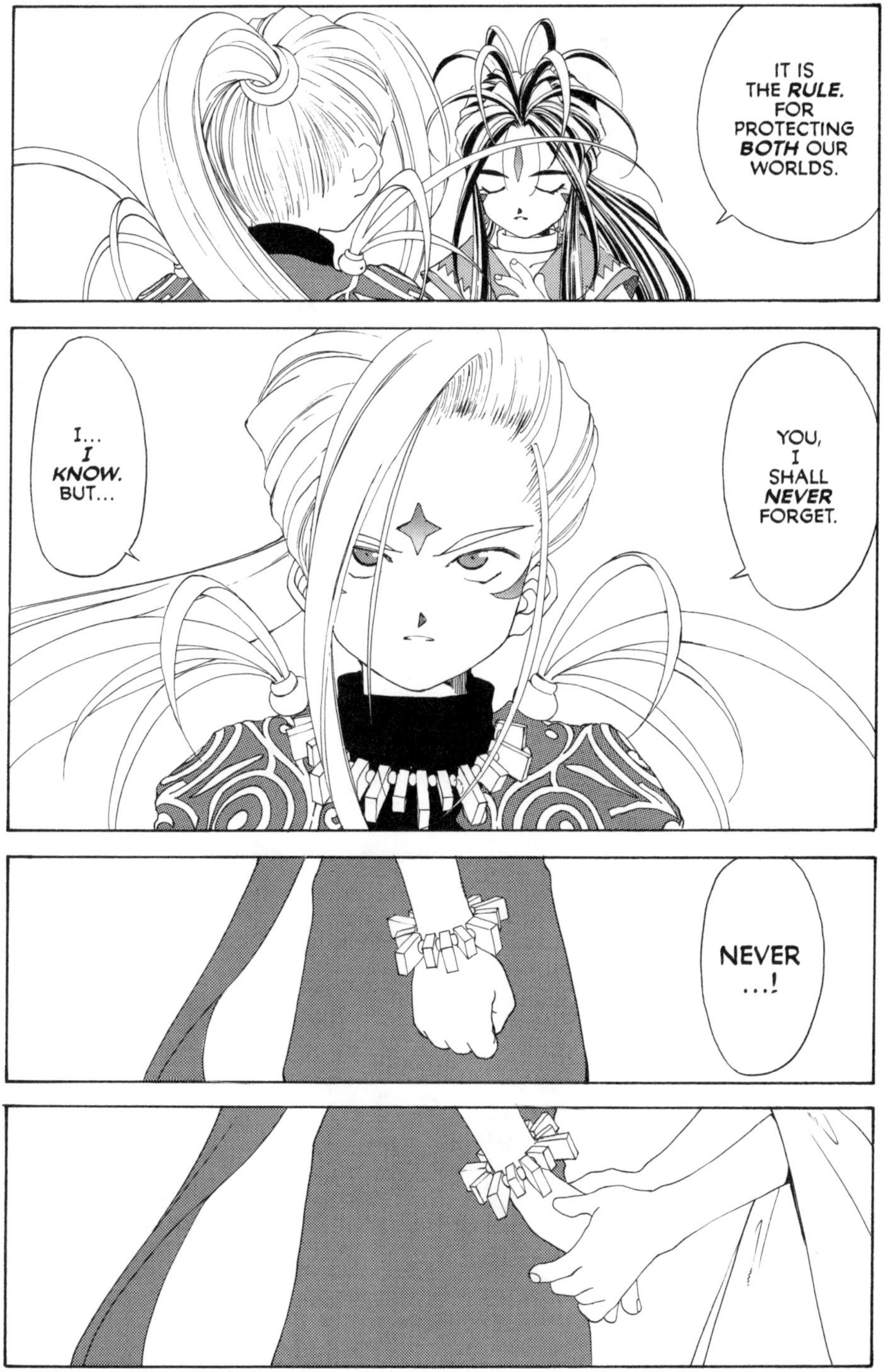
IT IS THE **RULE.** FOR PROTECTING **BOTH** OUR WORLDS.
I... ***I KNOW.*** BUT...
YOU, I SHALL ***NEVER*** FORGET.
NEVER ...!

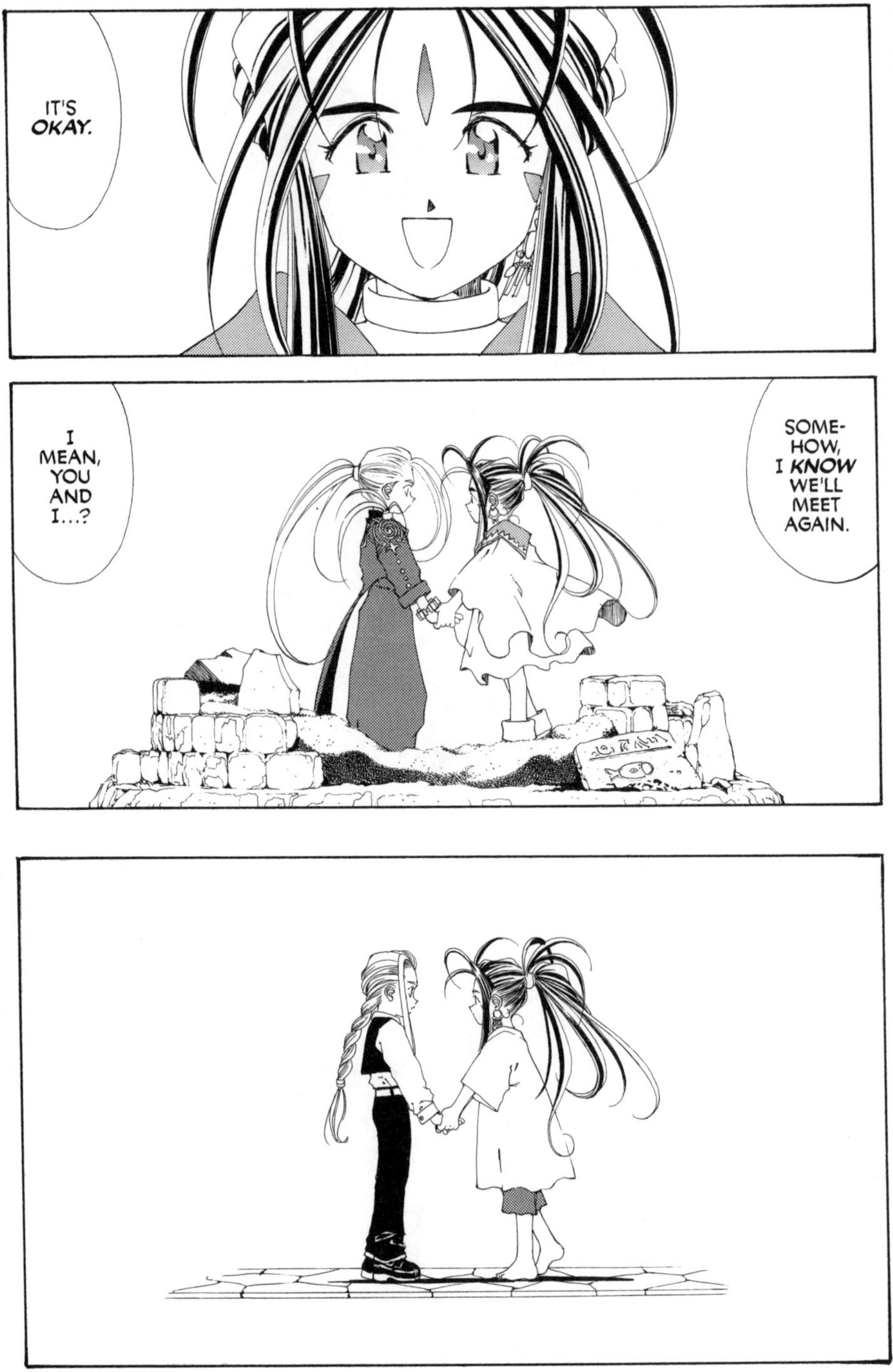
IT'S *OKAY.*
I MEAN, YOU AND I...?
SOME-HOW, I *KNOW* WE'LL MEET AGAIN.

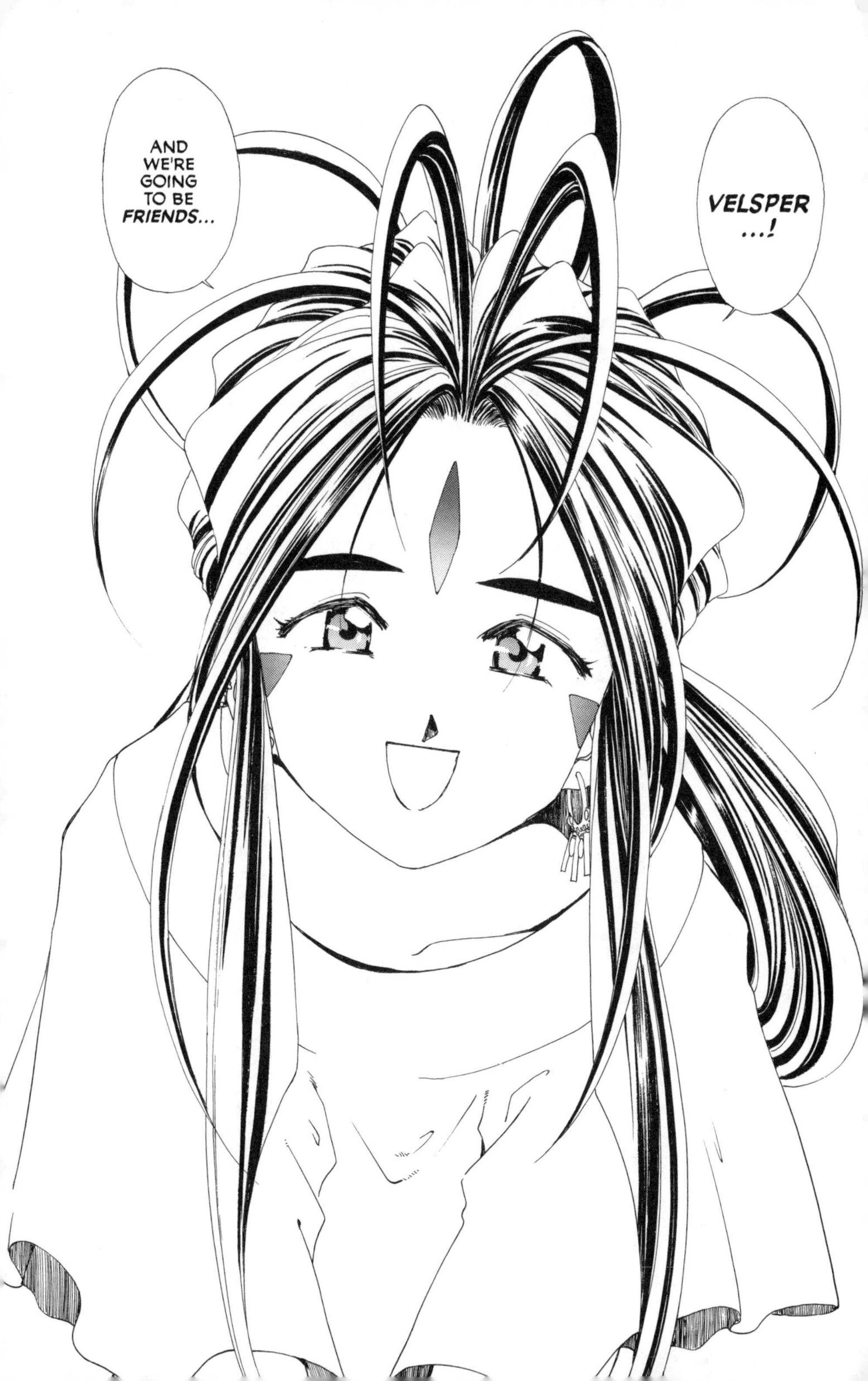
AND WE'RE GOING TO BE *FRIENDS...*
VELSPER ...!

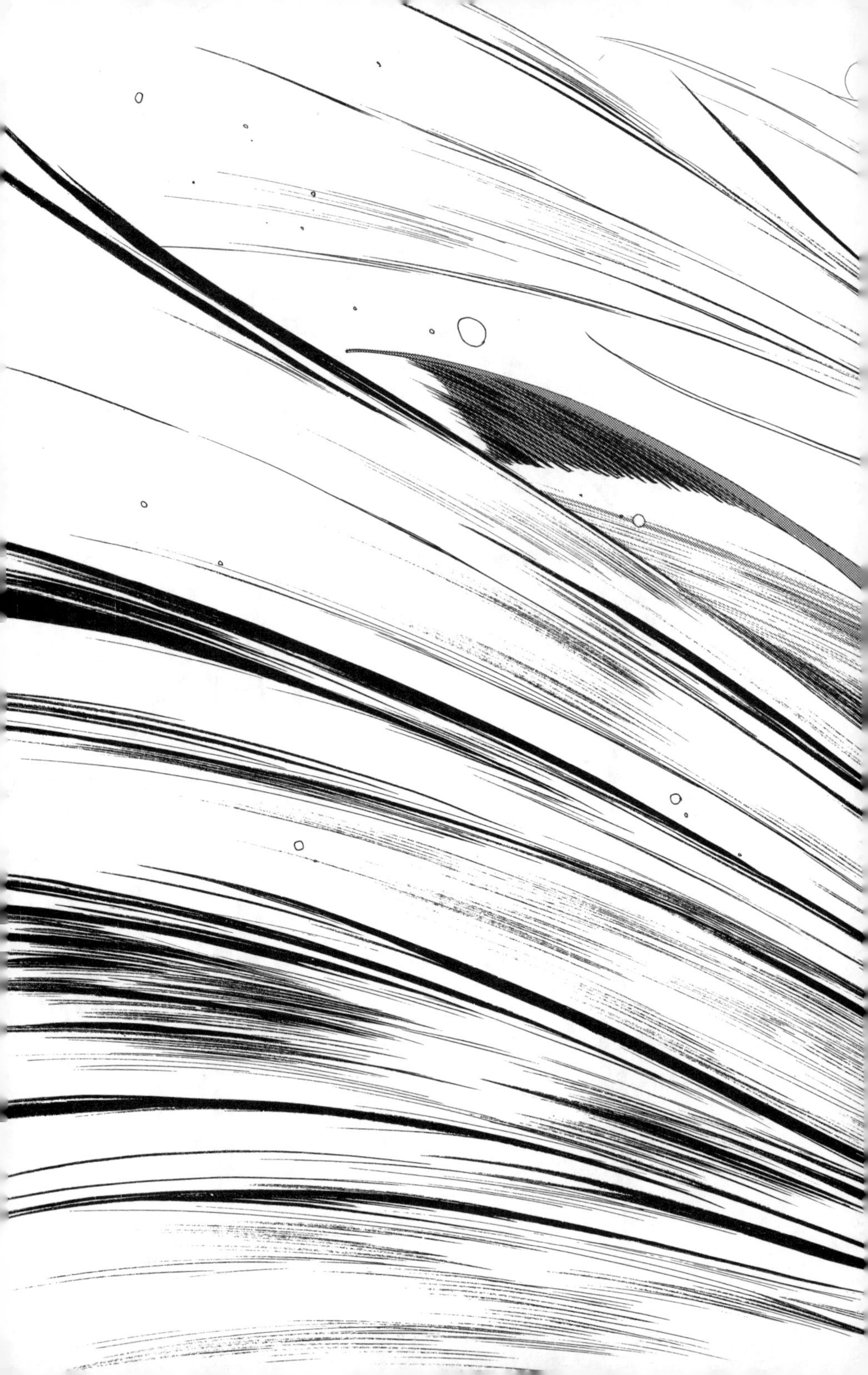

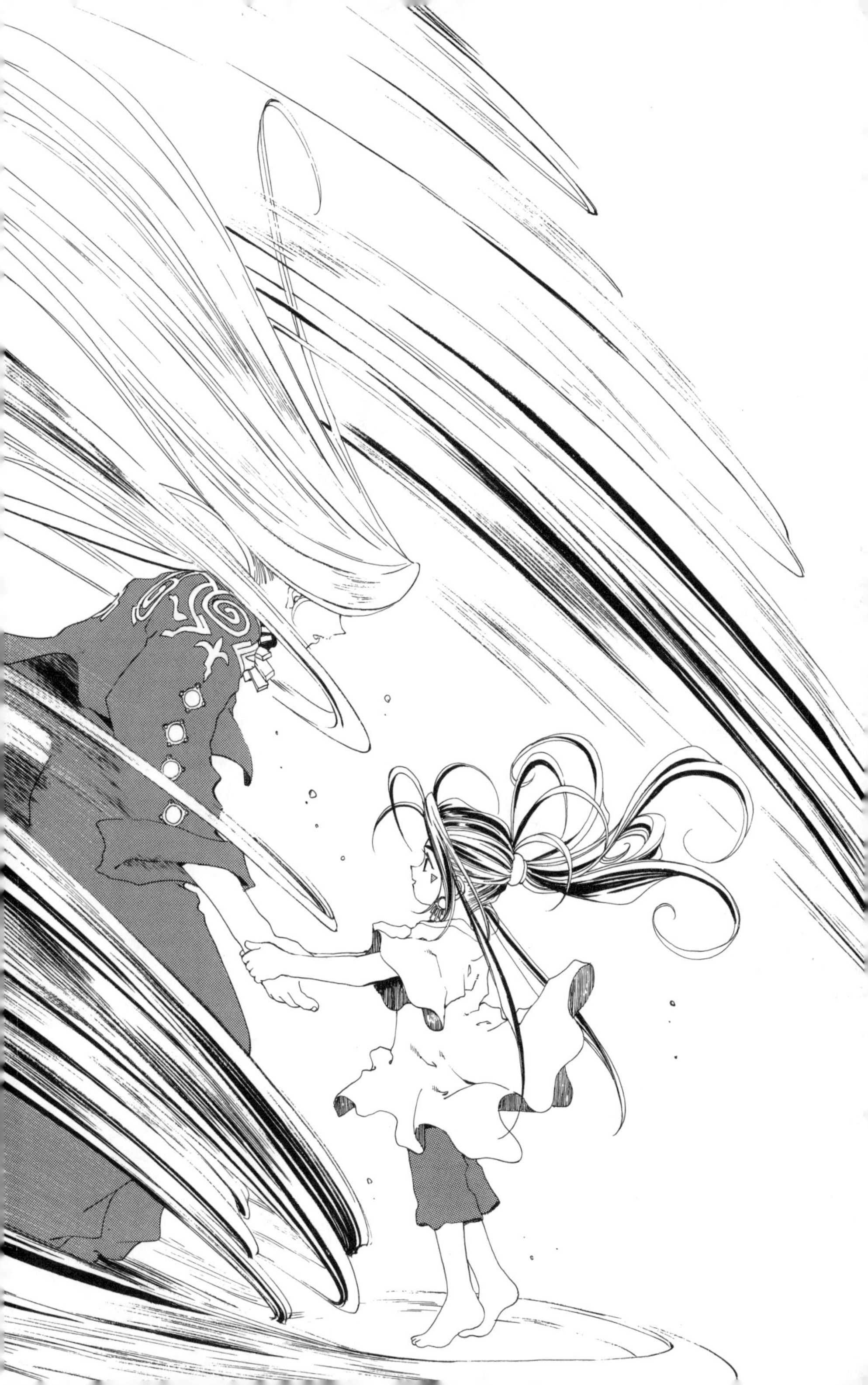

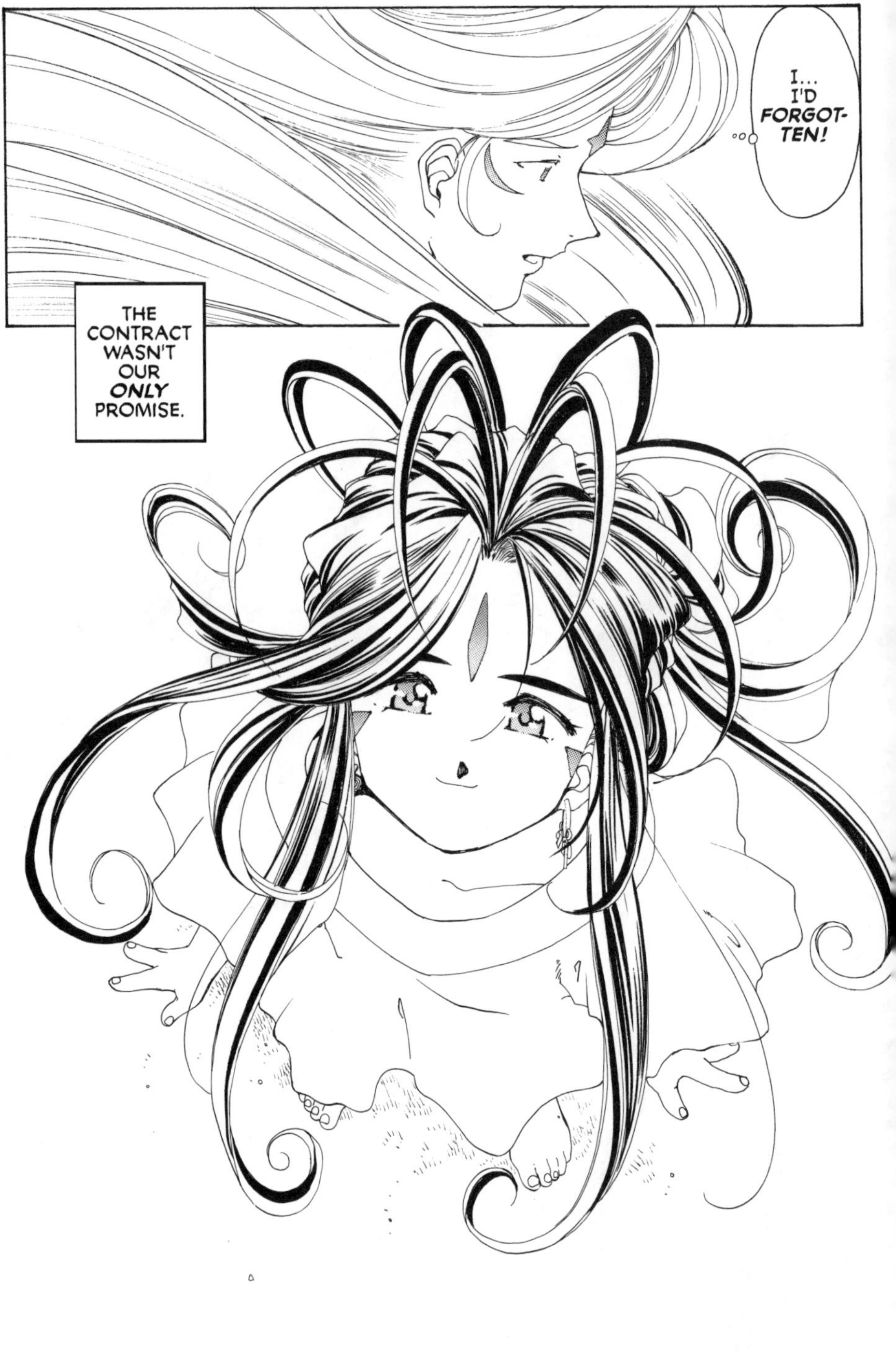
I... I'D FORGOTTEN!
THE CONTRACT WASN'T OUR ONLY PROMISE.

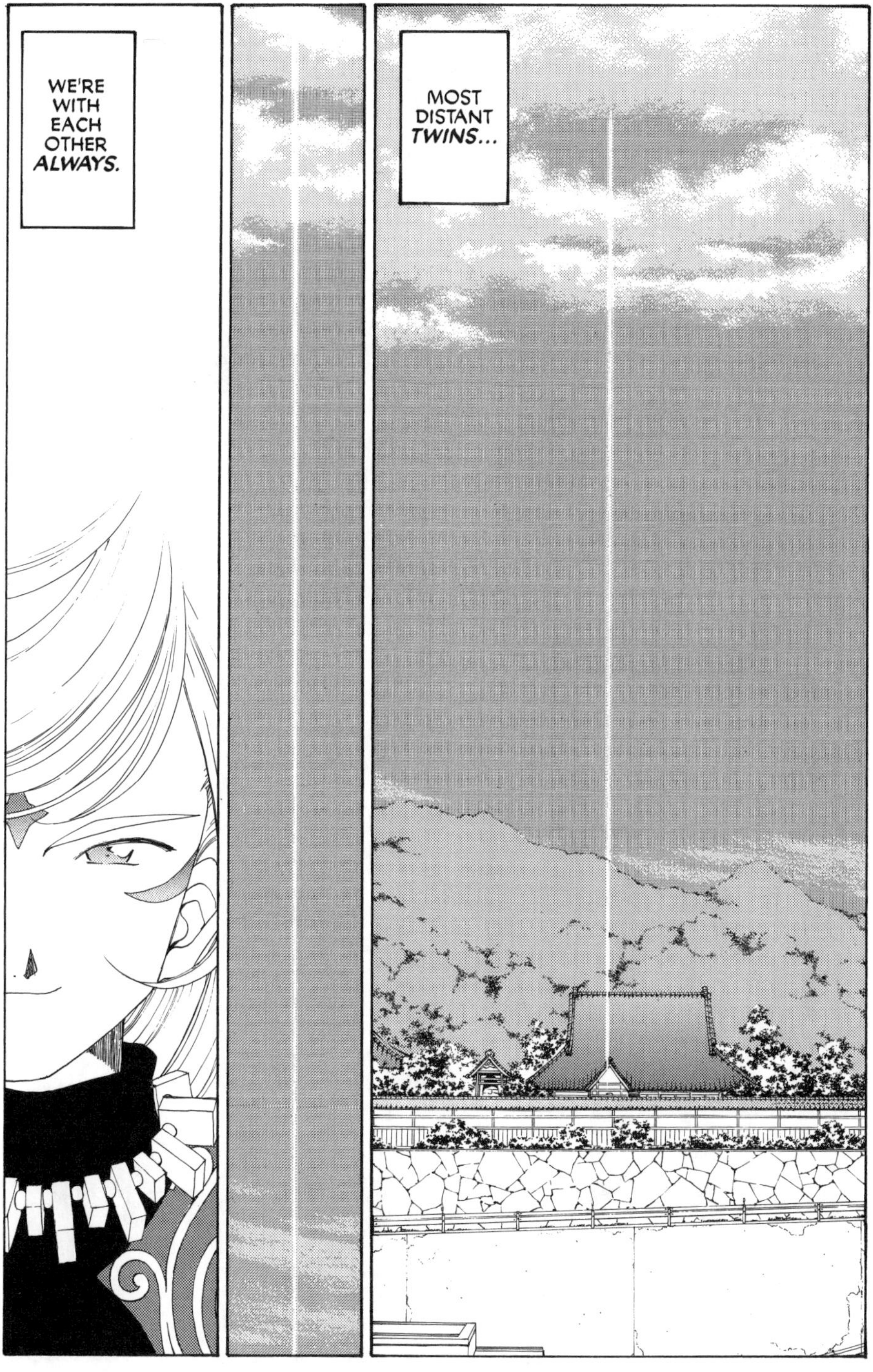
WE'RE WITH EACH OTHER *ALWAYS.*
MOST DISTANT *TWINS...*

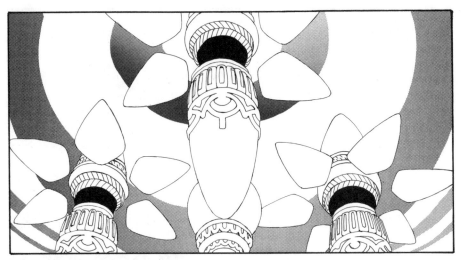

THE LOCKED FILES...

TH-THEY'RE *OPENING!*

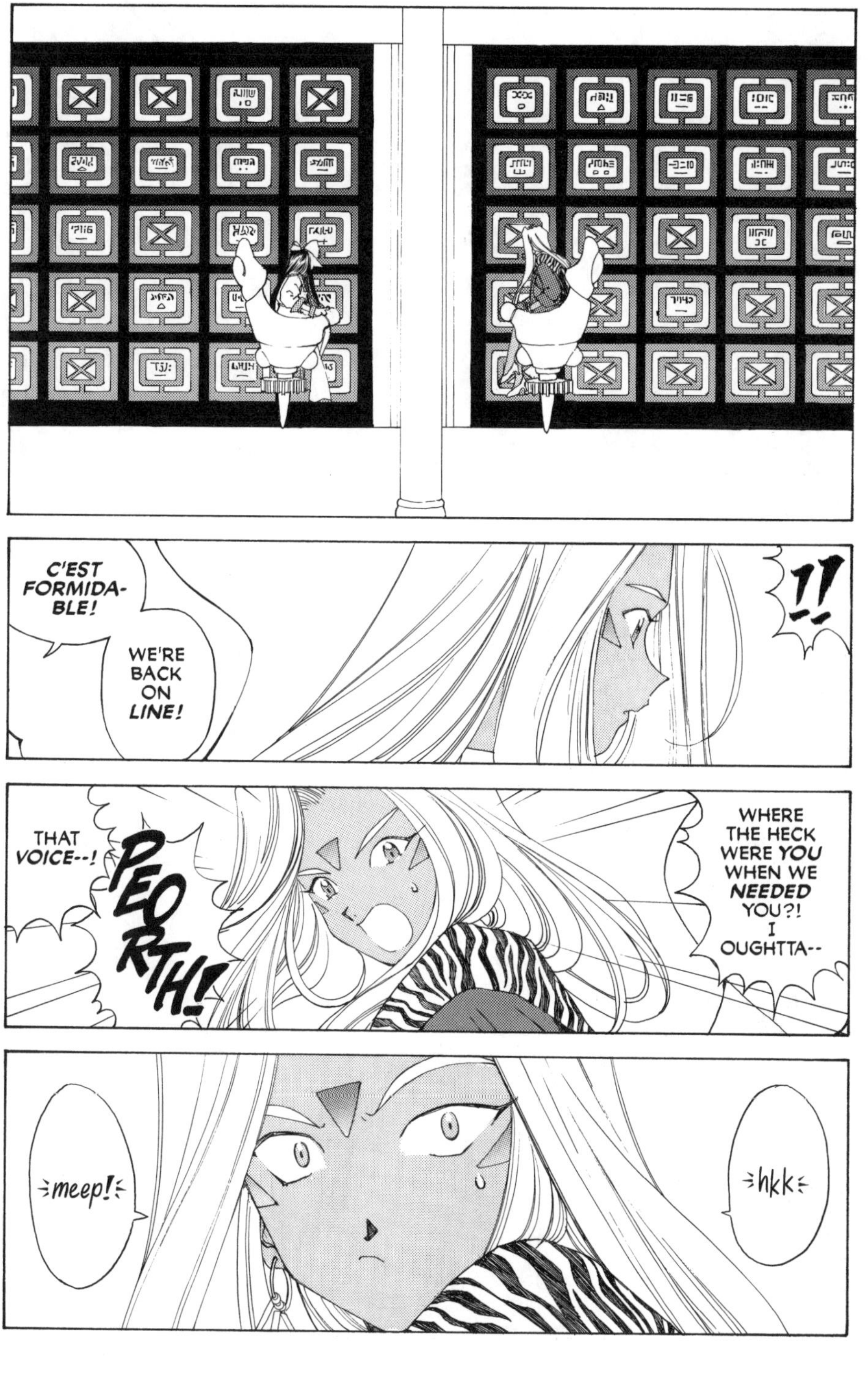
C'EST FORMIDABLE!
WE'RE BACK ON LINE!
!!
THAT VOICE--!
PEORTH!
WHERE THE HECK WERE YOU WHEN WE NEEDED YOU?! I OUGHTTA--
meep!
hkk

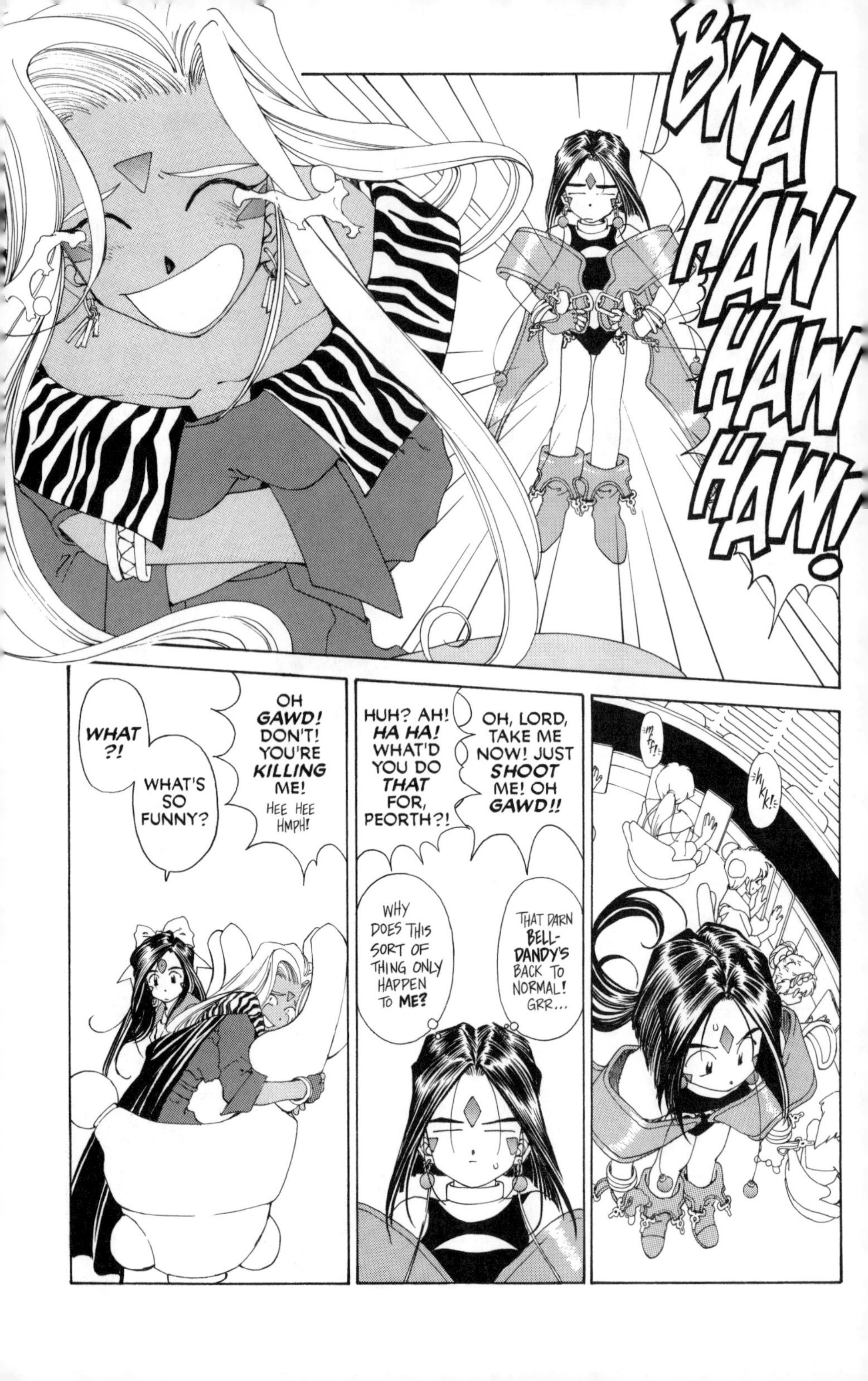
BWA HAW HAW HAW HAW!
WHAT?!
WHAT'S SO FUNNY?
OH GAWD! DON'T! YOU'RE KILLING ME!
HEE HEE HMPH!
HUH? AH! HA HA! WHAT'D YOU DO THAT FOR, PEORTH?!
OH, LORD, TAKE ME NOW! JUST SHOOT ME! OH GAWD!!
WHY DOES THIS SORT OF THING ONLY HAPPEN TO ME?
THAT DARN BELL-DANDY'S BACK TO NORMAL! GRR...
mff!
hnkk!

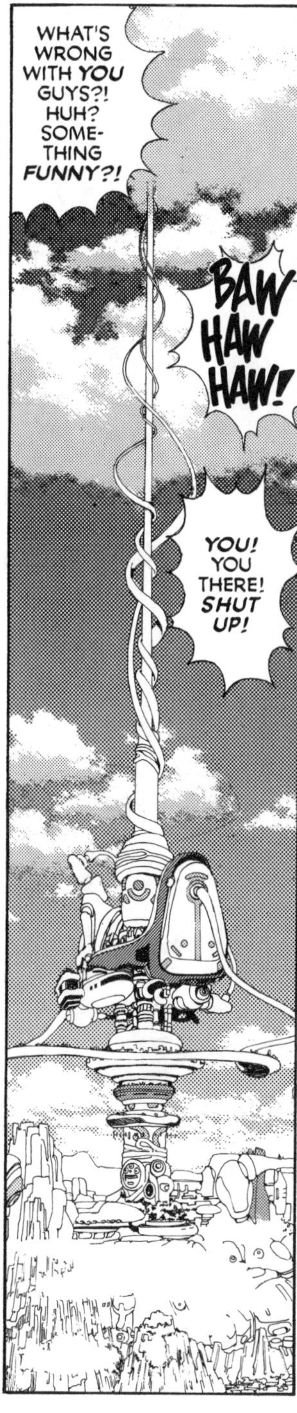
WHAT'S WRONG WITH YOU GUYS?! HUH? SOME-THING FUNNY?!
BAW HAW HAW!
YOU! YOU THERE! SHUT UP!
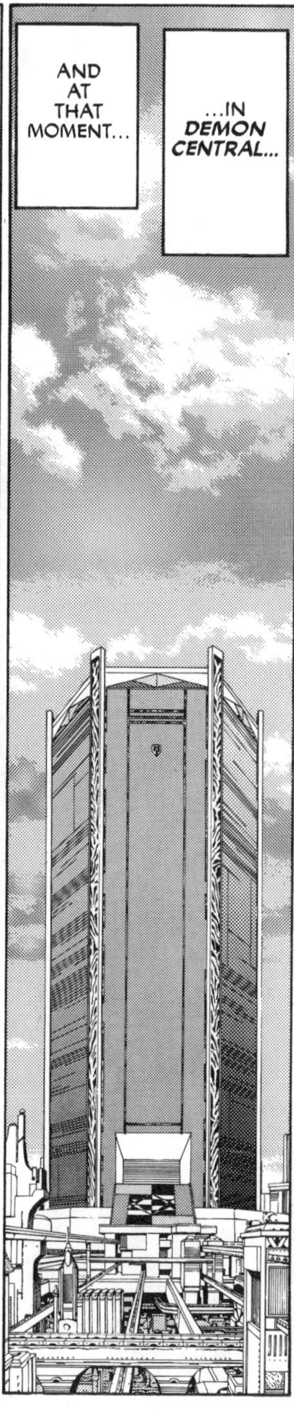
AND AT THAT MOMENT...
...IN DEMON CENTRAL...
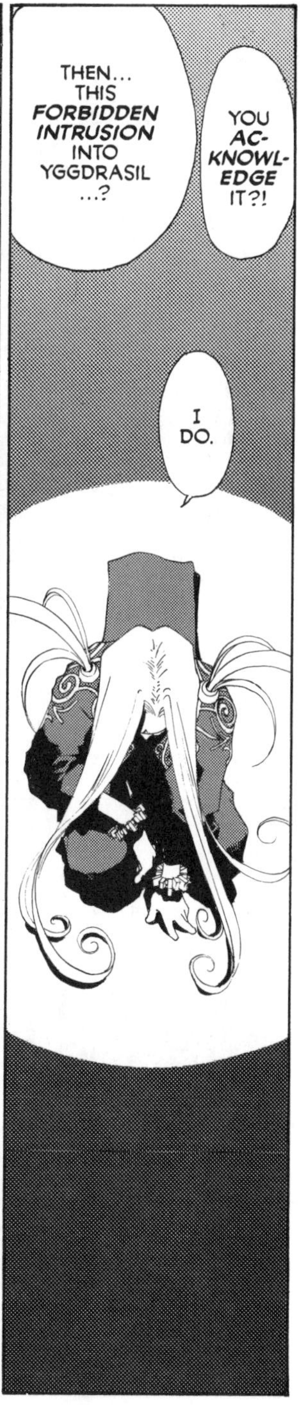
THEN... THIS FORBIDDEN INTRUSION INTO YGGDRASIL ...?
YOU AC-KNOWL-EDGE IT?!
I DO.

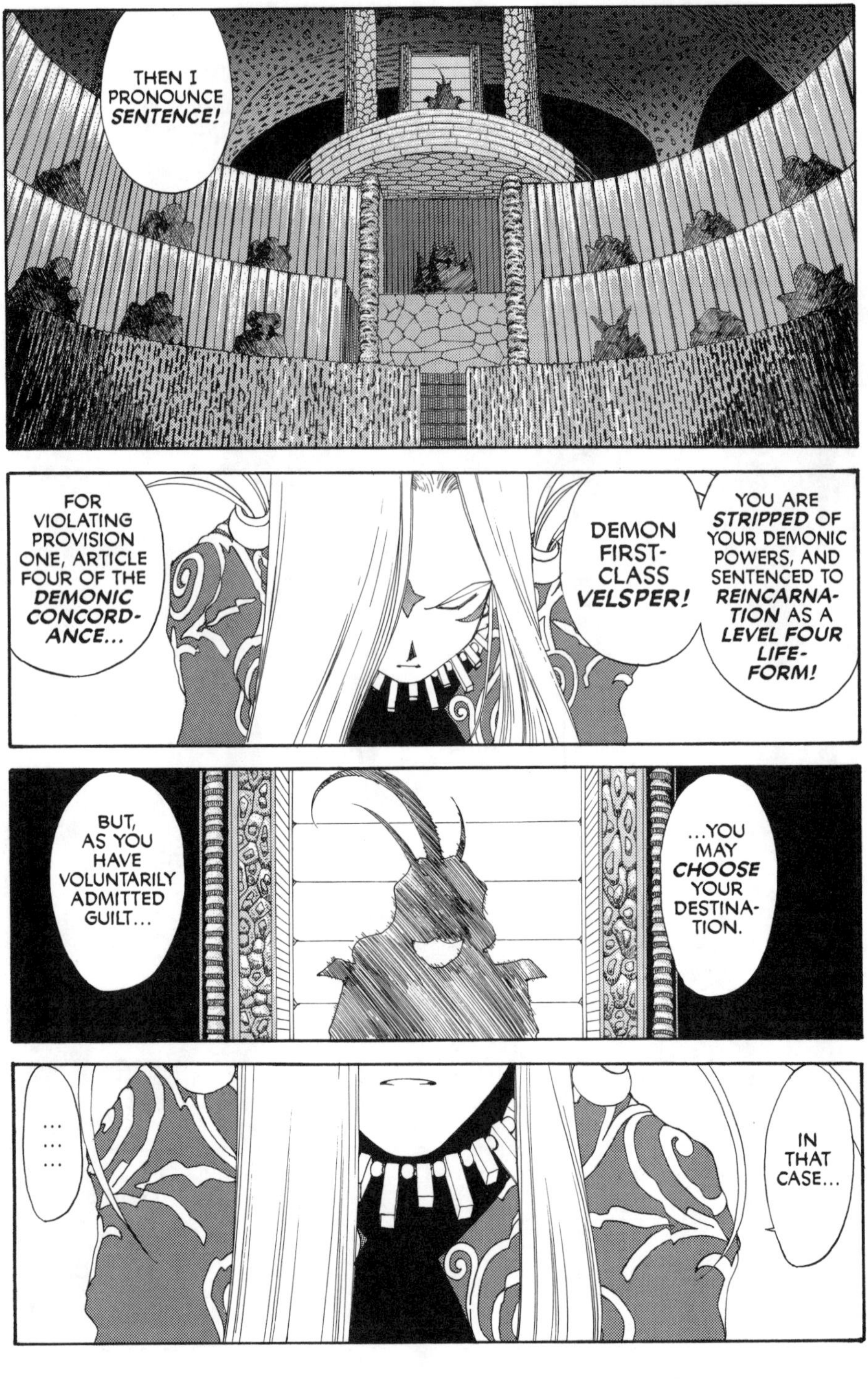
THEN I PRONOUNCE *SENTENCE!*
FOR VIOLATING PROVISION ONE, ARTICLE FOUR OF THE *DEMONIC CONCORDANCE...*
DEMON FIRST-CLASS *VELSPER!*
YOU ARE *STRIPPED* OF YOUR DEMONIC POWERS, AND SENTENCED TO *REINCARNATION* AS A *LEVEL FOUR LIFE-FORM!*
BUT, AS YOU HAVE VOLUNTARILY ADMITTED GUILT...
...YOU MAY *CHOOSE* YOUR DESTINATION.
... ...
IN THAT CASE...

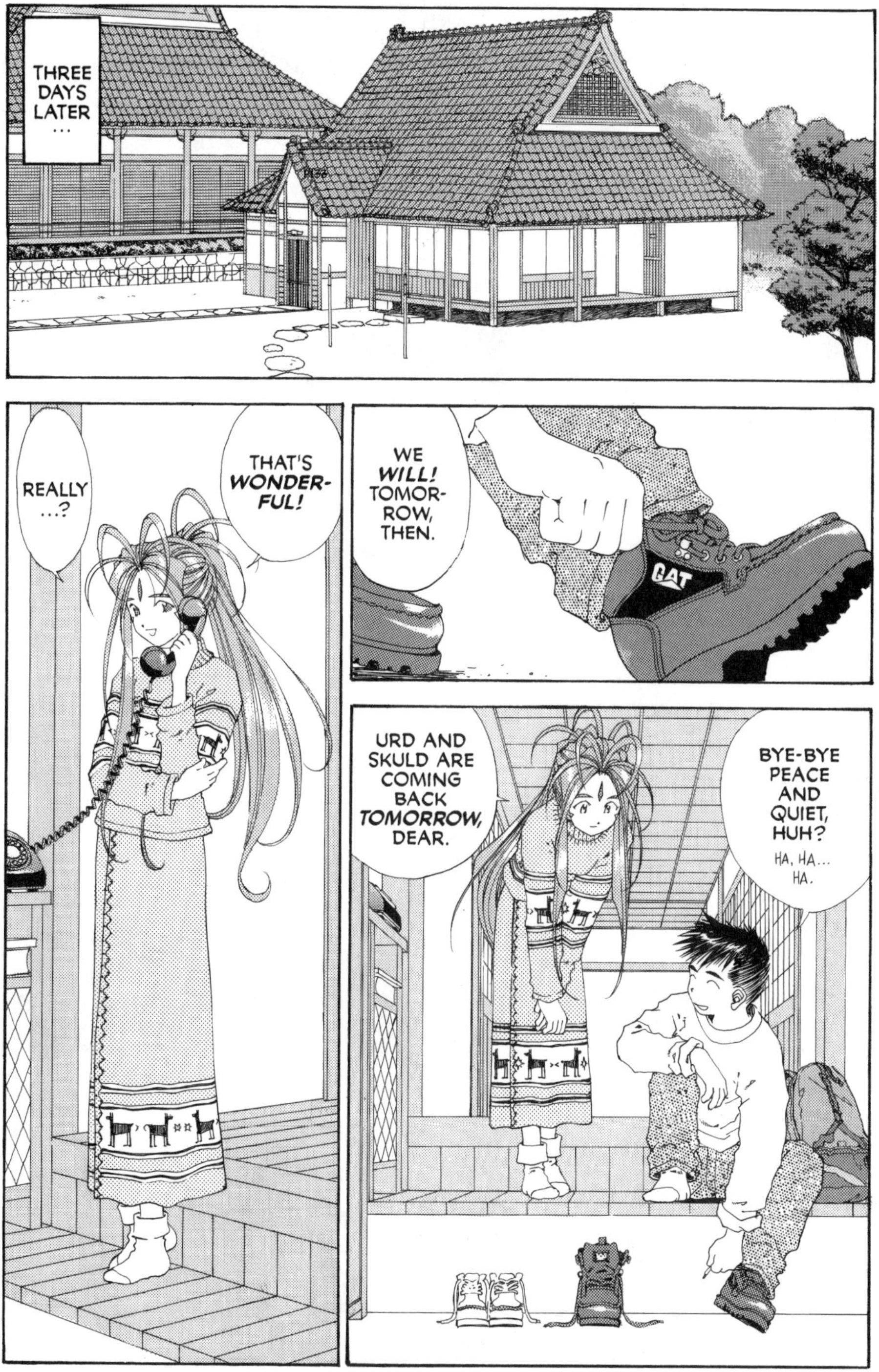
THREE DAYS LATER ...
REALLY ...?
THAT'S WONDERFUL!
WE WILL! TOMORROW, THEN.
URD AND SKULD ARE COMING BACK TOMORROW, DEAR.
BYE-BYE PEACE AND QUIET, HUH?
HA, HA... HA.

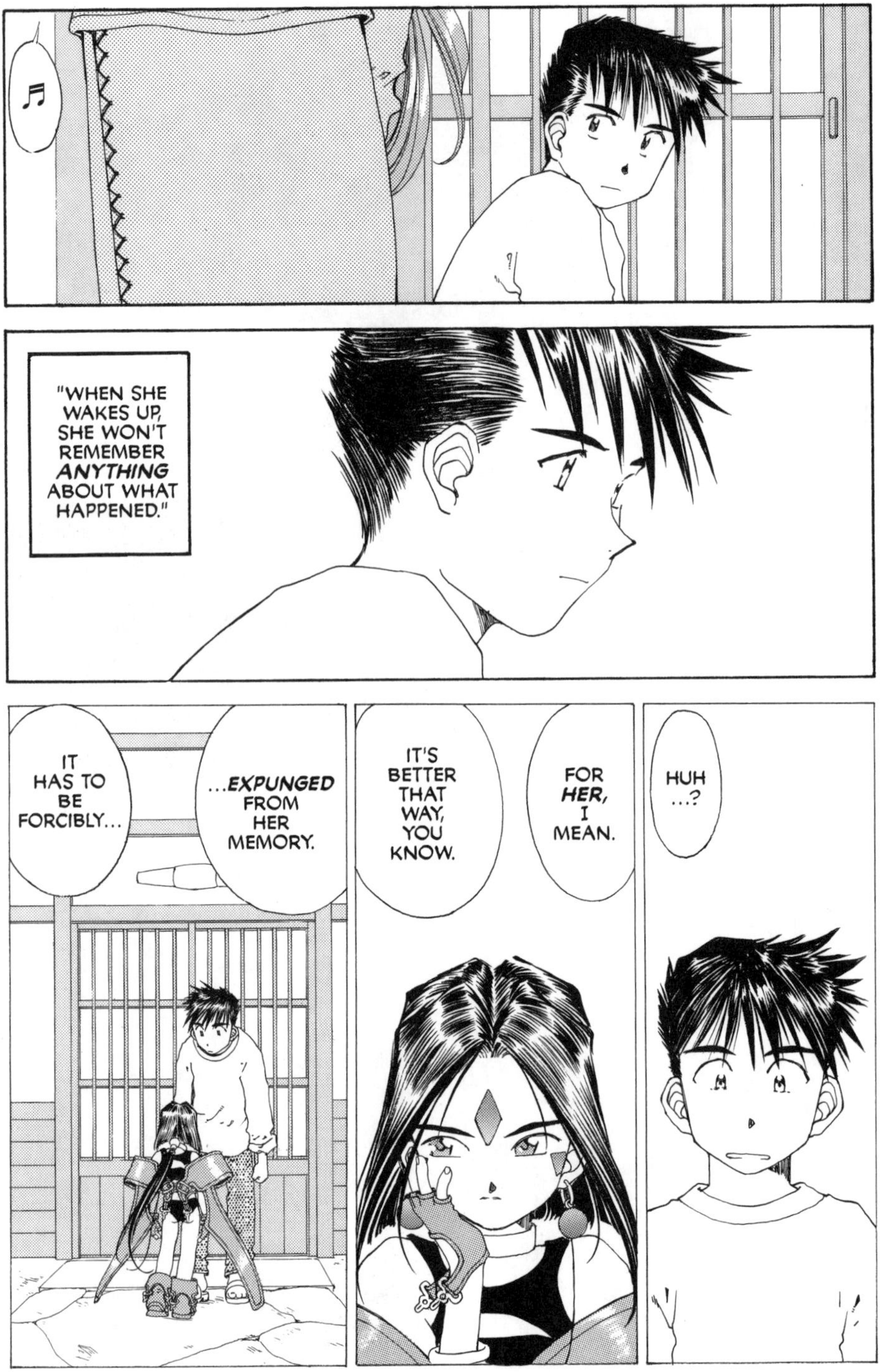
♬
"WHEN SHE WAKES UP, SHE WON'T REMEMBER ***ANYTHING*** ABOUT WHAT HAPPENED."
IT HAS TO BE FORCIBLY…
…***EXPUNGED*** FROM HER MEMORY.
IT'S BETTER THAT WAY, YOU KNOW.
FOR ***HER,*** I MEAN.
HUH …?

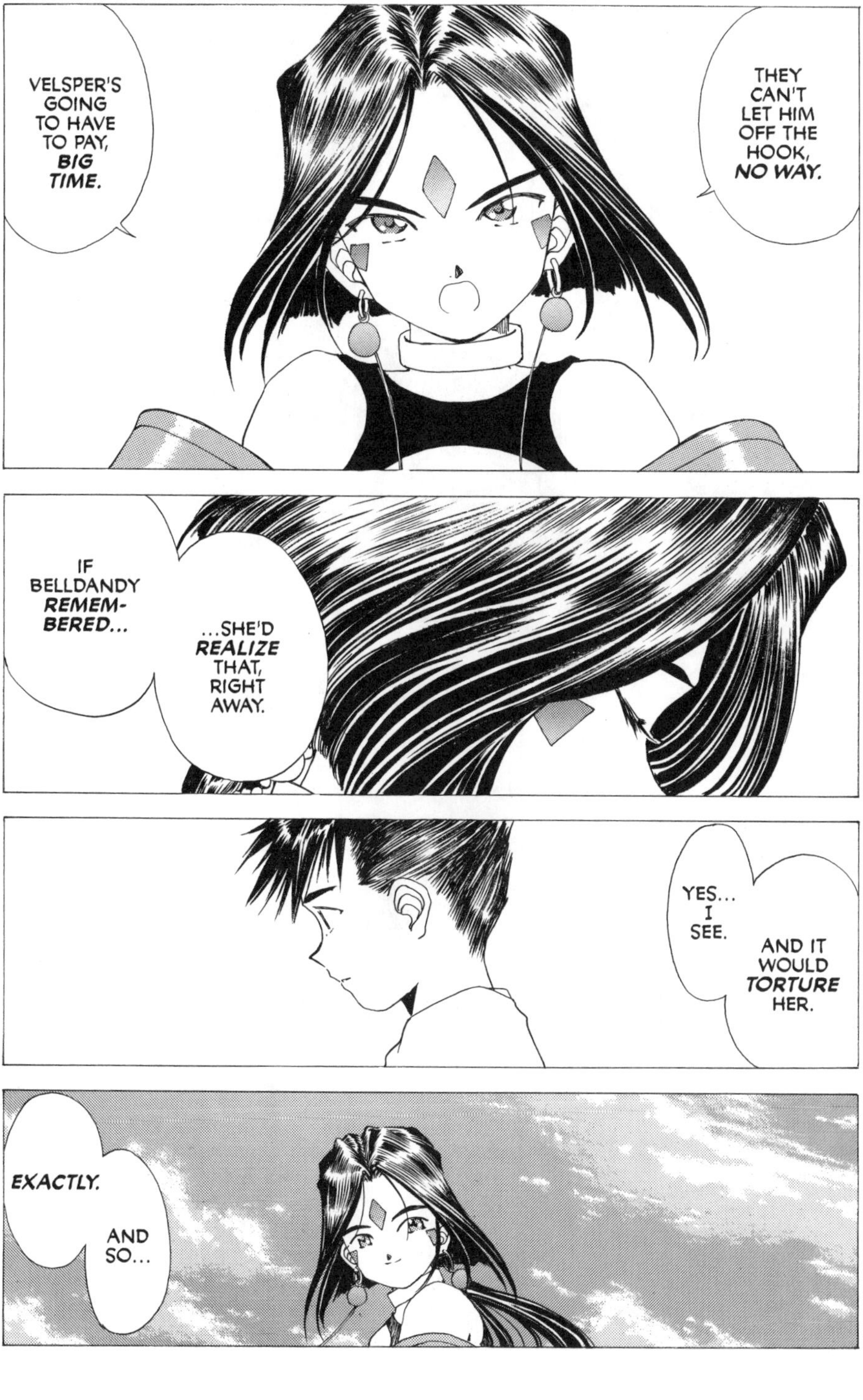
VELSPER'S GOING TO HAVE TO PAY, BIG TIME.
THEY CAN'T LET HIM OFF THE HOOK, NO WAY.
IF BELLDANDY REMEMBERED...
...SHE'D REALIZE THAT, RIGHT AWAY.
YES... I SEE.
AND IT WOULD TORTURE HER.
EXACTLY.
AND SO...

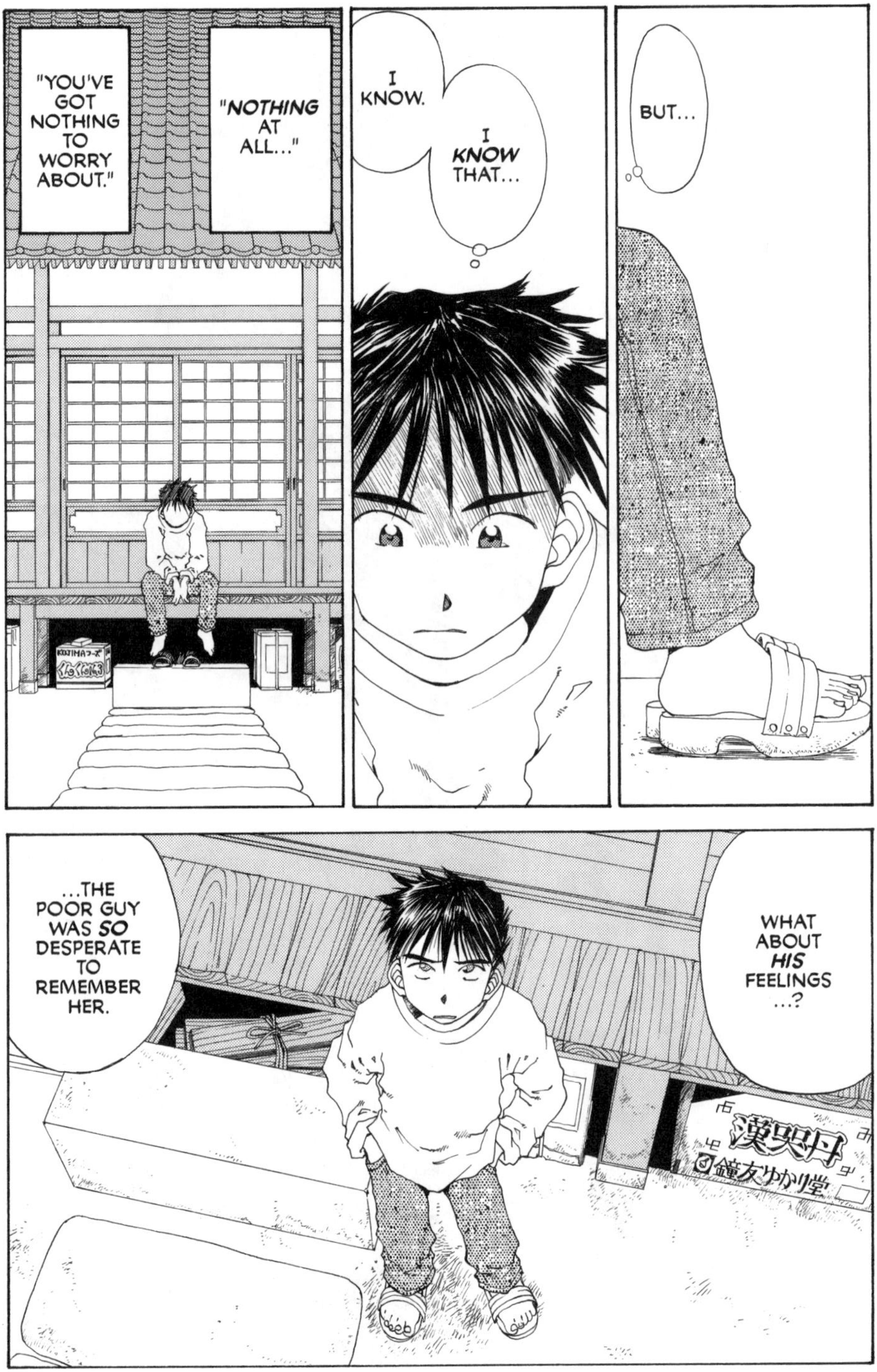
"YOU'VE GOT NOTHING TO WORRY ABOUT."
"*NOTHING* AT ALL..."
I KNOW.
I *KNOW* THAT...
BUT...
...THE POOR GUY WAS *SO* DESPERATE TO REMEMBER HER.
WHAT ABOUT *HIS* FEELINGS ...?

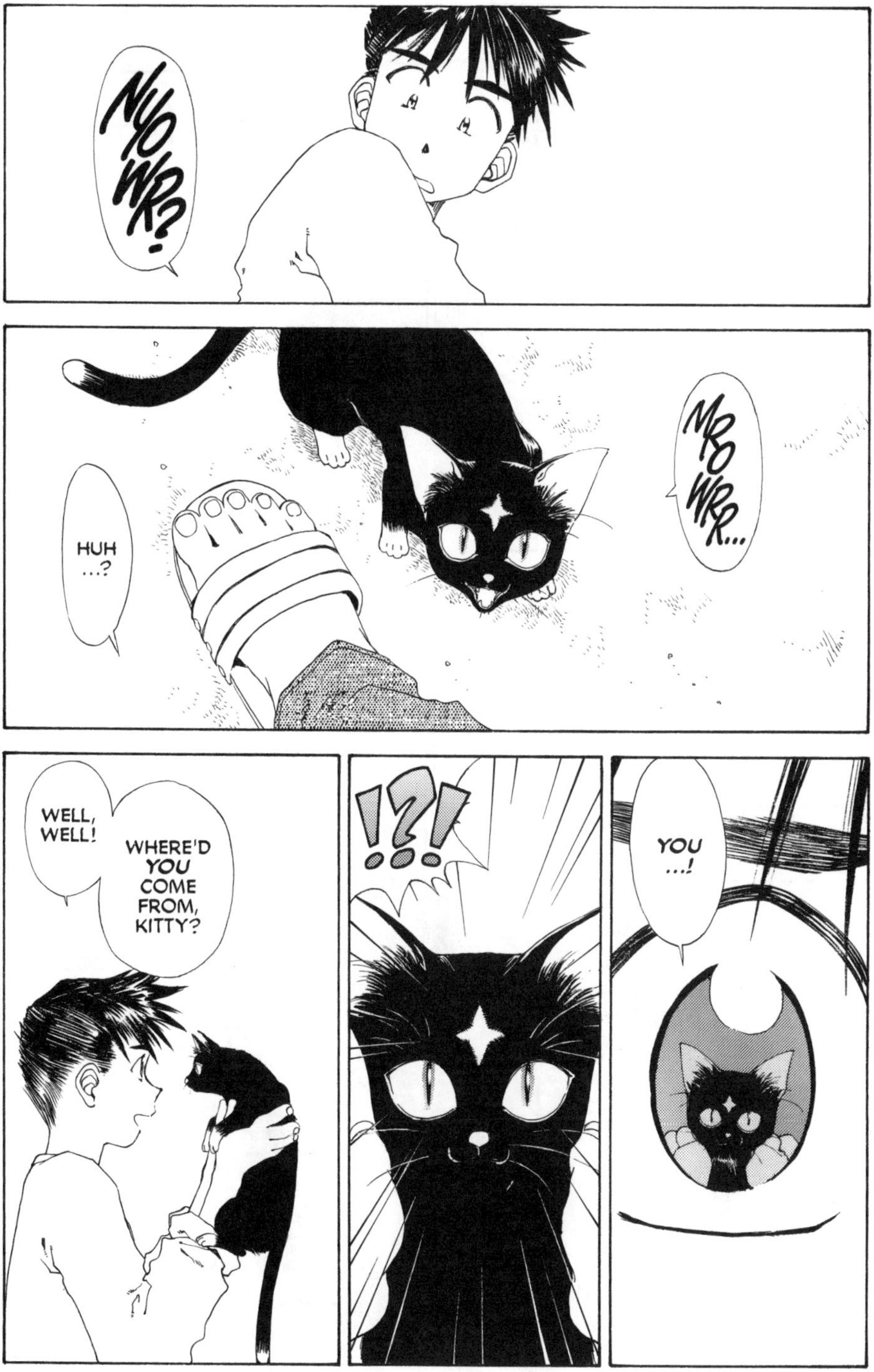
NYOWR?
HUH ...?
MROWRR...
WELL, WELL!
WHERE'D YOU COME FROM, KITTY?
!?!
YOU ...!

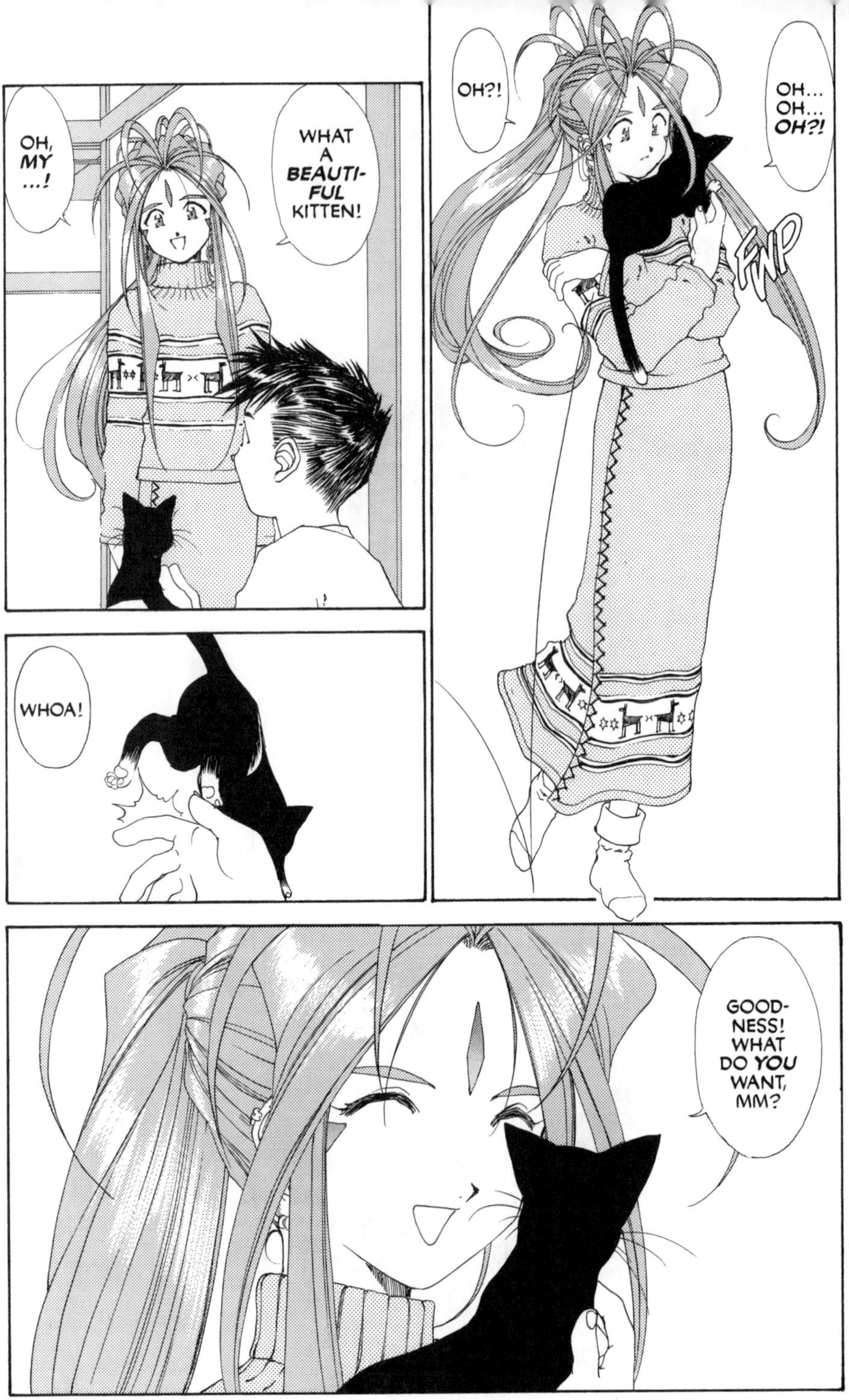
OH, MY ...!
WHAT A BEAUTI-FUL KITTEN!
WHOA!
OH?!
OH... OH... OH?!
FWP
GOOD-NESS! WHAT DO YOU WANT, MM?

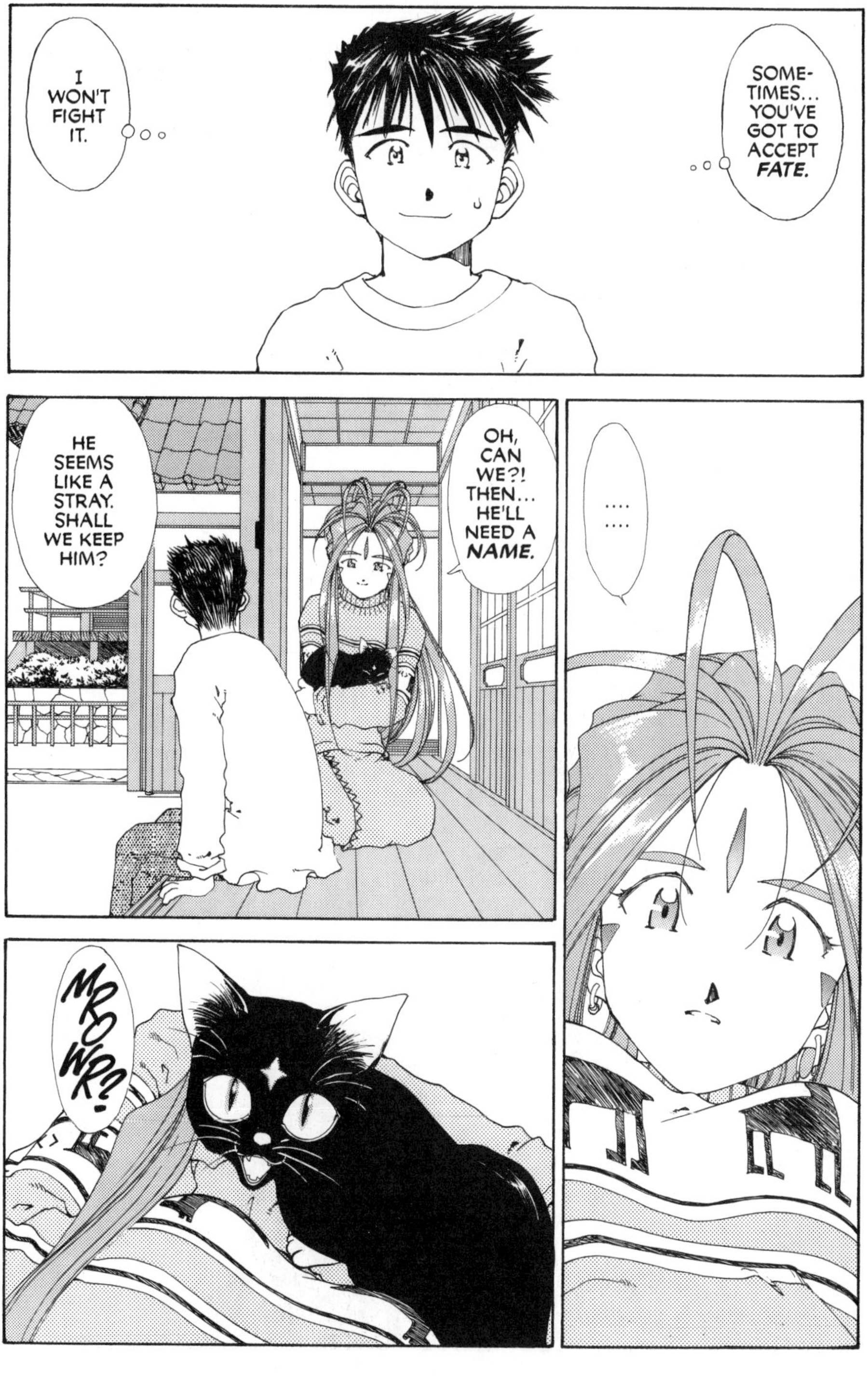

I WON'T FIGHT IT.
SOME-TIMES... YOU'VE GOT TO ACCEPT *FATE.*
HE SEEMS LIKE A STRAY. SHALL WE KEEP HIM?
OH, CAN WE?! THEN... HE'LL NEED A *NAME.*
MROWR?!
....
....

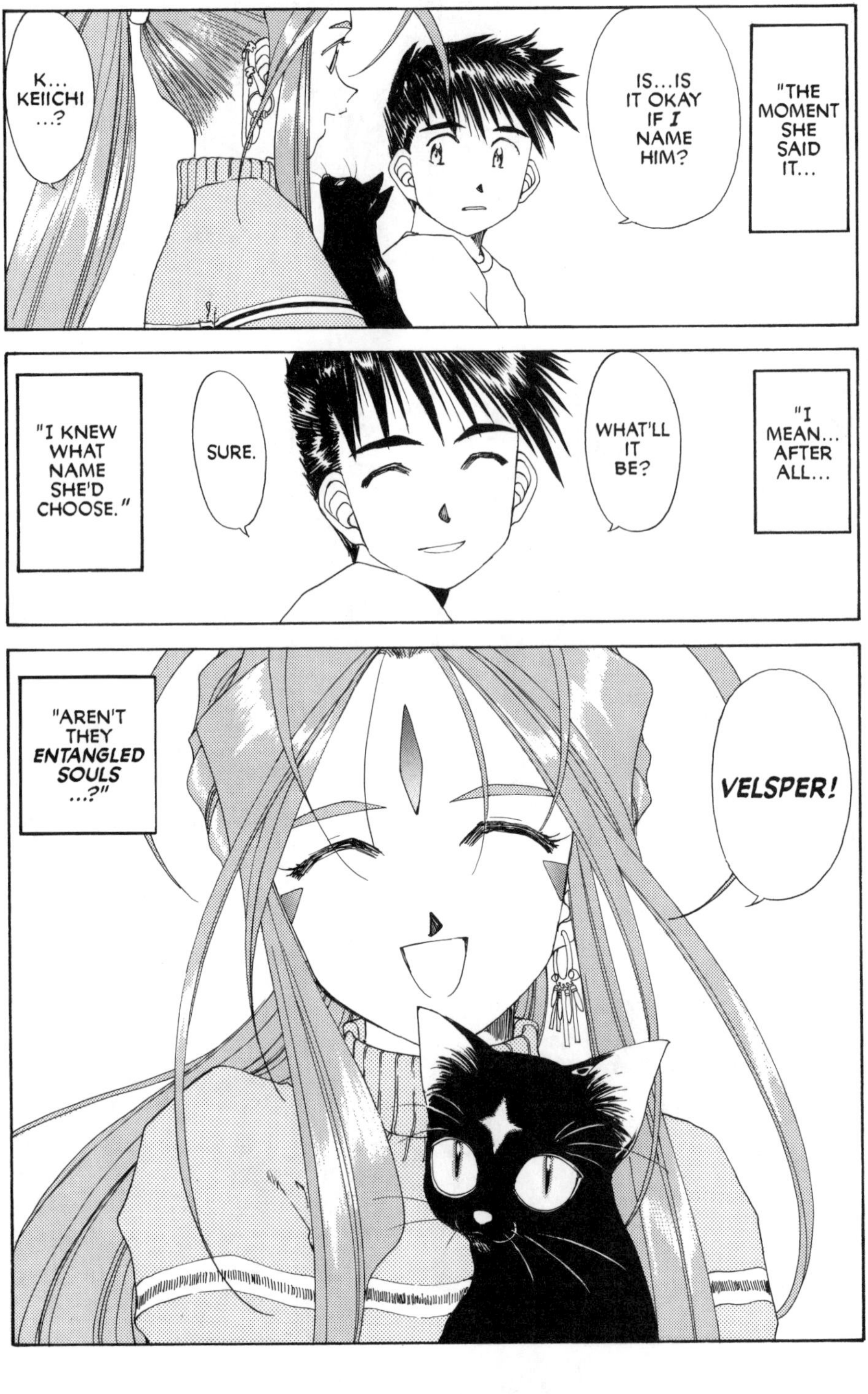
K... KEIICHI ...?
IS...IS IT OKAY IF *I* NAME HIM?
"THE MOMENT SHE SAID IT...
"I KNEW WHAT NAME SHE'D CHOOSE."
SURE.
WHAT'LL IT BE?
"I MEAN... AFTER ALL...
"AREN'T THEY *ENTANGLED SOULS* ...?"
VELSPER!

Kosuke Fujishima

Born in 1964, Kosuke Fujishima began his comics career just after graduating high school as an editor for comics news magazine, *Puff*. An interview he conducted with *Be Free!* creator Tatsuya Egawa led to becoming Egawa's assistant, which led to Fujishima's first professional panel work, a comics-style report on the making of the live-action *Be Free!* film. Fan mail he received for the piece inspired him to create *You're Under Arrest!* which was serialized in *Morning Party Extra* beginning in 1986.

In 1988, Fujishima created a four-panel gag cartoon that featured the *YUA!* characters praying to a goddess. Fujishima was so pleased with the way the goddess turned out that she became the basis for Belldandy and inspired the creation of the *Oh My Goddess!* series for *Afternoon* magazine, where it still runs today after more than a decade.

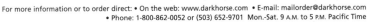

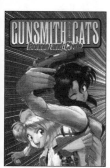

MANGA! MANGA! MANGA!
DARK HORSE HAS THE BEST IN MANGA COLLECTIONS!

AKIRA
Katsuhiro Otomo
BOOK 1
ISBN: 1-56971-498-3 $24.95
BOOK 2
ISBN: 1-56971-499-1 $24.95
BOOK 3
ISBN: 1-56971-525-4 $24.95
BOOK 4
ISBN: 1-56971-526-2 $27.95
BOOK 5
ISBN: 1-56971-527-0 $27.95
BOOK 6
ISBN: 1-56971-528-9 $29.95

APPLESEED
Masamune Shirow
BOOK ONE
ISBN: 1-56971-070-8 $16.95
BOOK TWO
ISBN: 1-56971-071-6 $16.95
BOOK THREE
ISBN: 1-56971-072-4 $17.95
BOOK FOUR
ISBN: 1-56971-074-0 $17.95

BLACK MAGIC
Masamune Shirow
ISBN: 1-56971-360-X $16.95

BLADE OF THE IMMORTAL
Hiroaki Samura
BLOOD OF A THOUSAND
ISBN: 1-56971-239-5 $14.95
CRY OF THE WORM
ISBN: 1-56971-300-6 $14.95
DREAMSONG
ISBN: 1-56971-357-X $14.95
ON SILENT WINGS
ISBN: 1-56971-412-6 $14.95
ON SILENT WINGS II
ISBN: 1-56971-444-4 $14.95
DARK SHADOWS
ISBN: 1-56971-469-X $14.95
HEART OF DARKNESS
ISBN: 1-56971-531-9 $16.95
THE GATHERING
ISBN: 1-56971-546-7 $15.95
THE GATHERING II
ISBN: 1-56971-560-2 $15.95
BEASTS
ISBN: 1-56971-741-9 $14.95

BUBBLEGUM CRISIS
Adam Warren • Toren Smith
GRAND MAL
ISBN: 1-56971-120-8 $14.95

CANNON GOD EXAXXION
Kenichi Sonoda
VOLUME 1
ISBN: 1-56971-745-1 $15.95

CARAVAN KIDD
Johji Manabe
VOLUME 1
ISBN: 1-56971-260-3 $19.95
VOLUME 2
ISBN: 1-56971-324-3 $19.95
VOLUME 3
ISBN: 1-56971-338-3 $19.95

THE DIRTY PAIR
Adam Warren • Toren Smith
BIOHAZARDS
ISBN: 1-56971-339-1 $12.95
DANGEROUS ACQUAINTANCES
ISBN: 1-56971-227-1 $12.95
A PLAGUE OF ANGELS
ISBN: 1-56971-029-5 $12.95
SIM HELL
ISBN: 1-56971-742-7 $13.95
FATAL BUT NOT SERIOUS
ISBN: 1-56971-172-0 $14.95

DOMINION
Masamune Shirow
ISBN: 1-56971-488-6 $16.95

DOMU: A CHILD'S DREAM
Katsuhiro Otomo
ISBN: 1-56971-611-0 $17.95

GHOST IN THE SHELL
Masamune Shirow
ISBN: 1-56971-081-3 $24.95

GUNSMITH CATS
Kenichi Sonoda
BONNIE AND CLYDE
ISBN: 1-56971-215-8 $13.95
MISFIRE
ISBN: 1-56971-253-0 $14.95
THE RETURN OF GRAY
ISBN: 1-56971-299-9 $17.95
GOLDIE VS. MISTY
ISBN: 1-56971-371-5 $15.95
BAD TRIP
ISBN: 1-56971-442-8 $13.95
BEAN BANDIT
ISBN: 1-56971-453-3 $16.95
KIDNAPPED
ISBN: 1-56971-529-7 $16.95
MR. V
ISBN: 1-56971-550-5 $18.95
MISTY'S RUN
ISBN: 1-56971-684-6 $14.95

INTRON DEPOT
Masamune Shirow
INTRON DEPOT 1
ISBN: 1-56971-085-6 $39.95
INTRON DEPOT 2: BLADES
ISBN: 1-56971-382-0 $39.95

LONE WOLF AND CUB
Kazuo Koike & Goseki Kojima
VOLUME 1: THE ASSASSIN'S ROAD
ISBN: 1-56971-502-5 $9.95
VOLUME 2: THE GATELESS BARRIER
ISBN: 1-56971-503-3 $9.95
VOLUME 3: THE FLUTE OF THE FALLEN TIGER
ISBN: 1-56971-504-1 $9.95
VOLUME 4: THE BELL WARDEN
ISBN: 1-56971-505-X $9.95
VOLUME 5: BLACK WIND
ISBN: 1-5671-506-8 $9.95
VOLUME 6: LANTERNS FOR THE DEAD
ISBN: 1-56971-507-6 $9.95
VOLUME 7: CLOUD DRAGON, WIND TIGER
ISBN: 1-56971-508-4 $9.95
VOLUME 8: CHAINS OF DEATH
ISBN: 1-56971-509-2 $9.95
VOLUME 9: ECHO OF THE ASSASSIN
ISBN: 1-56971-510-6 $9.95
VOLUME 10: HOSTAGE CHILD
ISBN: 1-56971-511-4 $9.95

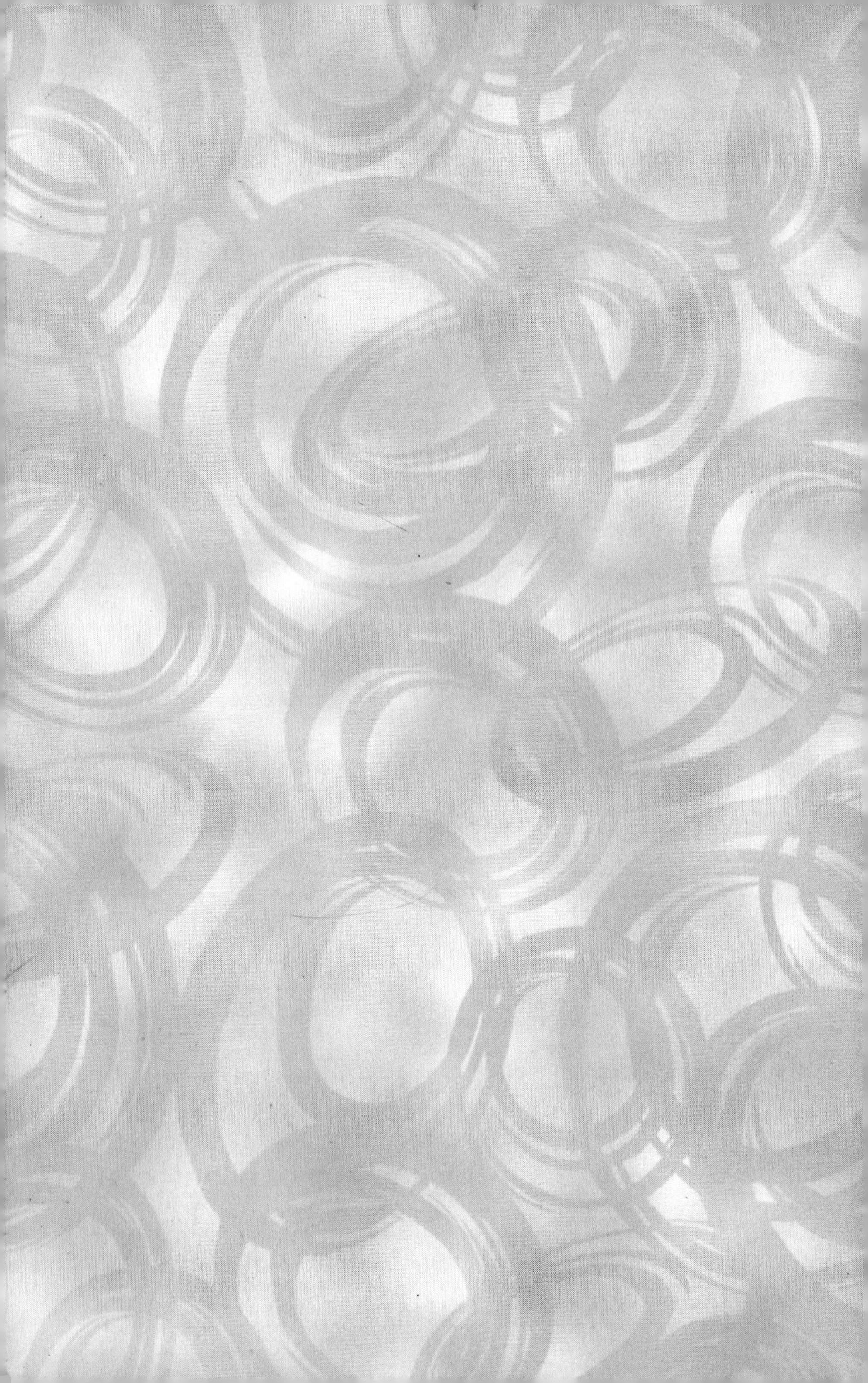